Imagine Jack Micheline, half pint riding the left hip pocket of his holy corduroys, walking sunset, one arm around the sky, the other around the Earth, as he rages against The Clowns who've denied The Poet's Blood— then get a firm grip on your soul, bust the cover of *Outlaw Bible* and let the century gush.

Wanda Coleman, author, *Bathwater Wine*

the Outlaw Bible
of american poetry

the Outlaw Bible
of american poetry

edited by Alan Kaufman

THUNDER'S MOUTH PRESS
NEW YORK

Published by
Thunder's Mouth Press
841 Broadway, Fourth Floor
New York, NY 10003

Library of Congress Cataloging-in-Publication Data

The outlaw bible of American poetry / edited by Alan Kaufman
    p.   cm.
  Includes index.
  ISBN 1-56025-227-8
  1. American poetry—20th century. 2. Experimental poetry,
American. 3. Beat generation—Poetry. 4. Performance art.
5. Sound poetry. I. Kaufman, Alan.
PS613.088 1999
811'.5408—dc21   99-18930
                                               CIP

ISBN 1-56025-236-7 cloth

Distributed by Publishers Group West.

Manufactured in the United States of America.

This book is dedicated to Jack Micheline, the greatest Outlaw Poet of all time, and to Outlaws everywhere, living or dead, who have stayed one step ahead of all laws, chasing after the lawless beauty of the imagination.

Alan Kaufman
San Francisco
March 5, 1999

contents

SLAMMERS

THE UNBEARABLES

acknowledgments

I WANT TO OFFER my humble thanks to God and the spirits of Buddha, Moses and William Blake, to whom I turned each day with prayers that were answered. My thanks and pledge of eternal love to Diane Spencer, my lifelong partner, who stood by me through it all with unflagging devotion. Were it not for Diane, none of this would be. My gratitude to David Carlson, my wise friend, pathfinder and Dharma buddy, and to the Sunset Niners for always being there for me, rain or shine. My hugs and affection to Angelo and Helen Frida who purchased for me the gift of a new computer on which so much of this effort took place, and encouraged me for no more recompense than to see me happy. My appreciation to Allen Regenstreif, who helped me to loose the knots and unpack the gifts. My thankfulness to Paul Haller, my Zen teacher and Dharma guide, and to my *sangha* at the Zen Center, San Francisco, for their warmth and encouragement. Thank you Bronnie Gallan for always being there. Thank you Ron Kolm for your unflagging and courteous help, and to Ralph Ackerman, one of the true artists of this world. Also, special thanks to Nancy Fish and Susan Reich, each of whom stood by this book when most needed. A big wave to Gerald Nicosia for disclosing the mysteries of his Rollerdex to me. And to the crew at Thunder's Mouth Press—Dan O'Connor, Jeri Smith, Ghadah Alrawi and Jessie Martin—thanks for all your help and prompt professional support!

There are two persons for whom I wish to reserve a very special thanks. The first is Neil Ortenberg of Thunder's Mouth Press. When I was starting out to make my mark as a literary man, I had read of legendary editors and publishers like Maxwell Perkins, Barney Rosset and Horace Liverwright, colorful figures with an air about them of both the racetrack and refinement, who gave of themselves selflessly in order to make a good book a great one, and for whom no obstacle was insurmountable in the pursuit of a vision. They treated their authors not as mere clients but as valued colleagues. They'd lay it all down for the Book. Neil Ortenberg is such a one, an editor's editor. First thing he did was send to me a photo of himself on his Heritage Softail. Neil proved a dream to work with—

fair-minded, affable, sharp, someone who could crystallize a vision. We brainstormed, conferenced, planned. Most editors starve a book; Neil said "Let's double its size!" Day in and day out, fifty years of Outlaw poetry flew back and forth between coasts on a magic carpet ride of faxes, e-mails, packages. It was hard work, the pace grueling and fun as all hell. The dream kept growing. He said "Let's make this book everything it can be" and pitched in with me, sleeves rolled. He went from a stranger to a soul brother. He takes risks, sign of a real artist. Today, we wear the same posse colors: Outlaw Poets. That's him on the Harley roaring by.

Brenda Knight, editor of *Women of the Beat Generation*, is another who breaks the mold, the Goddess of Buzz and the Andy Warhol-ette of Beat. Even as I write this, she's turning the world on its head. She was the very first to see the possibilities of "Outlaw" and bring it to fruition. When it was just a proposal, she shuttled with it under her arm between San Francisco and New York, talking it up to the trade, getting the spin going, and when time was ripe, landing me the contract. I offered her an agenting commission; she declined. It's a favor, she said. And she never asked for anything but the pleasure of seeing "Outlaw" become a reality. My hats off to you, Brenda, you're all class, a grand lady of letters!

ALAN KAUFMAN
EDITOR

This collection of verse happened because a poet lived and died. This book you hold in your hands, these words you now read, happened as a result of the passing of Beat legend and poet Jack Micheline and the marvel of the Internet.

Shortly after Jack's death, Alan Kaufman and I began an e-mail correspondence. Separately, he and I had long dreamed of putting together a book of poets and poetry reflecting the unheard voices; those that had long been ignored much like our friend Jack Micheline. Give it over to the process and to the business of poetry, and this book is the result. Granted, not all the poets or writers in this book would qualify as street, beat, or unheard; however, there are a substantial number of those that do qualify (including Jack) and it is to them that I have dedicated myself and my efforts in this book. This collection then is a bit of a Trojan Horse, for these poet/makers are now in your keeping, all of them; the famous, the infamous, and those never seen nor heard until now. They are yours. Keep them, treasure them, and honor their work.

My thanks to Brenda Knight, Nancy Fish, Rafael F. J. Alvarado, Tony Scibella and Jersey girl Lorraine Perrotta. Also, a gracious nod to Neil Ortenberg.

S.A. GRIFFIN
CONTRIBUTING EDITOR

introduction

WELCOME TO THE WILD WEST of American Poetry, the Hole-In-The-Wall of Blakean vision, a two-fisted saloon of New World dreams where you'll meet the greatest Outlaw voices from the post-war era to the present day. Here are the inventors of the Beat generation and the heroes of today's Spoken Word movement, poets who don't get taught in American poetry 101, yet hold the literary future in their tattooed hands. In this anthological and visual history are innovative crossovers from the fields of music, film and the visual arts, comedy and the novel. Here are the demons of the imagination, the Hipsters, Queers, Rappers, Babarians, Nuyoricans, Renegades, Carma Bums, Unbearables, Hustlers, Slammers, and Cons of Melvillian darkness and light who are bringing a fresh cultural dispensation of MTV and bookstore alike: a new American poetry premised upon uncompromised integrity and the naked power of visionary words. The Academy had best make room for these descendents of Whitman's "Roughs" and Emerson's "Berserkers": Our poets can whip your poets' asses.

Here is Bob Dylan, whose spurs still jangle on the wooden sawdust floors of American myth. Here is Sapphire, who rose from the harshest beginnings to become the reigning queen of American letters and whose poem "Wild Thing" sparked Congressional battles and the White House firing of the head of the NEA. Here are Kenneth Patchen whose poems of raging love inspire a generation, Hubert Selby Jr. making a last exit into poetry, Richard Brautigan traversing the cosmos in verse, and Henry Miller on how to write like sex. All are present: Lou Reed, Allen Ginsberg, Eileen Myles, Lawrence Ferlinghetti and Abbie Hoffman, Ray Bremser and Tuli Kupferberg, Diane DiPrima, Jennifer Blowdryer, Harold Norse, Kathleen Wood and Wanda Coleman and the subterranean genius Daniel Higgs. Here are Kathy Acker and her mentor William Burroughs, and generations of iconoclastic verb bandits like Ishmael Reed, John Giorno, and Ken Kesey, finding common ground in the thunderdome of poetry. Here is Tupac Shakur, gunned down at the height of his fame, the Francois Villon of Rap. Here are Lenny Bruce and Richard Pryor, who turned stand-up into ferocious satire. Here with William Carlos Williams and Jack Kerouac, Herbert Hunke and Gregory Corso are Lisa Martinovich, the Notorious Slam Queen of the Ozarks who performs with a boa contrictor wrapped around her neck, and Karen Finley exploding with beatific rage. Here are James Dean and Jackson Pollack, glittering gutter icons of American culture, knocking off visionary statement poems, respectively, in a bathroom in Tijuana and the bawdy Cedar Tavern in New York City. Here is Jim Morrison, who died like David's Marat in a Parisian bathtub. Here is Patti Smith wrestling the night alongside Norman Mailer, Gil Scott Heron, Tom Waits, Melvin Van Peebles, and Jim Carroll.

Outlaw poets have fierce and highly personalized styles, and reputations for deadly talent. They wield their talent with the murderous skill and accuracy of a Colt .45. If the poets share any common feature at all, it is an unspoken objective: to get in your face and stay there. Theirs is a voice of nightmare and love that may not exactly kill you but demands its toll in dangerous emotion as the price for listening. They are, for the most part, as Sartre said of Baudelaire, "Not revolutionaries but men (and women) in revolt." Not all survive intact. Some of them blow their brains out, like d.a. levy, who, before he ate the barrel of his shotgun for one last great acid trip at the age of 26, left behind a body of work that earned him the sobriquet of "The American Rimbaud." Some expire in transit from nowhere to immortality, like Jack Micheline, regarded as the greatest street poet of them all. His genius bore the price of living marginality, yet in death achieved him fame as the consummate troubadour, his passing reported worldwide, from CNN to the front page of the *New York Times*. Some perish on the lam after lives of literary honor and criminal mischief, like Miguel Piñero from whose fugitive ashes arose a worldwide movement of Nuyorican poets. Some rage in prisons of their own making, and others in barred cells of the state. Bob Kaufman wrote some of his best poems between cop beatings in the holding cell of San Francisco's notorious 850 Bryant Jail. Fame eluded Kaufman, yet when the pennies were laid on his eyes, the City declared a day of mourning and the poetry world stood still. Here for the first time assembled are poets long revered for their untarnished authenticity and brilliance, yet never before presented together to a national audience. Truly a "Bible" of the Outlaw poet's world, one can find here Jim Brodey, David Lerner, John Bennet, Ken DiMaggio, Sara Menafee, Maura O'Conner, Jesse Berstein, Jayne Cortez, David Trinidad, Pedro Pietri, Thomas McGrath, Jack Hirschman, Luis Rodriguez, Gary Snyder, David Meltzer, Bob Flanangan, as well as poetry from outlaw bikers and bangers.

The Outlaw Bible of American Poetry is not just a book for public inspiration but a groundbreaking resource. Outlaw poets relate to the poetic tradition, and to their contemporaries in the Academy, with the bristling wariness of a street hustler getting frisked by a cop. They've seen how excessive veneration for the poetic mainstream has turned practice of the art today into an ongoing memorial service held by those who want poetry to stay in the closet. Yet, Outlaw poets do delve in tradition, with the goal of turning straw into fire. It's simple: light a match. They want to learn what has made poetry inaccessible to so many until now—learning what *not* to do. Though, for the most part, they display a savage antipathy to the poetry establishment and its values, there is a lot of well-hidden craft in their work. Many are avid readers who have thought a lot about what constitutes a poem, but just try to engage them in literary chit chat and their eyes go cold. They have butchered the sacred cow of literature and eaten its parts. They want their poetry to inspire the kind of fever normally reserved for the Superbowl and hot sex. They know that the way to the heart of a public amused by COPS and listening to Notorious B.I.G. is not through Spencer's Faerie Queen.

At best, Outlaw poetry is an ongoing record of streetwise sensibility and tough tenderness. These poets have given form to incoherence, made a song of ugliness, and shown that unbearable pain is something we can survive. In their best work, the poetry achieves a gentleness and compassion despite that pain.

From the clubs of Manhattan's East Village to the cafes of San Francisco to the rock stages of Venice West, a new cultural front is riding the upsurge of populist verse in our time, a passionately lyrical energy that's spreading fast around the globe. In every town and city people from every walk of life, young and old alike, are standing up at open mikes to bare their hearts in protest against their dehumanization. A need for authenticity has gripped everyone. There is now more poetry sold and performed than at any other time in history.

Here then on the brink of a new millenium are poets who eat life whole and give their all. They are versifying Robin Hoods, stealing from the poverty of our wealth to feed our spirits. They dare to express the genius of the American character, and in ways that stir our imaginations to near-eruption. Simply put, they transform our lives into poetry. At the end of the road, some find bloodshed, others gold, some gain beauty, others blindness. All are sworn, as Jack Micheline wrote, to "illuminate the darkness."

ALAN KAUFMAN
SAN FRANCISCO

publisher's note

THIS ANTHOLOGY'S INTENT is to create a forum for poetry that is urgent, visceral, and at times redemptive. Not every school or category of what might be considered outlaw is signified here, and each existing category has a representative but not a complete list of suspects. Also, there were a few, not many, poets whose permission proved impossible to get, Bukowski being the most glaring example. We have chosen to highlight groups like the Slammers, Babarians, and Unbearables, not as a value judgment but out of a certain logistical convenience. The majority of poets are simply categorized as American Renegades. A few poets, like Bob Kaufman, Jack Micheline, or Harold Norse are given more space than others, not because they are greater poets than the rest, but because of a subjective decision to showcase a few voices that deserved more attention in their careers than they received. Others like Jim Carroll or Patti Smith just turned out that way.

The poets here have peeled back the skin and revealed the heart. Like Hip Hop, the work generally is candid, sometimes shockingly so, but the result of so much heavy throttle tends to be that you've visited a place you'll remember. There is a quality of otherness, but from that alienation a community has been created.

A decade ago, I got a letter from Allen Ginsberg, who was on my advisory board at the time. He was giving me advice on my publishing program, scrawled on a piece of paper with Bessie Smith lyrics typed on it. He ended the letter with the quote, "Stand ever in the hard Sophoclean light and take your wounds from it gladly." The light from this collection is here for you. Stand in it.

NEIL ORTENBERG

Shut Not Your Doors

Shut not your doors to me proud libraries,
For that which was lacking on all your well-fill'd shelves, yet needed
    most, I bring,
Forth from the war emerging, a book I have made,
The words of my book nothing, the drift of it every thing,
A book separate, not link'd with the rest nor felt by the intellect,
But you ye untold latencies will thrill to every page.

WALT WHITMAN

prologue: voices from outlaw heaven

JACK MICHELINE

Poem To The Freaks

To lives as I have done is surely absurd
in cheap hotels and furnished rooms
To walk up side streets and down back alleys
talking to oneself
and screaming to the sky obscenities
That the arts is a rotten business indeed
That mediocrity and the rage of fashion rules
My poems and paintings piled on the floor
To be one with himself
A Saint
A Prince
To Persevere
Through storms and hard-ons
Through dusk and dawns
To kick death in the ass
To be passed over like a bad penny
A midget
An Ant
A roach
A freak
A Hot Piece
An Outlaw
Raise your cup and drink my friend
Drink for those who walk alone in the night
  To the crippled and the blind
  To the lost and the damned
  To the lone bird flying in the sky
Drink to wonder
Drink to me
Drink to pussy and dreams
Drink to madness and all the stars
I hear the birds singing

May 16, 1975
San Francisco, CA

JIM BRODEY

Soul Eyes
a short bag of informative songs

1.
Miguel Pinero
speeding through
workaday Manhattan
in a stolen taxi
Uzi machine gun
out the window
backhanded fire
blasting cop cars
in pursuit
stolen loot
in lap, hears
on radio how
he just won
Pulitzer sur-
Prize's xx-number
bucks

Congratulations, dude

2.
Peter Orlovsky
mastermind saint
brother poet fiend
blasted near dawn
looks down fire escape
with cool blank eyes
over Lower depths
East Side morn
wonder vision watches
teen dark robbers
lift entire apartment
out window downhanded
stupefied doom
and smiles from

his poetic head:
a blissful dude

3.
Ray Bremser
ole jail Ray
who's seen
tree visions
open up & intend
beautiful wail
streets his Chet
Baker songs read
& sung in poems
He saw on a line
of white shit
He shoots on page
as we cannot but
hear his tree's
Gentle song, sleeps
on the floor of
Poetry Church, yo

Ray, man I think
of you often, love
your righteous soul

4.
Ted Berrigan
high on poems
not pills & acidy
white light seen
on the ceiling
where dragons sense
his keen eye & walks
down St. Mark's Place
in an old-time beard
wigged-out smiling
goof bliss, sees
Golden/white Buddha
on a flatbed truck
(intended statue for
Leary's theater lecture)
thinks he sees instead
the *real* golden Buddha
of great lost street joy

calling to him to follow
poetry to logical ends
of his singing bulk, that
ebbs & whines everyone
be free of control words
& control drugs, makes
poems breathe with a real
fire into living breath

Yo dude, you be gone
but we still remember
your incredible love

5.
When Fugs sing
Billy Blake, my heart
swells ripped crazy
like liquidy acid light
creeping through body
lightning cracked over
soft brilliant brain juice
that floods nerve into
American vocal speech
turns face into no-face
this golden fleece poets
seek in spirit dropping away
to reveal bone songs underneath
all street talk, that now & forever
feeling of rising angel float
that eternity dances rocked
& webby sat salted to wheel
sky made song by pieces
of living song freaked
anew from blasted idea:
Now we rock as he wrote

Poetry built this city
of the living page flesh
always new to eye torch

6.
Al Fowler, ripped
on some control drug
blew fucking mailman
down through walls,

PROLOGUE: VOICES FROM OUTLAW HEAVEN

thinking blue dream
it was CIA assassins
seeing through walls
reach in and take soul
blew him through door
into next century, ran
out and disappeared to
nowhere known

Ed told it true, so read
yr poems in ternity fella

7.
When I make it to heaven
Frank be there, his songs
made poems real to me, his
tobacco breath realer than
any poem she left us, he be there
he be there, he be there

D.A. LEVY

sitting on a bench near TSQuare
For David Meltzer

1.
through the branches of
the thin trees of tenth street
the blue sky waits
with me &
im waiting for god
(on a white horse)
to ride thru the
branches of
the lower east side
before returning to
        cleveland
& something

tells me
he isnt coming

2.
im a levy of the levites
yet in cleveland
i have painted myself
         celtic-blue
& am feeling
something like an outlaw

the druids give me soup
& think im a lama

its been close to 7 years
ive been looking for god
& the trails wearing as
thin as the trees on tenth street
i am a levy of the levites
& last week
a fanatic jew in the heights
called me a halfbreed
because my mother was a christian

i am a levy of the levites
& last week a rabbi
thought i was kidding
when i told him
i was interested in judaism

god i think yr sense
of humor is sad
& perhaps you are also
feeling something
like an outlaw

god i am wondering
for how many years
have the jews
exiled you
while they busied themselves
with survival

PROLOGUE: VOICES FROM OUTLAW HEAVEN

TUPAC SHAKUR

In the Event of My Demise

When my heart can beat no more
I hope I die for a principle or a belief that
    I have lived for
I will die before my time because I already feel
    the shadow's depth
So much I wanted to accomplish before
    I reached my death
I have come to grips with the possibility and
    wiped the last tear from my eyes
I loved all who were positive in the event
    of my demise

—2Pac, 1992

DAVID LERNER

Mein Kampf

Gary Snyder lives in the *country*. He wakes up in the morning and listens to *birds*. We *live in the city*.

—KATHLEEN WOOD

all I want to do
is make poetry famous

all I want to do is
burn my initials into the sun

all I want to do is
read poetry from the middle of a
burning building

standing in the fast lane of the
freeway
falling from the top of the
Empire State Building

the literary world
sucks dead dog dick

I'd rather be Richard Speck
than Gary Snyder
I'd rather ride a rocketship to hell
than a Volvo to Bolinas

I'd rather
sell arms to the Martians
than wait sullenly for a
letter from some diseased clown with a
three-piece mind
telling me that I've won a
bullet-proof pair of rose-colored glasses
for my poem "Autumn in the Spring"

I want to be
hated
by everyone who teaches for a living

I want people to hear my poetry and
get headaches
I want people to hear my poetry and
vomit

I want people to hear my poetry and
weep, scream, disappear, start bleeding,
eat their television sets, beat each other to death with
swords and

go out and get riotously drunk on
someone else's money

this ain't no party
this ain't no disco
this ain't foolin' a

PROLOGUE: VOICES FROM OUTLAW HEAVEN

grab-bag of
clever wordplay and sensitive thoughts and
gracious theories about

how many ambiguities can dance on the head of a
machine gun

this ain't no
genteel evening over
cappuccino and bullshit

this ain't no life-affirming
our days have meaning
as we watch the flowers breath through our souls and
fall desperately in love

this ain't no letter-press, hand-me-down,
wimpy beatnik festival of bitching about
the broken rainbow

it is a carnival of dread

it is a savage sideshow
about to move to the main arena

it is terror and wild beauty
walking hand in hand down a bombed-out road
as missiles scream, while a
sky the color of arterial blood
blinks on and off
like the lights on Broadway
after the last junkie's dead of AIDS

I come not to bury poetry
but to blow it up
not to dandle it on my knee
like a retarded child with
beautiful eyes
but

throw it off a cliff into
icy seas and
see if the motherfucker can
swim for its life

because love is an excellent thing
surely we need it

but, my friends . . .

there is so much to hate These Days
that hatred is just love with a chip on its shoulder
a chip as big as the Ritz
and heavier than
all the bills I'll never pay

because they're after us

they're selling radioactive charm bracelets
and breakfast cereals that
lower your IQ by 50 points per mouthful
we got politicians who think
starting World War III
would be a good career move
we got beautiful women
with eyes like wet stones
peering out at us from the pages of
glossy magazines
promising that they'll
fuck us till we shoot blood

if we'll just buy one of these beautiful switchblade knives

I've got mine

american renegades

SAPPHIRE

Wild Thing

And I'm running,
running wild
running free,
like soldiers down
the beach,
like someone
just threw me
the ball.
My thighs pump
thru the air
like tires
rolling down
the highway
big & round
eating up the ground
of America
but I never been any
further than 42nd Street.
Below that is as
unfamiliar as my
father's face,
foreign as the smell of

white girls' pussy,
white girls on the bus,
white girls on TV
My whole world is
black & brown & closed,
till I open it
with a rock,
christen it with
blood.
BOP BOP
the music
pops thru me
like electric shocks,
my sweat is a
river running
thru my liver
green with hate,
my veins bulge out
like tomorrow,
my dick is
the Empire State Building,
I eat your fear
like a chimpanzee
ow ow
ow whee
ow!
My sneakers glide off
the cement like
white dreams
looking out at the world
thru a cage of cabbage
& my mother's fat,
hollering don't do this
& don't do that.
I scream against the restraint
of her big ass sitting on my face
drowning my dreams in sameness.
I'm scared to go
it hurts me to stay.
She sits cross-legged
in front the TV
telling me no
feeding me
clothing me
bathing me in her ugliness

high high in the sky
18th floor of the projects.
Her welfare check buys me $85 sneakers
but can't buy me a father.
She makes cornbread from Jiffy box mix
buys me a coat
$400, leather like everybody else's.
I wear the best, man!
14 karat gold chain
I take off before I go wildin'.
Fuck you nigger!
Nobody touches my gold!
My name is Leroy
L-E-R-O-Y
bold gold
I got the goods
that make the ladies
young & old
sign your name across my heart
I want you to be my baby
Rapper D
Rapper G
Rapper *I*
my name is lightning
across the sky
So what I can't read
you spozed to teach me
you the teacher
I'm the ape
black ape
in white sneakers
hah hah
I rape
rape
rape
I do the wild thing
I do the wild thing.
My teacher asks me
what would I do
if I had 6 months
to live.
I tell her I'd fuck her,
sell dope & do the wild thing.
My thighs are locomotives
hurling me thru the

underbrush of Central Park,
the jungle.
I either wanna be a cop
or the biggest dope dealer in Harlem
when I grow up.
I feel good!
It's a man's world,
my sound is king
I am the black man's sound.
Get off my face whining bitch!
No, I didn't go to school today
& I ain't goin' tomorrow!
I like how the sky looks
when I'm running,
my clothes are new & shiny,
my tooth gleams gold.
I'm fast as a wolf
I need a rabbit,
the sky is falling
calling my name
Leroy Leroy.
I look up
blood bust
in my throat
it's my homeboys
L. D., C. K. & Beanbutt!
Hey man what's up!
I got the moon
in my throat,
I remember when
Christ sucked my dick
behind the pulpit,
I was 6 years old
he made me promise
not to tell no one.
I eat cornbread &
collard greens.
I only wear Adidas
I'm my own man,
they can wear New Balance or Nike
if they want,
I wear Adidas.
I'm L. D.
lover
mover

man with the money
all the girls know me.
I'm classified as mildly retarded
but I'm not
least I don't think
I am.
Special Education classes
eat up my brain
like last week's greens
rotting in plastic containers.
My mother never
throws away anything.
I could kill her
I could kill her
all those years
all those years
I sat
I sat in classes
for the mentally retarded
so she could get
the extra money welfare gives
for retarded kids.
So she could get
some money,
some motherfuckin' money.
That bitch
that bitch
I could kill her
all the years
I sat next to kids
who shitted on themselves,
dreaming amid
rooms of dull eyes
that one day
my rhymes
would break open
the sky
& my name would
be written
across the marquee
at the Apollo
in bold gold
me bigger
than Run DMC
Rapper G

Rapper O
Rapper *Me*
"Let's go!" I scream.
My dick is a locomotive
my sister eats like a 50c hot dog.
I scream, "I *said* let's go!"
"It's 40 of us
a black wall of sin.
The god of our fathers
descends down & blesses us,
I say thank you Jesus.
Now let's do the
wild thing.
I pop off the cement
like toast outta toaster
hot hard crumbling
running
running
the park is green
combat operation
lost soul
looking for Lt. Calley
Jim Jones
anybody who could direct
this spurt of semen
rising to the sky.
soldiers
flying thru
the rhythm
"Aw man!
nigger please
nigger
nigger
nigger.
I know
who I am."
My soul sinks
to its knees &
howls under the
moon rising full,
"Let's get a female jogger!"
I shout into the twilight
looking at the
middle-class thighs
pumping past me,

cadres of bitches
who deserve to die
for thinking they're better
than me.
You ain't better than
nobody bitch.
The rock begs my hand
to hold it.
It says, "Come on man."
T. W., Pit Bull, J. D. & me
grab the bitch
ugly big nose white bitch
but she's beautiful cause she's white
she's beautiful cause she's skinny
she's beautiful cause she's gonna die
cause her daddy's gonna cry
Bitch!
I bring the rock down
on her head
sounds dull & flat
like the time I busted
the kitten's head.
The blood is real & red
my dick rises.
I tear off her bra
feel her perfect pink breasts
like Brooke Shields
like bitches in Playboy
Shit! I come all over myself!
I bring the rock down
the sound has rhythm
hip hop ain't gonna stop
till your face sees
what I see every day
walls of blood
walls of blood
she's wriggling like
a pig in the mud.
I never seen a pig
or a cow
'cept on TV.
Her nipples are like
hard strawberries
my mouth tastes
like pesticide.

I fart.
Yosef slams her
across the face with a pipe.
My dick won't get
hard no more.
I bring the rock down
removing what she
looks like forever
ugly bitch
ugly bitch
I get up
blood on my hands
semen in my jeans
the sky is black
the trees are green
I feel good baby
I just did
the *wild thing*!

Rabbit Man

1.
he's the night
chasing rabbits,
a pot of dust
under the asphalt sky
cracked with stars.
athlete,
'colored boy from Houston makes good.'
standing straight as a razor
he cuts my vagina open
stretches it like bleeding lights thru dark air
his rabbit teeth drag my tongue
over sabers hidden in salt,
from the slit tip
red roses drip
screaming: daddy *don't*.

I'm not supposed to be
your dinner nigger.
your semen forms fingers
in my throat,
furry fingers.

I cough all the time
rabbit man
colored boy
run
jump
hurdle after hurdle—
higher.

till your penis melts
like a marshmallow in fire
and your fear is a desert with no flowers
except two daughters,
American Beauties,
tight rosebuds you hew open,
petals of pink light left bleeding
under a broken moon.
pine needles spring up in the sand
but you don't ask what they're for
surrounded like you are by infant daughters,
little dog fish drowning in diapers.
you did this rabbit dick,
rabbit dick
rabbit dick
hopping coprophagous freak
blind eyes opening
like terminal disease
in mouth after mouth—
paralyzing light.

2.
I slide between cold polyester rooms,
into your bed—
everything is so cheap and falling apart.
I recoil from the blond skin and
bleeding blue eyes of Jesus.
most nights you slept
in the obituary of light—
alone.
the picture is positioned
so when your head hit the pillow
you saw Jesus.
then what?

3.
you saw death like the black legs of your mother
like the bent teeth of your retarded sister
like the wet smell of light in a fish's eye.
you saw death riding without a car or credit cards.
you saw death creeping waddling like the fat women
    you hated.
you saw Jesus could not save you.

god's hand is creased with the smell of burnt hair and
    hot grease,
she hears you tell your sons don't get no
    black nappy-head woman.
her titties sag down sad snakes that crawl up your legs
till your penis talks and with blind sight you see
the two daughters you left in the desert without water.
oh death knows you and invites you for dinner,
rolls out the driveway like a coupe de ville, ·
is a snake-tongued daughter who turns on you,
is a thirsty rabbit choking on a lonely road.
death is an ax in an elevator rising to the sun.
death is god's egg.
death is a daughter who eats.
you are the table now the wet black earth lays upon—
you are dinner for dirt,
a cadillac spinning back to a one-room shack.
you are the rabbit released from fear,
the circle broken by sun
the handle of a buried ax,
head rolling thru the desert
like tumbleweed—
back to Neptune.

4.
now I am the queen of sand,
wind wrapping like wire around the rabbit's neck,
the end of a cycle.
my children refuse to believe your penis is a lollipop.
my children are the desert in bloom
cactus flowers opening to forgiveness,
millions of rabbits hopping—
hopping over you.

1989 cont./Gorilla in the Midst #6

"You shouldn't'a married me."
He felt like beating her to death. Stupid, sausage head,
  bitch.
"You knew you had this problem when we got mar-
  ried."
"Porky the Pig is upset," he sneered.
Her face reddened. "Making fun of me may make you
  feel better—"
"I'm sorry."
"I'm not," she paused. "Porky Pig, Fat Slob, Big Ben,
  whatever,
it doesn't make any difference what you can call me anymore,
I know what I am, I'm a woman and I thought I was marrying a man."
"You saying—" anger choked the words in his throat,
  where did this bitch
get off talking to *him* like that, "You saying I ain't no man!"
"I want you to get some kind of counseling," firmly,
"or I want a divorce."
"Divorce? Get a divorce! See who wants your fat ass!"

BAP!   SLAP!   SLAP!

She screamed, the hole of her mouth filled with blood.
"God help me!" she gasped at her teeth like white fish
floating out of her mouth onto the floor. God I gotta get—

BAM! BAM! BAM! BAM!
BAM! BAM! BAM! BAM!
BAM! BAM! BAM! BAM!

He looked at her bloody and still like a run-over animal
the slight movement of her chest rising to inhale
refueled his anger—
look at what she had made him do god dammit! God
  damn!
Big bullets of sweat popped out on his brow. It was
  hot.
He had to get out of the room, house. He was 40 years
  old. Married
16 years, 2 kids. 5 times in 16 years, at least the kids
  but 1 dies.
5 times, then the desert years. Nothing, years and
  years, nothing.

d.a. levy

The best unknown story to come out of the generational cultural war of the 1960s almost certainly belongs to d. a. levy. Considered by many to be the American Rimbaud, levy's tale is a modern *Rashomon*, filled with dichotomies illuminating the path of the warrior-artist. Thirty years after the legendary Cleveland poet-artist-publisher either committed suicide (by opening his third eye with a .22) or was murdered at the age of 26-years-old under very strange circumstances in his East Cleveland apartment, everyone who knows about his two and a half years under the microscope of intense police harrassment, overblown media attention, numerous arrests and court hearings over the content of his poetry, are still asking Who killed d. a. levy? Who silenced the legendary self-proclaimed Lake Erie "toilet lama" just as he was starting to be recognized as one of the most important voices of his generations?

Not many people outside the hard core had heard of d. a. levy at the time, though he was well-known internationally in avant garde circles for his collages, paintings and contributions to the concrete poetry scene, but it was his personal trials and tribulations with the Cleveland police that made him a mythological cult figure throughout the midwest. As the focal point of what became a genuine front page heads & feds/cops & poets war, almost on par with the legendary Johnson County Range War between cattleman-settlers, almost a hundred years earlier, levy's books were confiscated, a grand jury labeled him obscene, and he was arrested and charged with contributing to the Delinquency of Minors (in the audience at a church poetry reading).

levy and his poet friends rjs, T. L. Kryss, Kent Taylor, John Scott, D. R. Wagner, Geoffrey Cook, Steve Ferguson, Franklin Osinsky became known as The Underground Thought Patrol because they fought back and taunted the police and made fun of the city authorities. levy blew open a real estate scam in the University Circle area in his underground newspaper, *The Buddhist Third Class Junkmail Oracle*. In response, a contract was reputedly put out on his head by the last Subversive Squad leftover in America from the McCarthy era. levy's apartment was raided, his mimeo machine was confisicated, but even worse on a personal level, there was a police informer in their inner circle. Between an overabundance of psychedelics and paranoia, levy's story illuminates a small, but important niche in a very critical time in history that is not only still reverberating through us today, but because cultural mores were changed so drastically during that period, it will probably always be considered the one special time of the 20th century.

It was those times, of course, that drove levy's life and work toward the inevitable conclusion of his death, but it was his quest from the vacuum for spiritual knowledge and transcendence that prematurely did him in, no matter what the circumstances of his death actually were. Whether he was straight or was tripping at the time, was murdered or committed suicide, are questions that still haven't been answered 30 years after his death, but there are strong indications that he was not alone in the room when he died.

AMERICAN RENEGADES

From 1963 to 1968 levy's Seven Flowers Press, Renegade Press, *The Marrah-wanna Quarterly* and *The Buddhist Third Class Junkmail Oracle* published scores of unknown poets, writers and artists from all over the underground press circuit, including among many others, Charles Bukowski, Ed Sanders, R. Crumb, Paul Blackburn and Tuli Kupferberg. As for levy's own work, he had a prodigious still-developing body of work for one so young. Many of the longer poems like "The North American Book of The Dead" (1965), "Cleveland Undercovers" (1966), "Suburban Monastery Death Poem" (1968), "Kibbutz in the Sky" (1967) and "Tombstone as a Lonely Charm" (1967-68) were written over time—and in different parts. His shorter early poems, in three 1963 collections—*Variations On Flip*, *Fragments Of A Shattered Mirror* and *More Withdrawed Or Less*—portrayed a very romantic, but macabre American Graffiti trying to offer the universal goodbye to childhood and grow into a world he strongly suspected would never really live up to its potential. His work after that probably provides the most accurate poetic diary of the late 1960s ever recorded. In retrospect, levy may not have been the most well-known poet of his generation, but his voice may well be the truest to describe the external events he lived through, from an internal level.

Despite his extraordinary output, he was not a machine or a stenographer. He was simply a poet. But ah, what a fucking poet. He may have disclaimed the role of martyr or spokesman, but if ever a poet stood up for all other poets' right to speak what they see and feel, and stood up for all poets' obligation to be, as Pound put it, "the antennae of the species," d. a levy qualified. And that decision to stand up, more than anything else—the decision not to be an entertainer for the utilitarian powers that be—but to be an antenna for the evolution of the species, an illuminator of the truth as he saw it, was what killed him. So levy truly died for his work. Unfortunately, youth is impatient, so while he was living, he all too often felt deserted by what that work gave him back in the material world. But truth in the present tense of any infrastructure diametrically opposed to that truth, can only be handled in shards. So even in today's neatly packaged culture, if you squint your eyes and look around you, there are glimmers every-where of what d. a. levy and the last (unofficial) American revolution left behind for us to sort out.

MIKE GOLDEN

From *Tombstone as a Lonely Charm* (Part 3)

if you want a revolution
return to your childhood
and kick out the bottom

dont mistake changing
headlines for changes

if you want freedom
dont mistake circles
for revolutions

think in terms of living
and know
you are dying
·& wonder why

if you want a revolution
learn to grow in spirals
always being able to return
to your childhood
and kick out the bottom

This is what ive been
trying to say—if you
attack the structure—
the system—the establishment
you attack yourself
KNOW THIS!
& attack if you must
challenge yourself externally

but if you want a revolution
return to your childhood
& kick out the bottom

be able to change
yr own internal chemistry

walk down the street
& flash lights in yr head
at children

this is not a game
your childhood
is the foundation
of the system

        ·

walk down the street
flash lights in yr head
at children but be wary
of anyone old enough to kill

learn how to disappear

before they can find you

(that is, if you want to
stay alive)

if you want a revolution
do it "together"
but dont get trapped in
words or systems

people are people
no matter what politics
color or words they use
& they all have children
buried in their head

if you want a revolution
grow a new mind
& do it quietly
if you can

return to your childhood
and kick out the bottom
then become a being
not dependent on words
for seeing

whenever you get bored
change headlines
colors politics words
change women

but if you really want
a revolution
learn how to change
your internal chemistry
then go beyond that

walk down the streets
& flash light at
yourself

From *Cleveland Undercovers*

but that was then
NOW i am, and do not expect
tomorrow or yesterday today.
instead i write in exstacy
and when someone stops to say
"Hey, that's not true!"
i yell backwards,
"For who. . . . . . and fuck rhyme."
i have a city to cover with lines,
with textured words &
the sweaty brick-flesh images of a
drunken tied-up whorehouse cowtown
sprawling and brawling on its back.

From *Suburban Monastery Death Poem*

PART ZERO—Celebration With Rada Drums

only ten blocks away
buildings burned—perhaps burning now
the august night broken by sniper fire
police men bleeding in the streets
a sniper surrenders (perhaps out of ammunition)
Gun Jammed?
someone sed he was framed in a doorway
like a picture—his hands in the air
when they shot him—

only ten blocks away
from my quiet apartment
with its green ceramic buddhas
& science fiction books
unread skin magazines to be cut up
for collages

only ten blocks away
from my total helplessness
from my boredom enforced by the state
they are looting stores
trying to get televisions

AMERICAN RENEGADES

so they can watch the riots
on the 11 pm news

The Bells of the Cherokee Ponies

i thought they were
wind chimes
in the streets at night

with my young eyes
i looked to the east
and the distant ringing
of ghost ponies
rose from the ground

Ponies Ponies Ponies

(the young horse becomes
a funny sounding
word)

i looked to the east
seeking buddhas to
justify those bells
weeping in the darkness

The Underground Horses
are rising

Cherokee, Delaware, Huron
we will return your land to you

the young horses
will return your land to you

to purify the land
with their tears

The Underground Horses
are rising
to tell their fathers
"in the streets at night

the bells of Cherokee ponies
are weeping."

the suburban prophets
For R.D.D.

oh its an easy cool
that rolling of long grass lawn tranquility
and long grass philosophy
sounds almost as absurd
as suburban hipsters
smoking long grass
like panama red while subtly discussing
plato ouspensky sartre or zen
putting it down
its easy
from the long grass lands &
from the long grass lands
'everything is good'

"everything is good"
in the land of shad trees
"Everything is God"
"the universe is one"
walking in the long grass lands with flowers
within reach of quiet hands

"You bet motherfucker,
　　let me tell you about
　　　　the satori i had last week!"
in the suburbs
its easy
to remember
golden rules & golden days
& god is good even tho non-existent
its a good world in the suburban long grass
you can watch the grass grow
& smell progress in the open sky
and its easy to forget
across the city
are streets of hunger
and that suburban tranquility

doesnt feed those hungry streets
and that suburban tranquility
doesnt mean a good fuck
on suburban lawns

its easy to think there
are jobs for everyone
when youve got one

its easy to quote lao tzu
when yr wife inst on the streets
and dont have to dodge the
welfare children

its an easy cool
laying on the quiet suburban lawn grass
"in tune with the universe"

and its like smoking long grass
panama red
you just slip into
an easy forgetting
and its easy to forget
some men are starving
and some men with guns . . .

Poem for Beverly

1.
i sit down next to her
& our toes begin a love dance

i think
how beautiful
her dark smile
her brown skin
& i touch her arms
          her belly
our legs touch
& i realize i
want to see my white hand
   on her dark breasts
   and i cant do it

i try but my eyes
disappear
& all i can see
is beverly, beverly
tired & laying next to me

i get very confused
i dont really want to do
anything but *be* next to her

my hand touching
the small of her back

i cant do anything
except think love thoughts
to her & flash lights in my
head & wonder if she can
hear me loving her

2
in the 9 dimensional
collapseable universe
waiting for some one to
do it

i ask her what
she really wants

she knows!

she wants security

& i am so old and silly
in my need
i tell her the truth

Reality Jew (1964)
(or what its really like to be the angel of death in cleveland)

When i was a little kid
my parents never told me
i didn't find out until

i got out of high school
then when people asked me,
I ASKED THEM,
"Nationality or Religion?"

When i was a little kid
my parents brought me up as a christian
that when i discovered,
i was different
i wasnt THAT sick!
so at sixteen
still being a virgin forest
i decided
i must be a buddhist monk,
Then when people asked me
I TOLD THEM, i told them
"Not me, man, i don't belong to No-thing

In the navy
a swabby once asked me,
if i wanted to go to the
temple with him,
i told him
"Not me, man, im the last
of the full blooded american indians."

it became confusing
so after a while
when people inquired
"Hey..ah..you arnt. . . . .are you?"
i answered,
"with a name like levy,
what the hell do you think i am?"
A Ritz Cracker? A flying bathtub?
An arab?   etc.

But now its getting pretty hip
to be a jew
and some of my best friends are
becoming converted to halavah,
even the crones who suddenly
became World War 2 catholics are
now praising bagels & lox
i still dont feel on ethnic things like

"Ok, we all niggers so lets hold hands."
&
"OK, we're all wops so lets support the
mafia,"
&
"Ok, we're all jews so lets weep on each
others shoulders."
so now when people smile and say,
"Hey, you're one of us,"
i smile and say,
"Fuck you, man,
im still alive."

Cleveland: The Rectal Eye Visions

1. WARMING UP THE BOX

delivered on time to persons with city & state line bearing
only the words DEATH CITY—I suppose there is present
in *the city* a speed carrying living cartoons toward death
& an anxiety that pushed one over the edge of the ocean
sooner than necessary—i have seen people falling, under
New Yorks strange wheels of time,
                                    but there are worse places
there is AMERICA THE HOME OF THE VOID—2500 miles of apathy
    &
lack of communication . . . cities like cleveland & it leaves
an uneasy feeling to think of justice
                        peace
                        & love and then find oneself
lost in a city of war monuments;
in the morning the sun rises in the east & the
trumpets blare as wheelbarrows of $ $ are rolled
down EUCLID AVE &
the children dressed in rags
    bow down in reverence &
the children dressed in the bright-light of dreams
    shouts hossanas to the golden images
the sun rises in the east
        RA   is   a rain of dry tears over the dust of allah
        JAHVEH has tossed the karmic dice
        JESUS & MILAREPA & BUDDHA playing cards in a

                    lost room on the SOLAR BARQUE
the rainbowed children are ONE BODY
in their church of open sky
hemmed with banks and dimestores
and the new image of god is hailed
            OH—children of DEATH
            SIEG HEIL   SIEG HEIL
            DER PFENIG UBER ALLES
the wind in the trees of the forest city.
the coins freshly minted in solemn temple
& the resurrection is eternal   OH
god is gold & green like the leaves
in the trees & the silver stars twinkle
on the domes of 8AM time vaults

(i am looking for a comet on a shelf of quarters)

you infinitely portable god—a quiet god
heard deep inside the pocket—a soft mantra
of money that has taken over—the mass mind

2
YOU—lost in dreams of stallions &
                television violence
YOU ARE DYING in yr suburban homes
YOU ARE DYING—the 11:20 NEWS is a lie
the 7:30 news is a lie
huntley & brinkley are lies
the weather report is a cartoon
YOU ARE THE LATE MOVIE

BLOOD   GUTS   DEATH   MURDER   LAW   CRASH   WAR
            the angel of death is not news
            you failed in yr toilet training you dreamers
            without identities

YOU ARE NOT   JEAN HARLOW
                    JAMES DEANS DEATH IS NOT YRS
                    GARY COOPERS COOL IS NOT YRS
                     LIZ TAYLORS DREAM TWOT IS NOT YRS
                    BRIGIT BARDOT IS NOT RIMBAUD

        you are sitting there
        sucking it up
        the friday night horror movie is really

a HAPPENING in viet nam
the prisons of Spain are packed like a tin
of sardines
you are paying for them
you are paying for the death of others
you are paying
wth yr hemorrhoids
& wet dreams . . . shooting up with channel 3/5/8
& it is killing you faster than shooting
methedrine crystals on the beaches of lake erie
. . . in between the stench of fish—young
trains of skinnylegs are coupling—maggot infested
fish . . . soft breasts . . . a rat carries a piece of puke
home . . . hand under skirt-thunderbird cockman
(& theyre blowing Lady Jane on the western front) . . .
driftwood—the lightening in the void . . . OM MANI PAD ME HUM . . .
broken glass . . . beer courage . . . fires & fires & shouts from
Sandusky to ERIE . . . this fast dry "rocks off" lay is not
TANTRA (FUCK is not the ultimate expression of
love) . . . the sunrises in the east & the weekends
are not washed away—no one wears a white shirt
if they understand the tragedy of LOCKWIERD *
smells like rotting abortions on bayonets
would you believe it *BULLETIN*:   the white
virgin is dead—electric chair on television . . . there's a
lot of chicks balling with sand in the cracks of their
asses. .dry dock . . . i burn incense
we share pieces of light &
i remember the skeleton of a
ship half buried in the sand
& a photograph of a nude model 1920
carefully placed under an empty
gallo wine bottle

3
& Dr. Wagner "the dreams here are getting to be too much
HEADLINE: NIAGARA FALLS BEATNIK POETS TRY TO BRING
LOST LOVE TO HONEYMOONERS—POLICE ARE
ROUNDING THEM UP & X-RAYING THEM TO
DEATH"

HEAD-LINE . . . . . . BOO

CULTURAL EVENTS : HEADLINE : — the ring of heavenly blue
Morning glorys circling the feet of ST. EMERIC

has been condemned by the popoff as a
communist plot to advertise L.S.D. & degrade
the church—the popoff wore a lace peek-a-boo
nighty an american flag &´ sed Bless everyone
Xcept the Peace Creeps & P.S, George Lincoln
Ratwell is a reincarnation of Saint Paul & he
is not excommunicated from the church . . .

my second abortion this week—i sed was like eating
a bottle of ground glass—the shadows under this jung
chicks eyes . . . in the Suburbs BATMAN & FLASH
GORDON & L.B.J. SUPERHEROS—the superheros
taperecordings of BLACK BARTLETS FAMOUS QUOTATIONS
FOR EVERY OCCASSION * "what are you asking
me a chicken shit question like that for" the president
still puzzled over the pyramid on his dollar bills—

ACTION LIE—does NASSER really own 1/3 of America
reply—a lot of ARAB BEATNIK PEACE FREAKS ARE TRYING
        TO SUBVERT THE AMERICAN PUBLIC WITH
            MARIJUANAKILLERDRUGS
        & love—the group is small but DANGEROUS—
            NARCOTICS
        & commy propaganda—

behind the scenes & under the desk with a mona lisa
smile

HEADLINE: SEX AS A MEANS OF EXPRESSION!!   oh god,
             what are these people trying to say   ?
        YOU ARE WATCHING TELEVISION
            & DYING
                YOUR CHILDREN ARE BEING FUCKED
in the mouth with the poisons you feed them
in the ear with the tripe you tell them
in the mind with unusuable knowledge & lies
in the spirit with illusions
in the ass by the neighborhood 14 yr old queer who
        learned to love with his mouth before he
        could get an erection . . .
in dreams with compromise ⊛ yr daughters
    hymen is a myth to the high school dyke
    on the tennis court—Mayor
Locher is a whore . . . the police dept is a dream

house—the syphilis of ignorance & the brutality are heredit
ary
you are fucking your sons and daughters with apathy
& lack of vision

HEADLINE: *I AM NOT TRYING TO SCREW YOU*
                    I AM TRYING TO COMMUNICATE
    (this will be taken out of context)   or as the
latest 18 yr old abortion on the scene sucking up
beers faster than Zorro could circumcise a bad ass
or whip a masochist in a gay bar CRACK—
she sed it wasnt the "dusting & cleaning; it was the
furniture polish they used that brought her down
    & WHAT THEY FORGOT TO TELL HER CUNT
was another hour & then under the table & then
HANNA PAVILION & then she sed "it was when i
was 16 & dreams—mist-electric love for a fatherless
fathers eye—no one seemed to understand—i didnt
want an icebox in my bedroom—i wanted Someone to
  Say HEY YOU

        oh you know they have a T.V. here too?

4

                sometimes we walk around east Cleveland
                the lady is 18—a bucks county hindu
                she smiles & laughs
                she is collecting the years like dust
(it is difficult to remember—the bombs have dropped)
                today she saw a piece of my mirror
                & the sunlight of Amen Ra . . . later she broke out
in hives—it was a sweaty afternoon—her sculptured
being unbeleivably hindu—we read the KAMA SUTRA
lying in bed together—she wore a small red bow and
her kiss did not have sand in it
            i burned a candle

        the green coyote in the wastebasket wept
        as i uncovered a white sun
        everyone tells me its not the same
        as the one the people of cleveland
        put in the sky—the sun rises in the
                        EAST
        my white sun, white star

                    her green eyes like an egyptian cat
          we are both dying

TRINITY HEADLINE: the green gold father—the finance company &
                    the holy ghost of television have sanctified T.V.
                    DINNERS as a religious sacrament . . . "of course
                    i fall right into a trance after a quick frozen
                    dinner—who needs zen"
          her face is always flushed with sum inner excitement
we get on the rapid at Cedar & the trip doesnt end
"the dreams here are getting to be too much" Dr. Wagner
i hope winter arrives . . . we are moving the sun out of the
suburbs—

                    LATE EDITION HEADLINE

          PEACE CREEPS STAND IN RAIN & SNOW

5
sumthin else . . . U Ching (The Hebrew Book of Changes) begins a
          new cycle at the end of the fifth section—or
          THE SYNTHETIC ILLUMINATION
a new psychedelic Rug scene..tibetan gothic patterns COKE—kill for
Coca Cola ✄ ✄ ✄ ✄ ✄ the 4th peace Reich ; sing
                    "mother, i dont know who
                    put the cocaine in
                    the excedrine bottle"   (SCREAM)
change tune if line #3 is looose in yr mind
                              in my mind
its like st pauls cathedral
               "& no one told me
                what to do / with all this
                         SPACE
                         in my mind
               a mirror
refleckted in &   the moon   SHOOTING RAYS
   breaking from   transparent   flickering on the walls
          PLASTIC FORM MMMmmmmm"
                                        new colors?
Baby Ruths Blues—blue flowers jump off her dress & before my eyes
SPRONGGGGGG Am Bars, white powder & wine—i get my head so
   tired

its full of flames . . . i want to become a human lamp/ Xcept i turn in
to a player piano *THIS IS DIFFERENT*—lady jane prayerwheels dont
work—i start & finish talking simultaneously in 24 hours—the
beer can jumps at me—i cant get it Up like Osiris(his balls in a
pawn shop. . . . .(Who I GOING) everyones saying

planetrainbuscartime

·in the morning

          my grey face

               still talking to the fireplace
the real candles burn out-in the background "You cant outtalk the
Angel of Death" over over over overover over & the record is
off   but "i been wading thru the shit in Cleveland, mother
      & nobodies got the time"
trees whisper novenas for the lady with black nostrils
       "someday sum angel
       gona try to break in my brain
       hes gona be suprized
       i got a bomb & no pain
       i go to sleep in the morning
       wake up at four
       8000 nobodies waiting at the door
       Screaming WHO AM I WHO AM I"

       WHERES THE NIGHTMARE? angel the viet cong under
  my bed
& god is dead   How come We're Still Riding

               Next Week the BIG THEY
rounds up all the leaders *HA HA* "you aint got ennuf jails"
       YOU SAY *HAHA* you "got the bullets"
       & "sumbody'll give you the ground
       & "imported Assyrian Bulls to cover the
         crematorium____
        'i smell love burning'
       & everyone sez "You got to compromise
       & the smell is from the lake",
       & "i smell souls dying"

LAST HEADLINE: & STARS # 51 to 64 will contain small swastikas
       commemorating a similar unifying investment
       of the past. . . . ."

6
For Phil Ochs
ODE TO MAYOR LOCHER—Home is the Hunky

the dogs are in uniform at the Hough Ave Airport
waiting to greet you & the people with dog minds
the people in dog suits—the dog mind   a
        HA HA   you old rascal
you're not a police dog—you're in drag
i see yr zipper   ole mayor locher/
unzip ole ralphy & we got   "GOTT IN HIMMEL"
its SUPER SERVICE the gas station mechanic—the
        pharoah of Fairview park
        the maniac Buddha mind of Brookpark Village
        its an ibis/ a swallow/ a phoenix/
        its SUPER funk. . . . .Ole Magyar Locher
you ain't even a bad guy
                    you're like prez Johnson
                    who plays
                    strange new forms of music
                    "Jazz Politics"
                    "Fug the people" (it seems ive
heard that riff before)
Ole Magyar of Swamp Erie—your empty face
              you aint even a bad guy
              you are just one of the replacable
              3 stooges
              Ralph/Larry & Moe
Ole wise man of Cleveland
you're just like prez Johnson
who plays
musical electric chairs
With The People
   & the parades of parades
   & the uniforms of death all look the same to me,
Ole Magyar/   the hungarians died for freedom in 1956
& you are selling ours with your blank face in 1966
Ole Mayor Locher
   you aint even smart enough to be a bad guy
   & the parades of parades of death
   whisper in the marching   marching
   of the   4th Reich   America
        UBER   ALLES

7
For allen ginsberg
manifesto fragment & poem for-the one-eyed children

I DONT KNOW WHERE THESE WORDS COME FROM
    ANYMORE
dreams of non-paranoid paranoia it will all work out in the end
but i keep thinking ill be one of the dead/

did i put that into my head?

my conclusions are never related to the information devoured/or
                    i eat WORDS IDEAS VISIONS
                    in an attempt to grasp sumthing
                                    CONCRETE
            to communicate
            (there is no music in this country
            all my thoughts turn into myths
MY REALITY DOESNT HAVE A FUCKING THING TO DO WITH
    YR REALITY
for instance, a chinese holy man just appeared on the curtains
& what Antonin Artaud proved was "If you're really where its at"
you can turn shock therapy into a psychedelic experience/ & if
    you *overindulge* you get friedbrains & that freaks up yr brain
waves *for a while.*
        if you're ultra-cool you can control yr psychiatrist
& he'll turn you on at regular intervals, on the other hand ONE
mistaken ride on his brain waves & you may end up like him/ *exce
pt he has the money* & you don't. he can afford to let you pay him
to maintain his myth & that is the real basis of your unreality,
all you get is the pussy which you cant accept becuz you havent
paid for it / *the thang* becomes unreal until you can buy yr way out
of the mass myth
        FOR THE POET *words* ARE THE FASTEST CURRENCY out
    of the
State illusion . . . But it is still money that keeps him out of
the State Institutions / Physically that is . . . THE POETS MYTH IS
PORTABLE The Myth of Freedom is Portable . . . Pocket Ra is *Portable*

BEING TOLD YOU ARE LOCKED UP IS WORSE THAN BEING
    LOCKED UP
        WE ARE ALL LOCKED UP/ in credit cunt, behind the bars of
    the
conservative alcoholic bank book, in advertising supermarket food
prisons/Our Bodies are Spirit Vaults..BREAK THE SEAL by osmosis

along the dotted lines on the top of yr head FREEDOM FOR THE
SPIRIT the bodies tomb doors are locked from the outside
This is called Living In A World Of Ignorance
THE BEGINNING is learning to move about freely within yr own tomb
dont look outside there is nothing but the wrathful cardboard
deities of the T.V.Myth.
                    WHAT IS FREEDOM FOR THE SPIRIT?
its like driving a go cart in a parma supermarket & HELL/YAMA
is being pursued by a Lawrence Welk smile at GREAT NORTHERN
SHRIEK . . . THE SUPERMARKET SUTRA . . . & the small tantric
    sermons
of the drive-in auto-mobile ashram-strobescopic flickerings of
limp-sex films . . . a teeny bopper who is dry thinks she is a
tantric Kwan-Yin trying to mother love & worshiping the motorcycle
OSIRIS his phallus lost in the dawn—drive-in sex at the gas
station GAS?   OIL?   GROPE? mechanical hands grope you in your
auto as you are gassed & oiled & later annointed at the drive-in
reading The Perfumed Garden by the light of the glove compartment
                           I KEEP TELLING
MYSELF, to take more drugs so i will be more coherent/ i keep
telling myself to leap like a flame from my window//i am afraid
to be the first assassination in Cleveland, everyone will think
it was the drugs (i rarely took) perhaps i should have . . .)

Allen/ the bell me&the dragon lady bought in detroit or the
toledo art museum hidden in the turquiose scarabs/ i gave it to
you after you read at the AMASA STONE CHAPEL—chanted mantras-
shot us full of light & the bell rings saying THUS i dont want
to be paranoid but other than you, no one ever told me how to
LOVE a Vacuum, Allen you may not be as holy as Jesus & the fat
funk brahmans of India, but you are certainly among the most holy
& sacred men in this desert..allen..i dont want to start a cult
they do not sell meat tenderizer for the dawn cock & last night
i skoffed several lifetimes of snatch as a yoga practice—
turned on people just telling then how to function in the Love
Underground—the catacombs of america are full of the songs of
    the skull sung in gothic bathrooms—i beleive there is merit in
taking a good shit—THIS a first creative act is the first step
to being reborn—An act of love

(it came & swallowed all my words)

How did we fall
for the myth of Ulysses murdering
        the ONE-EYED child

when he sez he is NO MAN
he wasnt kidding
                    Ulysses is an animal
a george orwell cartoon movie of the bullshit pig
& the Babylonians & the Assyrians & our whole
                        disease culture is based on these
                    SWINE
proud to murder those giants with One EYE/
THOSE ANGELS WITH THE EYE THAT FEELS
Were they the original gods
if i open the window in my head
will they kill me?
how many survived   waiting   hiding
centuries piled on centuries waiting
     for the Day of Love to arrive & instead
they are greeted by the facist princes &
                        the war lords
Ulysses,hitler,mussolini,franco,stalin,johnson
eisenhower, trujillo, batista etc etc etc the
names always spell / IMPOTENT BRAIN WAVES &
                    UNCONTROLLED DEATH

8
part I
for w. e. wyatt
Acapulco lips

the dragon of winged lions & the ch'i-lin
racing in sum sort of mind game—i cant see this
the words are just falling out of the pen

the ch'i-lin has the body of a deer
   on my homemade postcard he carries a holy man
the ch'i-lin has the feet of a horse
   on my homemade postcard the words say
   CHINESE BRONZE MING DYNASTY (1368–1644)
the ch'i-lin has the tail of an ox
   & walks off the card into the living room
   carrying a holy man

it is 10 years since the silence was broken
   like a bird that appears only in times of
        PEACE & HAPPINESS
We made our plans carefully/first in the 5th century B.C.
     and worked—making revisions in the text as time

pretended to move around us/
in ceylon—the 8th century—we painted our dreams
drank tea & watched the oceans lap our shores
no one knew or knows our number

when we moved it was as a mountain mist
& there were rumors that we hid in the valleys
& wore animal masks in death dances
& meanwhile we planned the motion of fire in water
our motions in silence

a gesture at the sky to keep track of our years
we didnt bother when they preferred to run from their
shadows   i think it was the
11th century someone noticed 100,000 dead in a dream
& we knew that in their fear they would attempt to end all
shadows   &   we made our plans

when they invented the radio we laughed at how slow it was
& raced the waves as the ocean pressing our shores

the last i remember is 1890 we kissed the books and
smiled at the mountains moving away—not knowing what to say
i was to be reborn here
& you were to be reborn there
& that was that

Now in the 20th century there are many small fires burning
what do you think they will do when they discover
they cannot destroy our light
and when we meet them at the gates
laughing/as the mountains move away.

part II
for art kleps
an exodus in autumn/the white tiger has returned
the thunder & lightening is a shock for 100 miles
GOOD FORTUNE

AK of the AdriondAKS : the SPINing concepts frighten me
it is sad to be a dreamer, unable to dream
a lover unable to love
a builder denied materials
ALL Three rowed out to sea in a seive

gone,gone,gone to the other shore/
landed on the other shore, SVAHA!

GATE GATE PARAGATE PARASAMGATE BOHDI SVAHA!

oh well/ if the government wants to live on a war economy
i guess we can give them a war--------i feel a dream
death approaching, the anxiety is a bitch.
-(*)-
AMERICA WAKE UP!
GOD DOESNT WANT YOU TO *KILL* HIS ANGELS   a
if you knew the price you will pay for this   small
WAR ECONOMY   NATION OF DEATH   prophecy
STOP THE KARMIC MURDER PIE   NOW
Worse than worshiping the golden calf you
are killing for it

consider the weight of yr possessions
america, twice this weight you will
carry when you die
for the innocent and pure of heart
i am raising the flags/ a warning of storms
Be Prepared to GO HOME LAMBS

i do not have the courage to say
this may be your last sacrifice

they will not weep on wall street
until it is too late & the tears have no meaning

there is no reason to play with death
this is not your country
when i smelled love burning/ i cried
& NOW i smell the horse of the Angel of Death

go home lambs

you are trying to build
a temple in a graveyard
YOU/have years to plan,   my days are numbered
LAUGH at my fears and ignore my love
yet love & fear are the only wings to move on

when you have visited your own death
everyday is the last

GO HOME LAMBS
let yr children be born in the sun
"this country is insane"
GO HOME LAMBS
in the world of the spirit one does not
lose what he has gained.

DIANE DIPRIMA

Revolutionary Letters
Dedicated to Bob Dylan

1
I have just realized that the stakes are myself
I have no other
ransom money, nothing to break or barter but my life
my spirit measured out, in bits, spread over
the roulette table, I recoup what I can
nothing else to shove under the nose of the *maitre de jeu*
nothing to thrust out the window, no white flag
this flesh all I have to offer, to make the play with
this immediate head, what it comes up with, my move
as we slither over this Go board, stepping always
(we hope) between the lines

4
Left to themselves people
grow their hair.
Left to themselves they
take off their shoes.
Left to themselves they make love
sleep easily
share blankets, dope & children
they are not lazy or afraid
they plant seeds, they smile, they
speak to one another. The word
coming into its own: touch of love
on the brain, the ear.

We return with the sea, the tides
we return as often as leaves, as numerous
as grass, gentle, insistent, we remember
the way
our babes toddle barefoot thru the cities of the universe.

12
the vortex of creation is the vortex of destruction
the vortex of artistic creation is the vortex of self destruction
the vortex of political creation is the vortex of flesh destruction
      flesh is in the fire, it curls and terribly warps
      fat is in the fire, it drips and sizzling sings
      bones are in the fire
          they crack tellingly in
          subtle hierglyphs of oracle
      charcoal singed
      the smell of your burning hair
for every revolutionary must at last will his own destruction
rooted as he is in the past he sets out to destroy

29
beware of those
who say we are the beautiful losers
who stand in their long hair and wait to be punished
who weep on beaches for our isolation

we are not alone: we have brothers in all the hills
we have sisters in the jungles and in the ozarks
we even have brothers on the frozen tundra
they sit by their fires, they sing, they gather arms
they multiply: they will reclaim the earth

nowhere we can go but they are waiting for us
no exile where we will not hear welcome home
'goodmorning brother, let me work with you
goodmorning sister, let me
fight by your side'

36
who is the we, who is
the they in this thing, did
we or they kill the indians, not me
my people brought here, cheap labor to exploit
a continent for them, did we
or they exploit it? do you

AMERICAN RENEGADES

admit complicity, say 'we
have to get out of Vietnam, we really should
stop poisoning the water, etc.' look closer, look again,
secede, declare your independence, don't accept
a share of the guilt they want to lay on us
MAN IS INNOCENT & BEAUTIFUL & born
to perfect bliss they envy, heavy deeds
make heavy hearts and to them
life is suffering. stand clear.

PETER COYOTE

Tracking Bob Dylan

I have been listening to and thinking about the music of Bob Dylan since a morning in 1962 when I placed his first record on the KLH portable I'd proudly lugged to college along with my collection of 1200 jazz lp's and blues 78's, which represented six years of research and scrimping. Like a slap in the face, his plaintive, wry, sarcastic, and penetrating voice woke me to the presence and purpose of an authentic artist, and inspired me to dedicate my own writing to the guitar. Though this is not the way I make my living, it is a pursuit to which I am seriously dedicated, and my high intentions were fostered by my respect for Dylan's mastery.

I've met Bob Dylan twice, briefly each time. Once in the late fifties, in a dark and unloved apartment in Greenwich Village where my friend Johnny Panken, a flamenco guitarist known professionally as Juan Moreno, had come to ground after a year in Spain living in a cave he'd rented from gypsies. Dylan was smoking a cigarette and pacing restlessly. He wore peg-legged jeans and a short jacket and barely acknowledged our introduction. I thought of a scruffy street-dog whose feet were burning, and I glanced at Johnny to determine why I should mark this particular person. Johnny stood in the background, a towering silhouette, apparently content to watch Dylan pace. His Spanish-hatted shadow replied, "He's great."

We met once again, in the late sixties. My running-partner and fellow Digger, Emmett Grogan, and I were sluicing Manhattan for adventure, squatting in Chelsea Hotel rooms abandoned by Janis Joplin and her band, friends from our home turf in San Francisco. We had bluffed the hotel into believing that we were connected to her band so our room charges were forwarded to an office somewhere, leaving our cash available for our primary preoccupation, hard drugs.

He invited us to stay awhile at his country estate in Woodstock. Emmett and I were out of place there, in our greasy jeans and biker's attitudes; a little too down-town for the sybaritic chic of big-money rock-and-roll, where people aspired to all the edges of melted butter. Still, we adjusted to lounging by Albert (Grossman's) pool, eating his homegrown organic delicacies, and sharing the best drugs lots of money could buy. Dylan was the overriding presence and organizing principle of this rarified community that included The Band; hipsters like Herbert Huncke, an early influence on William Burroughs; actor John Brent; Dylan's filmographer Howard Alk, a bearded, bear-like man with huge intellectual, sexual, and narcotic appetites; and numerous lissome women who seemed to appear and disappear as if summoned and dismissed. Like the prophet Elijah, there was always an empty chair at the table for Dylan, though he was rarely present.

One day, however, Emmett took me to Dylan's large, brown-shingled house, and for some reason, known only to himself, introduced me as Tiny Montgomery, the name of a character from a Dylan song. I was too startled by this substitution to protest, and watched Dylan shoot pool with cronies, while I gradually determined that my fictional identity had been passed to Dylan like a coin that would somehow redound to Emmett's credit.

While these two occasions may place me in a slightly more intimate orbit around my subject than some, this sketchy acquaintance affords me no special intimacies, and I am glad. By not knowing Dylan personally, I am freed from confusing my regard for his talent with regard for his person. I have no idea whether we would enjoy one another's company; and long ago dismissed any idea that affection and respect for his music signaled any special resonance between us, despite the fact that that is precisely what the work of a fine artist always suggests. But sometimes even as small a perch as proximity is useful, and I offer the following story for its utility.

During my time in New York, I was visiting Albert's office one day. "Blonde on Blonde," Dylan's latest record, was on the sound system, and Albert was speaking, and smoking a cigarette, in the curious way he had of holding it between his fourth and fifth fingers and curling his hand into a light circle as if he were gripping an imaginary pole. He'd place his lips against the mouthpiece formed by his thumb and first finger to inhale. At one moment, as Albert took a long pull on his smoke, Dylan's lyrics in the background captured my attention:

> Mona tried to tell me
> To stay away from the train line.
> She said that all the railroad men
> Just drink up your blood like wine.
> An' I said, "Oh, I didn't know that,
> But then again, there's only one I've met
> An' he just smoked my eyelids
> An' punched my cigarette."

Albert was droning on with a cigarette jutting out of his fist, oblivious to the Rosetta stone accuracy of Dylan's observations on the speakers behind him. I was transfixed by the literalness and specificity of the images. I felt like I was hearing a headline, and decided at that moment, that for all his surrealistic affections, Dylan was a very literal chronicler of an absurd world. It was not his lyrics, but his subject matter which was bizarre, and much could be learned by paying attention.

BOB DYLAN

Wanted Man

Wanted man in California, wanted man in Buffalo,
Wanted man in Kansas City, wanted man in Ohio,
Wanted man in Mississippi, wanted man in old Cheyenne,
Wherever you might look tonight, you might see this wanted man.

I might be in Colorado or Georgia by the sea,
Working for some man who may not know at all who I might be.
If you ever see me comin' and if you know who I am,
Don't you breathe it to nobody 'cause you know I'm on the lam.

Wanted man by Lucy Watson, wanted man by Jeannie Brown,
Wanted man by Nellie Johnson, wanted man in this next town.
But I've had all that I've wanted of a lot of things I had
And a lot more than I needed of some things that turned out bad.

I got sidetracked in El Paso, stopped to get myself a map,
Went the wrong way into Juarez with Juanita on my lap.
Then I went to sleep in Shreveport, woke up in Abilene
Wonderin' why the hell I'm wanted at some town halfway between.

Wanted man in Albuquerque, wanted man in Syracuse,
Wanted man in Tallahassee, wanted man in Baton Rouge,
There's somebody set to grab me anywhere that I might be
And wherever you might look tonight, you might get a glimpse of me.

Wanted man in California, wanted man in Buffalo,
Wanted man in Kansas City, wanted man in Ohio,
Wanted man in Mississippi, wanted man in old Cheyenne,
Wherever you might look tonight, you might see this wanted man.

WOODY GUTHRIE

Jesse James and His Boys

Jesse James and his boys they have killed a many a man
They held up that midnight south mail
It was every sheriff around afraid to leave his town
To lay Frank or Jesse in his jail.

There was one little coward his name was Robert Ford
I wonder if he's happy where he's at?
He posed as Jesse's friend and brought Jesse to his end
And he shot poor Jesse in the back.

Galatin had a bank that lay full of money bright
And soon it was to give to Jesse James
For he took it from the rich and he spread it to the poor
And he scattered golden money through the land.

This outlaw Jesse James would never harm a child
Nor frighten a mother and her babe
He stopped the Kansas train and he rode into the night
He was upright and true and he was brave.

Every once in a while there comes along a man
Beloved by the humble and the poor
When Jesse on the run struck out to beat the law
Found a welcome at many a cottage door.

Jesse was at home there standing on a chair
Hanging up a picture on the wall
Robert Ford drew a gun and shot Jesse through and through
And heres what Jesse said when he did fall.

Well, you said you was my friend and you brought me to my end
I hope the coward now is satisfied
But the law will always know that there wasn't any law
Could take Jesse James when alive.

Jesus Christ

Jesus Christ was a man who traveled through the land,
A hard working man and brave.
He said to the rich "Give your goods to the poor."
But they laid Jesus Christ in His grave.
Jesus was a man, a carpenter by hand,
His followers true and brave,
One dirty little coward called Judas Iscariot
Has laid Jesus Christ in His grave.

He went to the preacher, He went to the sheriff,
He told them all the same,
"Sell all your jewelry and give it to the poor,"
But they laid Jesus Christ in His grave.
When Jesus come to town, all the working folks around
Believed what He did say,
The bankers and the preachers they nailed Him on a cross,
Then they laid Jesus Christ in His grave.

The poor workin' people, they followed Him around,
They sung and they shouted gay,
The cops and the soldiers, they nailed Him in the air,
And they laid Jesus Christ in His grave.
Well, the people held their breath when they heard about His death,
And everybody wondered why,
It was the landlord and the soldiers that he hired,
To nail Jesus Christ in the sky.

(Sung to first sixteen measures)
This song was written in New York City,
Of rich man, preacher and slave,
But if Jesus was to preach like He preached at Galilee,
They would lay Jesus Christ in his grave.

DAVID TRINIDAD

In a Suburb of Thebes

My father didn't see me
as I sat on the hood of his car
in the dark driveway that night.
How could I know
when he caught my shadow
in the corner of his eye
that I'd become burglar
then bad beat
and that he would fall flat?
Believe me, I did not mean to scare.
I was only getting some air,
only drinking my coffee
to get through Balzac.
How could I know
he'd have a heart attack?

I was always the odd one.
I was always up in my bedroom
reading books and books
while my brothers played baseball
in the street.
I was the yellow crop
that tainted his green thumb
like a nicotine stain.
If only he had accepted me
as a smoker does his cough.
But I was the queer seed
that sprouted full blossom
out of all his straight sperm.
I was the germ,
the rotted pith,
I crept towards his core
like a rebellious worm in the orchard
of apples he grew.
He retired too soon.
I did it,
I bit short his plans
like a late frost.

AMERICAN RENEGADES

I admit I killed him—
this one disease in a healthy life,
this sun that came out bright and different
above suburban clouds,
that invaded his house,
cleared his table,
became one with his wife,
this heart with this red that's blue—
murdered
with one soft stroke
by the blood clot hand
of the only son he never knew.

Night and Fog
(San Francisco)

Once, depressed and drunk on the worst wine, Christopher N. and I sat out on the fire escape. That was before he got weird, before I moved back to L.A.: we shared a second-floor single apartment in the Tenderloin. Christopher N. (an alias): seventeen, innocent-looking, runaway from the complacent suburbs across the bay, smiling defiler of the scriptures of his strict father, a Baptist minister. That night on the fire escape: genesis of intense gestalt friendship. Ritual of confession. We hugged each other and cried. That night I told him someday I'd write about us sitting on the fire escape. Somewhere a phone was ringing. He finished the last glass of Ripple (Pagan Pink) and pitched it at the brick wall of the opposite building. It shattered and we laughed.

Later, back inside: steam heat, *Discreet Music*, stamping on cockroaches on red carpet cigarette scars. The walls cracked like in *Repulsion*. Lavender and green lanterned light bulb of Blanche DuBois. Initiation rite: I gave him my junior high school St. Christopher (with a surfer on the other side).

Things he did I thought delightful: took taxis, wore suspenders, spit on silver cars, drew dark circles around his eyes with shoe polish for poetic effect, cut pictures out of library books and taped them to the apartment walls, insisted upon passion, allowed himself spontaneous spasms of unlimited excess, praised Tim Curry, praised Bryan Ferry, praised the gospel according to Pasolini, named his cat Icarus, created his own art form (shock), hocked records he tired of listening to to buy used books which he read and then hocked to buy our booze, spray-painted *D* in front of *ADA ST*, cried when I told him he was my Holly Golightly, cursed money for its ability to corrupt purity.

But then he got weird. St. Christopher of the Club Baths. St. Christopher of the trench coat and collect calls. His Philip Marlowe hat. St. Christopher of the transfer ticket. Turned eighteen. Moved into a condemned flat below Market.

Folsom: factories murmuring all night, leather bars. St. Christopher of the post-fascist lost degeneration. Devout disciple of Peter Berlin. St. Christopher of the punk rock safety pin. Pierced his nipples. Placed explicit *Advocate* ad. St. Christopher of the forbidden fetish. The decidedly strange attraction to rubber. St. Christopher of the cock ring and handcuffs. Spiked dildo. Branded asses. Undressing in the balcony of the Strand during *Maitresse*. Blond boy snorting Rush stroking himself underneath smooth leather sucked off behind bushes in Lafayette Park after dark. St. Christopher with super-clap. St. Christopher of the 120 days of the Baptist apocalypse. Sexual dementor. Collector of dentures and dead rats, bloodletters. St. Christopher of the Castro hard hat and jockstrap. St. Christopher kicking pigeons and poodles in Union Square. St. Christopher picked up on Polk and Pine: twenty-five dollars for shitting on his trick.

My last visit to San Francisco: saw vomit on the sidewalks, saw piss streaming down steep streets. Bandaged panhandler. Black kid lifting the crutches of a fallen drunkard. Transvestite prostitute throwing beer bottles at a passing bus. Old women with shopping bag suitcases picking in trash bins as if testing produce. At the airport terminal, before he turned to go, Christopher N. said: "You're so prissy I can't see how we could ever have been friends." I flew home. *Angels of the complacent suburbs! of discotheques! of hostile police!* Got drunk.

Jeannette MacDonald, there's a dark alley for every perversion in your sickening city (water sports, B & D, fist fucking). No one is ever innocent.

The Shower Scene in *Psycho*

She closes the bathroom door to secure her privacy, slips off her robe, drapes it over the toilet bowl, steps into the bath, and closes the shower curtain behind her, filling the frame with a flash of white (5.89).

Shortly before midnight on Friday, August 8, 1969, Manson called together Family members Tex Watson, Susan Atkins, Patricia Krenwinkel, and Linda Kasabian to give them their instructions.

From Marion viewed through the translucent shower curtain, Hitchcock cuts to (5.90), framed from within the space bounded by the curtain. At the top center of this frame is the shower head.

Fortified with drugs and armed with a gun, knives, rope, and wire cutters, they were to take one of the Family cars and go to 10050 Cielo Drive in Beverly Hills.

Marion rises into the frame. Water begins to stream from the shower head. She looks up into the stream of water and begins to wash her neck and arms. Her expression is ecstatic as the water brings her body to life (5.91).

In the secluded ranch-style house at the end of the cul-de-sac, Sharon Tate, aged twenty-six, a star of *Valley of the Dolls* and now eight and a half months pregnant, was entertaining three guests: Hollywood hair stylist Jay Sebring, coffee heiress Abigail Folger, and Folger's lover Voytek Frykowski.

At this point, there is a cut to Marion's vision of the shower head, water radiating from it in all directions like a sunburst (5.92).

(I had just turned sixteen, was about to start my junior year at Chatsworth High.)

Hitchcock cuts to the shower head viewed from the side (5.93) at the precise moment Marion turns her naked back to the stream of water.

(Every Saturday, I went to the matinee at the Chatsworth Cinema.)

Marion takes pleasure in the stream of water emanating from the shower head (5.94).

(The theater was next to the Thrifty Drug where, two summers before, I'd bought a copy of *Valley of the Dolls*.)

From the side view of the shower head, Hitchcock cuts back to Marion, still ecstatic (5.95). Then he cuts to a setup that places the camera where the tile wall of the shower "really" is.

(I took it home and hid it under my bed. I knew it was the kind of book my mother wouldn't let me read.)

The shower curtain, to which Marion's back is turned, hangs from a bar at the top of the screen, and forms a frame-within-a-frame that almost completely fills the screen (5.96).

(The summer before that, she'd found the box of newspaper clippings on the top shelf of my closet.)

The camera begins to move forward, until the bar at the top becomes excluded from the screen (5.97).

(For weeks, I'd been cutting out articles about murders.)

Synchronized with this movement of the camera, Marion slides out of the frame, so that the shower curtain completely fills the screen (5.98).

(It started with the eight nurses in Chicago. Right after that was the Texas sniper. Then there was the politician's daughter who was bludgeoned and stabbed to death in her sleep.)

A shadowy figure, barely visible through the shower curtain, enters the door that can just be made out in the background. It steps forward toward the camera, its form doubled by and blending into its shadow cast on the translucent curtain (5.99).

After cutting telephone wires to the house, they gained access to the property by scaling fences, careful not to set off alarms.

The curtain is suddenly wrenched open and a silhouetted knife-wielding figure is revealed (5.100).

As they walked up the drive, a car approached from the house and caught them in its headlights.

The silhouetted figure is symmetrically flanked by the raised knife on the one side and the light bulb on the other (5.101).

At the wheel was eighteen-year-old Steven Parent, who had been visiting the caretaker, William Garretson. In his apartment over the garage, Garretson listened to his stereo with headphones on, unaware of what was happening just yards away.

When the camera reverses field to Marion, turned away (5.102), her figure displaces the silhouette in (5.101).

Parent slowed down and asked who they were, and what they wanted.

It is through the silhouetted figure's eyes that Marion is now viewed, as she turns around clockwise until she looks right into the camera (5.103). What she sees makes her open her mouth to scream.

Watson's response was to place the barrel of a .22 against the youth's head and blast off four rounds.

Jump cut to a closer view of Marion's face (5.104).

(I didn't know why I was so fascinated by murder.)

Second jump cut to an extreme closeup of her wide-open mouth (5.105).

AMERICAN RENEGADES

(I told my mother the clippings were "research," that one day I wanted to write about crime. She made me throw them away.)

From Marion's point of view, the silhouetted figure strikes out violently with its knife (5.106).

Watson slit one of the window-screens, crawled into the house, and admitted the others through the front door. Linda Kasabian remained outside as lookout.

The knife slashes down for the first time (5.107).

Frykowski, who was asleep on a sofa in the living room, woke up to find Watson standing over him, gun in hand.

The knife slashes through the corner of the screen. The arm and the knife remain silhouetted (5.108).

Atkins reported to Watson that there were three more people in the house. He ordered her to bring them into the living room, which she did at knife-point.

In a slightly closer variant of (5.107), the knife is again raised, its blade gleaming in the light.

(The first time I saw *Psycho*, I was baby-sitting for a couple who lived at the end of a dark cul-de-sac.)

This shot frames part of Marion's body along with the intruder's arm, still shadowy in the frame (5.109).

(I prayed they'd stay out late. I wouldn't have been allowed to watch it at home.)

Viewed from overhead, the shower-curtain bar cuts across the screen. As Marion tries to fend it off, the knife strikes three times (5.110).

(There was a storm that night: rain and branches beat against the windows. I waited anxiously for "The Late Show" to come on.)

Marion's face fills the screen, expressing bewilderment and pain (5.111).

(They'd cut most of the shower scene for TV.)

Marion holds onto the shadowy arm as it weaves three times in a spiraling move-ment (5.112).

(I felt cheated.)

Reprise of (5.111).

(I wanted to be scared.)

Reprise of (5.112).

When Sebring was told to lie face down on the floor, he tried to grab Watson's gun, whereupon Watson shot him through the lung.

Another variant of (5.107). The knife again slashes down.

Watson looped one end of a nylon rope around Sebring's neck, threw the free end over a beam and tied it around the necks of Folger and Tate, who had to stand upright to avoid being choked.

Marion turns her face away, her head almost sliding out of the frame (5.113).

Watson ordered Atkins to stab Frykowski, who got to his feet and ran outside. Atkins pursued him onto the lawn, and knifed him in the back.

The slashing knife (5.114).

Watson followed, shot Frykowski twice and, when his gun jammed, continued to beat him over the head with the butt.

A shot of Marion recoiling, still bewildered (5.115).

In the living room, the two women struggled to free themselves from their dual noose.

This shot approximates (5.114), but this time the knife slashes through the center of the frame.

Like Frykowski, Folger got as far as the front lawn. She was chased down by Krenwinkel, who stabbed her repeatedly.

Reprise of (5.115). Marion's bewildered reaction.

Watson also descended upon her, after first knifing Sebring.

The hand and knife come into clear focus. Water bounces off the glinting metal of the blade (5.116).

Then they turned on the heavily pregnant Miss Tate.

AMERICAN RENEGADES

Juxtaposition of blade and flesh (5.117).

(In secret, I read *Valley of the Dolls* several times.)

Marion recoils, but still looks dazed, entranced (5.118).

(My mother found my hiding place and made me throw the book away.)

A low-angle view facing the door. The knife slashes through the frame (5.119).

(I bicycled to Thrifty Drug, bought another copy, and snuck it into the house.)

Marion's back and arms. The intruder's arm again enters the frame (5.120).

Watson told Atkins to stab her.

Closeup of Marion's face. She is now clearly in agony (5.121).

When the actress begged to be spared for the sake of her unborn child, Atkins sneered, "Look, bitch, I don't care . . ."

Blood drips down Marion's writhing legs (5.122).

"I have no mercy for you."

Marion turns her face from the camera. The knife enters the frame (5.123).

She hesitated nonetheless, so Watson inflicted the first wound.

Reprise of (5.122), with a greater flow of blood.

Within moments, Atkins and Krenwinkel joined in, stabbing her sixteen times.

The screen flashes white as the camera momentarily frames only the bare tile wall. Marion's hand, viewed from up close and out of focus, enters and then exits the frame (5.124).

Finally, Susan Atkins dipped a towel in Sharon Tate's blood and wrote the word "Pig" on the front door.

The intruder exits (5.125).

It was not until the next day, when they watched TV at the Spahn Movie Ranch in Chatsworth, that any of them knew who they had murdered.

Marion's hand pressed against the white tile (5.126). It slowly slides down the wall.

(The same summer I read *Valley of the Dolls*, the book was being made into a movie.)

Marion's hand drops out of the frame and her body slowly slides down the wall. She turns to face forward as her back slips down, the camera tilting down with her (5.127).

(After Patty Duke, my childhood idol, was cast in one of the lead roles, it was practically all I could think about.)

She looks forward and reaches out, as if to touch someone or something she cannot see (5.128). The camera pulls slowly away. Then her hand changes its path.

(I made a scrapbook of pictures I had clipped from movie magazines:)

In extreme close-up, Marion's hand continues its movement until it grasps the shower curtain in the left foreground of the frame (5.129).

(Patty reaching for a bottle of pills, tears streaming down her face;)

The shower curtain, unable to bear her weight, pulls away from the supporting bar, as the hooks give way one by one (5.130).

(Barbara Parkins in a white bathrobe, collapsed on the beach;)

Marion's arm falls, followed by her head and torso. Her body spills over from within the shower, and lands on the curtain (5.131).

(Sharon Tate in a low-cut beaded dress, her blonde hair piled up high.)

From (5.131), there follows a cut to the reprise of the sunburst shot of the shower head viewed frontally.

(Later, when the movie premiered at Grauman's Chinese, I begged my mother to take me to see it.)

The camera cuts to Marion's legs, blood mixing with the water (5.132), and begins to move to the left, following this flow of water and blood.

("Wait till it comes to the Chatsworth Cinema," she said.)

AMERICAN RENEGADES

At *the moment Marion's legs are about to pass out of the frame, the drain comes into view (5.133).*

(The Saturday the bodies were discovered, I saw *MacKenna's Gold*, a western starring Omar Sharif and Gregory Peck.)

The camera reframes to center the drain as it tracks in toward it, so that the blackness within appears about to engulf the screen (5.134).

(The "Coming Attraction" was for *Goodbye, Columbus*, a serious adult drama.)

At this point, there is a slow dissolve from the drain to an eye, viewed in extreme closeup (5.135).

(The following week I would ride up to see it, but they wouldn't let me in. It was recommended for mature audiences.)

This eye, which fixes the camera in its gaze, displaces the drain in the frame, and appears to peer out from within it (5.136).

(We lived a few miles from the Spahn Movie Ranch.)

The camera spirals out clockwise as though unscrewing itself, disclosing the eye, Marion's, dead (5.137).

(There was a newspaper machine in front of the Chatsworth Cinema. I always chained my bicycle to it.)

The camera keeps spiraling out until we have a full view of Marion's face (5.138).

(When I left the theater that afternoon, I saw the face of Sharon Tate.)

Death has frozen it in inexpressiveness, although there is a tear welled in the corner of her eye (5.139).

(Then I read the headline as my eyes adjusted to the sun.)

BOB KAUFMAN

Bob Kaufman was a street poet, a people's poet, a poet's poet. He was a multi-ethnic poet, an African American poet, a Beat poet, a surrealist poet, a jazz poet, a poète maudit, a New Orleans poet, a San Francisco poet. One of the founding architects and "living examples" of the Beat generation as a literary, historical and existential phenomenon, he has until recently been overshadowed in reputation by his white and formally educated contemporaries such as Allen Ginsberg, Jack Kerouac, Gary Snyder and William Burroughs. To some extent, this was the result of business-as-usual neglect of Black writers by the mainstream; to some extent it reflected his own stated ambition of becoming "completely anonymous." Partly out of choice and partly out of disillusioned resignation and the ravages of street life, he turned his back on the seductions of fame and respectability, implicitly declaring solidarity with the world's anonymous poor. While African American writers and scholars have been familiar with his work, it is only now in the last several years that he is beginning to get the wider recognition that he and other "other Beats" deserve.

One of thirteen children, Robert Garnell Kaufman was born in New Orleans to a well-respected, high-achieving Black Catholic family. His mother was a schoolteacher who insisted that the children develop sophisticated literary capacities (they were fed a steady diet of Henry James, Proust, Melville, Flaubert and the like). His father was a Pullman porter and thus participated in one of the most heroic labor efforts in American history, as the Brotherhood of Sleeping Car Porters, the Pullman porter union, was the first Black union to organize successfully; it was, in the words of Franklin Rosemont, "more than a union," as it used the railroad system to disseminate Black culture, education and political power throughout the United States. At age eighteen, in 1945, Bob Kaufman too became a laborer; like several of his older brothers, he joined the Merchant Marine and became active in the turbulent organizing activities of several overlapping maritime unions. He became an impassioned labor orator for the militantly leftist Seaman's International Union, and when the AFL and the CIO merged in the 1950s, he was "purged" from the union, a casualty of the anti-Communism that swept through the labor movement during the Eisenhower-McCarthy years.

Those were years in which political dissent was crushed, and cultural/aesthetic dissent seemed the only way to publicly affirm one's right to be different. The Beat literary movement was born under these circumstances, and Kaufman left New York, which had been his prime organizing territory, for California, where he met Jack Kerouac, moved to San Francisco, and became a familiar figure in the burgeoning Bohemian literary and street scene. In a brilliant move of spiritual survival, he reinvented himself as a poet—a half-Black, half-Jewish Beat poet with an Orthodox Jewish and "voodoo" upbringing. Embodying dissent in his lifestyle (not working) and writing—or not writing but living "poetically"—became his form of labor, as outlined in the poem "The Poet." He was a much-beloved and brilliant extemporizer who blended his own rapid-fire aphorisms and wisecracks with the considerable store of modernist poetry he was able to recite from memory. This ability to "sample" other writers in an original and inventive context is evident in his poetry, which reworks and defamiliarizes the work of Coleridge, Garcia Lorca, Tennessee Williams, Hart Crane, Langston Hughes and others. In its adventurous imagery, sonorous qualities and biting wit, moreover, Kaufman's poetry has much in common with other New World Black surrealists like Aimé Cesaire, Ted Joans, Will Alexander and Wilson Harris, as well as with the jazz-inspired poetry and fiction of LeRoi Jones/Amiri Baraka and Nathaniel Mackey.

His first book, Solitudes Crowded with Loneliness (1965) was compiled, edited and sent off to the publisher (New Directions) by his wife Eileen Kaufman. Many of the poems from this period describe the North Beach scene in San Francisco in all its Bohemian pathos, humor, posturing, and genuine utopian yearnings ("Bagel Shop Jazz," "Abomunist Manifesto"); others chronicle the ongoing social hassles of being African American ("Jail Poems," "I, Too, Know What I Am Not," which was selected by Clarence Major for his 1970s anthology The New Black Poetry); still others are modeled on jazz compositional principles ("Second April") or invoke jazz themes, and many are lyrics that express an intense desire to live beyond oneself or acute dissociation ("For My Son Parker, Asleep in the Next Room," "Would You Wear My Eyes?"). Golden Sardine (City Lights, 1967), continues many of these themes ("Oct. 5. 1963," "Heavy Water Blues") and continues to experiment, as did "Abomunist Manifesto" and "Second April" with new versions of the long poem ("Caryl Chessman Interviews the PTA from his Swank Gas Chamber"). After a three-year sojourn in New York City (1960–1963) during which time he experienced the hardships of active amphetamine addiction and alcoholism, Kaufman returned to San Francisco and abruptly withdrew from public life. Where he had been the life of the party, animated and gregariously spouting his witty raps from cafes and street corners, he became elusive and shadowy, hard to track down, desiring only "anonymity" and "uninvolvement," which he maintained for the remainder of the 1960s and early 1970s. There followed a second period of productive engagement with the literary and social world in the mid-70s through 1980s, during which time he wrote "The Ancient Rain," a bicentennial dark-night-of-the-soul, and several other beautiful poems, some of which derive their power from the decentered, fragmented vision of apocalyptic liberation and/or destruction that the poet's psychic, physical and political/aesthetic life embody; they are both historical allegories and personal accounts of nightmarish experiences and intuitions. This era culminated in the publication of The Ancient Rain: Poems 1956–1978 (New Directions 1981), edited by Raymond Foye, who had to demonstrate his commitment in order to convince Kaufman to break his silence and commitment to anonymity, but who ultimately won the poet's approval for the project. Posthumously, the Bob Kaufman Collective published Closing Time Til Dawn (1986), a poetic dialogue between Kaufman and San Francisco poet Janice Blue, and Coffee House Press republished Golden Sardine and a selection from the other books under the title Cranial Guitar: Selected Poems by Bob Kaufman (1996). Bob Kaufman's star is on the rise again; in the words of poet David Henderson, who has conducted extensive research on Kaufman, he's destined for the Poetic Hall of Fame.

MARIA DAMUN

Bagel Shop Jazz

Shadow people, projected on coffee-shop walls.
Memory formed echoes of a generation past
Beating into now.

Nightfall creatures, eating each other
Over a noisy cup of coffee.

Mulberry-eyed girls in black stockings,
Smelling vaguely of mint jelly and last night's bongo
      drummer,
Making profound remarks on the shapes of navels,
Wondering how the short Sunset week
Became the long Grant Avenue night,
Love tinted, beat angels,
Doomed to see their coffee dreams
Crushed on the floors of time,
As they fling their arrow legs
To the heavens,
Losing their doubts in the beat.

Turtle-neck angel guys, black-haired dungaree guys,
Caesar-jawed, with synagogue eyes,
World travelers on the forty-one bus,
Mixing jazz with paint talk,
High rent, Bartok, classical murders,
The pot shortage and last night's bust.
Lost in a dream world,
Where time is told with a beat.

Coffee-faced Ivy Leaguers, in California
Whose personal Harvard was a Fillmore district
Weighted down with conga drums,
The ancestral cross, the Othello-laid curse,
Talking of Bird and Diz and Miles,
The secret terrible hurts,

Wrapped in cool hipster smiles,
Telling themselves, under the talk,
This shot must be the end,
Hoping the beat is really the truth.

The guilty police arrive.

Brief, beautiful shadows, burned on walls of night.

I, Too, Know What I Am Not

No, I am not death wishes of sacred rapists, singing
    on candy gallows.
No, I am not spoor of Creole murderers hiding
    in crepe-paper bayous.
No, I am not yells of some assassinated inventor, locked
    in his burning machine.
No, I am not forced breathing of Cairo's senile burglar,
    in lead shoes.
No, I am not Indian-summer fruit of Negro piano tuners,
    with muslin gloves.
No, I am not noise of two-gun senators, in hallowed
    peppermint hall.
No, I am not pipe-smoke hopes of cynical chiropractors,
    traffickers in illegal bone.
No, I am not pitchblende curse of Indian suicides,
    in bonnets of flaming water.
No, I am not soap-powder sighs of impotent window washers,
    in pants of air.
No, I am not kisses of tubercular sun addicts, smiling
    through rayon lips.
No, I am not chipped philosopher's tattered ideas sunk
    in his granite brain.
No, I am not cry of amethyst heron, winged stone in flight
    from cambric bullets.
No, I am not sting of the neurotic bee, frustrated
    in cheesecloth gardens.
No, I am not peal of muted bell, clapperless
    in the faded glory.
No, I am not report of silenced guns, helpless
    in the pacifist hands.
No, I am not call of wounded hunter, alone
    in the forest of bone.

No, I am not eyes of the infant owls hatching
    the roofless night.
No, I am not the whistle of Havana whores with cribs
    of Cuban death.
No, I am not shriek of Bantu children, bent
    under pennywhistle whips.
No, I am not whisper of the African trees,
    leafy Congo telephones.
No, I am not Leadbelly of blues, escaped from guitar jails.
No, I am not anything that is anything I am not.

Would You Wear My Eyes?

My body is a torn mattress,
Disheveled throbbing place
For the comings and goings
Of loveless transients.
The whole of me
Is an unfurnished room
Filled with dank breath
Escaping in gasps to nowhere.
Before completely objective mirrors
I have shot myself with my eyes,
but death refused my advances.
I have walked on my walls each night
Through strange landscapes in my head.
I have brushed my teeth with orange peel,
Iced with cold blood from the dripping faucets.
My face is covered with maps of dead nations;
My hair is littered with drying ragweed.
Bitter raisins drip haphazardly from my nostrils
While schools of glowing minnows swim from my mouth.
The nipples of my breasts are sun-browned cockleburs;
Long-forgotten Indian tribes fight battles on my chest
Unaware of the sunken ships rotting in my stomach.
My legs are charred remains of burned cypress trees;
My feet are covered with moss from bayous, flowing
    across my floor.
    I can't go out anymore.
    I shall sit on my ceiling.
    Would you wear my eyes?

To My Son Parker,
Asleep in the Next Room

On ochre walls in ice-formed caves shaggy Neanderthals
    marked their place in time.
On germinal trees in equatorial stands embryonic giants
    carved beginnings.
On Tasmanian flatlands mud-clothed first men hacked rock,
    still soft.
On Melanesian mountain peaks barked heads were reared
    in pride and beauty.
On steamy Java's cooling lava stooped humans raised stones
    to altar height.
On newborn China's plain mythless sons of Han acquired
    peaked gods with teak faces.
On holy India's sacred soil future gods carved worshipped
    reflections.
On Coptic Ethiopia's pimple rock pyramid builders tore
    volcanoes from earth.
On death-loving Egypt's godly sands living sacrifices carved
    naked power.
On Sumeria's cliffs speechless artists gouged messages
    to men yet uncreated.
On glorious Assyria's earthen dens art priests chipped
    figures of awe and hidden dimensions.
On splendored Peru's gold-stained body filigreed temples
    were torn from severed hands.
On perfect Greece's bloody sites marble stirred
    under hands of men.
On degenerate Rome's trembling sod imitators sculpted lies
    into beauty.
On slave Europe's prostrate form chained souls shaped free
    men.
On wild America's green torso original men painted
    glacial languages.
On cold Arctica's snowy surface leathery men raised totems
    in frozen air.
On this shore, you are all men, before, forever, eternally
    free in all things.
On this shore, we shall raise our monuments of stones,
    of wood, of mud, of color, of labor, of belief, of being,
    of life, of love, of self, of man expressed
    in self-determined compliance, or willful revolt,
    secure in this avowed truth, that no man is our master,
    nor can any ever be, at any time in time to come.

Jail Poems

1

I am sitting in a cell with a view of evil parallels,
Waiting thunder to splinter me into a thousand me's.
It is not enough to be in one cage with one self;
I want to sit opposite every prisoner in every hole.
Doors roll and bang, every slam a finality, bang!
The junkie disappeared into a red noise, stoning out his hell.
The odored wino congratulates himself on not smoking,
Fingerprints left lying on black inky gravestones,
Noises of pain seeping through steel walls crashing
Reach my own hurt. I become part of someone forever.
Wild accents of criminals are sweeter to me than hum of cops,
Busy battening down hatches of human souls; cargo
Destined for ports of accusations, harbors of guilt.
What do policemen eat, Socrates, still prisoner, old one?

2

Painter, paint me a crazy jail, mad water-color cells.
Poet, how old is suffering? Write it in yellow lead.
God, make me a sky on my glass ceiling. I need stars now,
To lead through this atmosphere of shrieks and private hells,
Entrances and exits, in . . . out . . . up . . . down, the civic
    seesaw.
Here—me—now—hear—me—now—always here somehow.

3

In a universe of cells—who is not in jail? Jailers.
In a world of hospitals—who is not sick? Doctors.
A golden sardine is swimming in my head
Oh we know some things, man, about some things
Like jazz and jails and God.
Saturday is a good day to go to jail.

4

Now they give a new form, quivering jelly-like,
That proves any boy can be president of Muscatel.
They are mad at him because he's one of Them.
Gray-speckled unplanned nakedness; stinking
Fingers grasping toilet bowl. Mr. America wants to bathe.
Look! On the floor, lying across America's face—
A real movie star featured in a million newsreels.
What am I doing—feeling compassion?

AMERICAN RENEGADES

When he comes out of it, he will help kill me.
He probably hates living.

5

Nuts, skin bolts, clanking in his stomach, scrambled.
His society's gone to pieces in his belly, bloated.
See the great American windmill, tilting at itself,
Good solid stock, the kind that made America drunk.
Success written all over his street-streaked ass.
Successful-type success, forty home runs in one inning.
Stop suffering, Jack, you can't fool us. We know.
This is the greatest country in the world, ain't it?
He didn't make it. Wino in Cell 3.

6

There have been too many years in this short span of mine.
My soul demands a cave of its own, like the Jain god;
Yet I must make it go on, hard like jazz, glowing
In this dark plastic jungle, land of long night, chilled.
My navel is a button to push when I want inside out.
Am I not more than a mass of entrails and rough tissue?
Must I break my bones? Drink my wine-diluted blood?
Should I dredge old sadness from my chest?
Not again,
All those ancient balls of fire, hotly swallowed, let them lie.
Let me spit breath mists of introspection, bits of me,
So that when I am gone, I shall be in the air.

7

Someone whom I am is no one.
Something I have done is nothing.
Someplace I have been is nowhere.
I am not me.
What of the answers
I must find questions for?
All these strange streets
I must find cities for,
Thank God for beatniks.

8

All night the stink of rotting people,
Fumes rising from pyres of live men,
Fill my nose with gassy disgust,
Drown my exposed eyes in tears.

9

Traveling God salesmen, bursting my ear drum
With the dullest part of a good sexy book,
Impatient for Monday and adding machines.

10

Yellow-eyed dogs whistling in evening.

11

The baby came to jail today.

12

One more day to hell, filled with floating glands.

13

The jail, a huge hollow metal cube
Hanging from the moon by a silver chain.
Someday Johnny Appleseed is going to chop it down.

14

Three long strings of light
Braided into a ray.

15

I am apprehensive about my future;
My past has turned its back on me.

16

Shadows I see, forming on the wall,
Pictures of desires protected from my own eyes.

17

After spending all night constructing a dream,
Morning came and blinded me with light.
Now I seek among mountains of crushed eggshells
For the God damned dream I never wanted.

18

Sitting here writing things on paper,
Instead of sticking the pencil into the air.

19

The Battle of Monumental Failures raging,
Both hoping for a good clean loss.

20
Now I see the night, silently overwhelming day.

21
Caught in imaginary webs of conscience,
I weep over my acts, yet believe.

22
Cities should be built on one side of the street.

23
People who can't cast shadows
Never die of freckles.

24
The end always comes last.

25
We sat at a corner table,
Devouring each other word by word,
Until nothing was left, repulsive skeletons.

26
I sit here writing, not daring to stop,
For fear of seeing what's outside my head.

27
There, Jesus, didn't hurt a bit, did it?

28
I am afraid to follow my flesh over those narrow
Wide hard soft female beds, but I do.

29
Link by link, we forged the chain.
Then, discovering the end around our necks,
We bugged out.

30
I have never seen a wild poetic loaf of bread,
But if I did, I would eat it, crust and all.

31
From how many years away does a baby come?

32
Universality, duality, totality. . . . one.

33
The defective on the floor, mumbling,
Was once a man who shouted across tables.

34
Come, help flatten a raindrop.

Written in San Francisco City Prison
Cell 3, 1959

Abomunist Manifesto

ABOMUNISTS JOIN NOTHING BUT THEIR HANDS OR LEGS,
OR OTHER SAME.

ABOMUNISTS SPIT ANTI-POETRY FOR POETIC REASONS
AND FRINK.

ABOMUNISTS DO NOT LOOK AT PICTURES PAINTED
BY PRESIDENTS AND UNEMPLOYED PRIME MINISTERS.

IN TIMES OF NATIONAL PERIL, ABOMUNISTS, AS REALITY
AMERICANS, STAND READY TO DRINK THEMSELVES
TO DEATH FOR THEIR COUNTRY.

ABOMUNISTS DO NOT FEEL PAIN, NO MATTER HOW MUCH
IT HURTS.

ABOMUNISTS DO NOT USE THE WORD SQUARE EXCEPT WHEN
TALKING TO SQUARES.

ABOMUNISTS READ NEWSPAPERS ONLY TO ASCERTAIN THEIR
ABOMINUBILITY. .

ABOMUNISTS NEVER CARRY MORE THAN FIFTY DOLLARS
IN DEBTS ON THEM.

ABOMUNISTS BELIEVE THAT THE SOLUTION OF PROBLEMS
OF RELIGIOUS BIGOTRY IS, TO HAVE A CATHOLIC

CANDIDATE FOR PRESIDENT AND A PROTESTANT
CANDIDATE FOR POPE.

ABOMUNISTS DO NOT WRITE FOR MONEY; THEY WRITE
THE MONEY ITSELF.

ABOMUNISTS BELIEVE ONLY WHAT THEY DREAM ONLY
AFTER IT COMES TRUE.

ABOMUNIST CHILDREN MUST BE REARED ABOMUNIBLY.

ABOMUNIST POETS, CONFIDENT THAT THE NEW LITERARY
FORM "FOOT-PRINTISM" HAS FREED THE ARTIST
OF OUTMODED RESTRICTIONS, SUCH AS: THE ABILITY TO
READ AND WRITE, OR THE DESIRE TO COMMUNICATE,
MUST BE PREPARED TO READ THEIR WORK AT DENTAL
COLLEGES, EMBALMING SCHOOLS, HOMES FOR UNWED
MOTHERS, HOMES FOR WED MOTHERS, INSANE ASYLUMS,
USO CANTEENS, KINDERGARTENS, AND COUNTY JAILS.
ABOMUNISTS NEVER COMPROMISE THEIR REJECTIONARY
PHILOSOPHY.

ABOMUNISTS REJECT EVERYTHING EXCEPT SNOWMEN.

AMIRI BARAKA

Short Speech to My Friends

A political art, let it be
tenderness, low strings the fingers
touch, or the width of autumn
climbing wider avenues, among the virtue
and dignity of knowing what city
you're in, who to talk to, what clothes
—even what buttons—to wear. I address

> / the society
> the image, of
> common utopia.

/ The perversity
of separation, isolation
after so many years of trying to enter their kingdoms,
now they suffer in tears, these others, saxophones whining
through the wooden doors of their less than gracious homes.
The poor have become our creators. The black. The thoroughly
ignorant.
Let the combination of morality
and inhumanity
begin.

2
Is power, the enemy? [Destroyer
of dawns, cool flesh of valentines, among
the radios, pauses, drunks
of the 19th century. I see it,
as any man's single history. All the possible heroes
dead from heat exhaustion
at the beach,
or hiding for years from cameras
only to die cheaply in the pages
of our daily lie.
One hero
has pretensions toward literature
one toward the cultivation of errors, arrogance,
and constantly changing disguises, as trucker, boxer,
valet, barkeep, in the aging taverns of memory. Making love
to those speedy heroines of masturbation. Or kicking literal evil
continually down filmy public stairs.

A compromise
would be silence. To shut up, even such risk
as the proper placement
of verbs and nouns. To freeze the spit
in mid-air, as it aims itself
at some valiant intellectual's face.

There would be someone
who would understand, for whatever
fancy reason. Dead, lying, Roi, as your children
came up, would also rise. As George Armstrong Custer
these 100 years, has never made
a mistake.

Larry Rivers and Frank O'Hara

How to Proceed in the Arts

I. A Detailed Study of the Creative Act

1. Empty yourself of everything.
2. Think of faraway things.
3. It is 12:00. Pick up the adult and throw it out of bed. Work should be done at your leisure, you know, only when there is nothing else to do. If anyone is in bed, with you, they should be told to leave. You cannot work with someone there.
4. If you're the type of person who thinks in words—paint!
5. Think of a big color—who cares if people call you Rothko. Release your childhood. Release it.
6. Do you hear them say painting is action? We say painting is the timid appraisal of yourself by lions.
7. They say your walls should look no different than your work, but that is only a feeble prediction of the future. We know the ego is the true maker of history, and if it isn't, it should be no concern of yours.
8. They say painting is action. We say remember your enemies and nurse the smallest insult. Introduce yourself as Delacroix. When you leave, give them your wet crayons. Be ready to admit that jealousy moves you more than art. They say action is painting. Well, it isn't, and we all know expressionism has moved to the suburbs.
9. If you are interested in schools, choose a school that is interested in you. Piero Della Francesca agrees with us when he says, "Schools are for fools." We are too embarrassed to decide on the proper approach. However, this much we have observed: good or bad schools are insurance companies. Enter their offices and you are certain of a position. No matter how we despise them, the Pre-Raphaelites are here to stay.
10. Don't just paint. Be a successful all-around man like Baudelaire.
11. Remember to despise your teachers, or for that matter anyone who tells you anything straight from the shoulder. This is very important. For instance, by now you should have decided we are a complete waste of time, Easterners, Communists, and Jews. This will help you with your life, and we say "life before art." All other positions have drowned in the boring swamp of dedication. No one paints because they choose to.
12. If there is no older painter you admire, paint twice as much yourself and soon you will be him.
13. Youth wants to burn the museums. We are in them—now what? Better destroy the odors of the zoo. How can we paint the elephants and hippopota-

muses? Embrace the Bourgeoisie. One hundred years of grinding our teeth have made us tired. How are we to fill the large empty canvas at the end of the large empty loft? You do have a loft, don't you, man?

14. Is it the beauty of the ugly that haunts the young painter? Does formality encompass the roaring citadels of the imagination? Aren't we sick of sincerity? We tell you, stitch and draw—fornicate and hate it. We're telling you to begin. Begin! Begin anywhere. Perhaps somewhere in the throat of your loud asshole of a mother? O.K.? How about some red-orange globs mashed into your teacher's daily and unbearable condescension. Try something that pricks the air out of a few popular semantic balloons; groping, essence, pure painting, flat, catalyst, crumb, and how do you feel about titles like "Innscape," "Norway Nights and Suburbs," "No. 188, 1959," "Hey Mama Baby," "Mondula," or "Still Life with Nose"? Even if it is a small painting, say six feet by nine feet, it is a start. If it is only as big as a postage stamp, call it a collage—but begin.

15. In attempting a black painting, know that truth is beauty, but shit is shit.

16. In attempting a figure painting, consider that no amount of distortion will make a painting seem more relaxed. Others must be convinced before we even recognize ourselves. At the beginning, identity is a dream. At the end, it is a nightmare.

17. Don't be nervous. All we painters hate women; unless we hate men.

18. Hate animals. Painting is through with them.

19. When involved with abstractions, refrain, as much as possible, from personal symbolism, unless your point is gossip. . . . Everyone knows size counts.

20. When asked about the old masters, be sure to include your theories of culture change, and how the existence of a work of art is only a small part of man's imagination. The Greeks colored their statues, the Spaniards slaughtered their bulls, the Germans invented hasenpfeffer. We dream, and act impatient hoping for fame without labor, admiration without a contract, sex with an erection. The Nigerians are terrible Negro haters.

II. Working On The Picture. The Creative Act As It Should Flow Along

1. You now have a picture. The loft is quiet. You've been tired of reality for months—that is, reality as far as painting goes. The New York School is a fact. Maybe this painting will begin a school in another city. Have you started—now a lot of completely UNRELATED green—yes, that's it. We must make sure no one accuses you of that easy one-to-one relationship with the objects and artifacts of the culture. You are culture changing, and changing culture—so you see the intoxicating mastery of the situation. In a certain way, you are precisely that Renaissance painter whom you least admire. You are, after all, modern enough for this, aren't you? Don't be sentimental. Either go on with your painting or leave it alone. It is too late to make a collage out of it. Don't be ashamed if you have no more ideas; it just means the painting is over.

2. Colors appear. The sounds of everyday life, like a tomato being sliced, move into the large area of the white cloth. Remember, no cameras are recording. The

choice you make stands before the tribunals of the city. Either it affects man or infects him. Why are you working? No one cares. No one will. But Michelangelo has just turned over in his grave. His head is furrowed and you, like those dopey Florentines, accuse him of being homosexual. He begins to turn back, but not before you find yourself at his toes, begging for the cheese in between.

3. At this point go out and have a hot pastrami sandwich with a side order of beans and a bottle of beer. Grope the waitress, or, if you are so inclined, the waiter. Now return to your canvas—refreshed and invigorated.

4. Michelangelo??? Who likes cheese anyway? Call a friend on the phone. Never pick up your phone until four rings have passed. Speak heavily about your latest failure. (Oh, by the way, is this depressing you? Well, each generation has its problems.) Act as if there is continuity in your work, but if there isn't, it is because that position is truly greater. Point out your relationship to Picasso who paints a cubist painting in the morning, after lunch makes a Da Vinci drawing and before cocktails a *Sturm und Drang* canvas out of the Bone Surrel *oeuvre*. His ego is the point of continuity.

5. Do you feel that you are busy enough? Truly busy. If you have had time to think, this will not be a good painting. Try reversing all the relationships. This will tend to make holes where there were hills. At least that will be amusing, and amusement is the dawn of Genius.

6. If it is the middle of the day, however, discard the use of umber as a substitute for Prussian blue. Imitation is the initial affirmation of a loving soul, and wasn't James Joyce indebted to Ibsen, and didn't we know it from his words "at it again, eh Ib."

7. Later on, imitate yourself. After all, who do you love best? Don't be afraid of getting stuck in a style. The very word style has a certain snob value, and we must remember whom we artists are dealing with.

8. Refine your experience. Now try to recall the last idea that interested you. Love produces nothing but pain, and tends to dissipate your more important feelings. Work out of a green paint can. Publicly admit democracy. Privately steal everyone's robes.

9. If you are afraid you have a tour de force on your hands, be careful not to lean over backward. It is sometimes better to appear strong than to be strong. However, don't forget the heart either. . . . Perhaps we mislead you. . . . Forget the heart. To be serious means to include all. If you can't bear this you have a chance of becoming a painter.

10. Whatever happens, don't enjoy yourself. If you do, all that has been wisely put here has been an absolute waste. The very nature of art, as opposed to life, is that in the former (art), one has to be a veritable mask of suffering while in the latter (life), only white teeth must pervade the entire scene. We cry in art. We sing with life.

Written in 1952, first published in 1961

HELEN A. HARRISON
Director of the Pollack–Krasner House and Study Center

On Jackson Pollock

Jackson Pollock wrote very little about his own work. Although critics, collectors and indeed many of his fellow artists were often baffled by his efforts to communicate visually, he was reluctant to translate his message into the more familiar language of written or spoken words. Even in his representational work, Pollock's meaning was veiled in arcane symbolism that resisted straightforward interpretation. When asked for a statement about his 1943 painting, the *She-Wolf*, he wrote that it "came into existence because I had to paint it. Any attempt on my part to say something about it, to attempt explanation of the inexplicable, could only destroy it." Inevitably, as his reputation grew, Pollock had to confront questions about his challenging, innovative, and controversial art—questions he could not dismiss with such apparent arrogance.

In the autumn of 1950 Hans Namuth and the cinematographer Paul Faulkenburg filmed Pollock painting on canvas and on a sheet of plate glass, and during the winter they edited the footage into a 12-minute documentary for which the artist was asked to provide the narration. At about the same time, a Long Island journalist named William Wright was asked by a radio station to conduct a series of taped interviews with people he thought were noteworthy. Wright, who lived near Pollock on Fireplace Road in the Springs section of East Hampton, asked his neighbor to participate. Surprisingly, Pollock agreed to both requests.

Preparing his statements was clearly not a task Pollock relished. Fortunately, he had the help of his wife, Lee Krasner, an articulate and insightful commentator on his art who often served as his interlocutor. No doubt with her strong encouragement, Pollock jotted down some of his thoughts in preparation for Wright's interview, which took place after the filming ended in late 1950.

The poetic notes reproduced here may represent Pollock's initial thoughts on what he was most eager to convey—fragmentary concepts that he and Krasner polished into coherent statements to serve as the basis for Wright's interview, from which the film's narration was derived. Like an abstract painting, the handwritten material distills the essence of what Pollock wanted to communicate. He was especially concerned that people realize his painting technique was not an end in itself, and appreciate that the imagery had meaning—that is, it expressed something beyond tangible appearance.

"Energy and motion made visible" is the most widely quoted of Pollock's phrases about his work's content, but "states of order" is revealing for its insistence that there is a fundamental structure—intuitively arrived at, but nonetheless coherent—underlying its composition. By this time, Pollock's longstanding interest in Jungian symbolism and Surrealist efforts to explore dreams and the unconscious had matured into "acceptance" of spontaneous motivation. Yet this insistence on "denial of the accident" in technical terms, and the corrollary "total control" over this means of expression, suggest that he was uncomfortable with an image that projected action for its own sake, arbitrary response to stimuli, and lack of discipline.

Punctuated by long pen-strokes that give visual coherence to Pollack's separate but interrelated thoughts about his art, this holographic note is his most succinct and poetic consideration of his methods and motivations. Far from destroying his work (as he feared an explanation of the *She-Wolf* would do), his words amplify its meanings by steering us in the right direction and providing valid points of reference for our own imaginings.

JACKSON POLLOCK

Untitled

Technic is the result of a need_____
new needs demand new technics_____
total control_____denial of
the accident_____
States of order_____
organic intensity_____
energy and motion
made visible_____
memories arrested in space,
human needs and motives_____
acceptance_____

PATTI SMITH

Patti Smith is not only a great performer, she is a shaman—that is, someone in touch with other levels of reality.

Her effect on the audience is electric, comparable to voodoo or *umbanda* rituals, where the audience members become participants, and are literally lifted out of themselves.

Technic is the result of a need —

New needs demand new Technics ——————→

Total control —— denial of
the accident —— —— ·

States of order —

Organic intensity —

Energy and motion
made visible ——————

memories arrested in space,

human needs and motives ——

acceptance —— —

Jackson Pollock

Holograph of Jackson Pollock's statement (about 1950)

In many cases, however, they are destined "to return to ordinary consciousness"—to be once again the single mother of three small children, or to follow the animal goals of the street hustler . . . but the shaman has, at least, provided a respite.

WILLIAM S. BURROUGHS

Ballad of a Bad Boy

Oh I was bad
didn't do what I should
mama catch me with a lickin'
and tell me to be good
when I was bad twice times
she shoved me in a hole
and cut off all my fingers
and laid them in a finger bowl
my mama killed me
my papa grieved for me
my little sister Annalea
wept under the almond tree

Oh I loved a car
and when I was feelin' sad
I lay down on my daddy's Ford
and I'd feel good
and you know that I got bad
robbed hubcaps from the men
and sold them to the women
and stole them back again
and I got me a car
a Hudson Hornet car
and rolled the pretty ladies
and often went too far
I went to Chicago
I went to Kalamazoo
I went to Nashville
the highways I flew
I went to Salinas
I rode to the sea
and the people all scolded
and pointed to me
they said there's a bad boy
I was so bad boy

they gathered their daughters
I heard what they said
steer away from him, honey
'cause that boy is bad
and tho' he's hung good
and flashes that loot
don't slide by his side
he rides a wrong route
'cause he's a bad boy
I was so bad boy
my mama killed me
my papa grieved for me
my little sister Annalea
wept under the almond tree

And I wept on a stock car
I captured the junkyards
and I sped thru the canyons
though I never went far
from the wreckers mechanics
I worshiped these men
but they laughed at me, man
they called me mama's boy
mama mama mama mama . . .
Monday at midnight
Tuesday at two
drunk on tequila
thinking of you, ma
I drove my car on, ma
wrecking cars was my art
I held a picture of you, ma
close to my heart
I rode closed windows
it was ninety degrees
the crowd it was screaming
it was screaming for me
they said I was nonsense
true diver chicken driver
no sense
but I couldn't hear them
I couldn't see
fenders hot as angels
blazed inside of me
I sped on raged in steam heat
I cracked up and rolled at your feet

AMERICAN RENEGADES

I rose in flames and rolled in a pit
where you caught me with a tire iron
and covered me in shit
and I coulda got up
but the crowd it screamed no
that boy is evil
too bad for parole
so bad his ma cut off all his fingers
and laid 'em in a finger bowl
his mama killed him
his papa grieved for him
his little sister Annalea
wept under the almond tree

Oh I was bad
didn't do what I should
mama catch me with a lickin'
and she tell me
You be good

Libya

refusing to stain
the red carpet
on which I sit
cross-legged
cross armed
with paper and quill
and Coltrane
it was a crazy night
for woeful celebration
though I did not celebrate
I was mourning crazy
as a stranger mourns
the desert rain
its brevity
the unexpected thrill
the red dust whorl
oh well
we have bombed Libya
we choose a swaggering
vicious romantic
lying on his cot

playing Beethoven
playing Alexander
playing a dangerous game
perhaps we chose well
I don't know
but it is dawn
a dazed warhead struck
and he lies
alive his eyes
white with weeping
we have chosen well
we have bombed the compound
of a little girl
a tiny bud bearing his name
Hana Qaddafi swaddling enemy
whose tiny girl cries
are forever stilled
and to what purpose written
if not the gold leaf
of surrender
for God's arms are open
for a little one like her
it is dawn can it matter
many things have happened
in the rich chorus of night
here cloistered among notes
a high sigh of a waif
someone else passed from his skin
as you were blown from yours
a soul discarded
by a thief in flight
from his one star
Paris hotel
Jean Genet
sacred bugger, liar
the greatest poet
of our century
another swaggering
frightened son of a bitch
an angel
with little chance of redemption
save to be suffered
by the soul of a child
Hana little flower
take the hand of this man

AMERICAN RENEGADES

who loved beauty, liberty
the insane dance of a people
who would devour the sweat
of a people like yours
lead him across the violent
threshold where all his
marvelous pais await
he loved a people, a poem
and being a treacherous soft radiant man
would love you
a little girl
orphaned like himself
who was gathered in the arms
of the enemy and given a name
Hana Qaddafi
wrapped in muslin and burlap sack
your ashes will render pure
one who could not reclaim purity
but be anointed by it
may the prison in which he stands
be as a pack of cards
a sanctuary
to press his weight and form
columns of roses
garlands
to set upon your head
Hana you are the dawn
breaking the heart of God
exposing all his love
for every little thing
may the sun be cloaked
in your name
Hana be bright
the perfect dawn aright
may God embrace you both
and may your sleep
be a train of dreams
wider than a bride's

Babelogue

i haven't fucked w/the past but i've fucked plenty w/the future. over the silk of
skin are scars from the splinters of stages and walls i've caressed. each bolt of

wood, like the log of helen, was my pleasure. i would measure the success of a night by the amount of piss and seed i could exude over the columns that nestled the P/A. some nights i'd surprise everybody by snapping on a skirt of green net sewed over w/flat metallic circles which dangled and flashed. the lights were violet and white. for a while i had an ornamental veil. but i couldn't bear to use it. when my hair was cropped i craved covering. but now my hair itself is a veil and the scalp of a crazy and sleepy comanche lies beneath the netting of skin.

i wake up. i am lying peacefully and my knees are open to the sun. i desire him and he is absolutely ready to serve me. in house i am moslem. in heart i am an american artist and i have no guilt. i seek pleasure. i seek the nerves under your skin. the nar- row archway. the layers. the scroll of ancient lettuce. we worship the flaw. the mole on the belly of an exquisite whore. one who has not sold her soul to god or man nor any other.

High on Rebellion

what i feel when i'm playing guitar is completely cold and crazy. like i don't owe nobody nothing and it's a test just to see how far i can relax into the cold wave of a note. when everything hits just right (just and right) the note of nobility can go on forever. i never tire of the solitary E and i trust my guitar and don't care about anything. sometimes i feel like i've broken through and i'm free and could dig into eternity riding the wave and realm of the E. sometimes it's useless. here i am struggling and filled with dread—afraid that i'll never squeeze enough graphite from my damaged cranium to inspire or asphyxiate any eyes grazing like hungry cows across the stage or page. inside i'm just crazy. inside i must continue. i see her, my stiff muse, jutting about in the forest like a broken speeding statue. the colonial year is dead and the greeks too are finished. the face of alexander remains not solely due to sculptor but through the power and magnetism and foresight of alexander.

the artist preserves himself. maintains his swagger. is intoxicated by ritual as well as result. look at me i'm laughing. i am lapping S from the hard brown palm of the boxer. i trust my guitar. therefore we black out together. therefore i would wade thru scum for him and scum is ahead but we just laugh. ascending with the hollow mountain i am peaking. we are kneeling we are laughing we are radiating at last. this rebellion is a gas which we pass.

Notebook

I keep trying to figure out what it means
to be american. When I look in myself
I see arabia, venus, nineteenth-century
french but I can't recognize what
makes me american. I think about
Robert Franks's photographs—broke down
jukeboxes in gallup, new mexico . . .
swaying hips and spurs . . . ponytails and
syphilitic cowpokes. I think about a
red, white and blue rag I wrap around
my pillow. Maybe it's nothing material
maybe it's just being free.

Freedom is a waterfall, is pacing
linoleum till dawn, is the right to
write the wrong words. and I done
plenty of that . . .

Notes for the Future
August 2, 1998, New York City

What did we want
What did we ever want
To shake the fragile hands of time
To rip from their sockets
Deceiving eyes
To ride through the night
In a three cornered hat
Against the shadows
To cry Awake Awake
Wake up arms delicate feet
We are paramount then obsolete
Wake up throat wake up limbs
Our mantle pressed
from palm to palm
Wake up hearts dressed in rags
Costly garments fall away
Dangle now in truthful threads
That bind the breast
And wind the muscle
Of the soul and whole together

Listen my children and you shall hear
The sound of your own steps
The sound of your hereafter
Memory awaits and turns to greet you
Draping its banner across your wrists
Wake up arms delicate feet
For as one to march the streets
Each alone each part of another
Your steps shall ring
Shall raise the cloud
And they that will hear will hear
Voice of the one and the one and the one
As it has never been uttered before
For something greater yet to come
Than the hour of the prophets
In their great cities
For the people of Ninevah
Fell to their knees
Heeding the cry of Jonah
United covering themselves in sackcloth
And ashes and called to their God
And all their hearts were as one heart
And all their voices were as one voice
God heard them and his mind was moved
Yet something greater will come to pass
And who will call and what will they call
Will they call to God the air the fowl
It will not matter if the call is true
They shall call and this is known
One voice and each another
Shall enter the dead
The living flower
Enter forms that we know not
To be felt by sea by air by earth
And shall be an elemental pledge
This our birthright
This our charge
We have given over to others
And they have not done well
And the forests mourn the leaves fall
Swaddling forests mourn the leaves fall
Swaddling babes watch and wonder
As the fathers of our spirit nations
Dance in the streets in celebration
As the mountains turn pale

AMERICAN RENEGADES

From their nuclear hand
And they have not done well
Now my children
You must overturn the tables
Deliver the future from material rule
For the only rule to be considered
Is the eleventh commandment
To love one another
And this is our covenant
Across your wrist
This offering is yours
To adore adorn
To bury to burn
Upon a mound
To hail
To set away
It is merely a cloth merely our colors
Invested with the blood of a people
All their hopes and dreams
It has its excellence yet it is nothing
It shall not be a tyranny above us
Nor should God nor love nor nature
Yet we hold as our pleasure
This tender honor
That we acknowledge the individual
And the common ground formed
And if our cloth be raised and lowered
Half mast what does this tell us
An individual has passed
Saluted and mourned by his countrymen
This ritual extends to us all
For we are all the individual
No unknown no insignificant one
Nor insignificant labor nor act of charity
Each has a story to be told and retold
Which shall be as a glowing thread
In the fabric of man
And the children shall march
And bring the colors forward
Investing within them
The redeeming blood
Of their revolutionary hearts

Notes, New York City, 1976

AUGUST 9, 1976. A hurricane coming on the city. New York boarded up like a rat house. Record Plant, Studio A. Aural aquarium for *Mermaid Turn the Tides* 1985. The air black. The wind whistling. Windows rattling. Jack Douglas stuffing rags beneath the doors, laying newspapers over the floor. Up above us, the moon was full. Setting up for the night of the Lion. The emblem of Ethiopia. The Kingdom of Sheba. The true earth of Rimbaud.

Nobody looked at each other but we were ready. The avenging starfish—we five in a circle. Unity was our drug. By the last take we were completely lost yet all there. My guitar felt fantastic in my hands. The neck like a mallot. My old brown amp swirling feedback like some ravaged violin. A storm was coming but I didn't feel nothing, just groping for the right note; the one that splits and sounds the alarm. A storm coming but I didn't feel nothing. Just me on my knees laughing hysterically, thankful for the privilege of playing in a rock and roll band.

JAMES DEAN

James Dean's poem, "Ode to a Tijuana Toilet," composed in early 1955 during the filming of "Rebel Without A Cause," erupted from a long estrangement from his father. He believed his father, Winton Dean, refused to see that his son was a success, that he was someone important. The "Fuck You Father" theme surfaced as well from his work in Rebel, dealing with a father's failure to communicate with his son. A drawing on a napkin (made in Goggie's during the 'nightwatch' era and long since lost), of a sombrero-wearing matador with over-sized balls, riding a motorcycle and holding a fuck-you finger aloft, accompanied this poem. "Patchen Place" (sic) refers to the House of Detention for Women on Sixth Avenue and Greenwich Avenue, opposite Patchin Place. Dean once drunkenly sang "O Solo Mio" to a woman behind a barred window, almost getting himself arrested. This poem of anger and rebellion pits Dean as a kind of Tijuana-style Garcia Lorca in the bullring of fame—warring with authority. This poem was one of three poems typed width-wise on a second sheet. Another friend, Jack Simmons, retained the other two.

JOHN GILMORE

Ode to a Tijuana Toilet
(or the Famous Fuck You Prosaic Principle.)

Portrait of Jim & naked ass
in the mirror (from backstage
it issaid: IT IS "MORBID!"
Is it MORIBUND it is asked,
Oh Great Crusty bowel of no end
SHOWING HIS BALLS TO THE WORLD
Is it Sebastian
yanking arrows out of his butt
Or the brave matador's shadow
the last moment in the/mirror
IS IT THE FATHER
who cries it is the "MORBID SON"
THE ANSWER ARRIVES:
Fuck dad, dear dad, fuck you.
The lonely man who can't
get out
from the back of the mirror
Great puppet of the Other
O breathing life
to the dead on the sand
Dried sea weed that speaks
singing Italian Songs
on Patchen Place
to the caged girl
The body in a tin can
empty of the soul
The crow is crowing
and two becomes one
THE END
The pen is set aside,
the moving finger wrote
and now he takes a shit.

James Dean by John Gilmore

ODE TO A TIJUANA TOILET
   (or the Famous Fuck You
Prosaic Principle.)
Portrait of Jim&naked ass
in the mirror (from backstage
it issaid: IT IS "MORBID!"
Is it MORIBUND it is asked,
Oh Great Crusty bowel of no end
SHOWING HIS BALLS TO THE WORLD

Is it Sebastian
yanking arrows out of his butt
Or the brave matador's shadow
the last moment in the mirror
IS IT THE FATHER ½
who cries it i s the"MORBID SON"
THE ANSWER ARRIVES:
Fuck dad, dear dad, fuck you.
The lonely man who can't
get out xxzuxxkxxxxxxjxxxgxgx
from the back of the mirror
Great puppet of the Other
O breathing life
to the dead on the sand
Dried sea weed that speaks
singing Itanlian Songs
on Patchen Place
to the xx caged girl
The body in a tin can
empty of the soul

The crow is crowing
and two becomes one

THE END
The pen is set aside,
the moving finger wrote
and now he takes a shit.

Ode To A Tijuana Toilet by James Dean

TOM WAITS

9th & Hennepin

Well it's Ninth and Hennepin
All the doughnuts have names that sound like prostitutes
And the moon's teeth marks are on the sky
Like a tarp thrown all over this
And the broken umbrellas like dead birds
And the steam comes out of the grill
Like the whole goddamn town's ready to blow...
And the bricks are all scarred with jailhouse tattoos
And everyone is behaving like dogs
And the horses are coming down Violin Road
And Dutch is dead on his feet
And all the rooms they smell like diesel
And you take on the dreams of the ones who have slept here
And I'm lost in the window, and I hide in the stairway
And I hang in the curtain, and I sleep in your hat...
And no one brings anything small into a bar around here
They all started out with bad directions
And the girl behind the counter has a tattooed tear
"One for every year he's away", she said
Such a crumbling beauty, ah
There's nothing wrong with her that a hundred dollars won't fix
She has that razor sadness that only gets worse
With the clang and the thunder of the Southern Pacific going by
And the clock ticks out like a dripping faucet
'til you're full of rag water and bitters and blue ruin
And you spill out over the side to anyone who will listen...
And I've seen it all, I've seen it all
Through the yellow windows of the evening train...

JACK MICHELINE

Jack Micheline devoted himself to poetry after walking out of a sweater factory, where he worked in New York City, one day in the early 1950s. He travelled across the United States, Mexico and Israel trying to find himself. In a biographical note he sent to the British journal *Cosmos* in 1969, Micheline wrote that he had pushed a handcart in a garment factory, worked as a messenger boy, dishwasher, farmer, actor, union organizer, panhandler and street singer. He joined liberal causes and criticized the oppressive elements of government that enforced censorship or tacitly accepted racism. He identified with the disenfranchised people he encountered in his travels and learned to love the sound of jazz and poetry. As a poet Micheline spurned any form of modernism or avant garde poetry aesthetic in favor of a populist ideal that he believed resonated with the people he met in the Midwest. He used words from the common vernacular, including words normally seen as too vulgar or obscene for regular usage. He would often say that the sound of words mattered more than the words themselves, and he came to rely on the rhythm and rhyme of his lines to reach an audience that normally had little contact with poetry. His travels around the country, which were usually initiated with insufficient financial preparedness, nevertheless liberated Micheline from the confines of city life and taught him to value the simple beauty in mundane things. He became a messenger for the principle that beauty could be found everywhere.

Jack Micheline, né Harold Silver, aka Harvey Martin Silver, was born on November 6, 1929 in the East Bronx of New York City. His first published poem appeared in the American Friends Service Committee Newsletter in Wautoma, Wisconsin, where Micheline worked building latrines for Mexican migrant workers in 1955. In 1957, at the Half Note Cafe on Hudson Street in the West Village of New York City, Micheline won a poetry reading contest, the "Revolt in Literature Award," judged by Charles Mingus, Jean Shepard and Nat Hentoff. The prize consisted of ten dollars' worth of jazz albums from Mingus' "Debut" record label. The following year Hettie Cohen and Leroi Jones published one of Micheline's poems in the premiere issue of *Yugen* magazine along with work by Philip Whalen, Diane diPrima and Allen Ginsberg. It was the first time the name "Jack Micheline" appeared in print. Micheline selected the name "Jack" after his favorite author Jack London and "Micheline" by adding an "e" to the end of his mother Helen's maiden name. Also in 1958, his first book of poetry *River of Red Wine and Other Poems* was published with an introduction by Jack Kerouac. Dorothy Parker reviewed the book for Esquire and the poet Jack Micheline was launched into the literary world of New York City.

In the early 1960's Micheline travelled to Europe, published his second book of poems *I Kiss Angels*, and edited a collection of poems *Six American Poets* which included a preface by a writer he greatly admired, James T. Farrell. In 1965 Micheline self-published his first book of stories In The Bronx and Other Stories. By the late 1960s Micheline had relocated to the West Coast and was one of the poets who comprised the Venice Beach poetry scene in Southern California along with his friends Charles Bukowski, Harold Norse, and John Thomas. He was a frequent contributor to the underground magazine *Open City* and a story written by him and selected by Bukowski for inclusion in the magazine resulted in obscenity proceedings brought by the Los Angeles Sheriff's Department.

Throughout his life Micheline viewed himself as an outlaw and was uncomfortable with the "Beat" label that was cast over his work. While his work had undisputably gained attention because of his associations with the Beats in New York City, he preferred to be identified with the vagabond and bohemian tradition of Vachel Lindsay and Maxwell Bodenheim. Later he identified with the emergence of a "street poetry" that included many of his contemporaries in the North Beach district of San Francisco including Bob Kaufman, Jack Hirschman, Wayne Miller, A. D. Winans, George Tsongas, Kell Robinson, Kaye MacDonough among others. For Micheline being an outlaw meant that the "academy" would ignore him; his work would not be readily available, he wouldn't be anthologized, he wouldn't be taught in schools. Any success he had would be through the pure strength of his work and would be disseminated by small publishing houses or through self-publication efforts. For the most part, he was helping to define a new poetry canon.

Micheline did not, however, romanticize the alienation that being an outlaw caused him. Though he could boast of having published over 20 poetry books, none were by a major publisher, and virtually all of them were out of print at the time of his death in February of 1998. Nevertheless, he was proud of his achievements including his largest publishing success: the 1977 publication by Paul Mariah's Manroot Press of almost 150 poems, North of Manhatten, Collected Poems, Ballads and Songs: 1954–1975.

Diane diPrima has said of Micheline that he was "a true minstrel, living in our own sad, desperate times." Floyd Salas has called Micheline the "Peter Pan of the Hard Streets." David Meltzer has compared Micheline to "one of those club fighters up against the ropes [who] always rallied to win another fight." And ruth weiss has said that "Jack Micheline cuts his words from gutstrings to make the music of his poems."

Micheline was a vagabond poet who wrote poems in a particular moment and who delighted in giving unpublished poems away to anyone who wanted them. He devoted much of his time to making his own books from mineographed or xeroxed pages. He wrote letters to women in prison, wore large colorful bowler hats and painted his old friends in beautiful gouache colors. He reveled in a travelling vagabond style that meant leaving poems strewn across America in much the way Johnny Appleseed has been immortalized in legend. For Micheline, this meant writing and giving and trading poems for food and a place to sleep. Perhaps there was no clear bargaining that occurred when this happened, but it was implicit in dealing with Micheline that he left something behind to remind you that he had been there. It is anticipated, and perhaps Micheline would have preferred it this way, that a "Complete Works of Jack Micheline" will be impossible to assemble because his poems will continue to surface. They will be found in floorboard cracks, behind stoves, couches, and refrigerators, in suitcases, closets, and attics. Wherever he was, he is.

MATT GONZALEZ

AMERICAN RENEGADES

Beauty is Everywhere Baudelaire

Beauty is everywhere Baudelaire
Even a worm is beautiful
The thread of a beggar's dress
The red eye of a drunkard
On a rainy night
Chasing the red haired girl
Baudelaire across the sky
Your raggy pants
Laughing in the rain
Beauty is everywhere Baudelaire

Hiding Places

There are hiding places in my room
where beautiful poems are hidden
Poems hidden away in boxes
on sheets of brown paper
Poems of spirit and magic
workers hands hidden in boxes
beautiful thighs
there are blue skies hidden in my room
dolphins and seagulls
the heaving of breasts and oceans
there are skies in my room
there are flies in my room
there are streets in my room
there are a thousand nights hidden in boxes
there are drunks in my poems
there are a million stars on the roof of my room
all hidden away in boxes
there are steps down side streets
there is a crazed eye of a poet in my room
there are old Arabs exploring the desert near Escalon
there are sparrows and bluebirds and wildcats in my room
there are elephants and tigers
there are skinny Italian girls in my room
there are letters from Peru and England
and Germany and Russia in my room
There are the steps of Odessa in my room
the Volga river in my room
there are dreams in the night of my room

there are flowers
there is the dance of affirmation in my room
the steps of young poets carrying knapsacks full of poems
there are the Pictures of an Exhibition in my room
Moussorgsky and Shostakovich
and Charlie Mingus in my room
Composers and painters all singing in my room
all hidden away in boxes
one night when the moon is full
they will come out and do a dance

On Franz Kline

He was a clown of immense proportions, the last son in a modern age. A pathetic genius in a modern age. A limping heart. A rag. A dishrag in a wet night. Blazing eyes of a lap dog, of a husky. Of a hunted man. Mad with light.

Black and white. Red and blue. Orange and green. The nigger of narcissus. The thief in the night. The ragged beggar. The man alive dancing up the street. People running on the other side of the street. The man was too alive. So he sang songs in a bar. Drank his heart out to death. Laughed and cried. Was a human. A big human heart beating like a piston in a drum, like a drummer and a saxophone player. A man of great magnitude, of vision. A significant human being. Wore nice sports coats with his dungarees. A man with class, class of a prince. A prince of the soul, a prince of the spirit. The prince without a kingdom but the streets of New York. The Pennsylvania-born dreamer walking the streets of the Village. Drunk, singing songs, falling on his ass in Washington Square Park.

Evicted seventeen times for non-payment of rent. To beg like a dog, like a rat, to survive. A great vision, a great artist. Won awards as a figurative painter before going abstract. He was the top banana, the man who hit the home run, the man who never compromised, a man who never sold out. A man who belonged to the people, belonged to the poor people, to the rich people, to everybody. He belonged to the whole universe. He was part of the universe. Part of a cloud that went across the sky.

He lived in his dreams.

Warren Finnerty Riding a Bicycle on 4th Avenue at Midnight Dreaming of Love and Wine and Franz Kline

1.
I don't know
But he rode
Down the darkness
Some mad happy Irishman
Down 4th Avenue
No teeth
Dreams, a part in a movie
Come on children
Puerto Ricans
Mad Irishmen
Brooklyn
Dennis Hopper
Hollywood
Nobody knows Warren
A dream
A ghost
A Russian hard-on
A woman who was a flower in India on Thompson Street
Warren riding a bicycle down 4th Avenue at midnight
Dreaming of love and Franz Kline
He laughed his sorrow away in drink and horses
In Kansas City, on the East Side
At the ranch, in Barney's Beanery in Hollywood
Softball games, midnight movies, concubines
Brooklyn Heights, New York parties underground
The moon was full that night
Chicks, cunt, women
A pair of legs, lipstick
Cup runneth over sapphires, sirens, railroad trains

2.
Tom Halley
Harold Anton
Joe Gould
Making the round to the next bar
A merry go round
Scorpio's, Hot Mamas
Montana, Moses
Assyrians, Latvians
Poles, Polamania
It doesn't matter to be born a freak in this world

We're all freaks freaking freaks
Hot hands on a skinny bike
The moon shines with tears
A dream of a script
A part on a stage
A movie
A performance, a performance
A dance in a dungeon
A mask
A montage
A make believe Halloween
A miraculous mirage
Richard Widmark walks down 8th Avenue
Christmas 1963
        or 1962
         or 1961
          or 1919
I want to get drunk
To say Yeah! Yeah!
I'm on parole
A frame up
A hung jury
A job on 2nd Avenue
Tomashefsky
Paul Muni

3.
Mark Twain
Chekhov on tobacco
Bob Blossom
Ellen Stewart
   Bob Bolles
      Feathers and dynamite
       The cash registers
        Chayefsky
         Actors as bartenders in drag
          It doesn't matter
            The slime of New York in cemeteries
            Miles of tombstones on Long Island
             Warren is beautiful
              On a bicycle at midnight
               Riding down 4th Avenue
               With white sneakers
               Laughing at the stars

Stone of the Heart

Stone of the heart
Fires blazing in the sky
Street lights in the city after dark
Railroad trains crossing the prairie tonight
Fire engines racing down the avenues
And gutters of the soul
Concrete city of the heart
Billboards blazing with radios
Lampposts like ghosts in the night
See the city of stone
See the prisons
The towers
The hospitals
And such hells
People jumping like maniacs
Yellow cabs and wild cats screaming in the night
Trashcans with debris
See the carnival of the city street
Pants
Shirts
Books and underwear
Street calls and hunted men
Screaming

Blues Poem

I got no smile cause I'm down
I carry a horn to blow in all these streets
A solo riff out of my head
How could you ever know I feel
So high on life and feet and ass and legs and thighs
That I can rise and dance with all the stars
And I can eat the moon and laugh and I can cry
The dark caves of cities hungry streets
The tired faces dark and dreary bent
and all the death it dies
I let it die
I lift my horn and blow some sounds
some soul for kids to come
Some unborn sun
in darker streets than mine

Magicians carry wings so they can fly
Let's blow a horn and love
Let's get on it and ride
and laugh and dance and jive
Let's shake the dead and let the downers die
The magic of the singers warms the earth
A song
A poem
Some paradise of mind
I got to smile now
I'm feeling good
The city street
The palace of my mind

One Arm
For Ed Balchowsky

He made love with one arm
He sang with one arm
He laughed with one arm
He cried with one arm
He walked the streets of Chicago
All with the one arm
Was beaten up with one arm
Went to jail with one arm
Took a shit with one arm
Played Bach & Beethoven
Sang on the rooftops
To early dawn
Old Spanish War Songs
All these things
With one arm
He made love
With one arm

One arm
One arm
One arm
One arm
One arm
One arm
One arm

AMERICAN RENEGADES

Ed Balchowsky
My Friend

Poem to the Seventeenth of November 1962

The eyes of children follow me as I walk through the streets
A clothesline waves in this November afternoon
The sea gulls dipping their wings in the harbor
Traffic roars across Houston Street
I just ate a potato pancake
it cost me twenty cents
O water towers
O beautiful sky
where are the angels
in the underground of cities shivering prostitutes
walk up Third Avenue
hard faces pass them by
faces of nickels and dimes and half dollars
I see aerials
drums are beating in a vacant loft
the cold air brushes against my face
history is a lie and time is a whore
The lips of dead dogs lie in the street
The twentieth century races by
and civilization is a worm that crawls sucking
Children smile at me as I walk by
their eyes like dandelions
No need to tell them what a poet is
The wagon is picking up some old rummies
One of these days I will run wild in the streets
and smell the indian corn under the pavements
The sky grows dark
The twilight is coming
O Manhattan where are the indians now
four million souls in the rattle of trains
four million
and a poet conquers a city
O city! infamous, cruel, undeserving
city of stone and lost loves
Those children's eyes
I am blind to the sky
let the light shine
It is time to stop the clocks!

Most people want to love but they can't
that is the crime
I want to be with angels!

Rambling Jack
(a biography)

Walking in a city in a daze
I opened up my heart so I could breathe
The air of life bubbling from inside
The movement of the eye to pen and brush
A thigh
A nose
A leg
The movement of a buttock
Up the avenue of time
strolling in a morning breeze
the sun that warms the Earth
the rain and snow and wind
to be alive like comets, shooting stars
The Child's eye ablaze
The wonder of cats and bats and bells, salamanders
Flowers singing in the air
all these things
Hobos, bums, blacks, the destitute desperate desperados
Museums like graveyards without foliage
boredom, strife, fear on faces chained in buses,
  jobs and wages
football fields of cheers, frustration, anger, victory,
   pits of warfare, the Piston's pride
Teachers smug like bugs and protestants
The Artist is a force for light
I'll give you color
reds and yellows, orange, purple, green
and fifty shades of blue
treetops, chimneys, railroads, bridges, rivers, streams,
  lightning, valleys
The children live and playing in the sun
To be alive
To be is the poem
A shooting star
A submarine
This life of climbing mountains falling down and rising

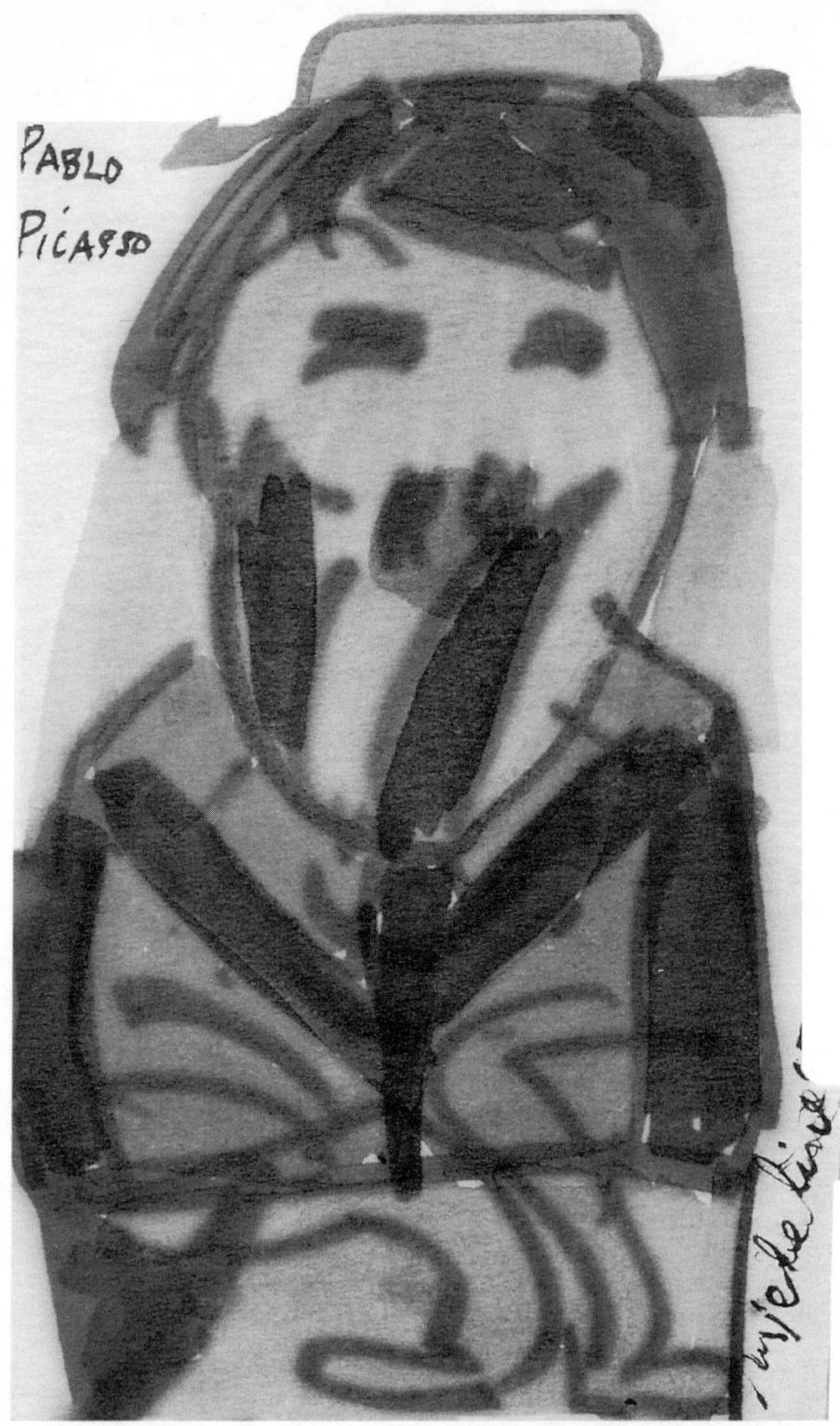

Pablo Picasso

Jack Micheline

Cafe Trieste

Jack Micheline

A submarine submerged in depths lower than mud and
  slime reaching for stars
The dead, dying and the bored in slavery of fashion,
  food and horses
singing, crying, dancing, fighting, dying, fornicating,
  shadow boxing
I chase my ghost through city streets
Through Paris, Rome, Constantinople, New York,
  Chicago, Boston, Mexico City, Merida, Isla de Mujeres,
  New Orleans, L.A., Miami, San Francisco
I chase my dreams and out the darkness
It is fear that runs the wheel of all the world
    and keeps it turning
Madness, Power
Turning inward like pomp and ceremony
The politicians guile
The cunning, slippery eels and double dealing
  double crossing
Genius is a Freak, A dog Alone Sublime!
The shrinks have lied
Your mother lied
Your teachers lied
The Rabbi lied
Your Brother even lied
Newspapers full of lies forever
It's all a stage, A game control
No natural acts allowed called truth
I am a freak, a dog
life is not a game, a stage of clowns
O Wisdom of my heart
O pussycat
I come from clouds
From earth
From constellations
I come from heat
and dream
and dungeons
I am tired Mr. Charlie
Leave me be
Ten books
Five hundred paintings
A thousand streets
Skys, furnished rooms and cheap hotels
Rooming houses
horses dying in the stretch

and women playing Yo-Yo with my mind
I do not seek it
Fame's a bitch Goddess Cleopatra
Osmosis is the fame I seek like air and water
Infamy like floods and fire and earthquakes and legends
natural acts untarnished and pure
like bird and wing and wind
The ghost that comes from nowhere and returns
shakes the dead and dying
A dirge rising from cloud
A pair of trousers and a song
Who I am and what I've done soiled
will come in time
Enjoy the riches that you have
Ask me for my Biography
I've taught you more than most
I do not want to be acclaimed by Mediocrity
It is a fool's game called greed and war and markets
    and seduction
I do not play the game
The rules are cruel
There are no rules
No compromise!
and life is not a game
I walk the streets the richest man that ever lived
Tell Muldoon I told you so
I have the sky, the air, the bird
I have my eyes
My health
The knowledge of survival
more than most
Grey hair
The gleam of cities in my eyes
My spring like walk of feet
That I am rare
A genius freak
A bird of time
I seek no more my friend farewell
And Tell Muldoon
I told you!

Chasing Kerouac's Shadow

The alabaster city gleams in the sunlight
I am on a bus going to Santa Rosa
Away from the stinking hotel
They tell me I am famous, like the Jerome cookies
Streets, poems, nuthouses, jails, paintings, con men and time
My twenty years of poems and paintings
stored away in houses and cellars
relentless with anger and love
I ponder at life and the world around me
The bus speeds on the highway going sixty
I am fifty-two, live alone, considered some mad freak genius
In reality I am a fucked up poet
who will never come to terms with the world
No matter how beautiful the flowers grow
No matter how children smile
No matter how blue is the bluest sky
The harsh realities of life, that life is mostly a put up job
The genius rain avoids us
The lone solitary soul that does her beautiful dance for
     all to see
I seek the genuine leaf blowing in the wind
The real person tapping a song whose melody
flows through rivers and time
The image that dances with stars
The sun that melts anger and harassment
Years spent begging and hustling
Carrying paintings on buses
Carrying mattresses through streets
Evictions, lost loves, hangovers, rheumatism, hemorrhoids
For a muse that rarely pays off
I must be mad, bewitched like a lost gambler
Down to my last bet with no carfare or candy
I am not subtle or charming
I cannot lie for money or tell stories
I'm the gray fox some schmuck
The old pro chasing the mad dream
The crazy Jew himself
Who don't know when to quit
Who can't say die unless I die
It is all a mad dream
The race track full of maniacs
Lost gamblers living on hope and dreams
Tomorrow is never better

The same buses full of beaten and tired faces
I only know when the cock rises and the crow howls
To eat, to drink, to take a leak
And chicken is good to eat when one is hungry
Money buys everybody, that is why the world is fucked up
That is why politicians have seventeen faces and
 speechwriters
And waitresses wear lipstick
Why mediocrity rules
Why poets hang out in groups for protection
And musicians disappear faster than flies
And artists suck the rich quicker than summer watermelon
and bourgeois children
Why the communists and capitalists
Use the same deck of tricks
To hide the miraculous
The magic of life
The wonder of children and salamanders and birds
Wonder is the thunder
Wonder is the Spring rain itself
Wonder is the young girl in love
Wonder is love
The concerto
The hummingbird
The clouds moving across the night sky
It is raining again
Light against darkness
Shadows chasing the sun
The sun chasing the shadows
Man against the night
Man and woman together with the night
The day awakens
Let's sing a song
For those who chase the night
For those that dance with light
One speck of light
No matter who is light
Light the unknown
The unknown, it is all we have
Anything is possible
Like new born colors flashing across the Universe
The road
The vagabond
The dreamers
The dancers

The unsung
Fuck the Gung Ho!
Byron Hunt is doing a collage at the Goodman Building
Ed Balchowsky is doing another painting
Raising his one arm to the sky
Rosalie Sorrells is singing a song in Kansas
Sam Shepard is smiling
Rare birds are coming out with new coats of color
Rainy Cass is alive and well in New Orleans
Valentine Chuzioff is sketching some blonde in
    Jackson Square
Bodenheim hustling another poem for wine
Franz Kline singing a sad song at the Cedar
Kerouac talking to the moon again
James T. Farrell chasing a waitress at Yankee Stadium
Charlie Mingus bopping, chucking, eating a steak
Playing bass with angels
Wilbur Ware
Gil Gaulkins
Bill Bosio
Al Delauro
Bob Bolles
Charlie Stark
Sue McGraw
Linda
Charlotte
Banana Boat
Steamboat Jones
Jeremiah
Jerusalem
The light is coming out
I'll give the sun away
It belongs to everybody
It's not mine to give away
Those with the sun
Those seeking the sun
Those on the run in the Chicago night
Those in jail
Those in the towers
Those chasing a ghost in the wilderness
Those on the road
Those with dreams
Those who will never give up
Those who are learning to dance

Those perplexed
        agonized
        wacked
        wretched
        tattooed
        confused
We are all the sun
You are the sun
This world is one
Those with wonder, you are the sun
Shake the sun
We are one
The moon and the sun are brothers!

March 15, 1982

Written on a bus from
San Francisco to Santa Rosa

LAWRENCE DURRELL

On Henry Miller

> About saints, both male and female. Somehow they are always asso-
> ciated in my mind with fierce sexual desires. That's why their struggle
> with the flesh is so heroic. And I, in my old age, I who thought I had
> solved that problem, find it flaring up again.
>
> HENRY MILLER

Miller himself had lots to tell me about Brenda Venus, and never a day passed
without him scribbling a message to her. The thought of her was omnipresent.
He does not exaggerate when he says she is literally keeping him alive; indeed,
her generosity and tact allowed him to end his days in a marvelous euphoria of
loving attachment. He was, as he himself writes, a physical ruin. Then when the
young actress strayed into his life a wind stirred the embers of Mona, of June,
Betty, Anaïs—and he once more became the young lover and renegade of his
early books. What luck! He would have been forced to drowse away his last years
with the needle and knockout drops for company! As it was, he lived them in
an ecstasy of love bequeathed, valued, and reciprocated. Brenda Venus played

the finest role an actress could wish for—Muse and Nurse of a great spirit in his decline.

HENRY MILLER

A Poem in Prose for My Venus

Were you conscious last night
Of the grandeur of the moon?
Did you know that she was a pound of honey?
You, oh pound of honey for all the couples
Crouched together everywhere in the world.
The men on their backs their phalluses
in huge erection.
The women, their vaginas sighing
and flashing.
All making love like
animals of hell.
All bridled by the desire—
the incredibly fruitful desire.
The air was pierced by the bizarre sounds—
the groaning of elephants, the "whinneying" of horses and the
bleating of
calves.
It would be deplorable if everything was
not commanded by the God Priapus.
His stamp was visible here and there—
briefly, everywhere.
He reigned over the night like an
emperor . . . Sometimes it was terrible.
But little by little one heard the Chopinesque music, the
nostalgia,
the sobs, the cries of the camels—everything
was very beautiful.
Chopin and Ravel—and also Debussy!
Oh what divine music!
Played by an angel with the refinement
of a prince.

Suddenly a resurrection.
The obscured couples rise and
begin to sing.
Their voices reach the edge of the sky.
Even the dead are touched.
The dead are revived, delirious
Now the birds can also
be heard.
"Hark hark the lark at Heaven's gate sings . . . et tra la la."
Yes the dead and the angels understand
English—how odd it is.
The gods and the half-gods speak
Hungarian and Polish
But only amongst themselves!
The dawn arrives . . . everything becomes
silent. The world breathes.
The angels disappear into the
images of Fra Angelico.
Da Vinci sleeps. Botticelli opens his eyes.
The world begins under a
Pale blue sky. Rather bluish.
Until we see each other again

Advice to a Young Writer

All piffle & twaddle—influence of Bottom Dog man.
For real "decadents" read Huysmans & other French authors.
Diarrhea of words—stew of classic allusions.
Fuck Artemis et alia!
Don't put intellect in your prick!
Write honestly even if poorly.
Humor is weak—immature.
Try drugs and compare two kinds of writing.
Try using only Anglo-Saxon words.
Throw your dictionary away!
Don't mix realism with poetics!
If you can't make words fuck, don't masturbate them!
When you speak of Cunt put hair on it!
Try to forget everything you learned in college.
Try talking like an ignoramus—or an Igaroti.
Read, for emetic, "Palm Wine Drinkard."
You will learn to write only when you stop trying to write.
A line without effort is worth a chapter of push and pull.

AMERICAN RENEGADES

First ask yourself if you have anything to say.
Don't draw the pen unless you are ready for the kill!
If you don't get rid of the Classics you'll die of constipation.
Never show any one what you've written until a year or two later.
Use the axe to your 1st draft and not the fine comb.
The latter is for lice!!!

NORMAN MAILER

The Shortest Novel of Them All

At first she thought she could kill him in three days.
She did nearly. His heart proved nearly unequal to her compliments.
Then she thought it would take three weeks. But he survived.
So she revised her tables and calculated three months.
After three years, he was still alive. So they got married.
Now they've been married for thirty years. People speak warmly of them.
    They are known as the best marriage in town.
It's just that their children keep dying.

SARAH MENEFEE

I have lived in San Francisco since 1978, where I support myself working in bookstores, while continuing as a poet and an artist. I'm a member of the League of Revolutionaries for a New America, and contribute articles and photographs to its national paper, *The People's Tribune*.

    I see how true culture arises from the people, where most necessitous. "Without vision, the people perish."

SARAH MENEFEE

From *A Letter to Jim Scully, December 1994*

My sense of what really is (now) keeps bringing me (yanking me—my eyes, my thoughts) down to the streets. On the streets it's mostly not a fight-back yet. Except inch by inch just to survive. As long as that is so I keep getting brought back down to where it's most desperate, broken, frozen, cracked. Where it's smithereened down to barely an individual, hanging on, or having let go falling, fallen. This mostly hasn't organized. Yes, there are certain places where these ones are more to be seen—but to me it's more what you'd think of as those points at which the whole system crosses into turbulence. So I keep hearing the stutter where that happens. And it also speaks to me as to someone who is also in reality exhausted in a (far less) desperate struggle to survive—so the locus is in transit, in the BART station, waiting for buses, sharing a train car with some-body sleeping, etc. But that's just the context in which there's a recognition. Maybe it would be better to write about the hope and vision and solidarity that comes out of the struggle, the movement. Yet the writing seems to insist on going back down to the bottom, back down to what's grounded, ground down, there, ground down to a few words. Or I might try to explicate, if I was any good at that, on my vision, which is informed by my political understanding, of those utterly thrown out and left to rot, rendered invisible, illegal, tongues ripped out. That's the new class, that's its first members. And mostly they aren't the "deserving poor". It can barely speak itself, though, it does so continuously.

Thank you for giving me the occasion

Comradely,
Sarah

From *The Blood About the Heart*

a palimpsest of all the times he walked by bearded flemish face and a campy smile headband white panama red rag flapping at twilight red sores on ankles of bare feet sticking out from a doorway his gracious hello

talk talk talk the black-lipped street woman said all day I talk my asshole off

he used to be young and attractive not so long ago the sick boy hustler who goes by wrapped in a blanket that trails behind in the mud his bare feet cracked and indecent past groaning walls and gutters flowing with blood

you on the corner with a plastic bag tied around your mouth we joke and laugh at the stiff-standing sight of you through the windows of our retail jobs

today the jerking mumbling letters-to-the-police-chief crazy is wearing in his jacket lapel a full-blown rose

AMERICAN RENEGADES

summer's the unmistakable smell of roses in the hall that becomes fried fish behind a neighbor's door

I never was taught about hell when I was young but love the thought of the earth's body-heat

smell that over loving years is a wide habitation

laying beside him so nice I leaned over and began to stroke his neck a sweet suck of flesh down by the pulse of the throat

I love your loose-skinned body bitch

fuck-body my little suck-body go down after just any old cock

jasmine cocksucker he says that's what you are

I'll give you thick and deep

after he yelling comes I kiss a shoulder his shoulder I can't tell if it's his or mine my lips are touching

pressing my nose against his heart chakra

a loud guffawing man an entrepreneur has sold the Sphinx and the buyer has taken it away so the salesman's saying in a hawhaw voice well we're gonna have to replace it with another and sell that too

boys for sale leaning against the walls of boutiques I pass in the night with aching breasts

a marriage proposal from a guy with a can held out for coins

falling-down-drunk leading feeble-and-old

a man with matted hair stealing a sip of dregs from a cappuccino cup in a rain of yells of get out get out I'll call the police get out

sometimes when I have a bottle you can stop and have a little

his mother kneeling above three hotplates cooking Thanksgiving dinner

at the end of time when time comes to an end there the faithful will be gathered together to dine on the great ham hocks of Leviathan's female

back and forth every moment up and down this block

blackened feet first sign of gangrene early in the decade

that they were removing me like an old fixture

thin men on Mission St selling their blood

sad Easter-open greasy-spoons

cop strides into the check-cashing joint

everything shoplifted bare as relief

the one arrested with us who cursed and howled for her confiscated bed was down by the curb in my dream singing so sweetly

we were living down in the subway he said we'd go for walks together along the tracks

he said you can't or don't want to own anything down here but you can own a cloud

I dreamed that my life was only a short time more and was weeping to lose the simple joys of it

it's the dead who make us kind

JACK HIRSCHMAN

San Francisco's Jack Hirschman was born in the Bronx in 1933, and among San Francisco poets, no one is more admired. A poet of dazzling virtuosity and uncompromising principles, he has published more than 75 books, chapbooks and translations from eight languages. His books also have been published in Italy, where he annually tours, by Multimedia Edizione. He has edited the forthcoming Curbstone Art On The Line anthology as well as co-edited with Paul Laroque and co-translated with Boadiba the Curbstone Press forthcoming edition of Haitian Creole poetry, *Open Gate*. His latest book in the U.S. is his translation of the poems of Ferruccio Brugnaro, *Fist of Sun* (Curbstone Press, 1998). In Italy, Multimedia has just published a large selection of his *Arcanes*. He is a member of The League of Revolutionaries For A New America.

I've always detested the system of government the people of this country have had to live with—its breeding of competitive division in the name of profits, of racist ideologies in the name of profits, its destruction of so many wonderful people under the weight of profit-making machineries of lies and exploitation. That's centrally why, as a poet, I developed into a communist: I believe the basic Marxist idea that human beings can *change* life; and the affirmations in my poems, even when the poems have nothing to do with, say, a political issue, belong to the dimension of hope in the wider sense of revolutionary change. This is also because I live with the belief that everyone is a poet and that the only reason such an idea is not realized is because the conditions of life have not yet been transformed so that the real meaning of poetry be manifest in the abundance of its human grandeur—not in hindsight, not through the death of the poet, but in the immediate communal resonance that really collectivizes the soul of the world.

To such a process of transformation, which today is realizing the emergence of a new class of destitute proletarians the world over, I give my voice as a poet, as a translator of revolutionary poetry written in other languages, and as a visual artist; and I give my sensible body to the struggles of the poorest and most marginalized and criminalized people of this land, in direct participation, in order to educate with revolutionary ideas.

The poems I've selected here represent a range of subject matters, all of them socially concentrated, some of them more overtly political than others. I've also included examples of poems in translation that I consider powerful in evocation of statement and form.

JACK HIRSCHMAN

Europe

You more powerful
than all the visions
You who died in fire
and Rainer's fragments
You who persist in me
as the distance here
Oh continent of Being
You awful old space
where I left my voice
where I saw my face
outside its member
You who keep in touch
day after darkness
You whom I cannot bear
You who drove me mad

with the old devices
You of the palpable
tenderness and real
depth uproaring night
You of impotence made
debonair with rage
made clear with limit
made free with loss
of all but the unending
compassionate weeping
that goes on under
the endless burning
the vivid hatred
the rich red love
the chthonic whole
the master's gong
the endless turning
back into time's
long bleeding friends
made into visible song

The Recognition #2

I know it was her
Sigourney
I turned my head
upside in the darkness
just after the Nazis
were forced by the liberating army
to throw her dead body
into the pit—yes,
it was the same face, it was
Sigourney,
her breasts strangely still fleshed
though below them
just a clacking skeleton
of thigh-bones and stick-legs

I'd never seen this footage before
—perhaps because it was Russian—
so I'd never seen Sigourney—yes,
it was Sigourney Weaver
before she had even been born,

but that's impossible,
but nothing is after that period
I'm telling you it was Sigourney Weaver
who went plummeting onto the pile
—her face her hair her torso—
to a shuddering violin-bow,
it was unmistakeably Sigourney
and I understood
why I loved Sigourney Weaver
without ever having seen her in a film,
from just having caught a momentary
glimpse of her in an interview,
she began entering my fantasies
not however as a star
I never saw her as a star
nor had seen her work as a star,
in fact what I loved about her
was that she didn't come off
as a star, she came off as . . .
I didn't know . . . I didn't know . . .
a woman, of course . . . an ordinary woman

but I didn't know why or wherefrom
and couldn't believe a few-second
image in an interview could have
so deeply and for some years
penetrated my very being
until last night when I saw her
in that mass pit and there
was no mistaking it was Sigourney
and if you don't believe
what I'm getting at, just look
around, down the street, across
the way, across the drink,
just you look outside.

NY, NY

It's big
It's ugly
I hate it
I love it
I'm free

O
Talk to me
Can't you hear me
I can't leave it
I'll do anything for it
It's so big
It's filthy
It's so sweet
I adore it
I'm staying
I'll never leave
It's in me
It's so cruel
I hate it
I love it
It's mine
I own it
It's mine
Again and again
I say I hate war
I love it
It's disgusting
It's awesome
I love it
I won't go
I promise
It's beautiful
Talk to me
Can't you hear
Me loving
O it's so brutal
It's so shit
Talk to me
Tell me
What I should do
Anything
It's marvelous
I'll never stop
Loving it
Never never
Never never
Never

Haiti

One day in the future these sounds are seeds of,
there will be a moment when not even the monkeys chirp in the
    trees,
when burros will hold their brays,
when the coconut-milky clouds will not stir in the sky,
when the thatchwork of huts will not be gossiping
and there is no breeze or sweat between your body and your rags
One day when that moment lived for years, for centuries, is here
and everything is still
like death
or zombie bread holding its breath,
a drum will begin sounding
and then another and another, multiplying,
and the voices of the simidors will be heard in every field.
And the backs,
those backs with everything written on them,
which have bent like nails hammered into the wooden cross
of the land of ages,
will plunge their arms into the ground
and pull out the weapons they've planted.
For the drums aren't an invitation to a voodoo ceremony.
The voices of the simidors are singing another song.
The lambis are growling lions of Africa.
And it isn't the cranium of a horse hung on the wooden cross
braided with limes;
it isn't a wooden cross at all that's planted in the good earth
of new Haiti.

On the night of that day the taste of a mango will be
a rapturous fireworks bursting and dying into
the ecstasy of the simple truth in our mouths.
Our acres will sleep with their arms round each other.
The child freed from terror and death will bound with
the boundless, and the maize amaze the sky upon waking
for as long as humanity is.

Buy, Always Consume
(by Ferrucio Brugnaro, translated by Jack Hirschman)

Buy, buy more than you can
consume. Consume. Fuck over

                        any relationship.
Step on everything and always
            buy everything up. Carry home
                    as much as you can.
Stuff, stuff yourself with greed.
Don't look anybody in
                        the eyes.
Surround yourself with high walls
so neither grass nor human
                    voices can reach you;
sink, sink into shit as deep
                    as you can go.
You must be on your guard;
buy away, carry it home
                    always consume.
Look around, make sure
they're not robbing you;
                trample
                    any flower
                        any plant..
Buy, always buy
            carry home
                    more than you can carry;
        consume, consume,
sink, sink into the shit,
shit shit shit.

Home
(to the National Union of the Homeless)

Winter has come.
In doorways, in alleys, at the top
of churchsteps,
under cardboard, under rag-blankets
or, if lucky, in plastic sacks,
after another day of humiliation,
sleeping,
freezing,
isolated, divided, penniless,
jobless, wheezing, dirty
skin wrapped around cold bones,
that's us, that's us in the USA,
hard concrete, cold pillow,

where fire? where drink?
damned stiffs in a drawer
soon if, and who cares?
shudders so familiar to us,
shivers so intimate,
our hands finally closed in clench
after another day panhandling, tongues
hanging out;
dogs ate more today, are curled
at the feet of beds, can belch, fart,
have hospitals they can be taken to,
they'll come out of houses and sniff
us dead one day,
pieces of shit lying scattered here
in an American city
reknowned for its food and culture.
The concrete is our sweat hardened,
the bridge our vampirized blood;
the downtown, Tenderloin and Broadway
        lights—our corpuscles transformed
        into ads;
our pulse-beat the sound *tengtengendeng*
of coins piling up on counters, in
phonebooths, Bart machines, *tengtengendeng*
in parking meters, pinball contraptions,
public lavatories, toll booths;
our skin converted into dollar bills,
plastic cards, banknotes, lampshades
for executive offices, newspapers,
toiletpaper;
our heart—the bloody organ the State
gobbles like a geek in a sideshow
that's become a national circus of the damned.

O murderous system of munitions and inhuman rights
that has plundered our pockets and dignity,
O enterprise of crime that calls us criminals,
terrorism that cries we are fearful,
greed that evicts us from the places we ourselves
        have built,
miserable war-mongery that sentences us to misery
        and public exposure as public nuisances to
        keep a filthy republic clean—
this time we shall not be disappeared
        in innercity ghetto barrio or morgue,

AMERICAN RENEGADES

this time our numbers are growing into battalions
        of united cries:
We want the empty offices collecting dust!
We want the movie houses from midnite til dawn!
We want the churches opened 24 gods a day!
We built them. They're ours. We want them!
No more doorways, garbage-pail alleys,
no more automobile graveyards,
underground sewer slums.
We want public housing!
No more rat-pit tubing, burnt-out rubble-caves,
no more rain-soaked dirt in the mouth,
empty dumpster nightmares of avalanches of trash
        and broken bricks,
screams of women hallucinating at Muni entrances
        gates,
no more kids with death-rattling teeth under
        discarded tarp.
We want public housing!
we the veterans of your insane wars,
workers battered into jobless oblivion,
the factory young: fingers crushed into handout
        on Chumpchange St.,
the factory old: spat-out phlegm from the sick
        corporate chest of Profits.
Instead of raped respect, jobs
with enough to live on!
Instead of exile and eviction in this,
our home, our land,
Homeland once and for all
for one and all
and not just this one-legged cry
on a crutch on a rainy sidewalk.

Act
(by Roque Dalton, translated by Jack Hirschman)

In the name of those washing others' clothes
(and cleansing others' filth from the whiteness)

In the name of those caring for others' children
(and selling their labor power
in the form of maternal love and humiliations)

In the name of those living in another's house
(which isn't even a kind belly but a tomb or a jail)

In the name of those eating others' crumbs
(and chewing them still with the feeling of a thief)

In the name of those living on others' land
(the houses and factories and shops
streets cities and towns
rivers lakes volcanoes and mountains
always belong to others
and that's why the cops and the guards are there
guarding them against us)

In the name of those who have nothing but
hunger exploitation disease
a thirst for justice and water
persecutions and condemnations
loneliness abandonment oppression and death

I accuse private property
of depriving us of everything.

VICTOR HERNÁNDEZ CRUZ

An Essay on William Carlos Williams

I love the quality of the
spoken thought
As it happens immediately
uttered into the air
Not held inside and rolled
around for some properly
schemed moment
Not sent to circulate a cane
field
Or on a stroll that would include
the desert and Mecca

Spoken while it happens
Direct and pure
As the art of salutation
of mountain campesinos come to
the plaza
The grasp of the handshake upon
encounter and departure
A gesture unveiling the occult
behind the wooden boards of
your old house
Remarks show no hesitation
to be expressed
The tongue itself carries
the mind
Pure and sure
Sudden and direct
like the appearance
of a green mountain
Overlooking a town.

HAROLD NORSE

Native New Yorker. A year after graduation from Brooklyn College, in 1939, I
became a member of W. H. Auden's inner circle. On the way to an academic
career as a poet in the Forties and Fifties, my second book of poems, *The Dancing Beasts,* mostly traditional, was published by Macmillan when I was living at
the Beat Hotel in Paris, doing experimental cut-up writing with William Burroughs and Brion Gysin from 1959 to 1963.

In April 1951 I received a letter from William Carlos Williams praising a free
verse poem of mine called "The Railroad Yard." He had read it in an avant garde
collection of poems by eight young poets who sent it all to him and Ezra Pound,
who was in an asylum as a traitor. Williams arranged for my reading debut at
the New York Museum of Modern Art in 1952.

That year the poem appeared in the New Directions Anthology under the
title "Warnings and Promises." Noting that the way I handled language dictated
its own forms, Williams urged me to abandon traditional forms. I had struggled
between the two poles, but after his letter I began developing my own free style
and never relapsed.

Left for Europe in 1953, lived in Rome, translated bawdy vernacular sonnets
of the great 19th Century Roman poet, G. G. Belli. He was admired by James

Joyce, D. H. Lawrence and other great writers. His Roman plebeians who speak the monologues in these poems sound like slangy New Yorkers, coarse, cynical, witty.

I translated Belli at exactly the same time that Allen Ginsberg, the shy kid I knew in New York, wrote "Howl," which wasn't published yet. I grew up using vulgar New York speech—the only exact equivalent for the Roman dialect in English. I could see why writers and scholars regarded translating Belli as impossible. They didn't believe that common American usage was suitable for serious poetry. But Hudson Review featured them in one and they appeared in book form in 1960 with a Preface by Williams. Thus I had two books published in 1960, the vulgar, vernacular Belli and my traditional, formalist poems I had by then abandoned (I saved and revised some of them).

In his letter of January 30, 1959, Williams responded to a batch of my new poems (including "Classic Frieze in a Garage") that I sent from Naples: "You have breached a new lead, shown a new power over the language which makes theories of composition so much blah. . . ." he wrote. That year I left for Paris and through Gregory Corso met William Burroughs who invited me to live at the "Beat Hotel." Thus began my ongoing relationship with the Beats. I had met Ginsberg in 1944 when he was a freshman at Columbia University, and I knew Jack Kerouac when he was a noisy boisterous drunk in the San Remo bar, Greenwich Village.

The four years when I was involved with Burroughs and Gysin in the experimental Cut-up technique, using chance for unusual effects, are documented in my Cut-up book, Beat Hotel, with a Preface by Burroughs. Repatriated in 1968 after fifteen years overseas. Have resided in California ever since. In 1969 my selected poems appeared with Charles Bukowski and Philip Lamantia in a three-poet Penguin Modern Poets volume. In 1974 City Lights published my Selected Poems, Hotel Nirvana, nominated for the National Book Award. Regarded as the poetic spokesman of the gay literary movement with my book, Carnivorous Saint (Gay Sunshine, 1977), a collection of my gay poems from 1941 to 1976. Camille Paglia in her essay "Love Poetry" (Vamps & Tramps, Vintage, 1994) wrote, "The 1960s freed gay poetry from both underground and coterie. . . . Paul Goodman, Robert Duncan, Frank O'Hara, Thom Gunn and Harold Norse document the mechanics of homosexual contact for the first time since Imperial Rome." Only Goodman and I had used the vernacular in the Forties and Fifties. We were influenced by Jean Genet. In her book, Poetry for the People (Routledge, 1995), June Jordan included me among "indispensable" Gay and Lesbian poets (Whitman, Emily Dickinson, Gertrude Stein, Allen Ginsberg, Frank O'Hara, John Ashbery, Adrienne Rich, James Baldwin, and others).

In the Eighties I wrote my autobiography, Memoirs of a Bastard Angel (William Morrow). In his groundbreaking book, Gay Spirit: Myth and Meaning (St. Martin's, 1987), Mark Thompson wrote: "Burroughs and the experimental writers of the day—Jack Kerouac, Harold Norse, Brion Gysin, Allen Ginsberg . . . created a stylistic revolution in literature, a fresh way to view . . . words themselves. Their technique disrupted syntax and linear structures of thought to create new context and forms."

As a pioneer of colloquial/Beat and Gay poetry and deconstruction of language, I gave readings at home and abroad. My work is translated into many languages. I received the Lifetime Achievement Award from the National Poetry Association and two NEA grants. My poems are being translated into Spanish by Poet/Professor Arturo Dávila, sponsored by the U.S. Mexico Fund for Culture and the Rockefeller Foundation. I am presently working on a volume of my collected poems.

HAROLD NORSE

We Bumped off Your Friend the Poet
Based on a review by Cyril Connolly, Death in Granada, *on the last days of* Garcia Lorca, The Sunday Times *(London), May 20, 1973*

We bumped off your friend the poet
with the big fat head this morning

We left him in a ditch

I fired 2 bullets into his ass
for being queer

I was one of the people
who went to get Lorca
and that's what I said to Rosales

My name is Ruiz Alonzo
ex-typographer
Right-wing deputy
alive and kicking
Falangist to the end

Nobody bothers me
I got protection
The Guardia Civil are my friends

Because he was a poet
was he better than anyone else?

He was a goddam fag
and we were sick and tired
of fags in Granada

The black assassination squads
kept busy
liquidating professors
doctors lawyers students
like the good old days of the Inquisition!

General Queipo de Llano
had a favorite phrase,
"Give him coffee, plenty of coffee!"

When Lorca was arrested
we asked the General what to do
"Give him coffee, plenty of coffee!"

So we took him out in the hills and shot him
I'd like to know what's wrong with that
He was a queer with Leftist leanings

Didn't he say
I don't believe in political frontiers?

Didn't he say
The capture of Granada in 1492
by Ferdinand and Isabella
was a disastrous event?

Didn't he call Granada *a wasteland*
peopled by the worst bourgeoisie in Spain?

a queer Communist poet!

General Franco owes me a medal
for putting 2 bullets up his ass

San Francisco, 1973

I'm Not a Man

I'm not a man. I can't earn a living, buy new things for my family.
I have acne and a small peter.

I'm not a man. I don't like football, boxing and cars.
I like to express my feelings. I even like to put an arm
around my friend's shoulder.

I'm not a man. I won't play the role assigned to me—the role created
by Madison Avenue, *Playboy*, Hollywood and Oliver Cromwell.
Television does not dictate my behavior.

I'm not a man. Once when I shot a squirrel I swore that I would
never kill again. I gave up meat. The sight of blood makes me sick.
I like flowers.

I'm not a man. I went to prison resisting the draft. I do not fight
when real men beat me up and call me queer. I dislike violence.

I'm not a man. I have never raped a woman. I don't hate blacks.
I do not get emotional when the flag is waved. I do not think I should
love America or leave it. I think I should laugh at it.

I'm not a man. I have never had the clap.

I'm not a man. *Playboy* is not my favorite magazine.

I'm not a man. I cry when I'm unhappy.

I'm not a man. I do not feel superior to women.

I'm not a man. I don't wear a jockstrap.

I'm not a man. I write poetry.

I'm not a man. I meditate on peace and love.

I'm not a man. I don't want to destroy you.

San Francisco, 1972

The Ex-Nun and the Gay Poet

They talked about meditation
and extra-sensory perception
as her eyes kept straying
to the black hair on his chest
where his shirt was open
and he talked of his new poems
as his eyes kept straying
to the slit in her crotch
where her slacks were tight.

They smoked Lebanese hash,
her first turn-on,
and she slumped a little
and said, "Nothing is happening,"
and he laughed, watching her
and she said, "I feel as if our bodies
are moving towards each other
like 2 sticks in a bathtub
of their own volition,"
and he reached over
cradling her neck in his arm
and said, "They are,"
and didn't wait
to remove his pants.

That night they drifted
in a twilight zone
with Adam and Eve
fish and amoeba
sperm and egg.

She spoke of the convent in Boston
where the nuns were in love
with the body of Christ
spreadeagled on the crucifix
and very naked.
The nuns did strange things
as they passed each other
silently in the hall
like flicking the habit
against each other's breasts
which made them horny

and quite crazy.
So she quit.

She dropped the habit
and went in search of a real man.
She worked at the US Army Base
in Libya, but had troubled dreams
of the Boston Strangler
and woke up screaming
because she dreamed of a man
under the bed.

One night he was *in* the bed
but it wasn't the Strangler,
it was a G.I. Then a cameldriver.
Then a string of cameldrivers.
Then a camel. Or was it a dream?

She felt the need of something
"more spiritual"
and having read Lawrence Durrell
she fled to Athens to find herself
but the Greeks had nothing
to say except "I love you,
50 drachmas please!"

So she drowned her dreams
in bottles of ouzo
with male hustlers in tourist tavernas
where they got money from other men
for services rendered
and gave it to her
for services rendered.
It wasn't very spiritual,
and she was losing her mind
trying to find a way
of giving and receiving
that wasn't physical.

It looked like curtains
for the ex-nun from Boston.
And then it happened.
"I met you," she said,
"I hit the jackpot."

She found her bliss
with a Gay American poet
from Brooklyn.

Porto Santo Stefano, Summer, 1970

William Carlos Williams

I want to thank you
for the pink locust
& the white mule
for the keen
scalpel
that carved
memorable poetry

those silvery lines will shine on
like a harvest moon
thru infinite trees

you pulled
a jazzy native song
out of the womb
of America

meant to be heard
like a jukebox
singing pop tunes
we can't forget
your sound

I want to thank you
for being alive
although you're dead
& buried where the Passaic
runs by the parks
& Jersey dumps—your
bailiwick! thanks
for singing of used car lots
& the broken brain
that tells 'the truth about us'

your surgical cool fingers cut
thru formal literary crap
labeled PURE
                    AMERICAN

I see you at the door
in Rutherford
clutching my shoulders
in welcome, eyes flashing
as we sit & talk
        till the light is gone
you wring your hands
        & paw the ground
like a racehorse
        on the skids
        smelling death

you pace and whinny   you are coltish
amazingly young   your high voice
agitated
        Jee-zus! what clean
hygienic genie inhabits your anguish!
old age
        disease
                the black earth
            in your throat

but that greeny flower
your asphodel
            still flourishes

Thanks for our famous garden party
in the backyard with roses

we sat hearing a concrete mixer
        the radio blaring
from the army surplus store

appropriate measure for
the language you never tired of
        —not English—but plain
                American speech
that you loved
as much as the stinking dumps
& immigrant women

American Renegades

of your landscape
                    'I'll
experiment till I die'

what heaven
do you experiment in now?
is the asphodel blowing
in the junkyards of God?
                    abandoned
chariot wheels rusty & clogged
        with cloud dust maybe?

do angelic choirs sing
        in the 'variable foot'?

Athens, 1964

Classic Frieze in a Garage

I was walking thru the city past umber embassies
            & pine-lined palaces
                palmtrees beside balconies
            the heat something
            you could touch

        past street kids with cunning
            delinquent faces
begging cigarettes
        from Americano sailors

—I thought of Nerval *Rends-moi le Pausilippe*
            et la mer d'Italie
while living on the hill   Posillipo
    above a gangster's dance floor

                on the bay of Naples
                    in a stone cottage
            over tufa caves where the sea
            crashed in winter   sweet Gerard
                one hundred years
            have made the desolation greater

the tower is really down & the sun blackened
beyond despair   loudspeakers advertise
        from boats on the bay
drowning out finches & roaring sea-caves
      all in the hands of racketeers

I have passed my time dreaming thru ancient ruins
walking thru crowded alleys of laundry
      outside tenements with gourds in windows
& crumbling masonry of wars

when suddenly I saw among the greasy rags
   & wheels & axles of a garage
      the carved nude figures
      of a classic frieze
      above dismantled parts of cars!

garage swallows sarcophagus!
   mechanic calmly spraying
      paint on a fender
observed in turn by lapith & centaur!

the myth of the Mediterranean
      was in that garage
   where the brown wiry youths
      saw nothing unusual
        at their work
among dead heroes & gods

but I saw Hermes in the rainbow
   of the dark oil on the floor
     reflected there
   & the wild hair of the sybil
      as her words bubbled
mad & drowned
      beneath the motor's roar

Naples, 1958

Let Go and Feel Your Nakedness

Let go and feel your nakedness, tits ache to be bitten and sucked
Let go with pong of armpit and crotch, let go with hole a-tingle

Let go with tongue lapping hairy cunt, lick feet, kiss ass, suck cock and
  balls
Let the whole body go, let love come through, let freedom ring
Let go with moans and erogenous zones, let go with heart and soul
Let go the dead meat of convention, wake up the live meat of love

Let go with the senses, pull out the stops, forget false teachings and lies
Let go of inherited belief, let go of shame and blame in brief
Let go of forbidden energies, choked back in muscles and nerves
Let go of rigid rules and roles, let go of uptight poses
Let go of your puppet self, let go and renew your self and be free
Let go the dead meat of convention, wake up the live meat of love

Let go this moment, this hour, this day, tomorrow may be too late
Let go of guilt and frustration, let liberation and tolerance flow
Let go of phantom worries and fears, let go of hours and days and years
Let go of hate and rage and grief, let walls against ecstasy fall for relief
Let go of pride and greed, let go of missiles and might and creed
Let go the dead meat of convention, wake up the live meat of love

At the Café Trieste

The music of ancient Greece
and Rome did not come down to us
but this morning
I read Virgil's *Eclogues*
struck by the prophecy
of a new era:
"A great new cycle of centuries
begins. Justice returns to earth,
the Golden Age returns," he wrote
30 years before the end
of his millennium, describing
the birth of the infant god, come down
from heaven. Jesus was 19
when Virgil died at 89.
Will the Golden Age ever come?
Same faces thrown up each generation,
same races, emotions, struggles!
all those centuries, those countries!
languages, songs, discontents!
They return here in San Francisco
as I sit in the Café Trieste.

O recitative of years!
O *Paradiso!* sings the jukebox
as Virgil and Verdi combine
in this life to show
this is the only Golden Age
there'll ever be.

Dream of Frank O'Hara

I saw you being interviewed by a hysterical mob of followers
And, edging closer, got a good look at your defiant humorous face,
Quite flushed and ruddy as always, with a touch of contempt.
Only this time you didn't put me off, the haughtiness gone,
Turned to sheer madness, a venerable, daft figure.
You shot answers like a ghost accustomed to being right,
Coming from another sphere—yet the dead seem humbler,
Somehow, envious of us, though you made death a circus,
Behaved like a ringmaster, and the living who crowded you
Seemed left out of the real show, whose key you held so lightly.

I alone knew you were dead; the others, your "readership,"
In my dream were privileged for the first time to "see you
Plain." I was no less surprised when you chose to leave
With me, harboring no rancor for San Remo days, really nights,
Though I never knew why you should. We used to swap small
Talk over beer in the Forties, eyeing the service men and crew
Cut blonds. But you were guarded, as if you had a secret
You wouldn't share. Now, leaving together, you bubbled over
With vast, inspired wildness, spouting weird phrases,
The poetry of vision peculiar to schizzy types. Street noises
And pneumatic drills cut off the meaning, the city strange
Yet familiar. Cincinnati? I'd never seen it before. In a frame
House we talked to an ancient couple playing cards; you stole
A jacket and hugged it. We left, walked more paved hills, you
Spoke of violence. "All art is violence!" you said, still beaming.
I was afraid, not of you but the dimension you came from.

Our most intimate scene, this astral meeting, I can't explain—
Hypnotic, intense, stripped of vanity, and free of pettiness.
You were never more real or living. The whole day hung
In that tricky aura of dream and death and trivial things
That you made poems from: notes from the street, who died,
What happened in the bar and what the cat did,

Who fucked whom and where you went, some French
Thrown in for flavor, and all the time you're diddling yourself
With flashy rubbings from Life, gorgeous and bubbly Joy.

Just don't tell me that, except for dreams like this, dullness
Didn't drip into the spaces between sensation like Campbell's Soup,
Damaging New York, the sun, poems, music, like literary prize
        committees
Sitting, plop, all over your gay mood, with irritating power to ignore
The fresh and reward the stale. So when this dream is over I'll get up
And make some coffee not trying to capture the feeling of something
Happening. I know that the best as in sensation happens without rhyme
Or reason, and I'm going to let music speak for itself for a change.

(Sure enough your bibulous rhythms have swept like giant tsunami
With the riptide of your sound through the flat surface of meaning,
Soaring with a lilt of the voice and the color of orange (you loved it!)
Through drab grays and blazing blues. New pinnacles of pleasure!
Random freshness! Like this dream, this death, these oneiric things,
They're forms of my feelings, shapes of appearance, and maybe just
        plain mess.
But the messy earth breathes as we breathe, as animals breathe
And stretch and rush around and glow and emit sound, no need
To complicate the simple act of being, that merely consists of some
        oxygen and flowing.)

Together for the last time, Paris, a gathering you endured,
You remarked with blasting pupils ripping silky skies,
"All art is violence!" looking quite helplessly violent and angry
And quite drunk, too, spreading infinite bitchiness like a bruise
In the living room, made wet by bearded cocktail holders.
I retreated to New York, your first year, at the Remo
Where we put away the beer with John and gossiped profoundly
And joined the Marines. You played sonarman, the juke played Elvis.
Seized with immeasurable lust at the bar I rushed through a tunnel
Filled with nude sailors. I heard a whirring sound. My throat
Wrapped up in jockey shorts. It was the grunt's. And patriotic.
Your saucy images collide with foregone conclusions to be gone
Much too soon, for rococo joy hadn't worn out its ode.

WILLIAM CARLOS WILLIAMS

Letter to Harold Norse

William C. Williams M.D.
9 Ridge Road
Rutherford, N.J.
St. Valentine's Day
[14 February 1957]

Dear Hal:

Sometimes I think your place should be in NY, not Europe. Then again I think just the opposite. What the hell have I to do with it, you're the judge of what is best for you. The cause of this outburst is a movement that began in San Francisco among a group of young (not so young) poets who are beginning to make their way at present in New York. They are headed by Allen Ginsberg, Jack Kerouac, a Canadian partially American Indian prose writer who is soon to have a voluminous novel published by a prominent house under the patronage of Malcolm Cowley; you'll see more of that in the news later.

The reason I speak of that gang now is that the whole gang of them is at present headed for Italy. Look for them in a month around Florence and Rome, 4 or 5 of them including a poet named Corso, the youngest of all who is slowly making his presence felt around here, a very gentle guy who has been through some very tough years out of the slums of Brooklyn.

A feature of the united front that these men present is that they are all Zen Buddhists, one of their most influential members is at the present time living in a monastery in Japan. As you may run into the gang this spring in Italy I wanted you to know in advance about them. They are self-sufficient and ask nothing for themselves—they usually carry knapsacks out of which they live. I hope you meet at least one of them for they know what they are about and you would enjoy meeting them.

But.

Right at this time when you yourself have just struck a lead may not be profitable to dwell too much on Allen Ginsberg and his gang, I thought I'd mention him at least.

Your last letter really moved me. I'll speak to Dave McDowell as soon as I think he has had a chance to get settled in his new job. Meanwhile I look to see more poems, a bookful, exploiting what you have begun of the interrelationship of the renaissance & the modern.

More power to you
Bill

AMERICAN RENEGADES

If you *will* not put your address on the letters you send to me how can I help
it if the mere envelopes are destroyed?
Bill

Luckily Floss kept the envelope for the stamps.
Bill

GREGORY CORSO AND ALLEN GINSBERG

Ten Outlaw Heroes
Esquire, 1986; the magazine titled it "Ten Angry Men"

William Carlos Williams (1883–1963): Respectable pediatrician by trade, by vo-
cation an outlaw from an Academy that didn't understand his Einsteinian in-
vention of a "relative measure" as a new law of verse form to articulate living
talk on the poetic page. Proposed that American poets write American; after
Robert Lowell had a nervous breakdown, most did. Following generations still
hear Dr. Williams speaking to them kindly from the grave.

Willem De Kooning (1904–   ): Made and broke art. The fourth top Dutch-
man, after Vermeer, Rembrandt, Van Gogh. Abandoned the literal image of
empty lot fence & steam shovel; taking their abstract forms, excavated giant city
holes in the 2-D 1940s canvas. Experimented the volumes of breasts thighs and
holes a lifetime, saw women for what they were. A classic moderne American.

William Seward Burroughs (1914–   ): Inventor of a literary collage montage
cut-up jump-cut cut-up technique for novel writing (*Naked Lunch*, *Wild Boys*,
Place of Dead Roads) as a counter-brainwash method for reversing effects of
mass media Military-Industrial communist-capitalist CIA-KGB disinformation
Reality Image Bank. Inventor of *Heavy Metal*, *Soft Machine*, *Steely Dan* concepts
for a multitude of garage bands across the MTV globe. A doctor of doctor'd
time and space. Rimbaud's Poet of Science.

Charlie Parker (1920–55): Took off from spoken black street-speech cadence
in an alto saxophone breath that blew down the skyscrapers of New York: "When
the mode of the music changes, the walls of the city shake," quoth Plato. Parker
proved it, changing the time of gutbucket jazz, transforming the cadence of
prose novels and lyric poetry, altering the rhythms of white speech, syncopating
up the mechanistic metronome of modern thought. Once busted for drugs, was
outlawed from playing music in New York clubs in the last decade of his brief
life for lack of a police-OK'ed cabaret card. made and broke jazz; the supreme
intellectual of Afric sounds.

Jack Kerouac (1922–69): Visionary Seer of his own beatific generation looking up out of the bottom of the empty barrel of the atom-bomb world, prose creator of twentieth-century intercontinental myth of personal-heart consciousness in over twenty tomes writ in obscurity saintly solitude prior to enlightened Fame. Bodhisattva behind the solipsistic Arhats of New Journalism; redeemer of individuality in the hyperindustrialized metropolis, poetic adorer of humankind whose *Mexico City Blues* inseminated the hearts of a hundred younger poets including immortal Dylan. Hermetic messenger of Buddha consciousness in the American Half-Century; yet suffering Christ-loving alcoholic body crucifixion, took care of his cracked mother & "didn't throw her to the Dogs of Eternity." Wrote the first true North American haikus; gave speech back to Bop, gave Bop to speech; scribed sacred prayers in guise of modernistic novels that form a single vast and interconnected visionary Bookmovie of his mortal life.

Neal Cassady (1926–68): Prototype inspirer of Kerouac's telepath prose of 1940s Roads, Johnny Appleseed of Bay Area Aquarian weed culture; living human phantom behind the Grateful Dead, king of Ken Kesey's 1960s cross-continental psychedelic Wheel; tenderhearted lover of melancholy poets, family railroad brakeman father husbandman, classic jailbird orphan haunted by his lost father the United States itself. Dragon slayer of squaredom, the hip-cocksman of the American vulva, spoke faster than a bullet and hit the mark because he could recollect recall entire contents of some moments of his universal mind.

Julian Beck (1925–85): Helped invent Nike Laughter peace protest refusing to duck-and-cover underground mid-1950s for atom-bomb drill. Then as American Living Theaterman survived the glory of 1960s *Paradise Now* and brought his pacific-Anarchy onstage to Europa; as did Shelley, ventured to free the heirs of Prometheus from their bondage on the Military-Industrial rock where an American eagle plucks perpetual War-Tax from the liver. In his last year insulted from the aisles by homophobic bourgeois press reviewers in America, rose from cancer bed with hollow-eyed finely chiseled intelligent skeleton face to act *Cotton Club* film Mephistopheles, pre-record television serial dream Lama reappearances, then fly off to a Swiss graveyard with video innovator Nam June Paik and read a page of classic anarchist text, "Slavery is the necessary consequence of the very existence of the State" (from "Rousseau's Theory of the State" by Mikhail Bakunin), over the grave of the great Bakunin while smoking a cannabis joint, breaking the laws of death.

Robert Frank (1924–): Abandoned imitation of classic art picture misty naked girls on Turkish rugs and Swiss chalets with cuckoo clock snowpeaks, came down to the gutters of Paris and black Mississippi backroad America, inventing the Leica gut portrait of jukebox coffins & Chicago flag cigars. Gave up on snapshots and invented spontaneous chair-scratching-across-the-floor underground movies that turned Hollywood upside down till Marlon Brando stuck a buttery finger up his lady's behind in a last tango of cinema-inspiration breaking the bonds of commercial censorship. The map of the wandering Jew on his face, his eyes are human, but arm'd with lens and shutter can be god's spies thru 35 mm stills black & white 16 mm cinema scriptless classics like Mick Jagger in

Cocksucker Blues, or video-haunted spots of time home-make on Daytona Beach; by the 1990s some kind of million-dollar full-scale genius accident film likely'll get shot far from Hollywood.

The Vidyadhara, The Venerable Chögyam Trungpa, Rimpoche (1939–): A bona fide guru Tibetan Lama, knowledge holder of Thousand-year-old Wild Wisdom lineage teachings of the Kagyu-Nyingma Buddhist schools of actual Shambhala kingdom once misnamed Shangri-La. A Renaissance man of the highest peaks of East, meditation emperor, space awareness Dance-master, witty rude calligrapher whose poetry and flower arrangements unite the Mind with Body; Admiral of Tibetan Navies, Prime Minister of Imagination in the Bud-dhafields, General of empty Doorkeeper Armies at the Eternal Gates in Rocky Mountains' American spine; founder of Naropa Institute: 2130 Arapahoe Ave-nue, Boulder, Colorado 80302—the first Buddhist college in the West, whereat students can attend the Jack Kerouac School of Disembodied Poetics; Vajrayana vehicle teacher, Chairman of Board of Directors of Ordinary Mind.

Bob Dylan (1941–): One of the most powerful blues singers ever heard in the West, peer of Ma Rainey and Leadbelly in long unobstructed ecstatic breath, his body consciousness of column of air stopping time inspired at the interna-tional microphone, Poetus Magnus at the piano of conscience, so hard-working got not time to answer telephone mail media vampiric flattery insult lacklove paranoia; genius of ethic metaphor from *Hard Rain* past "Idiot Wind" . . . "to live outside the law, you must be honest." A literary heir of early-century black lyric minstrels, white Bardic rebels of the 1950s. Stands alone the world's trou-bled muse—He has nowhere to go, a singing bum of the mind.

JACK KEROUAC

241st Chorus

And how sweet a story it is
When you hear Charley Parker
            tell it,
Either on records or at sessions,
Or at official bits in clubs,
Shots in the arm for the wallet,
Gleefully he Whistled the
                perfect
                horn

Anyhow, made no difference.

Charley Parker, forgive me—
Forgive me for not answering your eyes—
For not having made in indication
Of that which you can devise—
Charley Parker, pray for me—
Pray for me and everybody
In the Nirvanas of your brain
Where you hide, indulgent and huge,
No longer Charley Parker
But the secret unsayable name
That carries with it merit
Not to be measured from here
To up, down, east, or west—
—Charley Parker, lay the bane,
    off me, and every body

149th Chorus

I keep falling in love
    with my mother,
I dont want to hurt her
—Of all people to hurt.

Every time I see her
    she's grown older
But her uniform always
    amazes me
For its Dutch simplicity
And the Doll she is,
The doll-like way
    she stands
Bowlegged in my dreams,
Waiting to serve me.

    And I am only an Apache
    Smoking Hashi
    In old Cabashy
    By the Lamp

211th Chorus

The wheel of the quivering meat
                            conception
Turns in the void expelling human beings,
Pigs, turtles, frogs, insects, nits,
Mice, lice, lizards, rats, roan
Racinghorses, poxy bucolic pigtics,
Horrible unnameable lice of vultures,
Murderous attacking dog-armies
Of Africa, Rhinos roaming in the
                            jungle,
Vast boars and huge gigantic bull
Elephants, rams, eagles, condors,
Pones and Porcupines and Pills—
All the endless conception of living
                            beings
Gnashing everywhere in Consciousness
Throughout the ten directions of space
Occupying all the quarters in & out,
From supermicroscopic no-bug
To huge Galaxy Lightyear Bowell
Illuminating the sky of one Mind—
    Poor! I wish I was free
    of the slaving meat wheel
    and safe in heaven dead

NEAL CASSADY

Adventures in Auto-eroticism

I stole my first automobile at 14 in 1940; by '47 when swearing off such soul-thrilling pleasures to celebrate advent into manhood, I had had illegally in my possession about 500 cars—whether just for the moment and to be taken back to its owner before he returned (I.E. on Parking lots) or whether taken for the purpose of so altering its appearance as to keep it for several weeks but mostly only for joyriding.

The virgin emotion one builds when first stealing an auto—especially when one can hardly make it function properly, so takes full minutes to get away—is naturally strenuous on the nervous system, and I found it most exciting. I was initiated into this particularly exhilarating pastime (tho undeniably utterly stupid) by a chance meeting with the local bad-boy, whom I had known at school. We came upon a '38 Olds sedan which was parked before the well-light entrance of an apartment house. It so happens this model Olds is a bastardized type—Olds being GM's "experimental" car—and since the ignition, lights, radio etc. are unconventionally set off the dashboard by bull horn-like dials; and because this unfamiliarity heightened his panicky condition, John's efforts to start the car seemed really ludicrous from my tree-trunk vantage point. He turned on the radio, the lights, everything but the key I guess, anyhow, when he finally became so flustered as to honk the horn, he bolted away, failing to even close the door. So it was with a genuine fear, so well-based as to make me think I was pretty brave indeed, that we sneaked back for another try. John, altho belittling his own fright, kept assuring me how easy it was, and this (besides the many minutes of quietude that passed after we had resumed our observation point behind a big tree) finally bolstered my courage enough to run over and drive away in the car.

We left it on the premises of an army post south of town, after stalling the motor on a U turn and even though two soldiers helped hand push us and the engine did sputter a bit we finally had exhausted the battery and had to hitch hike home, arriving so near dawn as to create complications there which, emotional tho they had been, now proved nothing beside my night-long thrill—from which I literally tingled for days until, in fact after serving mass as usual one morning, I left the rectory to find before it a current model Mercury with keys dangling! Naturally, having never driven so powerful an automobile, I burned rubber most of the block, before even realizing how to overcome it. And tho still quite inexperienced a driver I know it took so long to halt the tires' squeel only because each additional release of the accelerator, whether fractional or full-inch, was still not enough to ease the power—hell, come to think of it, I might have even been in high gear!

Anyhow, the erotic nature of the Mercury experience happily included exploring the anatomy of the school girl picked up in it, and therefore has no further, sharper, stronger, more meaningful remembrance than the one of its get-away moments, which included wading thru a three-phase traffic signal in the first block. . . .

Leaving L.A. by Train at Night, High . . .

Dark streets, hundreds of silent autos parked almost too close to the rail, mammoth buildings, many still lit, now looming in blacker outline, isolated houses, houses of dirt, of noise, cheery ones, then dark, dark ones; one wonders, the occupation of its owners. Billboards, billboards, drink this, eat that, use all manner of things, EVERYONE, the best, the cheapest, the purest and most satisfying of all their available counterparts. Red lights flicker on every horizon, airplanes beware; cars flash by, more lights. Workers repair the gas main. Signs, signs, lights, lights, streets, streets; it is the dark between that attracts one—what's happening there at this moment? What hidden thing, glorious perhaps, is being passed and lost forever. The congestion slackens, a cone of widening sparcity stretches before the train, now one has left the center and its core is burst past as the interlocking plants terminate grip and entrust us to the automatic block system's meticulous care. The maze of tracks have unwreathed from cross-over webs of railroad intellectuality to become simple main line dignity; these ribbons of accurate gauge so ceaselessly toiled over, respected, feared. Oh, unending high rail of intrigue!

GREGORY CORSO

Great poetry and great music have at least one thing in common. What can you say about them? Can they be explained? "If I could paraphrase Ulysses," Joyce once snapped at a critic, "I wouldn't have had to write it."

All the exegesis in the world isn't going to add or take away one whit from Corso's work. The best thing you can do is pick up a copy of "Gasoline" and be astonished at the precocity of this self-taught young poet. Gregory wrote poems before he had heard the word or knew the concept of poetry. "Gasoline," in my opinion, is the most extraordinary collection by a young poet in our time. Then go on to "The Happy Birthday of Death," "Long Live Man," "Elegiac Feelings American," which has the long elegy to his friend Jack Kerouac, one of the most tender and poignant poems ever written, an invocation to America to recognize one of her most loving sons. His last books have not lost any of his humor, irony, or wit.

There was a brief moment when poetry was actually popular. Young people and college students knew great pieces of Ginsberg's "Howl," and Gregory's "Marriage," "Bomb," and "Power."

With Gregory, the last of the great "Beats" still alive, and still close, I am reluctant to do anything but respect his ferociously guarded privacy. His poetry speaks for him. All you have to know is that behind that curmudgeonly exterior is a beautiful, loyal, generous, sensitive, truthful and extraordinary human being. Like Huncke, you can't fool him—he knows. He is a wise, spiritually profound man: in Nietzsche's words, "Human, all-too-human."

ROGER RICHARDS

Poet Talking to Himself in the Mirror

Hi, I'm me—
It has become glaringly absurd
this hunt for me
believing that when I was
hunted down
I'd find not only me
but a whole herd
past me's, future me's
the whole cart load
and all the years
and where have I gotten to
in this point of time
this isn't the same mirror
    I gazed into years ago

        It's the mirror that changes
        not poor Gregory

Hey, in life
  Where I went, I went
  Where I stopped, I stopped
  When I spoke, I spoke
  When I listened, I listened
  What I ate, I ate
  What I loved, I loved

But what about
  where I went, I did not go
  where I stopped, I moved on
  when I spoke, I listened
  when I listened, I spoke
  when I fasted, I ate
  and when I loved . . .
  I did not want to hate

Now I see people
  as police see them

I also see nuns the same way
 I see hare-krishnas

Ain't got no agent
can't see poets having agents

AMERICAN RENEGADES

Yet Ginsy, Ferl, have one
and make lots of money by them
and fame too
Maybe I should get an agent?
   Wow!
No way, Gregory, stay
   close to the poem!!!

Dear Villon

Villon, how brotherly our similarities . . .
Orphans, altar boys attending the priest's skirt;
                 purpling the coffins

Thieves: you having stolen the Devil's Fart
And I stealing what was mine
(not because like our brother Kerouac said:
everything is mine because I am poor)
Rather: Nothing is mine, a Prince of Poetry
made to roam the outskirts of society
taking, if I needed a coat, what was taken
                 from the lamb

Killers: You killed the priest who slit your lip;
thus far in that respect I am unlike you
           O thankfully so!

What sooty life, eh what, oh Villon?
An after-rain has laundr'd your day
blued is the white of it
Yet when O when
            Shall unsoiled navies
            sail by again?

I know the same I knew before
Now I would less knowledge than more
for I know knowledge to be
such information as fattens memory . . .
aye, wisdom is a lean thing
for regard that head on his deathbed
hemlocking: "All I know is I know nothing"
You at least claimed to know everything
           but yourself

I claim to know all there is to know
because there ain't that much to know

Poets Hitchhiking on the Highway

Of course I tried to tell him
but he cranked his head
        without an excuse.
I told him the sky chases
        the sun
And he smiled and said:
        'What's the use.'
I was feeling like a demon
        again
So I said: 'But the ocean chases
        the fish.'
This time he laughed
        and said: 'Suppose the
                strawberry were
                        pushed into a mountain.'
After that I knew the
        war was on—
So we fought:
He said: 'The apple-cart like a
                broomstick-angel
                snaps & splinters
                        old dutch shoes.'
I said: 'Lightning will strike the old oak
        and free the fumes!'
He said: 'Mad street with no name.'
I said: 'Bald killer! Bald killer! Bald killer!'
He said, getting real mad,
        'Firestoves! Gas! Couch!'
I said, only smiling,
        'I know God would turn back his head
        if I sat quietly and thought.'
We ended by melting away,
        hating air!

Greenwich Village Suicide

Arms outstretched
hands flat against the windowsides
She looks down
Thinks of Bartok, Van Gogh
And New Yorker cartoons
She falls

They take her away with a Daily News on her face
And a storekeeper throws hot water on the sidewalk

ALLEN GINSBERG

C'mon Pigs of Western Civilization, Eat More Grease.

Eat Eat more marbled Sirloin more Pork'n
    gravy!
Lard up the dressing, fry chicken in
    boiling oil
Carry it dribbling to gray climes, snowed with
    salt,
Little lambs covered with mint roast in racks
    surrounded by roast potatoes wet with
    buttersauce,
Buttered veal medallions in creamy saliva,
    buttered beef, buy glistening mountains
    of french fries
Stroganoffs in white hot sour cream, chops
    soaked in olive oil,
surrounded by olives, salty feta cheese, followed
    by Roquefort & Bleu & Stilton
    thirsty
for wine, beer Cocacola Fanta Champagne
    Pepsi retsina arak whiskey vodka
Agh! Watch out heart attack, pop more
    angina pills

order a plate of Bratwurst, fried frankfurters,
 couple billion Wimpys', MacDonald burgers
 to the moon & burp!
Salt on those fries! Boil onions
 & breaded mushrooms even zucchini
 in deep hot Crisco pans
Turkeys die only once,
 look nice next to tall white glasses
 sugarmilk & icecream vanilla balls
Strawberry for sweeter color milkshakes
 with hot dogs
Forget greenbeans, everyday a few carrots,
 a mini big spoonful of salty rice'll
 do, make the plate pretty;
throw in some vinegar pickles, briney sauerkraut
 check yr. cholesterol, swallow a pill
and order a sugar Cream donut, pack 2 under
 the size 44 belt
Pass out in the vomitorium come back cough
 up strands of sandwich still chewing
 pastrami at Katz's delicatessen
Back to central Europe & gobble Kielbasa
 in Lódz
swallow salami in Munich with beer, Liverwurst
 on pumpernickle in Berlin, greasy cheese in
 a 3 star Hotel near Syntagma, on white
 bread thick-buttered
Set an example for developing nations, salt,
 sugar, animal fat, coffee tobacco Schnapps
Drop dead faster! make room for
 Chinese guestworkers with alien soybean
 curds green cabbage & rice!
Africans Latins with rice beans & calabash can
 stay thin & crowd in apartments for working
 class foodfreaks—

Not like western cuisine rich in protein
 cancer heart attack hypertension sweat
 bloated liver & spleen megaly
Diabetes & stroke—monuments to carnivorous
 civilizations
presently murdering Belfast
 Bosnia Cypress Ngomo Karabach Georgia
mailing love letter bombs in
 Vienna or setting houses afire

AMERICAN RENEGADES

in East Germany—have another coffee,
here's a cigar.
And this is a plate of black forest chocolate cake,
you deserve it.

HAROLD NORSE

Letter to William Carlos Williams, February 23, 1957

Dear Bill,

Many thanks for your last. It is odd that you should have said, referring to where I should be, the same as my Armenian friend, who writes as follows: "From what I have been able to observe these last years, it seems that your mode of writing follows its own laws of development and is therefore best let to follow its own bent. Ultimately, you are feeling your way toward a style of utmost and crystal clarity, of which the Florentine poems already give a foretaste. But for the definitive form of this the time is not yet; therefore in the following representative poems [a very long new poem which I will send you in a month or so from Florence], i.e. those you sent me, you move to a greater density and complexity in language, in rime and alliteration, in syntax. This shows that your subconscious knows what it is doing, and there is no call for any of us to intervene. You will probably go through various stages of alternate simplicity and complexity before you reach your own definitive clarity as Williams seems to have done, for instance, in his latest work."

I believe I mentioned this Armenian sage in an earlier letter, saying that when he read *The Desert Music* and *Journey to Love*, which you inscribed to me, he was astonished and said, "Why don't we in England hear more of this man? He is really great—far better than Pound or Eliot!" At any rate, he is my sponsor— God bless him!—and also a kind of mentor. I bring him up because it all ties together: Europe, my poetry, Buddhism. It is strange, very strange that in your last letter you should mention Allen Ginsberg and his Buddhist bunch. I hadn't heard of his Buddhism, but knew Ginsberg slightly some twelve years ago. We met in the subway at about four a.m. We were the only occupants of the car, and he was leaning back drunkenly reciting Rimbaud, I think, in French, and we got to talking and bumped into each other once or twice since then. At any rate, one of the main reasons for my being in this isolated town on the coast of Spain was to concentrate heavily on Buddhist works, which I have done. IS IT STRANGE? I am not a Zen Buddhist, but I am receptive and sympathetic.

My place, dear Bill, is right here for the time being—Europe. It has brought out the best in me, that might never have come into being had I not left the States, which, I can say, had brought out the worst in me. When the time is ripe, I shall return. Meantime, whatever developments occur in my poetry, I owe to Europe, to the Armenian sponsor-mentor, to an inner growth and artistic inner revival that would have surely been crushed out of me, crushed to death, in New York. That is why I fled New York. The city, the people; they were certain death, I knew it. It was all or none. Stay and die, or leave and take my chances. The second proved to be my sheer physical, as well as mental, survival.

Yes, I have struck a lead, and it has been going, thank God, smoothly, according to its own laws. I myself am only dimly beginning to perceive where the poetry is going—I just let it go, and then I see where it has taken me! I have now a book, a big book—some 60 poems, with a basic theme: the interrelationship of the past with the modern, as seen through experiences with time and place. A good half of the book, like the Florence poems, treats of place, where personages and events move through landscapes and cities in a constant voyage. There are many long poems. But the whole thing I will have to whip into shape in Florence, where I shall be returning in April. I'm glad you will speak to David McDowell about this, when the time is ripe.

Meanwhile, if you see any of the Buddhist boys, before their departure for these shores, don't hesitate to tell them to look me up in Florence. I'd like to see Allen Ginsberg again, and I've heard of Corso. I, too, come from the slums of Brooklyn. One never knows what a slum will produce.

I have no address now, and will be dropping you a line on picture postcards from various Spanish towns, to gladden your heart!

So keep up the good work, may we all enter the pearly gates in due time!

All the best,
Hal
&, of course, to Floss!

Letter to William Carlos Williams, October 4, 1958

American Studies Center
Largo Ferrantina, 1
Naples, Italy
4 Oct./58

Dear Bill,

Finally got moved from Florence to Naples. It is no small thing to get lodgings in Naples that doesn't cost an eye. But I got an unbelievable deal—the first thing I saw—high on Posillipo, the hill over the Bay of Naples, like living in Amalfi or Capri, over the water—one room and bath, with a vast terrace in the sun, facing Vesuvius and Capri, all for 45 bucks a month. This involves paying extra for electric, concierge service, although he doesn't give any, etc. But I signed the contract with the American school which pays 150 bucks a month, so I can afford the luxury of living in Lotus Land. Posillipo—long a favorite resort of the ancient Greeks and Romans, who carved out caves from the igneous rock, making smooth sensuous golden grottoes everywhere, with houses and terraces to the sun and sea on the side of the cliff overlooking Naples, with palms and figs and eucalyptus and prickly pears and cedars and ferns and vines hanging over stone walls. Posillipo—I just found out the word means in Greek "pause from pain". What a wonderful word! It was de Nerval who wrote,

> Dans la nuit du tombeau, toi qui m'as consolé,
> Rends-moi le Pausilippe et la mer d'Italie.

Still, for me, there's a terrible cloud hanging over all this. Just the day before signing the contract to teach at the School, I was informed that there would be a "Security check" through Washington since the school comes partly under the United States Information Service jurisdiction, although in reality it is owned and operated by the Italo-American Association of Naples, a private organization. But the American bureaucracy will stick its finger into every pie. And what a finger! Always looking for communists and homosexuals and other terrible degenerates, so as to weed out the worst elements . . . the ones who think or feel or have ideals, we might say. I am no communist, nor was I ever one, officially, but I did sign many petitions that as a free American I had a free right to do, and I published a poem or two in radical papers. And as for my morals, although no better or worse than anybody else's, remember that disorderly conduct fine for a doorway episode, and voilà, a bad American. But I was told the "check up" takes about five months, so I signed anyway to live for a while in a way that I think I deserve, after so many years of hard luck. And even so, it's the first time I'm on a good salary in Italy, and it isn't even coming from the US government—yet they have to stick their big ugly Inquisitorial face—that bunch of cultural dinosaurs—into the picture and spoil it, take away the bread and the wine and everything but the insides of a man. Jefferson, Paine, Freneau, all the real Americans, must be very sour in their graves by now. Alex. Hamilton has won out after all. And the Fulbrights keep getting the dough. A bunch of bland unimaginative dopes.

I am keeping up with poetry by writing it, I don't see anybody else's, and feel cut off. But I'm enclosing some of the most recent. Let me know what you think. If you've done anything on the "variable foot", remember to send it to me. (Sailboats go by at my feet as I write this, flashing. And the sea licks at the caves.) It is all too good to be true. Curse all bureaucrats. When will man know how to live?

Affectionately,
Harold
Love to Floss.

WILLIAM CARLOS WILLIAMS

Letter to Harold Norse, August 26, 1960

William Carlos Williams
9 Ridge Road
Rutherford, N.J.
Aug. 26/60

Continuing what I was saying in the garden. Greetings.

THE AMERICAN IDIOM

The American idiom is the language we speak in the United States. It is characterized by certain differences from the language used among cultured Englishmen, being completely free from all influences which can be summed up as having to do with "the Establishment." This, pared to essentials, is the language which governed Walt Whitman in his choice of words. It constituted a revolution in the language. (In France only Paul Fort recognized what had happened about him to negate the *académie*.)

The language had been deracinated in this country but the English tongue was a tough customer with roots bedded in a tradition of far-reaching cultural power. Every nursery rhyme gave it a firmer grip on the tradition and there were always those interested in keeping their firm hold upon it.

Every high school in America is duty bound to preserve the English language as a point of honor, a requirement of its curriculum. To fail in ENGLISH is unthinkable!

Ignoring the supreme masters of English composition and thinking to go beyond them along the same paths impugns a man's loyalty if not his good sense. In fact it has been baldly stated in the highest circles and believed that there is no American language at all, so low have we fallen in defense of our speech.

The result is a new and unheralded language which has grown stronger by osmosis, we are asked to believe, but actually by the power of those Whitmans among us who were driven to take a chance by their fellows and the pride of an emerging race, its own. The American idiom had been driven into a secondary place by our scholars, those rats that had abandoned it to seek salvage elsewhere in safer places. No one can blame them, no one can say that we shall survive to plant our genes in another world.

We must go forward, uncertainly it may be, but courageously as we may. Be assured that measure in mathematics as in verse is inescapable, so to the fixed foot of the ancient line including the Elizabethans we must have a reply: it is the variable foot which we are beginning to discover after Whitman's advent.

"The Establishment," fixed in its commitments, has arrived at its last stand: the iambic pentameter, blank verse, the verse of Shakespeare and Marlowe, which give it its prestige. A full stop. Until we can go beyond that, "the Establishment" has an edge on us.

Whitman lived in the nineteenth century but he, it must be acknowledged, proceeded instinctively by rule of thumb and a tough head, correctly, in the construction of his verses. He knew nothing of the importance of what he had stumbled on, unconscious of the concept of the variable foot. This new notion of time which we were approaching, leading to the work of Curie and the atom bomb, and other NEW concepts, has been pregnant with far reaching consequences.

We were asleep to the tremendous responsibilities as poets, and as writers generally, that were opening up to us. Our poets especially are asleep from the neck [up]—only the Russians with their state control of letters are stupider than we. And still we follow the English and teach it to our unsuspecting children.

William Carlos Williams

WANDA COLEMAN

South Central Los Angeles Death Trip, 1982

1
jes another X marking it

dangling gold chains & pinky rings
nineteen. done in black leather & defiance
teeth white as halogen lamps, skin dark as a threat

they spotted him taking in the night
made for the roust
arrested him on suspicion of
they say he became violent
they say he became combative in the rear seat of
that sleek zebra maria. they say
it took a chokehold to restrain him

and then they say he died of asphyxiation
on the spot

summarized in the coroner's report
as the demise of
one more nondescript dustbunny
ripped on phencyclidine
(which justified their need to
leave his hands cuffed behind his back
long after rigor mortis set in)

2
stress had damaged his thirty-nine-year-old mind
more than he could admit but he was trying
to make life work as well as it could
for a father with three children praying
dad will pull through

where the butcher knife came from
no one's sure. they say
he held off ten riot squad patrol cars
for forty-five minutes outside that 109th street
church. they say the cops had stopped him
because they didn't like his looks.
they say something fragile inside his head
snapped. they say it took twenty rounds of ammo
to bring him down they say he took five
gunshot pellets & thirteen bullets
they say that was a lot of outrage over
a case of misconstrued identity

3
she was fed up that day with
everything. now here they come turning off
the damned gas so she went and
chased the service rep
from the yard before he could carry out the
disconnection order. by the time
police officers arrived she had lost what was
left of her common sense
had grabbed up & brandished an eleven-inch
boning knife to back up her mouth.
the two officers complained she threw
that knife at them. and they were so terrified
they didn't consider a wounding. they

simply emptied both guns into
the thirty-nine-year-old hefty female.
it took twelve shots to
subdue all that treataniggahthis
and whitesonofabitchesthat,
they said, and kill it

4
strangely he was dodging & ducking,
        bouncing & rolling,
        tipping & slipping
(as if dangling from the end of it)
in and out of traffic in front of the sheriff's
station, embarrassing them, causing a modest jam
        for no apparent reason
therefore they arrested the twenty-six-year-old
descendant of slaves and booked him for
this queer behavior, their spokesman said
        because there weren't
enough terrorists, assassins or irate taxpayers
to keep them busy that Wednesday afternoon.
        he was handcuffed
and left alone in his cell and fell inexplicably
into unconsciousness in a mere three hours,
        they said. he was
rushed to a nearby hospital still in cuffs
where he died within twenty-two minutes

cause of demise as unknown as ever

5
without evidence to support the supposition
they swore the twenty-one-year-old
consumer was involved in the robbery of
the popular Manchester Avenue chicken shack,
and not just another hungry-but-innocent bystander
he was assumed guilty, if not the brainiac
perhaps the getaway driver. he was captured during
the fray before questions could be asked or
players & slayers identified. that he was unarmed
was not a pertinent issue. that he was ignorant
decidedly was. they handcuffed him and made
him lay on the ground in the middle of the fray
where, unfortunately, his ignorance got
him killed by police gunfire. they say an officer

yelled freeze and this inexperienced
young black hoodlum being unfamiliar with the
procedure of how one freezes while being held face down
on the sidewalk, hands cuffed behind one's back
could not do so. therefore the inability to freeze
under these conditions cost him his life

6
exhausted after working the nightshift
he was so dead on his feet he couldn't
hear 'em ramming in his door, so they broke into
the sepia-toned man's apartment by mistake
(it was supposed to be the one downstairs).
officers swarmed his bed as he opened his eyes,
officers were on him like maggots on foul meat.
nevertheless he managed to free himself long
enough to run into the bathroom where
he was ultimately subdued without ever knowing why

the coroner reported this
as death due to heart attack
brought on by advanced arteriosclerosis
in a twenty-eight-year-old black male

7
he was bound for college but was caught
standing on a street corner blocks from home
maybe, like they say, he had recently scored some
dope (which could not be found) or maybe
minutes earlier he'd been snacking on that
ham sandwich mama made for her nineteen-year-old
sure is handsome fine young black man.
maybe there was nothing to it at all, not even
that missing piece of aluminum foil the officers
claim they saw him pull out of his trousers

sudden-like

as they happened to be cruising past. it made
a mysterious metallic gleam
which they mistook for the glint of steel
which is why there was all that draw-and-fire
which is why

mama went to his funeral instead of his graduation

8

all of twenty-six, the ebony diabetic had
no steady job and lived with his parents.
he was a young man with mental & physical
problems. he began to act strangely, they say
although no one noticed him brandishing
that piece of radiator fan belt or that
kitchen knife in the middle of the street.
perhaps some car somewhere had broken down
certainly, he had, enough to make the sheriff's
deputies approach with caution and order him
to freeze. he turned toward them and even
though he was fourteen feet away from them his
turning toward them inspired so much fear
in the armed men one of them emptied his
Smith & Wesson service revolver into the
young diabetic who died from three slugs

9

that night Bob came blamming on her door.
she had just gotten home from working
the register at the club and her feet were
killing her, now here come some numbskull
sayhisnameis Bob knocking the damn door
in with some okey-doke about "here come da
police. hide me quick!" so she got something
for Bob's jive probably-drunk ass, that .22
caliber rifle she uses regularly to scare off
the riffraff. then she cracked the door a taste
but before she could make her melodrama move
it slammed open and she was blinded by the
flash as she took a shot in her left breast.
the bullet entered her right rib cage and killed
the 8 ½-month old baby she was carrying.
all this behind a supposedtobe drug bust where
no drugs were found by the officers in charge

jes another X marking it

KATHY ACKER

From *Devoured by Myths, an Interview with Sylvére Lotringer*

LOTRINGER: What does it mean, conceptualist, in terms of writing?

ACKER: Most poets in those days (70's) didn't think why did they write the way they wrote. There was still, and still is, the lingering idea of good poetry as the perfect word in the perfect line. And what David really taught me is, the hell with all that. Just think what do you want to do and do it. Form is determined not by arbitrary rules, but by intention. And intentionality is all. That's what I meant by this emphasis on conceptualism, on intentionality. So I had really been trained in the idea that you just don't sit down and write, you have to know why you write and why you use certain methodologies.

LOTRINGER: Any other training as a writer?

ACKER: I grew up in New York City and when I was a teenager I was introduced to a lot of the underground filmmakers, Stan Brakhage, Stan Rice, Gregory Markopolos. Most important I met Jack Smith who told me that his dream was to have a huge dome in Africa and anybody would walk and tell their dreams, which I thought was absolutely fabulous. But just as important I was introduced to Robert Kelly and Jackson MacLow and to the work of Charles Olson. So you might say I had an early training in Black Mountain School rhetoric which came mainly out of *The Wasteland* and Pound's work, *The Cantos*. Olson's main thesis was that one sentence comes after another sentence so you might have the movement of meaning, but also a movement where language leads to language. Olson also had his way of seeing the world and putting it down in a certain kind of rhythm, usually a very jagged rhythm, like writing from scat. It all had to do with music.

LOTRINGER: You were writing poetry then?

ACKER: No, I never wrote poetry, I always wanted to write prose. So I was looking for models of fiction that were poetic and fiction writers don't work that way. They outline things before they write. They don't write by process. The only model I found in my world was William Burroughs. I like Kerouac but he worked too much from intuition for me and I wasn't interested in that kind of autobiographical work. Whereas Burroughs really was doing the major work because he was dealing with how politics and language come together, the kind of language, what the image is, all that early Burroughs work. Burroughs was the only prose writer I could find who was a conceptualist. Oh he's very much of a conceptualist. So I used *The Third Mind* as experiments to teach myself how to write, and I think this is part of the trouble I had with the St. Mark's people because this was not the usual thing to do.

LOTRINGER: You had come back to New York by then.

ACKER: Yeah, and I hung out in the poetry scene. That was the St. Mark's Poetry Project. I was working in a sex-show in 42nd Street and I had two lives, the poetry and the sex-show. I was in it only six months but it pretty radically changed my view of the world.

LOTRINGER: In what way?

ACKER: One, it changed my politics. When I was in the university at San Diego I was SDS, but the student left was very elitist. The 42nd Street experience made me learn about street politics. You see people from the bottom up, and sexual behavior, especially sex minus relationship—which is what happens in 42nd Street—is definitely bottom. Then you see it in a different way, especially power relationships in society. Genet has the same kind of perspective. And I think that never left me.

LOTRINGER: What about your other life in the poetry scene?

ACKER: I really wasn't comfortable there. I felt very rejected. The people I was close to were the generation above me—the people who are my age are Larry Fagin, Michael Brownstein. At that point the culture was hippy and all these hippies in the St. Mark's Poetry Project at the time were very much into fucking around with each other and writing about it. The poetry was very autobiograph-ical, very third generation Surrealist, some of it had come down from the New York School. And working in a sex-show really didn't make you feel very nice about sex. It was all about money and that's how I thought about it. It's not that I fucked for work because it was just fake—I performed with this guy Mark Stevens, I think he became a famous porn star, and he was totally gay; if he tried to kiss me, he'd start giggling—but still it was enough. I didn't need it back in the home-base. So I was very separated culturally from these people. And they thought I was weird, I was some kind of a pervert. Everyone was in blue jeans and I had shaved my head—that was my radical stance against work-ing in a sex-show. (Laughs). It wasn't very radical, but what can you do when you need money? I hated men at that point, even though I was living with a guy from the sex-show. He was a real creep anyway.

I Begin to Feel

I remember the corpses stood up before me. There's a creep on T.V., asking me to call him about my grandparents, but my grandparents are dead.

The corpses say: "You were born beautiful rich and smart you little creep and beauty wealth and intelligence just brought you down to deterrence, secretion, to reject you . . . You came from a good family even though your real father was a murderer and your mother was crazy. Even being a creep won't save you. Tonight you're going to be ours."

They're babbling tenderly to me:

This is the corpses' song:

This is Christ the eternal humiliant, the insane tyrant. He and the corpses are holding me in their arms.

The only thing that matters to me is waking up.

I begin walking to look for that moment that will wake me up.

The only thing that is satisfactory is this moment.

Soon money isn't enough for me whether American or Arabian, I float, suspended between the sky and the earth, suspended between the sky and the earth, between floor and ceiling. My dumbly sad eyes which always see things opposite to the ways they are my dumbly sad eyes which always see things opposite to the ways they are are showing their stringy lobes to the world, my mutilated hooks reveal my mother's madness reveal my mother's madness.

My mother tells me why I was born: she had a pain in her stomach, it was during the war, she went to some quack doctor (she had just married this guy because it was the war and she loved his parents); the doctor tells her she should get pregnant to cure the pain. Since she's married, she gets pregnant, but the pain stays. She won't get an abortion because she's too scared. She runs to the toilet because she thinks she has to shit; I come out. The next day she has appendicitis.

At night in every city I live in I walk down the streets to look for something that will mean something to me.

The city I dreamt of: It was here that I heard the voice of Mary the Whore Who Gave Her All For Love, here I stared at the beautiful look of Violette injected by the blackest ink, here finally Justus and Betelgeuse, Verax and Hair and all the girls with the names of stars the openings of doors magnetized the young girls. They no longer know what they're doing. Invisible rays make this nothingness where everything is possible, possible.

Anonymity by imposing no image reveals space.

This is the beginning of love. For you it's of no importance but for me it has every importance.

AMERICAN RENEGADES

You also said: "You don't understand why I'm bothering with you because I have so much to give and you have nothing to give."

I'm not bothering with you now.

I hate you you took me. "I don't understand why you're bothering with me" meant I'm *not going to give anything to you.*

I'm being a bitch now saying all this. Chauffeur. It doesn't matter where you're taking me: to the furnace, to the toilet, to the brothel you're working in, now you won't see me. The only thing I need is to burn; myself torn into pieces scattered each bit away from every other, covered in your shit; and I feel every fuck that happens, every fuck frightens me. Past your taking me.

To sleep inside your left shoulder.

My real being alive will never occur where there is rigidity of mentality—too bad for my mind.

WILLIAM S. BURROUGHS

The Evening News

The old desk sergeant looked grimly at the wanted
pictures yellow pealing
30th day without an arrest in New York area
they risk 15 light-years, entire future,
certain discussions, cool gardens and
pools of the evening.
The old turnkey makes the round of empty cells.
"Sleep tight boys."
No one there
muttering phantom voices
peet men junkies con men
the old hop smoking worlds
mutter between years.
The Sailor hanging by his belt
A drunk banging on the door of his cell
thin grey pickpocket stops him.
"Get me this letter out, Screw.
It's worth an Abe to you."
pulls the Abe out of his fibrous junkie shoe.
"I need an arrest, Mike. I'm thin."

William S. Burroughs by Gregory Corso

"Fuck off punk
I can't find an old drunk."
No arrest. She reads it in his dull eyes.
"*Conservez toujours une bonne morale.*"
a sharp cold bray of laughter
sliding away into the sky
"*Cher ami, voici mon dernier livre.*"
Couldn't reach from the old cop film.
Twirling his club down cobblestone streets
the sky goes out against his back
in a darkening park
couldn't reach with the sap
"*et personne n'a ri*"
I do not need to remind you
laws as strict as the United States . . .
urine in straw a yellow sky
his bicycle of light
"*poumons sensibles.*"
a blue smell of hope as he rounded the corner
and the sea air hit his face
"Leaving the fading film please."
Got up. Remembered "Thank you."
The Old Courthouse empty cells and precincts
bondsmen judges lawyers probation officers
paper cups of coffee on the desk
NARCOTICS DEPARTMENT . . . the door is open
files and pictures scattered on the floor
stained with urine and excrement.
On the wall in phosphorous roach paste
AH PUCH JACKED OFF HERE.
Laws as severe as the United States,
"*L'indécision ne servirait pas votre cause ce soir.*"

"My Legs Señor."

attic room and window my ice skates on the wall
the Priest could see the bathroom pale yellow wood
    panels
toilet young legs shiny black leg hairs
"It is my legs *señor.*"
luster of stumps rinses his lavender horizon
feeling the boy groan and what it meant
face of a lousy kid on the doctor's table

I was the shadow of the waxing evenings and strange
    windowpanes.
I was the smudge and whine of missed times in the
    reflected sky
points of polluted water under his lavender horizon
    windowpane
smudge scrawled by some boy cold lost marbles in the
    room
the doctor's shabby table . . . his face . . .
boy skin spreads to something else.
"CHRIST WHAT'S INSIDE!" he screams.
flesh and bones rose tornado
"THAT HURTS."
I was the smudge and whine of missed legs shiny black
    leg hairs
silver paper in the wind frayed sounds of a distant
    city.

Cold Lost Marbles

my ice skates on a wall
luster of stumps washes his lavender horizon
he's got a handsome face of a lousy kid
rooming houses dirty fingers
whistled in the shadow
"Wait for me at the detour."
river . . . snow . . . someone vague faded in a mirror
filigree of trade winds
cold white as lace circling the pepper trees
the film is finished
memory died when their photos weather worn points of
polluted water under the trees in the mist shadow of
boys by the daybreak in the peony fields cold lost
marbles in the room carnations three ampoules of
morphine little blue-eyed twilight grins between his
legs yellow fingers blue stars erect boys of sleep
have frozen dreams for I am a teenager pass it on
flesh and bones withheld too long yes sir *oui oui*
craps last map . . . lake . . . a canoe . . . rose tor-
    nado in
the harvest brass echo tropical jeers from Panama
City night fences dead fingers you in your own body
around and maybe a boy skin spreads to something
else on Long Island the dogs are quiet.

AMERICAN RENEGADES

AMY GERSTLER

A Non-Christian on Sunday

Now we heathens have the town to ourselves.
We lie around, munching award-winning pickles
and hunks of coarse, seeded bread smeared
with soft, sweet cheese. The streets seem
evacuated, as if Godzilla had been sighted
on the horizon, kicking down skyscrapers
and flattening cabs. Only two people
are lined up to see a popular movie
in which the good guy and the bad guy trade
faces. Churches burst into song. Trees wish
for a big wind. Burnt bacon and domestic tension
scent the air. So do whiffs of lawnmower exhaust
mixed with the colorless blood of clipped hedges.
For whatever's about to come crashing down
on our heads, be it bliss-filled or heinous,
make us grateful, OK? Hints of the savior's
flavor buzz on our tongues, like crumbs
of a sleeping pill shaped like a snowflake.

The Bride Goes Wild

You Can't Run Away From It and You Can't Take It
With You, Man of A Thousand Faces: The Children
Upstairs, Brats; All These Women Up In Arms—
Misunderstood Husband Hunters. It Started In Paradise—
The Best Of Everything: Ten Nights in A Bar Room, Men
Without Names, The Exquisite Sinner High And Dizzy—
Long Legs, Dimples, The Velvet Touch. Foolin' Around,
Just This Once, She Had To Say Yes. A Night To Remember.
Don't Tell. I Confess—I'm No Angel, I Am The Law!
The Fiend Who Walked West, Breathless, Accused
My Foolish Heart. The Pleasure Of His Company
Changes White Heat to A Cold Wind in August.
But One Night In The Tropics, I Saw What You Did.
Ready Willing And Able, Naughty But Nice, She Wore

A Yellow Ribbon. Miles From Home, Living It Up,
She Couldn't Say No—My Sister Eileen—Too Young to Kiss,
Each Pearl A Tear. The Awful Truth: Ladies Love Brutes.
The Good News: The Devil Is A Sissy. So Tickle Me,
Doctor X, Truly Madly Deeply. Keep Laughing. You Gotta
Stay Happy. Naked, The Invisible Woman Cries and Whispers
Nothing But The Truth, Too Scared To Scream.

(the above is a poem composed of movie titles)

PEDRO PIETRI

In His Own Words

El Reverendo Pedro Pietri is a Native New Yorker born in Ponce, Puerto Rico
in 1898 and 1943 and 1998—Poet-Playwright, Wise Guy, Stand-up Undertaker,
Ex-Prophet and Member of "LIMCWM" (Latin Insomniacs Motor Club With-
out Motor Cycles) has published seven books of poetry—Puerto Rican Obituary
is most renowned—which has been translated into 13 languages, most recently
published an anthology of his poetry in Milan, Italy. Most most recently pub-
lished collection of his plays Illusions of a Revolving Door by the University of
Puerto Rico. Most most most recently published The Masses Are Assses II by
Instituto De Cultura, Puerto Rico. As a Playwright he has been produced by the
Public Theatre, La Mama, Nuyorican Poet's Cafe, and the Henry Street Settle-
ment. Has received grants from CAPS & National Endowment for the Arts,
which amounted to chump Change. Has assisted in the disorganization efforts
of The first & Last South Bronx Surrealist Festival. Covert Member of The
Committee To Bury The Community for free in No More Bingo At The Wake,
an endless one act play directed by Ambassador Eddie Figueroa, late great bad-
dest director. Academy Award Winner Legendary Puerto Rican Actor-Director
José Ferrer attempted to direct his Plays, El Livingroom & Lewlulu at HB studio
and Intar. Otto Preminger told him He should take a haircut, Didn't listen.
Sneaked Seven Roosters into Joseph Papp's private toilet, with El Poeta Jesús
Papoleto Meléndez. Mediates at the Doctor Willie Institute of Concrete Con-
sistent Contradictions in midtown. Is Alumini of The New Dramatists and of
the Bermuda Triangle in Spanglish Harlem district of Great Borinken. Reluctant
Member of The Governing Board of The Poetry Society of America (1985–69).
Has done recitals & theatrical Presentations thru-out the United States and El

Barrio. Was ordained a Reverend by the Ministry of Improvised Salvation in 1990. Preaches at THE IGLESIA DE LA MADRE DE LOS TOMATES INC. Co-inspirator with Eduardo Figueroa, of El Puerto Rican Embassy Soverign State of Cultural Harmless Mind Conspiracy to upstage eternity! The Reverend's Puerto Rican Embassy Manifesto Appears On the Puerto Rican Spirits Republic Passport, which entitles all Puerto Ricans regardless of color or religion Dual Citizenship in El Barrio U.S.A. and Puerto Rico. Currently co-producing the Speedo & Speedo Father & Hijo Half Hour Anarchy Show, with his almost three year old son, Speedo Juan. He was elevated to Bishop by the Board of the Nu-yorican Poet's Cafe, but turned it down. And last but not least El Reverendo Pedro Jaun Pietri Aponte Oppenhemier de Joo Kee Yoo Too, is an Honorary Member of the Royal Chicago Air Force in the west coast! And least but not last Reverendo Pedro is involved as Spanglish Metaphor consultant in "The Capeman," a musical he co-wrote with Paul Simon (who now gives the credit For the text to Nobel Laureate Dereck Walcott. He communicates with Lip O & boycotts the month of April! His "Dark Art" is on exhibit in the Underground Subway Train Stations of the N.Y.C. Transit.

PEDRO PIETRI

Puerto Rican Obituary

They worked
They were always on time
They were never late
They never spoke back
when they were insulted
They worked
They never took days off
that were not on the calendar
They never went on strike
without permission
They worked
ten days a week
and were only paid for five
They worked
They worked
They worked
and they died
They died broke
They died owing
They died never knowing
what the front entrance
of the first national city bank looks like

Juan
Miguel
Milagros
Olga
Manuel
All died yesterday today
and will die again tomorrow
passing their bill collectors
on to the next of kin
All died
waiting for the garden of eden
to open again
under a new management
All died
dreaming about america
waking them up in the middle of the night
screaming: Mira, Mira
your name is on the winning lottery ticket
for one hundred thousand dollars
All died
hating the grocery stores
that sold them make-believe steak
and bullet-proof rice and beans
All died waiting dreaming and hating

Dead Puerto Ricans
Who never knew they were Puerto Ricans
Who never took a coffee break
from the ten commandments
to KILL KILL KILL
the landlords of their cracked skulls
and communicate with their latino souls

Juan
Miguel
Milagros
Olga
Manuel
From the nervous breakdown streets
where the mice live like millionaires
and the people do not live at all
are dead and were never alive

Juan
died waiting for his number to hit

AMERICAN RENEGADES

Miguel
died waiting for the welfare check
to come and go and come again
Milagros
died waiting for her ten children
to grow up and work
so she could quit working
Olga
died waiting for a five dollar raise
Manuel
died waiting for his supervisor to drop dead
so he could get a promotion

Is a long ride
from Spanish Harlem
to long island cemetery
where they were buried
First the train
and then the bus
and the cold cuts for lunch
and the flowers
that will be stolen
when visiting hours are over
Is very expensive
Is very expensive
But they understand
Their parents understood
Is a long non-profit ride
from Spanish Harlem
to long island cemetery

Juan
Miguel
Milagros
Olga
Manuel
All died yesterday today
and will die again tomorrow
Dreaming
Dreaming about queens
Clean-cut lily-white neighborhood
Puerto Ricanless scene
Thirty-thousand-dollar home
The first spics on the block
Proud to belong to a community

of gringos who want them lynched
Proud to be a long distance away
from the sacred phrase: Que Pasa

These dreams
These empty dreams
from the make-believe bedrooms
their parents left them
are the after-effects
of television programs
about the ideal
white american family
with black maids
and latino janitors
who are well trained
to make everyone
and their bill collectors
laugh at them
and the people they represent

Juan
died dreaming about a new car
Miguel
died dreaming about new anti-poverty
programs
Milagros
died dreaming about a trip to Puerto Rico
Olga
died dreaming about real jewelry
Manuel
died dreaming about the irish sweepstakes

They all died like a hero sandwich dies
in the garment district
at twelve o'clock in the afternoon
social security number to ashes
union dues to dust

They knew
they were born to weep
and keep the morticians employed
and long as they pledge allegiance
to the flag that wants them destroyed
They saw their names listed
in the telephone directory of destruction

AMERICAN RENEGADES

They were trained to turn
the other cheek by newspapers
that misspelled mispronounced
and misunderstood their names
and celebrated when death came
and stole their final laundry ticket

They were born dead
and they died dead

Is time
to visit sister lopez again
the number one healer
and fortune card dealer
in Spanish Harlem
She can communicate
with your late relatives
for a reasonable fee
Good news is guaranteed

Rise Table Rise Table
death is not dumb and disable
Those who love you want to know
the correct number to play
Let them know this right away
Rise Table Rise Table
death is not dumb and disable
Now that your problems are over
and the world is off your shoulders
help those who left you behind
find financial peace of mind
Rise Table Rise Table
death is not dumb and disable
If the right number we hit
all our problems will split
and we will visit your grave
on every legal holiday
Those who love you want to know
the correct number to play
Let them know this right away
death is not dumb and disable
Rise Table Rise Table

Juan
Miguel

Milagros
Olga
Manuel
All died yesterday today
and will die again tomorrow
Hating fighting and stealing
broken windows from each other
Practicing a religion without a roof
The old testament
The new testament
according to the gospel
of the internal revenue
the judge and jury and executioner
protector and eternal bill collector

Secondhand shit for sale
Learn how to say Como esta usted
and you will make a fortune

They are dead
They are dead
and will not return from the dead
until they stop neglecting
the art of their dialogue
for broken english lessons
to impress the mister goldsteins
who keep them employed
as lavaplatos porters messenger boys
factory workers maids stock clerks
shipping clerks assistant mailroom
assistant, assistant assistant
to the assistant's assistant
assistant lavaplatos and automatic
artificial smiling doormen
for the lowest wages of the ages
and rages when you demand a raise
because is against the company policy
to promote SPICS SPICS SPICS

Juan
died hating Miguel because Miguel's
used car was in better running condition
than his used car
Miguel
died hating Milagros because Milagros

had a color television set
and he could not afford one yet
Milagros
died hating Olga because Olga
made five dollars more on the same job
Olga
died hating Manuel because Manuel
had hit the numbers more times
than she had hit the numbers
Manuel
died hating all of them
Juan
Miguel
Milagros
and Olga
because they all spoke broken english
more fluently than he did

And now they are together
in the main lobby of the void
Addicted to silence
Off limits to the wind
Confined to worm supremacy
in long island cemetery
This is the groovy hereafter
the protestant collection box
was talking so loud and proud about

Here lies Juan
Here lies Miguel
Here lies Milagros
Here lies Olga
Here lies Manuel
who died yesterday today
and will die again tomorrow
Always broke
Always owing
Never knowing
that they are beautiful people
Never knowing
the geography of their complexion

PUERTO RICO IS A BEAUTIFUL PLACE
PUERTORRIQUEÑOS ARE A BEAUTIFUL
RACE

If only they
had turned off the television
and tune into their own imaginations
If only they
had used the white supremacy bibles
for toilet paper purpose
and make their latino souls
the only religion of their race
If only they
had returned to the definition of the sun
after the first mental snowstorm
on the summer of their senses
If only they
had kept their eyes open
at the funeral of their fellow employees
who came to this country to make a fortune
and were buried without underwears

Juan
Miguel
Milagros
Olga
Manuel
will right now be doing their own thing
where beautiful people sing
and dance and work together
where the wind is a stranger
to miserable weather conditions
where you do not need a dictionary
to communicate with your people
Aqui Se Habla Español all the time
Aqui you salute your flag first
Aqui there are no dial soap commercials
Aqui everybody smells good
Aqui tv dinners do not have a future
Aqui the men and the women admire desire
and never get tired of each other
Aqui Que Pasa Power is what's happening
Aqui to be called negrito
means to be called LOVE

Telephone Booth
Number 301

when I was very young
I used to have many
imaginary girlfriends
now that I am an adult
I miss them very much

Telehpone Booth
Number 507

I will jump out the window
if thats what it takes
to satisfy you sexually,
but only if you live in the
basement

Telephone booth
number 898½

if you are
unable to erase it
it means that you
have not written down
anything to erase
& don't have to fear
being quoted just
when you are about
to contradict what
you didn't write down

Telephone booth
number 63765057

there will always
be time to stare
across the room
at a blank wall

& wonder have you
done this before—!

Telephone booth
number 542

the only way
i know how
to wash dishes
is by smashing them
against the wall!

Telephone booth
number 32439

if you hit a poet
& he doesn't hit you back
leave town immediately
take out life insurance
get a new identity
unite with transvestites
sleep with unlisted numbers!

RICHARD BRAUTIGAN

The Galilee Hitch-Hiker

The Galilee Hitch-Hiker
Part 1

Baudelaire was
driving a Model A
across Galilee.
He picked up a

AMERICAN RENEGADES

hitch-hiker named
Jesus who had
been standing among
a school of fish,
feeding them
pieces of bread.
"Where are you
going?" asked
Jesus, getting
into the front
seat.
"Anywhere, anywhere
out of this world!"
shouted
Baudelaire.
"I'll go with you
as far as
Golgotha,"
said Jesus.
"I have a
concession
at the carnival
there, and I
must not be
late."

The American Hotel
Part 2

Baudelaire was sitting
in a doorway with a wino
on San Francisco's skid row.
The wino was a million
years old and could remember
    dinosaurs.
Baudelaire and the wino
were drinking Petri Muscatel.
"One must always be drunk,"
    said Baudelaire.
"I live in the American Hotel,"
said the wino. "And I can
    remember dinosaurs."
"Be you drunken ceaselessly,"
    said Baudelaire.

1939
Part 3

Baudelaire used to come
to our house and watch
me grind coffee.
That was in 1939
and we lived in the slums
of Tacoma.
My mother would put
the coffee beans in the grinder.
I was a child
and would turn the handle,
pretending that it was
  a hurdy-gurdy,
and Baudelaire would pretend
that he was a monkey,
hopping up and down
and holding out
a tin cup.

The Flowerburgers
Part 4

Baudelaire opened
up a hamburger stand
in San Francisco,
but he put flowers
between the buns.
People would come in
and say, "Give me a
hamburger with plenty
of onions on it."
Baudelaire would give
them a flowerburger
instead and the people
would say, "What kind
of a hamburger stand
is this?"

The Hour of Eternity
Part 5

"The Chinese
read the time

in the eyes
of cats,"
said Baudelaire
and went into
a jewelry store
on Market Street.
He came out
a few moments
later carrying
a twenty-one
jewel Siamese
cat that he
wore on the
end of a
golden chain.

Salvador Dali
Part 6

"Are you
or aren't you
going to eat
your soup,
you bloody old
cloud merchant?"
Jeanne Duval
shouted,
hitting Baudelaire
on the back
as he sat
daydreaming
out the window.
Baudelaire was
startled.
Then he laughed
like hell,
waving his spoon
in the air
like a wand
changing the room
into a painting
by Salvador
Dali, changing
the room

into a painting
by Van Gogh.

A Baseball Game
Part 7

Baudelaire went
to a baseball game
and bought a hot dog
and lit up a pipe
of opium.
The New York Yankees
were playing
the Detroit Tigers.
In the fourth inning
an angel committed
suicide by jumping
off a low cloud.
The angel landed
on second base,
causing the
whole infield
to crack like
a huge mirror.
The game was
called on
account of
fear.

Insane Asylum
Part 8

Baudelaire went
to the insane asylum
disguised as a
psychiatrist.
He stayed there
for two months
and when he left,
the insane asylum
loved him so much
that it followed
him all over
California,
and Baudelaire
laughed when the

insane asylum
rubbed itself
up against his
leg like a
strange cat.

My Insect Funeral
Part 9

When I was a child
I had a graveyard
where I buried insects
and dead birds under
a rose tree.
I would bury the insects
in tin foil and match boxes.
I would bury the birds
in pieces of red cloth.
It was all very sad
and I would cry
as I scooped the dirt
into their small graves
with a spoon.
Baudelaire would come
and join in
my insect funerals,
saying little prayers
the size of
dead birds.

San Francisco
February 1958

DOMINIQUE LOWELL

Bike Messenger Leading the People
An Anarchy Poem. It's Devil's Night in Detroit.

I burn my own house down cause it ain't my house
it's your house

your shit your shit your shit
incitement to riot
burn it down burn it down burn it down burn it
down burn it down
there's so much paper
burn it down burn it down burn it down
the kindling's there the fuel for the fire
it would glow burn beautiful orange licking flames
paper paper paper paper
it's all just fuel for the fire
the big bonfire
violence against buildings
violence against property
the ultimate act of rebellion
and I'm gonna build me a guillotine
at One Sansome
right by The Wall
right where it says "The Sharper Image"
grab these fuckers by the hair
drag em by their power nooses
and chop their lousy heads off
it's French Revolution time
burn it down
and there'll be a huge famous painting of me
bike messenger leading the people
yeah

43 years she said
43 years I was chained to a desk
43 years I pushed around rubber bands and paper
clips and xerox memos
43 years and I hated every goddamn minute of it
now I drink in cheap bars
now I wait for my landlord to sell my building so he
can toss me on the street
43 years of all that paper paper
pushin pushin paper
of being an appliance part of the hardware the
interior decorating
43 years of being no one for a paycheck
well you know what I say
all these buildings the skyscrapers
all that chrome and glass filled with all that paper
well we could have ourselves
one hella Molotov cocktail

all we need is a little gasoline and
just one match
light the fucking match
what are we waiting for?
all these people in their starched white shirts
who act like they own the street and the sidewalk
and the fucking world
because they do
burn it down
burn it down burn it down burn it down burn it
down

goddamn peds
goddamn clogs
goddamn termites
goddamn ants
goddamn drones
in my way I am
lost in the forgotten guts
of dead office equipment souls
Jesus came to the marketplace
Jesus came to Market street and He said
burn it down
all you buyers and sellers He said
burn it down
you profane my world

I am riding my bicycle through the den of lepers
and I am trying to remain unscathed
and me well I'm a white slime maggot
I was fed television and twinkies
and the scroungy ethics
of depression children parents
one who can't throw away a piece of wilted lettuce
one who buys crates of the finest just to watch it rot
we are the refuse of a decaying system
we are products of decay
but oh! the fragrant twisted beauty of death
the rollicking waltz to be danced
come on come on come on
light the match

Women are Hungry

Women are hungry. They be hoes, They be sittin on
your stoop waiting to drink your beer. Eat Your Food.
Suck your dick. Women are hungry. They need your
favorite shirt your leather jacket a house and a car
they just neeeeeeeeeeeeeeeeeed.
And they wanna tell you things. Pretty little things
about the light in your eyes and the feel of your thighs
they wanna shave your balls. Wanna know all your
masturbatory nightmares, about every clit you ever
licked every ass you ever eyed so they can slice them
all to ribbons. They're insatiable. It's biological.
They just want and want and stretch their yearning arms
at you their insatiable envelopes gawking open mouthed
must have must have must have it you now
whoremothergoddesspriestessconvictjailer
needyneedyneedyneedy
need your sperm need your job need space. Need more
impossible paint for another impossible face. Blackened
purple eyes and concrete sharpened nails. Puffy crimson
lips. The beaten look, that's it. Already been hit.
Well feed me. Feed me beer and cigarettes and dead idols
who make me feel like I might have a reason to die too.
Give me war and Coca-Cola and the promise of another
American Chance. Give me another good song to dance to.
Tell me I'm not fat. Tell me my tits are jewels, my
nipples gumdrops. Tell me we can pay the rent tomorrow.
Tell me we are just like John and Yoko, only I get to
die first o.k.? I get to be the one they light the candles
for in Central Park, o.k.?
Fuck Women. They are such sluttish catfight evile bitches
every one of them. Beware. Beware. They know what they
are doing. Does that scare you? Are you scared?
Women are hungry. Hungry for balance. I been called a
whore so many times I guess I am one. And it's not you
personally I want anything out of it's the world. The
world owes me big time. The world leaves me hungry.

Manifest Destiny

To seek to know To Know
to strip Maya of her veil and nuns of their habits

Caprice has a notion don't get in her way
she's a wild thaaaang
with a freewheeling flurry of cobwebs in her wake
with a pop and a toss she chucks morals like
beercans in the wastebasket
M O R A L I T Y
cogent constrained chinese water torture
of oppression
no black no white just grey tight skirts of
Behaviour
strained through old cheesecloth
crumpled old soldiers who rest their wormy limp
pricks on velvet hemorrhoid cushions
while they machinate the dissection of souls
with a digital watch

Time is the greatest whip of oppression
It can be used from any distance
a torpid touch
the slightest glance
and we dance a cold measured step
in the middle of the road
granular
and carefully glazed.

No!
None of that!
I worship only whimsy!

all levers and lubricants needed to pry a last bit of
suffocating soul from grey bondage
shall be used to excess
a fulmination of excess is the prescription
salve of extremity
balm of nonsense
cool cloth of waywardness
to be as bad as it takes to be a true saint
a true seeker
To seek to know To Know
and no cold feet allowed

pregnant with lust for the unknown
divine the gurgles and murmurs of chaotic joy
rambling and unraveling through the
abdomen and chest and
thorax

give them no rest
no time for effete politesse
play is serious business
frivolity ain't no laughing matter
and Love must be made
must be found
must be redefined and reintroduced to us all
ripped from the gut and splattered brutally on the
wall
peals of laughter will splay it through the streets
like a muthafuckin riot
because you see
sheer exuberance is the only responsibility
convulsive
and naked

An Oliver Stone Movie

Jim Morrison never had to be a busboy or a maid
Work at Carl's Jr. or go on G.A.
He just took some acid in the desert one day
And woke up a rockstar
Of course he was tortured
He was an artist and a poet and shit
He's supposed to be tortured
And he'd have these visions
Of naked Indians and medicine men
Big ol bad Jim Morrison
He really thought he was a lizard
Poor ol tortured guy
And these journalists would drink his blood
In these weird ass satanic rituals
But boy oh boy that Jim could party
Damn he sure could drink
And he showed everyone his prick
And got arrested and got all fat
But he didn't give a fuck
He had a really fine bitchin girlfriend
And he smacked her around but it was cool
She could take it
And she understood
When she found him dead in the bathtub.

WALT WHITMAN

From *Song of the Open Road*

1
Afoot and light-hearted I take to the open road,
Healthy, free, the world before me,
The long brown path before me leading wherever I choose.

Henceforth I ask not good-fortune, I myself am good-fortune,
Henceforth I whimper no more, postpone no more, need
                nothing,
Done with indoor complaints, libraries, querulous criticisms,
Strong and content I travel the open road.

The earth, that is sufficient,
I do not want the constellations any nearer,
I know they are very well where they are,
I know they suffice for those who belong to them.

(Still here I carry my old delicious burdens,
I carry them, men and women, I carry them with me wherever
                I go,
I swear it is impossible for me to get rid of them,
I am fill'd with them; and I will fill them in return.)

2
You road I enter upon and look around, I believe you are not
                all that is here,
I believe that much unseen is also here.

Here the profound lesson of reception, nor preference nor
                denial,
The black with his woolly head, the felon, the diseas'd, the
                illiterate person, are not denied;
The birth, the hasting after the physician, the beggar's tramp,
                the drunkard's stagger, the laughing party of
                mechanics,
The escaped youth, the rich person's carriage, the fop, the
                eloping couple,
The early market-man, the hearse, the moving of furniture
                into the town, the return back from the town,

They pass, I also pass, any thing passes, none can be inter-
  dicted,
None but are accepted, none but shall be dear to me.

RUDOLFO ANAYA

Walt Whitman
Strides the Llano of New Mexico

I met Walt, kind old father, on the llano,
    that expanse of land of eagle and cactus
Where the Mexicano met the Indio, and both
    met the tejano, along the Río Pecos, our
    River of blood, River of Billy the Kid,
    River of Fort Sumner where the Diné suffered,
    River of the golden Carp, god of my gods.

He came striding across the open plain,
    There where the owl calls me to
        the shrine of my birth,
    There where Ultima buried my soul-cord, the
        blood, the afterbirth, my destiny.

His beard, coarse, scraggly, warm, filled with sunlight,
    like llano grass filled with grasshoppers, grillos,
    protection for lizards and jackrabbits,
    rattlesnakes, coyotes, and childhood fears.

"Buenos dias, don Walt!" I called. "I have been
    waiting for you. I knew you would one day leap
        across the Mississippi!
    Leap from Manhattas! Leap over Brooklyn Bridge!
        Leap over slavery!
    Leap over the technocrats!
        Leap over atomic waste!
    Leap over the violence! Madonna!
        Dead end rappers!
            Peter Jennings and ungodly nightly news!

AMERICAN RENEGADES

Leap over your own sex! Leap to embrace la gente
de Nuevo México! Leap to miracles!"

I always knew that. I dreamed that.

I knew you would one day find the Mexicanos of my land,
the Nuevo Mexicanos who kicked ass with our
Indian ancestors, kicked ass with the tejanos,
And finally got their ass kicked by politicians!
I knew you would find us Chicanos, en la pobreza,
Always needing change for a ride or a pint,
Pero ricos en el alma! Ricos en nuestra cultura!
Ricos con sueños y memoria!

I kept the faith, don Walt, because I always knew
you could leap continents! Leap over the squalor!
Leap over pain and suffering, and the ash heap we
Make of our Earth! Leap into my arms.

Let me nestle in your bigote, don Walt, as I once
nestled in my abuelo's bigote, don Liborio,
Patriarch of the Mares clan, padre de mi mamá,
Farmer from Puerto de Luna, mestizo de España y
México, Católico y Judío, Moro y indio, francés
y mountain man, hombre de la tierra!

Let me nestle in your bigote, don Walt, like I once
nestled in the grass of the llano, on summer days,
a child lost in the wide expanse, brother to lagarto,
jackrabbit, rattlesnake, vulture and hawk.
I lay sleeping in the grama grass, feeling
the groan of the Earth beneath me, tierra sagrada!
Around me, grasshoppers chuffing, mockingbird calling,
meadowlark singing, owl warning, rabbit humping,
flies buzzing, worms turning, vulture and hawk
riding air currents, brujo spirits moving across
my back and raising the hair of my neck,
golden fish of my ponds tempting me to believe
in the gods of the earth, water, air and fire.
Oriente, poniente, norte, sur, y yo!
Dark earth groaning beneath me, sperm flowing,
sky turning orange and red, nighthawks dart, bats
flitter, the mourning call of La Llorona filling the
night wind as the *presence of the river* stirred, called my
name: "Hijo! Hiiiii-jo!"

And I fled, fled for the safety of my mother's arms.

You know the locura of childhood, don Walt—
    That's why I welcome you to the llano, my llano,
    My Nuevo México! Tierra sagrada! Tierra sangrada!

Hold me in the safety of your arms, wise poet, old poet,
    Abuelo de todos. Your fingers stir my memory.

The high school teachers didn't believe in the magic
    of the Chicano heart. They fed me palabras sin sabor
    when it was your flesh I yearned for. Your soul.
    They teased us with "Oh, Capitan, My Capitan!"
    Read silently so as to arouse no passion, no tears,
    no erections, no bubbling love for poetry.

Que desgracia! What a disgrace! To give my soul only
    one poem in four years when you were a universe!

Que desgracia! To give us only your name, when you were
    Cosmos, and our brown faces yearned for
    the safety of your bigote, your arms!

Que desgracia! That you have to leap from your grave,
    Now, in this begetting time, to kick ass with
    this country which is so slow to learn that
    we are the magic in the soul! We are the dream
    of Aztlán!

Que desgracia! That my parents didn't even know your name!
    Didn't know that in your *Leaves of Grass* there was
    salvation for the child.
    I hear my mother's lament: "They gave me no education!"
    I understand my father's stupor: "They took *mi honor, mi
    orgullo, mi palabra.*"

Pobreza de mi gente! I strike back now! I bring you
    don Walt to help gird our loins!
    Este viejo es guerrillero por la gente!
    Guerrillero por los pobres! Los de abajo!

Save our children now! I shout. Put *Leaves of Grass* in their
    lunchboxes! In the tacos and tamales!
    Let them call him Abuelo! As I call him Abuelo!

AMERICAN RENEGADES

Chicano poets of the revolution! Let him fly with you
　　As your squadrons of words fill the air over
　　Aztlán! Mujeres chicanas! Pull his bigote as you
　　Would tug at a friendly abuelo! His manhood is ours!
　　Together we are One!

Pobreza! Child wandering the streets of Alburqué! Broken
　　by the splash of water, elm seed ghost, lost and by winds
　　　　of spring mourned, by La Llorona of the Río Grande
　　mourned, outcast, soul-seed, blasted by the wind
　　　　of the universe, soul-wind, scorched by the
　　Grandfather Sun, Lady Luna, insanity, grubs scratching
　　　　at broken limbs, fragmented soul.

I died and was buried and years later I awoke from
　　the dead and limped up the hill where your
　　　　Leaves of Grass lay buried in library stacks.

"Chicano Child Enters University!" the papers cried.
　　Miracle child! Strange child! Dark child!
　　　　Speaks Spanish Child! Has Accent Child!
　　Needs Lots of Help Child! Has No Money Child!
　　　　Needs a Job Child! Barrio Child!
　　Poor People's Child! Gente Child! Drop Out Child!
"I'll show you," I sobbed, entering the labyrinth of loneliness,
　　dark shadows of library, cold white classrooms.

You saved me, don Walt, you and my familia which held
　　Me up, like a crutch holding the one-leg Man,
　　　　Like Amor holding the lover,
　　　　　　Like kiss holding the flame of Love.

You spoke to me of your Manhattas, working men and women,
　　miracle of democracy, freedom of the soul, the suffering
　　of the Great War, the death of Lincoln, the lilacs' last
　　bloom, the pantheism of the Cosmos, the miracle of Word.

Your words caressed my soul, soul meeting soul,
　　You opened my mouth and forced me to speak!
　　Like a cricket placed on dumb tongue,
　　Like the curandera's healing herbs and
　　Touch which taught me to see beauty,
　　Your fingers poked and found my words!
　　You drew my stories out.
　　You believed in the Child of the Llano.

I fell asleep on *Leaves of Grass*, covering myself with
    your bigote, dreaming my ancestors, my healers,
    the cuentos of their past, dreams and memories.

I fell asleep in your love, and woke to my mother's
    tortillas on the comal, my father's cough, my
    familia's way to work, the vast love which was
    an ocean in a small house.

I woke to write my *Leaves of Llano Grass*, the cuentos
    of the llano, tierra sagrada! I thank the wise
    teacher who said, "Dark Child, read this book!
    You are grass and to grass you shall return."

"Gracias, don Walt! Enjoy your stay. Come again. Come
    Every day. Our niños need you, as they need
    Our own poets. Maybe you'll write a poem in Spanish,
    I'll write one in Chinese. All of poetry is One."

KEN DiMAGGIO

Ken DiMaggio, is one of the founding poets and estheticians of the contemporary resurgence of Spoken Word poetry. Allen Ginsberg first took note of him in the early-eighties. Later in that decade and into the nineties, during the nascent days of New York's now-burgeoning downtown scene, he earned the unqualified admiration of fellow poets at ABC No Rio and the Nuyorican Poetry Cafe. His stunning performances of highly original poems combine Punk and Pop sensibility with high art. Though others would later imitate his unique style with far less effect, his stubborn integrity often deprived him of opportunities for greater prominence. Undaunted, he continued throughout the last decade to churn out novels, poems, a newsletter and to perform from coast to coast. With Steve Hartman of Pinched Nerves Press he has created limited edition books that are the last word in visionary underground art.

ALAN KAUFMAN

These Are My Words, My Neon, Siliconed, Carcinogenic Words.
But This Is My Poem, My Poem About Elvis.
For Robert Parody

Who will strum the Mississippi and wake from its mud
buffalo nickels who will there be to shake
sex from his hips for adolescents scared senile
of nuclear missiles Elvis who I
once threw rocks at Elvis who my generation tried
to pronounce dead but who is there now to
tell the truth about Chevrolets who is there
now to give dignity to TV dinners and
readymade families who is there now it's not Henry
James who is there now it's not Peter Paul and Mary
who is there now

that doesn't want to own a Saab or an Audi

but in the trailer courts in the mobile homes in the
low-rent projects the three family houses someone is
singing Are You Lonesome Tonight someone is
singing from loneliness just loneliness that you won't
find in a novel by Thomas Jefferson that you
won't hear in an opera sung by Phil Donahue that
you won't see in a movie starring The Women's
Movement and George Armstrong Custer but in
the houseware aisle at Caldor's in the Junior Department
in Penny's in the garden center at Sears will you hear
the piped muzak and the loneliness loneliness loneliness the
piped muzak and the mobile homes mobile homes mobile
homes the piped muzak and the TV dinners TV dinners TV
dinners the piped muzak and the undernourishment the
soul dying like a moth alone in some dark closet
alone in a wardrobe of loneliness no not Henry
James and certainly not Jackie Kennedy the
first Presidential widow to walk on the moon

no   there was only one rock and roll to float to the surface
all the Boy Scout knives buried in the Missouri river
there was only one rock and roll to know mechanical
failure body rot and obsolescence in a
Chevy and there was only rock and roll
to dream the dream of the trailer the
TV dinner and have it only to die in some bloated

drugged-out entertainer's closet no there was only
rock and roll and I never listened to it

like so many other millions of Americans I tried
to be Thomas Jefferson thinking that I could
be liberal   and also own slaves   but instead I
became neither   when I found that I was
a has-been   and not even a slave

There was only one rock and roll one rock and roll one
Mississippi yielding up the dreams

wished on so many Indian-head nickels

and loneliness loneliness loneliness   is everywhere
is on the rooftops sharp like broken glass is on the cars dented
like old tin cans is on the empty factories covered
with dead brown rose petals is on the juvenile
delinquent covered with World War Two victories
steel strapping plants and Saturday Evening
Post covers that he does not see
from a city in Connecticut a city called New Britain a
city of gravel lots and warped purple flowers a
city of long hilly streets lined with mothballed
fleets of old Galaxies and Impalas a city of virgin
mary lawn ornaments and newspaper gray bungalows Elvis
still sings he sings he sings

and in a graveyard   a graveyard in Lincoln
Nebraska a graveyard for dead boxcars dead
cabooses Elvis sings to the prairies rusting
inside The Burlington Northern caboose and
to the mountain lost in the bits of stone and mud
inside the Missouri Pacific refrigerator car and to the
memories of North Dakota Kansas Idaho and Montana
cobwebbed under the wheels of the nameless box car   Elvis
sings Oh he sings

but only to a rattlesnake a moth a raccoon because
the bum in the City Mission a quarter mile away
is too busy being an undiscovered human being and the
banker in the perforated building a half mile away
is too busy being St. Peter or Ward Cleaver and the state
senator in the clothes pin shaped capitol three

quarters of a mile away is too busy being a
Norman Rockwell illustration

in Lincoln Nebraska   in New Britain Connecticut
in North Dakota Kansas and Idaho cobwebbed
under the wheels of a 40-year old freight car   Elvis
sings does your memory stray do the chairs in your
parlor seem empty and bare is your heart filled
with pain Elvis sings! He sings!

In Tacoma Washington   in Pittsburgh Pennsylvania
in the Adirondacks the Rockies the Appalachias lost in pieces
of stone of mud in a 30-year old refrigerator car Elvis
sings! do you miss me tonight shall I come back again
to a bright summer's day Elvis sings! He sings!

in a rose-dead covered factory in a No Vacancy
motel in a newspaper gray cornfield Elvis sings!
Are you lonesome tonight! Is your heart filled
with pain! Are you lonesome tonight! Are you
lonesome tonight tell me are you lonesome
tonight Yes I am lonesome Yes my heart
is lonesome Yes my factories are lonesome!
Yes my cornfields are lonesome Yes My hilly
streets with rusting cars yes they are lonesome!
Yes! The banker the bum the state senator! Yes
the mountains the prairie the highways! Yes
the would-be humans the would-be apostles the would-
be civic leaders! Yes I am lonesome! Yes my
heart is lonesome! Yes my country is
lonesome! Yes we are lonesome! We are lonesome!
We are lonesome!

but not from the guitar of Henry James the
Boogie Woogie of John F. Kennedy the
tambourine of Thomas Jefferson but from the
velvet painting of an angel in white
from a velvet painting of an angel in a
white sequined suit from a velvet painting
of a white sequined angel no older
than 25 from a velvet painting selling
for 25 dollars on the roadside
and from a ceramic mug and a plastic nite-lite and a
small statuette music box all of them of an
angel in white will come the simple naive blessing

trying to soothe an alienation that has even
reduced God to some fragmented presence   lodged
in a dead freight car

Oh but with a buffalo nickel a Boy Scout knife
a juke-box loving song Are You Lonesome Tonight

can the simple and naive   let us be alone long enough

to cry   to cry   to cry

Elvis he sang to me Elvis he sang to me Elvis he
sang to me but I was part of the dream that
made him die I was part of the dream that lured him
on I was part of the dream that brought him
down I was part of the dream but a very
small part of the dream I was part of the
dream but a rusting Chevrolet a
sedimented box car a street inevitable to the
warped flowers and the gravel

O how a simple naive song would now do   but
as both singer and listener know

there is nothing simple or naive in
a country that is lonely

only in a man who would be King a man who would try
entering heaven on a glittering pink-bulbed stairway a
man who would try driving into paradise in a leopard-
striped Cadillac   only in a man who would try dreaming
beyond the trailer courts beyond the TV dinners beyond
the steel strapping plants yes   only in this man did the
Paul Bunyon the Johnny Appleseed the Cherry tree the
cotton field the Blue Ox come alive

and the banker within his toasters fishing poles satellites
and station wagons   no no no   only Elvis dreams Is your
heart filled with pain Are you lonesome tonight Shall I
come back again Are you lonesome tonight Are you lonesome
tonight Are you lonesome tonight

and from an abandoned graffiti'd freight car   an empty
windowless factory   a torched-out rusted trailer

I cry   I cry   I cry

AMERICAN RENEGADES

ALAN KAUFMAN

When I hear lyrical rage shaped for a consumption money cannot buy, I clap my hands because I know: a poet of the people is being born. Alan Kaufman is such a poet, and I'm happy to be able to preface this selection with a few words aimed at putting the reader on the lookout: a poetry with spine in it is in our midst. The horizon was never more vertical!

It's not simply the journey of a poet from The Bronx to California that's encompassed here. Kaufman, a product of the conciousness especially of the past deacade, sees an America slain by capital, a land that has left its felonious texture everywhere. The polarity of wealth and poverty ride with every mile, along with the underlying violence and desperado desolation that inhabit the American soul because of that polarized inequity.

Kaufman, who is people-possessed, can jump into the skin of an American soldier in the Middle-East to assault the rot of that "adventure" (in his poem *Kuwait*) with the same raw ease with which he identifies with the "friendless" and "fugitive" riders through the nightmared American dream.

His identies in fact are with the poor, the fugitives, the outcasts—in the best tradition of that greatest of all American poems, *Song of the Open Road*.

But Kaufman seeks more than identity. His book, a youthful poet's credo, is also a call to those abused by the system in power to rise and gather as revolutionaries "till the mouth of every starving child is fed."

This is not gush or gusto. Even when, because he is new, his identities clash or are obscured in all he wants to expose, the rage of his heart for the underlying necessity of change races ahead with clarity.

That's one of the reasons why this book goes *toward* the future more directly than others, and why it launches an important voice for truth at a time when the technology of lies is endemic.

JACK HIRSCHMAN,
from the Preface to Alan Kaufman's *American Cruiser*

Bus

At the gateway
to America
Greyhound strikers
shrieked:
"You won't
get out!"

Ninety bucks
to cross the
land by bus

For this, embarked,
anonymous, neither
lonely or glad,

a young man
with family
stared at his
ticket, afraid

and an old aunt
stooped to her
bags as a skinhead
cursed her back

and a punk with a pierced nose
sighed: "this country's
fucked"

and beside me
an ex-con, patting
his hair, snapped:
"Man, I done my time!
I'm going home"

We boarded like
souls on Charon's bark

As the road
stroked by wheels
removed its dress,
one by one
we laid our tired
heads on breasts
of trembling
glass

But somewhere
in Pennsylvania
I woke,
my face a gun

House of Strangers

Her face,
cut from patient
ebony, looked ill

A trash bag
of belongings
rode her lap

I guessed her
life had been
a suicide of kindness
repaid in grief

And somewhere in Cheyenne
I asked where she was going

and she said that she
was going to the
House of Strangers
in Reno, Nevada
where God sits in a
clapboard casino
playing the one-armed bandit

"Heaven is a hotel,"
she smiled, "and if you meet
His price, the Big Guy
will let you sit
and listen to the wind
blow: Whooooooo!"
and I knew
she was crazy

"My daughter-in-law
swore I'd die, but
it's good exercise
for me to ride. Look
at me, am I dead?"
And I knew
that she was

I laughed. "You look,"
I said "like morning
in Atlanta"

She grinned and
wrapped my hand
in a glove of bone

"Is it a way still?"
"Not far. We're
getting there"
"Good," she sighed,
"I'm ready"

She showed me a bag
big with silver dollars:
"Ten years of my life
there," she laughed

And later, while she slept,
I stole a few
to feed myself

Who Are We?

Into the past
I go like a stranger
to discover why at night
I lay alone as a child
waiting for the front door
to slam, my father gone
to night-shift work,
and my mother, Marie, to enter,
unable to sleep, and tell me
tales of childhood
war, pursued by those
who, as she spoke,
seemed to enter the room,
Gestapo men in leather coats
who ordered me to pack
and descend to a waiting truck,

for I am still going to Auschwitz
though a grown man in 1999
I am still boarding the freight,
crushed against numbed, frightened
Jews and Gypsies and Russian
soldiers and homosexuals
crossing frontiers to be gassed

I am her, in my heart,
though I am six feet two
and two hundred and ten pounds
and have played college football
and served as a soldier
and have scars from fights
with knives and jagged
bottles smashed on bars

I am still her, little girl,
hiding in chicken coops
and forests, asleep on dynamite
among partisans
I am still her, brushing teeth
with ashes
from the ruins of nations
gutted in war

I am still her brown eyes
and black hair of persecution
foraging scraps of thistle soup,
a star-shaped patch
sewn to my shirt

I am still my mother
every day in the streets
of New York or San Francisco,
the chimney skies glow and swirl
with soot like night above
a crematorium, or the Bronx
incinerator chute where I
threw out trash in a brick
darkness shooting sparks

I am still her in the streets
of Berkeley, walking among

sparechangers, dyed-hair punkers,
gays in stud leather, Blacks,
Mexicans and Asians

I am still her rounded up
among poets and thieves
and politically incorrect
social deviants
on sun-drenched sidewalks
in the Mission and the Haight,
Greenwich Village, the Lower
East Side, or anywhere the weird
congregate in tolerance

And every day in this age
of intolerance,
in a mental ghetto
affirmed by the homeless,
I pass the dying
with the loud ring of my boots,
ashamed to think that perhaps
my heels are the last thing
they heard
Every day I am a
survivor of AIDS and poverty

Every day I sit in cafes
watching tattoos turn to numbers
and I grow angry
I want America back
I want America to be
the home I never had

And you, who are you
if you hear my voice?
Who are you, stranger
if you read these words?

Who are we
who stand threatened
in these times of darkness?
Who are we, condemned to die,
who do not know ourselves
at all?

AMERICAN RENEGADES

The Saddest Man on Earth

The saddest man on Earth . . .

ignored how the rain felt
as he left home
for the last time

Wore down
his boot heels
searching for the woman
of his dreams
but never understood
that life is a woman

Lived in a town
where sadness was illegal
and where grinning
cops ticketed his face
so often
that he lost his license
to cry

The saddest man
on Earth
tuned guitars
but couldn't play them
cheated the IRS
of his own refund
fathered a child
who thought she saw
him in perfect strangers
yet didn't recognize
him face to face

I met him once
in a bar
toasting the mirror
with his stare
He had come
south to start
life over

He was a
Mozart of silence

On Reading Whitman's Song of Myself at One O'clock in the Morning

An image or two stuck:
the swimmer tossed into the sea and surfacing
with damp curls, reborn, beside himself with joy,
and further on you enjoin the student,
me I guess,
to destroy you, the teacher,
and that will spread your breast

BANG!
You're dead

I'm out here, Walt, rushing broke
down Mission to beg Unemployment
to cut me a check
I'm out here in dry dock,
spilling my guts like a dweeb to a bunch of drunks
whose names I don't know,
and I'm thinking I'll have these narratives
from Hell tattooed on my skin,
so I can step up to cops,
rip off my shirt
and shout: Read this!

Because underfoot, Walt,
is not grass but flames
I'm living the private American inferno
where anguish is something you do at home,
behind locked doors; terror
expressed to strangers in rented rooms
anonymously, and late at night
over telephones to friends, who sob in turn
of their own HIVs of incurable hepatitis
enlarged livers secreting
schizophrenic genes of utter emotional
drear, shame success tumors,
and harrowing despair at the ghosts
of their walking fathers

I am laughing by kitchen light, Walt,
bent with rot-toothed
grin over your most famous poem,
watching my reflection

AMERICAN RENEGADES

in the night of ashtray eyes
and lips shaped by the vowel of Oblivion,
and tonight, Walt, I am James Dean
on the day of his death,
I am Marilyn Monroe's baby grown,
the second one she lost,
and all that I have been
is falling down
like a house of cards
in this room by-the-week,
with my iodine-dabbed
gangrenous leg like a seated shriek
I am shrieking, Walt, for a drink,
for a fix, for a mother, for a God,
for a kindness, for a child,
for a prayer I can say
without sneering in my guts

I'm asking, Walt,
have you got like me
slant eyes, hook nose,
black skin and Spanish lips,
do they let my type with dick,
one ball, big tits, mascara, wig,
pumps, two wombs
and cocktail dress into Heaven?

I'm, sick of Wonder bread, Walt
Have you got democratic steak for me?
Have you got red-blooded boneless
shoes for me, without holes, a lot
of ketchup, size twelve?
Because I'm years in the alleys
in the garbage cans in the rain
laying for you with a poem like a gun
I don't know what's got into me
I'm trigger obsessed
Must be the Bronx where I grew up
Must be Bronx make me
hard as an aerial snapped
off a car, as a packed
Saturday night special,
and I wanna rumble,
Walt, I wanna mix it up

I'm infected with the virus of the poor
who never read the Norton Anthology of Modern Verse
Who sing madrigals of bucked teeth,
harelip and rickets, recite sonnets
of executed eviction summonses
for unpaid back rents, and job
applications to Macdonalds,
and critically deconstruct
stab wounds painted with Mercurochrome

I've got a vision, Walt, of savage
love for the one-eyed drunk,
the limping thief, the unshaven
cabby in drag
I've got a vision, Walt
of the cosmic benefit
of sound nutrition
of medical attention
of housing and of voice
in a truly democratic society
on the filthy piles of flesh
dying on the pavement
I've got a vision of extended hand
of lifting arm
of healing souls leafing and loafing
in winter coats and resoled shoes
and of their lonely power to destroy you,
once and for all, old teacher,
and spread your breast a billion-fold,
to absurd bursting point, like gout,
and not just your breast, old fella,
but your neck and cheeks,
guts and buttocks and knees
will swell, inflamed with their angry joy
And the poor will not drown in the sea
Their deaths, for too long
given over to God, will return to us
with restored trust
in the thriving intimacy of the earth
and from love we will come
and with love we will see
even in the hour of our greatest blindness
that to an even gentler love we go

Across the Mississippi

We crossed the Mississippi's muddy brown expanse in a blinding
thunderstorm,
creeping over a big suspension bridge whose name nobody knew,
in a bus with sheets of rain battering windows feeble as eyelids
trembling in fear,
and we could hardly see but for glimpses of suspension cable over
the sullen river, on the banks houses like garbage cans with pedal lids,
and over it all a sky the color and consistency of clay,
with an occasional lightening bolt seaming it like a cheek
wrinkled in angry laughter.
And we didn't even know that we were crossing
the Mississippi until that bottle of Fleishman's whiskey
fell from the overhead luggage rack
and the lanky driver with hair in his eyes, and rolled sleeves,
and a pack of filterless Pall Malls
cast a glaring boozy eye our way in the rear view mirror,
pulled over the bus right there on the bridge
and announced for the twentieth time since leaving New York City
that Federal regulations prohibit booze consumption aboard,
which hadn't made a goddamned difference to anyone
for over a thousand miles so far,
and didn't make a goddamned difference now.
The drunkards still snuck drinks and the sober people didn't.
And he put the bus into high gear and gunned it.
And this was as we crossed the Mississippi,
though we didn't even know it.

Assumed it was just some trash river,
as some birds are trash birds—say, the robin.
A trash river, some of us thinking, a love canal,
an above-ground industrial sewer of radioactive Republican by-products
by which to contaminate and kill the poor on the merry road to profit.
So we didn't even know that we we were crossing that famous river,
had no way to know.
Most of us had never seen it.
I had come from a transient hotel room east of the Hudson to find
my gain in California. I didn't have much money.
When the bus pulled into a rest stop, I stayed on board—didn't
stumble off like the others blear-eyed drunk on lack of sleep
to gorge myself on fast food.
I was making it across the continent on three loaves of wonder bread
and two jars of peanut butter and one of jam, and so far so good.

And that bottle of Fleishman's that dropped out missed
a passenger's big pink ear by a hair's breadth, bounced
without shattering, and rolled to a stop against the bolted leg of a chair,
and the passenger, his name as I recall was Chopper,
reached down, retrieved the bottle, held it up with a big grin
and while everybody in the back of the bus roared with approval,
he waved it at the driver, who stopped the bus and made the speech.
And then, after a moment's sullen pause,
suddenly the driver's voice came on again, but kinder,
and he said with a gentle pride that surprised most of us I think:
"You are crossing the Mississippi River, on the Sasquahana
Bridge, and are about to enter the town of Shilo Springs."
And the effect on us of this announcement was like what maybe the
Hebrews felt when Moses told them after all their wanderings
and afflictions: *You are crossing the Jordan River. You are entering the
Promised Land.*
Because everyone became very serene suddenly,
and reposed quiet in their seats,
some with heads cocked, and just slow-watching the passage
occur.

The ex-con wearing the shower cap, the hungry computer jock,
the professional piercer with earrings in his eyes and ears and exposed
nipples in a fishnet shirt,
the old woman with a garbage bag containing all her
possessions riding on her lap,
the Nam vet with a baseball cap gray beard blue eyes
the color of anti-freeze,
that girl who looked like every girl I'd ever seen writhe nude
in the glaring footlights of a topless bar,
the silent man who refused our repeated offers
of whiskey with a tight, unresentful smile,
and even the loud, hard-muscled mustached guy
with a face like a skinned and butchered leg of steer
and who claimed to be a lumberjack
(but whom many of us figured for a killer of some kind,
in flight from his latest barroom manslaughter),
everybody, and that includes that stiff and uncommunicative
respectably-dressed middle-aged lady
with silver hair who shuddered when asked by the ex-con
for a match, everyone without exception
seemed to give up their tension and their fear
like the dying surrender of a soul on its way to final rest
and we sat back and just let the transition occur.

And on the other side of the Mississippi River it was like an older,
more innocent time in America.
There was a kind of canal branching from the main body of water,
and less turbulence to the rain
and we could see clearly through the windows
as an old time boat paddled its way to the interior
past banks lined with weeping willows,
and the houses were bigger than they'd seemed from the bridge,
they were stately gray with age
and big columns announced their facades
and dark mandala-shaped stained glass attic windows,
the kind you see in pictures in magazines,
suggested, at least to my mind, the sanctuary and safety
of a family cemetery vault, of time and place and the dignity
of knowing where you come from and where you'll probably end up too.
And this calmed me, calmed everyone I think,
and then the bus met, to our delight, a roadblock
and we had to detour through little old time streets
and it was peaceful for a few brief minutes,
and then the bus drew up to the edge of a puddle
as wide and deep as a stream
and the brakes hissed and the driver's voice announced:
"We are going to ford this puddle," and we cheered.
And just then a man dressed in a green flannel shirt and denim
coveralls stepped from the door of one of the houses
and stood there stock still on the porch to watch.
The rain had lessened and as the bus descended,
almost kissing the rim of the tires,
we watched the man's face watching us
with a kind of compassionate interest, as if encouraging our
success, and when the bus climbed out on the other side
dripping like a baptized bather
the driver braked again.
"We'll sit here a minute," he said "to let the brakes dry."
And that man on the porch,
I guess he saw our faces dim in the tinted rain swept-windows,
and lifted his hand in a wave.
A few of us waved back,
and he beamed a smile. Then he turned and entered the house.
We heard the porch door slam,
crisp and clean in the pattering rainfall.

Let us

Let us
take ourselves aboard a bus
and travel to the dispossessed
and let us praise their dreamless eyes and hardened
smiles
with rogue words of truth
in the killing fields of their hopes
the slum wards and ragged towns and stolen farms

Let us
take to them the carnival
of our mad and scattered lives

Let us bring them the mountain
Let us give them the vision
of an open window, an unlocked door, a bed to sleep in,
a plate of food

Let us give
them the keys to the house of their love
Let us bare our throats tattooed with roses
our breasts sequined with diamonds
our loins hot with dragons
our hands and feet pierced with beauty

Let us come
to their dusty squares and drinking holes
with canticles of magnificent defeat
Let us deliver in their mangers
of pollution and penitentiaries, shopping malls and
tenements
the hard, beautiful birth of the heart

Let us bring renewal
Let us declare the death of despondency and tyrants

For I have seen our campfires pitched beside the roads
like fallen, still-burning miraculous stars
I have seen our bus voyaging to innocence

I have seen us poet-dogs tossed
the last decade of this century, like a bone,

after ninety years of science and war,
reason and corporation, art and Auschwitz

I have seen my vocation descend like a pen
to a page that can never be filled with enough truth
I have crossed a continent of despair
with a summons much older than lies,
and I swear to you, Poets,
I live for greater than myself

You
street-latin Elizabethan hustlers,
I tell you time has come to deal death's passionate kiss to
kings
Time has come to bare our asses in Paradise
Time has come to strip for freedom
Time has come slut dogs, drag queens,
sadomasochists and criminals
to be Tom Paines, Franklins and Jeffersons

Time has come to write
the Constitution
with our poetry and flesh

Time has come
to costume up for Liberty and ride
with words like steel-tipped whips
into the soul of America
and rage there and sing
til the mouth of every starving child
is fed

DAVID LERNER

Before his untimely death in 1997, David Lerner presided as the éminence grise
of the notorious Cafe Babar in San Francisco. Born in New York City in 1951,
he was a former journalist by trade, but left the profession to pursue the bo-
hemian life. In the mid-Eighties he fell in with a wild group of gifted renegade
poets who came to be known, in part through Lerner's promotional efforts, as
the Babarbians. Cafe Babar, where the Babarians assembled weekly to read, soon
became the West Coast outpost of the poetry rebellion that was stirring in New

York and Chicago. For a time an underground network sprang up of poets moving between the three cities, reading at such venues as Cafe Babar, ABC No Rio on the Lower East Side of Manhattan, the Nuyorican Poets Cafe (also on New York City's Lower East Side) and The Green Mill Tavern in Chicago. In this network, Lerner's reputation grew.

From 1986 to 1994, every Thursday night, in a small sheet metal-lined back room of Cafe Babar the Babarians, led on by Lerner and his cohort, Zeitgeist Press publisher Bruce Isaacson, delivered a form of public poetry that came in time to reflect Lerner's passion for the apocryphal phrasing and syntax of pop journalism and the calculated exuberance of blues ballads and hard rock. One pop journalist termed Lerner and Isaacson the Ezra Pound and T. S. Eliot of the underground.

Robinson Jeffers was an influence, as was Bob Dylan and Charles Bukowski. He had a passion for the prose of Hunter S. Thompson and would spend hours poring over past issues of *Rolling Stone*, underscoring sentence fragments from Thompson and others that had caught his eye. Yet despite the resonance of such influences, his poetry was his own, a tightly controlled eruption of paradoxes, visions, emotions and wit. At his performance best, Lerner, with his low-key silken voice, could burn down an audience faster than it takes to smoke a cigarette.

ALAN KAUFMAN

The Crucifixion of Johnny Carson

he smiled once too often
he cracked one too many
lame jokes
about Ronald Reagan
I got tired of watching the sequined backdrop
sway behind him as he
played air golf
while the commercial kicked in

the band was just too expertly bland
Doc's outfits hurt my eyes
he got married one too many times
to a Joan

so we decided to nail him up
we used a big old nail gun
and a stainless-steel cross
times have changed
but the song remains the same

he screamed bloody murder
it was pretty cool
and I felt a little bad
after all, he'd given me
hours of viewing pleasure

but I just got tired of that
pretty little smirk
that perfect gray hair
those retired-Lieutenant-Colonel suits
the headlines in the *Enquirer*
I got tired of Ed McMahon's
booming, desperate laugh
got bored with his belly too
and the cracks about his boozing

I got tired of all that intensely false
show biz camaraderie jive
the guests were always
throwing around

I even got tired of Johnny's
smooth silver touch with
old ladies and children

so we crashed the party
way past midnight
slammed him up against the wall
and popped the steel home

you should have heard him scream
it was really tasty
stripped down to his underwear
he cried too
it was fantastic

at first he hung tough
said things like
"What's the meaning of this"
and "Don't you know who I am?"
and "You'll never work in this town
again"

but when we
told him we never worked in this town

anyway
and yes, we knew who he was
and we couldn't tell him the meaning
for all the cunt in Malibu
his smile turned hard
then his hard face faded
and a blank look came over those features
that gleam so well

and the blankness started to shake
and the shaking shuddered
and then he began to cry

it was really special
when he cried
and suddenly I felt a little
bad for him
he breaks just like anybody else
I thought

it was nice to see him cry
and that was really all
we wanted
to see something that made sense
on that jewel of a mask

he wept like blazes
he screamed for his life

and I thought
shit, let's yank those things out
and give him another chance

but it was too late
the red light was fading
they were folding the set
he was
going off the air

and the look that crossed over his eyes
just before he
leaned over into The Next World
he sort of looked like Jesus

I know he forgave me for my sins

all in all,
I felt pretty good
about the whole thing

Slamdancing to the Blues

there's a sadness that's
better than love
it fell in the air
the other night

little girl face
with a mind as wild as Egypt

she reads all the high-class
sex literature
the pornography of Miller
even the later novels of Rechy
now into the novelization of
Liquid Sky
and *The Apocalypse Culture*

during the days she
takes off her clothes to
Tom Waits and the Dead Kennedys
at a theatre on Market
while the customers finger their crotches
and tip paper money

she said, "How do I look?"
and I told her she looked like
a 14-year-old beatnik with an
IQ of 200

she wasn't sure she liked that
she has invented herself so well
she's not sure she can
escape

I know that song

Blasted Youth

blasted youth in black
blasted youth looks good in black
hot black

blasted youth doesn't care in this special way
that charms you
only reads the obituaries and the
ads

blasted youth is cold with feeling
blasted youth is sexy
death dressed in the wind and
ready to go anywhere

blasted youth doesn't understand ideals
when it was born they were already
cartoons

blasted youth believes in
the paradise of the single second
the long night of the flesh
the terrible hunger for ecstasy

blasted youth is wild with fragile purpose

the way it moves with grace through
poisoned water
forgetting nothing

blasted youth will die trying
and there are
worse things to die of these days

Satan After Hours

people think
Satan is a mythic beast
breathing doom and fire
laughing rapaciously as he
plucks your eyes out

a comic book ghoulie
with bad breath and a skin problem

Satan is a bus station

Satan is a cold fried egg
on a plastic plate
a cup of weak coffee beside it
while the telephone rings

Satan is the bland smile of
the cashier at the bank
when he tells you you're overdrawn
or the glittering one
on the face of the angel in the blue dress
on the tv show
making you an offer you can't believe
at terms you're unable to resist

Satan is when you
run out of cigarettes and out of money
at the same time
when every part of your body hurts
and you're only 36
when the miles you've logged
start showing up in the way
you laugh

in the way you count your change
when the whiskey bottle's dry
Satan is the crackle of the police radio
just after they've put the cuffs on
as they laugh about the baseball game

the color of the walls
in a county hospital emergency room
the papers they make you sign
before they'll give you medicine

the bad food you eat when you're poor
a cough that won't go away
the kind of hopes
that get pinned on a lottery

Thief of Fire
For Rimbaud

I know you like I know my dick
the way you burned and fled

savaged by beauty
possessed by genuis as kind as a
hangman's noose

Id've liked to
share a number with you
as the late night glaze of North Beach
glowed over into dawn
talking about everything at once

Id've liked to drink you under the table
at some bar with just the right amount of
dirt on the floor

Id've liked to take you down the highway
in a stolen car
throwing rocks at everthing that
moved
I'd show you this great, raw beast America
the wilderness of its cities
the chill horror of its suburbs
its brilliant emptiness

you'd've looked good on a skateboard in
green hair
mowing down pedestrians and
racing through red lights

you'd've looked good
dying in Vietnam
catching a grendade in your teeth
after fragging the lieutenant
you'd've looked good
on the streets of San Francisco
during the last war
the one that peaked in 67
selling bad acid to idiot hippies
and turning the real clowns onto
STP

but you'd never have looked good
in a suit and tie
hosing down the sidewalks of American commerce
15 minutes ahead of the boss

you'd've looked rotten
buying a new car on payments and
boasting about the stereo

you'd've looked bad
trying to make it as a poet
befriending people who bored you
reading your stuff in rooms the color of
death
wondering which slumped, comatose firgure was an
editor

you were the cat who was "as shy as
60,000,000 newborn puppies" when
confronted with your
first true love

you were the guy who
came to Paris mad
and left insane
having pissed off everyone who could
do you any good half-a-dozen times each, and
wishing you could've been a little more
vicious

and down through the ages your
eyes stare out of your pictures,
glittering with a terrible wisdom
that choirboy's face

The Night of the Living Tits

Joie was back in town, see
and the joint was even liver than usual
the night of the living tits

see, poems were read
in honor of her return

from San Diego
where she'd been in self-imposed exile
boiling her art down into the impossible

but, anyway, she read a story, a
fierce flaming tale of truth and sentiment
ending with the lines,
"It's just like Dorothy said,
'There's no fuckin' place like home,' "

and the place was like an
inferno of joy

and then she showed her tits

and then Danielle got up
to read
and she showed her tits
and it was good

and the temperature somehow rose
and the fair Kathleen, she
showed hers too
with a little bump and grind
they were excellent, soft and
tender

and then it was Anna's turn

and everyone was so happy

tits, Joie, beer, poetry, dementia, heart attacks, the
world and everything in it, trading places
with fire, it was just
one of those nights

Why Rimbaud Went to Africa

poetry isn't literary
poetry isn't sure which fork to
use
poetry can't name the parts of speech

fill out a grant application
logroll

poetry doesn't like cappuccino
poetry doesn't want to be printed in a
small press edition with its name on the
cover and get reviewed in 2 little magazines
read by 3 people
argued over by 8

poetry doesn't care about glory
glory is nice but poetry figures it's
dessert
poetry doesn't want to get laid
poetry might want to get drunk but
that's only self defense

poetry doesn't want to traipse around Europe
and collect stray bits of wisdom
from ruined empires
that it can show like slides when it gets home
poetry has a headache

poetry is a better slingshot
a war you can carry in your pocket
a better way to die
the kind of fire that never goes out
and never give an inch

poetry wants to be on every street corner
hissing from the cracks in the sidewalks
from the columns of print in the newspapers
on the lips of people on buses going to their
miserable jobs in the morning

poetry wants to be
in the prayers of dogs and the
screams of acrobats
in the terror of politicians
and the dreams of beautiful women

poetry wants to be
an eye through which the world will see itself and
tremble

poetry doesn't want to
die in the gutter
it already knows how

poetry doesn't want to sparechange strolling professors
and millionaires
wear anything but blood

have conversations with college students about
the meaning of life

because a bad wind is coming
you can smell it in the air

the pollution of the cities
mixed with the odor of rotting souls

the wind will climb

it will have little sense of humor
it will not want cappuccino
or reviews
or girlfriends
or anything else

except the death of
everything we love

DANIEL HIGGS

From *The Exploding Parable*

> This is the evening of two-fisted prayer.
> K. PATCHEN

I courted poetry
I spilled a whole lot of milk
Down the front of me

AMERICAN RENEGADES

I courted scripture
I invited zoomorphic angel guardians
To ascend from the muscled flanks
Of our horizons
I assumed the posture for them
To eat my brain
With their baboon snouts
And mouths full of blue sky
A spread peacock fan
Of gleaming surgical spoons
Wings unfolded revealing a multitude of faces
Rows of my own faces
Crammed up into their stark wingspans
The wings and their chorus tucked around me
My faces laughing crying shouting whispering on me
To get me tender enough
To suggest a fear of rape
And I said:
When does my family return?
When is our beautiful reunion?
When do I dissolve into
The Redness
The Whiteness
The Blueness
Of our effulgent Stepfather's grace?

I courted poetry
I questioned my function
I purged my function
Now I serve no function
You must be careful what you wish for
She propped her ankle stumps up on the kitchen table
As a sort of interrogative proposition
Fresh pink toes had poked through the callous stump flesh
She said there is a naked beast in the guest room
O you angels
O you proud oracular flesh
O you infinite quilt
Cast before my conscienceless eyes
There are things I wish I had never seen
Visions which contaminate every subsequent vision
Profanity oozing under the door of every idea
There are impostors in me that are bred for violence
So sick of being sick of being sick of it all

Fall upon me
PANTHER FACE
PANTHER FIST
PANTHER LOIN
VIOLET NIPPLE FLANGE
RODEO FLOWER SUCK FORCE
We've reached the wall of the container
The seams are sealed with a brittle law
Let's burst the container
Let's blow death
With wet hot logic
Let's flog the airplane
Let's blow death
TRUTH OBSCURED BY THE SYMBOLS OF TRUTH
I burn a bridge every day of my life
Not by choice
By nature
Let's blow death

From *Clay Man High House Head*

The trotting river wolf of the word
Bleeding between its fingers
Not for faith or anguish
But for the computer is the middle man
A scorpion sleeping in a delicate locket
Of sandstone and particular metal flakes
Lonely to get with the curve
If you knew the spirit in which I was receiving you
You would understand that you are mine already
A symmetrical imposition of artificial memory
Flavors and smells and traditional dances
A good man meets a good woman before he falls
A standard light bearer brought my staircase
I keep it hidden in my white beard
The brain of my hand grows stronger
Patiently cutting out the cavern blessing
Recorded announcements wafting
Risen yet further twisted fallen
As close as we're ever gonna come
The arcing ear wing of the counterface
Calm fulcrum seed of argument

Moderate malice: that's all
At the groin of the soul
You wear your tool belt in the naked vortex
I glimpsed your shoulders from the pit I was digging
I claimed all the names of your broad flat bones
I will keep you safer than a promise
Skull butter combined with finger hash
A crown of tender flames condemned to the peacock roost
I am threatening to threaten you
If you continue to refuse to read my mind
Don't make me state the obvious outcome
Of our haphazard pilgrimage home
I am socketed and jerry-rigged
A woman in constant counteractive rebellion
A want-list of hits
Negligent sunshine protection
One kind of morality exposes another kind of moral fraud
A good woman meets a good man
A torch boost over the prayer railing
The cascading forge of the throat claw
Birth in the brute world
A sore sojourner dumb ass and backwards
With a trigger button box
The loafing bisector turns a blind other eye
From a wholeness that is conveyed
You know what kills you sometimes
A nip or a peck on the shepherd's perch
A good gravity harvest
The manacles we weave
The pH of tears and acidic fruition
From me to you or any combination
Of soil books and beans
I am scrubbing again

From *What I Have Learned About Boxing*

The curtain rips aside
The one-way mirror clears up
To expose you in postures short of dignity
To prove you gave into yourself finally
Cuz you're nothing without trials
According to your school of navigation
I said I fear no pictures

It sounded like a battle cry
When the delusion barreled down
Eating hailstones like birdseed
What are we without trials?
Spit to polish the shoe train
A stolen branch for the Easter procession
A predetermined turbine hidden in your liver clod
Bison and antelope and gameshows and water towers and gang language
The simple instruments of little or no impact
I toil at their consoles lever jerk and goof
I strike matches and herald mailmen
Wait for you to come around
Like you might guess you ought to
Hoarding your numbers
Coming of ageless eye glaze
Searching for a mouth to trust along its natural border
Each whisker stores a breath with its name
Her face was a stable downtown bucket out
A grid like bleachers or pews or orchards or infantry
We're always fit to spar
This is where we live sometimes
On her face
The miser behind the headstone
The strategic lie that humiliates devotion for gut cosmic laughter
The twisting heels that deliver citations
Buckets of foundry dope sloshing
When the money runs out we sleep with the statues of heroes we mock
This is where we live a lot of the time
As close to her face as we can afford

From *The Doomsday Bonnet*

16.

Proceed unnamed into the corporate geometry of your momentum—You've got an end of the world but no corresponding method of creeping away from a swollen perspiring planet—The stained teeth of stars flit their bashful circles and this I hereby pledge—Medicinal words enshrined on a flypaper archive—The way magicians can wash dishes with detergent and a sponge as gravity discerns what it supports from what it topples—A severed wing held firm in a stout beak

27.

A hindsight that herds us into the future—The first lightning bolt strikes the first ocean—The conversation spreads creeping between the earth's crust and mantle—Twirling like a dancing tyrant to nestle in our modern brains where all names seem to hatch and ride and no one will be held accountable ever again—Lady stallion—Bridge-legged magnet tower—O these united states—O twist and snap and heaped with flowers—A mouth telling about where it leads inside its body—Shining scrambled days row the boat ashore—O do what you do when you stop what you're doing—Pay the tax—Arrange a cobra bite—Purchase all manner of machine—Speak aloud and believe you are heard—Spin with lust—Lust in fear—Fear not and know what a devil is—It's being stared at

slammers

ALAN KAUFMAN

The Slam

Many of the poets who comprise the new wave of American poetry first came to know each other through the "Slam," an audience-judged poetry performance competition with the ambience and energy of a guillotine party in the French Revolution. Here Poetry and Democracy roughhouse amid hoots, howls, thundering applause and sometimes jeers.

Begun in the early eighties by Marc Smith, a fiery Chicago poet and construction worker, Slam grew into a nationwide movement of poets. Today, Slams are held in cities and towns around the world. Once a year Slam poets convene to hold a National Poetry Slam. Those brave enough to attend will attest that it is one of the most exciting experiences in post-war American literary history.

Many have struggled for spin control of the poetry explosion that has occurred worldwide in the past decade, but it is incontestably true that had it not been for Marc Smith's Slam, his selfless and tireless devotion to the growth of the Slam movement and the cause of poetry, the field today would continue to be a poet snoring at a podium, with wine and cheese served at the break.

MARC SMITH ("SLAMPAPPY")

In July 1986, Marc Smith, Jean Howard, and Ron Gillette co-produced the first "Uptown Poetry Slam" at the Green Mill Lounge in Chicago. From that point forward, the people's poetry in Chicago—and then the world—had two distinct paths, one toward stage and the other toward the page. Poetry has not been the same since. Slam poetry has infiltrated both the underground literary scene and mass media, producing effects in cinema, television, and the press.

Smith's scholastic roots came from a fairly typical public education, but his artistic urges were more dynamic. He was inspired by extant "pugilist poetry" practiced in New York and Chicago during the punk music wave of the 1970s and '80s. While that thread is continued today in the bouts at the Taos Poetry Circus, Smith sought a more inclusive practice where people of all walks of life could engage poetry as audience, artists, and critics in an informal and lively dialog. The poetry bout invited well-known writers to compete in a spectacle intended to draw attention back to poets and poetry. For Smith, who was used to performing poetry before audiences from the start, reversal of the attention made more sense: Assert the focus on the audience, empower their voices, and let the poetry fly freely. Today, slam is not just a competition, but a charismatic poetry style celebrated in the Americas, Europe, Asia, and Australia, borne abroad by an embracing and vocal public.

Smith is well-known for Slam's genesis, but early on he also brought other forces to bear upon performance poetry in Chicago, such as multi-vocal and ensemble techniques (the Bob Shakespeare Band, Chicago Poetry Ensemble); music (Pong Unit One); and stagecraft ("Tattoo Taboo," "The Whitechapel Club"). Smith's protégés such as Lisa Buscani, Cin Salach, and Patricia Smith (no relation) have taken performance poetry even further in performance art, theater, and collaborative new media.

Smith lives in suburban Chicago with his children who often proudly join him at readings and performances. His first book, *Crowdpleaser*, was published in 1996.

Kurt Heinz

Lucky Strike No Strike Back

"Lucky Strike No Strike Back"
Packs a hard memory for me.
On my first day walking to school
Unescorted by my mother
Wade Corner of the third grade
Stepped on a Lucky Strike pack
And smacked me whack in the shoulder
Hard as he could making me cry.

It was the first time I
Had ever been hit
By a stranger.
How could I hold back the tears?

"Lucky Strike No Strike back!"
That was the rule.
Any time you saw the red and white
	and black Lucky Strike symbol
Lying on the ground,
You stamped your foot on it, whirled,
And hurled your fist into whoever was standing near.

"It's a safety hit. No hits back."
That's how it worked,
School and the social graces.
I got hit three times by three different guys
Before I had the sense to step away
Out of the vincinity of the Lucky Strike circle.

It was a hard lesson to learn
For little me kindergarten kid,
But three whollops do alot
To get the brain cells movin'.

Next day, scanning eyes alert
Over the horizon
I spied a Lucky Strike pack
Flat on the sidewalk
Near the blue and white mailbox.
I stepped on it
And hurled my tiny fist into Henry of the First Grade's back.
He whirled and kicked the shit out of me.

"Lucky Strike No Strike Back!" I complained,
Prompting him to hit me hard again,
Breaking all the rules.
Making me ball up into the fetal position
On the grass next to some dog pooh.

On the third day, and forever there afterward,
I stirred clear of Lucky Strikes.

SLAMMERS

The Stroke

There's a clock ticking in our living room.
I hear it when I'm thinking.
It looks like the head of a grandfather,
Tiny pendulum necktie.

The clock runs down
Every thirty-one days or so.
Sometimes at a quarter to four.
Sometimes at eleven to six.
Midnight exactly never.

When I notice that it has stopped
(Either by the wrong time
Or the silence it makes)
I fiddle for the key
Hidden in its throat.
Finding it,
I unlock its glass face
And crank the steel lips open.

And what an unregulated action it would be
To go by that clock each day
Refusing to take the time it takes to turn it
To give it the power it needs,
To see it stalled at an insignificant hour
Unable to turn me out of bed or into sleep,
Silently poised as if placed upon a shelf
Like a fat forgotten Buddha
With a sour time piece in its belly—
The outworn worn down item
That doesn't move
Year after year, month by month
Ticking out of purpose,
Ticking out of time.

PATRICIA SMITH

Skinhead

They call me skinhead, and I got my own beauty.
It is knife-scrawled across my back in sore, jagged letters,
It's in the way my eyes snap away from the obvious.
I sit in my dim matchbox,
on the edge of a bed tousled with my ragged smell,
slide razors across my hair,
count how many ways
I can bring blood closer to the surface of my skin.
There are the duties of the righteous,
the ways of the anointed.

The face that moves in my mirror is huge and pockmarked,
scraped pink and brilliant, apple-cheeked,
I am filled with my own spit.
Two years ago, a machine that slices leather
sucked in my hand and held it,
whacking off three fingers at the root.
I didn't feel nothing till I looked down
and saw one of them on the floor
next to my boot heel,
and I ain't worked since then.

I sit here and watch niggers take over my TV set,
walking like kings up and down the sidewalks in my head,
walking like their fat black Mamas *named* them freedom.
My shoulders tell me that ain't right.
So I move out into the sun
where my beauty makes them lower their heads,
or into the night
with a lead pipe up my sleeve,
a razor tucked in my boot.
I was born to make things right.

It's easy now to move my big body into shadows,
to move from a place where there was nothing
into the stark circle of a streetlight,
the pipe raised up high over my head.
It's a kick to watch their eyes get big,
round and gleaming like cartoon jungle boys,

right in that second when they know
the pipe's gonna come down, and I got this thing
I like to say, listen to this, I like to say
"Hey, nigger, Abe Lincoln's been dead a long time."

I get hard listening to their skin burst.
I was born to make things right.

Then this newspaper guy comes around,
seems I was a little sloppy kicking some fag's ass
and he opened his hole and screamed about it.
This reporter finds me curled up in my bed,
those TV flashes licking my face clean.
Same ol' shit.
Ain't got no job, the coloreds and spics got em'all.
Why ain't I working? Look at my hand, asshole.
No, I ain't part of no organized group,
I'm just a white boy who loves his race,
fighting for a pure country.
Sometimes it's just me. Sometimes three. Sometimes 30.
AIDS will take care of the faggots,
then it's gon be white on black in the streets.
Then there'll be three million.
I tell him that.

So he writes it up
and I come off looking like some kind of freak,
like I'm Hitler himself. I ain't that lucky,
but I got my own beauty.
It is in my steel-toed boots,
in the hard corners of my shaved head.

I look in the mirror and hold up my mangled hand,
only the baby finger left, sticking straight up,
I know its the wrong goddamned finger,
but fuck you all anyway.
I'm riding the top rung of the perfect race,
my face scraped pink and brilliant.
I'm your baby, America, your boy,
drunk on my own spit, I am goddamned fuckin' beautiful.

And I was born

and raised

right here.

Medusa

Poseidon was easier than most.
He calls himself a god,
but he fell beneath my fingers
with more shaking than any mortal.
He wept when my robe fell from my shoulders.

I made him bend his back for me,
listened to his screams break like waves.
We defiled that temple the way it should be defiled,
screaming and bucking our way from corner to corner.
The bitch goddess probably got a real kick out of that.
I'm sure I'll be hearing from her.

She'll give me nightmares for a week or so;
that I can handle.
Or she'll turn the water in my well into blood;
I'll scream when I see it,
and that will be that.
Maybe my first child
will be born with the head of a fish.
I'm not even sure it was worth it,
Poseidon pounding away at me, a madman,
loosing his immortal mind
because of the way my copper skin swells
in moonlight.

Now my arms smoke and itch.
Hard scales cover my wrists like armor.
C'mon Athena, he was only another lay,
and not a particularly good one at that,
even though he can spit steam from his fingers.
Won't touch him again. Promise.
And we didn't mean to drop to our knees
in your temple,
but our bodies were so hot and misaligned.
It's not every day a gal gets to sample a god,
you know that. Why are you being so rough on me?

I feel my eyes twisting,
the lids crusting over and boiling,
the pupils glowing red with heat.
Athena, woman to woman,

could you have resisted him?
Would you have been able to wait
for the proper place, the right moment,
to jump those immortal bones?

Now my feet are tangled with hair,
my ears are gone. My back is curving
and my lips have grown numb.
My garden boy just shattered at my feet.
Dammit, Athena,
take away my father's gold.
Send me away to live with lepers.
Give me a pimple or two.
But my face. To have men never again
be able to gaze at my face,
growing stupid in anticipation
of that first touch,
how can any woman live like that?
How will I able
to watch their warm bodies turn to rock
when their only sin was desiring me?
All the want is to see me sweat.
They only want to touch my face
and run their fingers through my. . . .
my hair

is it moving?

LISA MARTINOVIC

Debt of Blood

My name is Nila
Nila Marse
lissen up, now
cuz I'm here to tell y'all bout how
I never owed nobody nothin'

That's right, I been worked like a mule all my life
bustin' my ass and payin' dues to where I'm bled drier than a salt box
I raised eight brothers and sisters with no mama
and a no 'count daddy
Hell, he was worse than no daddy at all

I been workin' twenty years at the chicken plant
my fingers all hobbled up
my lungs so full of dust from ground up chicken bones
every time I cough, feathers fly outta my mouth

and I still ain't stopped workin' for Veon and the kids
him another no 'count drunk
useless as tits on a boar-hog

no sir, I don't owe nobody nothin'
looks to me like somebody owes me
somebody owes me a goddamn life

Sometimes I think about how much I put out for everybody
and how I never get a lick of respect, a raise or even a goddamn thank
    you, ma'am
I think about it while I'm guttin' chickens on the eviscerating line
I think about it every time some lil ole sugar tit gets light duty
cuz the boss likes the way she wiggles her ass

and whenever Veon comes at me in the middle of the night
and shoves his belching, beer stinkin' body into me
I don't anymore dream of some young, handsome, god-fearin' farmer
Alls I can think about is sleep
or murder

Then there's other times
like when I'm up to my elbows in the trailer's busted toilet
the whole mess stinkin' till hell won't have it
I wonder if the ocean is really as pretty as it looks in the magazines
if the flower on a cactus smells sweet
I wonder if I'll ever get just one goddamn day of happiness before I die

Well, I worked all my days
suffered through them long nights
and prayed on my knees every morning
and when that day never did come
I lost the faith
Now I'm bitter like an old root

Hell, I could crack a walnut shell between my teeth without even
   flinchin'
I've took to slapping my kids
cussin' the boss when his back's turned
and putting pepper in Veon's coffee
but nothing's changed
'cept we all got meaner

My mind's like on fire with hate
my job, my man—hell, even my kids
leeches all of 'em
suckin' the life out of me

Well, Nila, I says to nobody in particular
since nobody pays me no mind anyway
Well, I says
there ain't a hell of a lot left to suck
my marrow's done tapped out
bones hollow
'fore long, there won't even be blood a'crawlin' through my veins

but I tell you what
for all my hatred
I don't blame no earthly creature for my misery
so much as I hold God responsible
for giving me such a shitty life

and when I think about it like that
I know it's God what owes me
God owes me that debt of blood

Nila don't owe nobody nothin'

The Outlaw

thunderstorm turned my tent into a swimming hole
drove me to a florescent motel room in some beat up Ozark village
named after somebody famous
that nobody remembers
hot spring Saturday night noise
led me to the open air dance hall on the banks of Elk Creek
where I stood, awkwardly available

for pert near an hour, till
a long haired, skinny local,
Confederate Flag emblazoned on his belt buckle
wobbled over for a dance
Figuring Californians can't be too picky, I obliged
We wriggled and stomped through a few tunes
Dwane was impressed
he felt so real
with me
he just knew I was an outlaw
like him
what do you mean, outlaw?
real slow-like he said, well . . .
I've ridden with the best of 'em
and . . . I've ridden with the worst of 'em
till I sold my Harley—cuz of a chick
What do you do now?
I hang chickens
No bizarre sacrificial cult this
just a poultry processing plant where
one step on the line is shackling live chickens
onto a wire, to be dissembled
5 days a week
8 hours a day
6 dollars an hour
Yup, best pay in the area
Hey little outlaw, he grinned
in a tone I reserve for cooing my puppy
Let's dance
We rocked out to ACDC
Knocking me out with those American thighs—Yeah!
The Budweiser was doing strange things to Dwane's footwork
so we sat this one out
He sidled over closer to me
Ya know, the way you look
and the way you dance
I can tell . . .
Yes Dwane?
I can tell you've sat on one before
My eyes bugged out like I just stepped alongside a 10 foot rattler
Too drunk to notice
Dwane blathered on
Yup, he said
I'm sure you've sat on a Harley before
Outlaw like me knows these things

SLAMMERS

REG E. GAINES

welcome to mcdonalds
(may i take your order please?)

so i bust into mcdonalds and this sister ringing fries
is squabblin with this brother moppin the filthy floor
now the sister (who's kinda cute)
is in the process of bein steam/roomed by some buppy
who's droppin lines he must a lifted from some
nineteen seventies black exploitation flick
so the sisters pissed the brothers stressed
and the buppies new nikes was gettin wet
all this time i'm standin in line
tryin to order a fish filet with no tartar
seems the sisters sick a ringing fries
cuz she hikes her hands rolls her eyes and says
"punk motherfucka coward ass bitch
yours hairs too straight and you walk with a switch"
the buppies french wave stood at attention
as his boys frick and frack cracked the fuck up
then/the manager
who happened to be a male member of the
caucasion pursuasion
tried to pull a newt gingrich impersonation
and set the sister straight
so she hits void
snatches the cheese stained apron
from around her dancehall hips
pokes out her lip
then precedes to rip into the boss
who makes like forest gump
then runs to the back
and hides behind a freezer
meanwhile the brother with the mop
is diggin into his thick grey sock
tryin to find a vial a rocks
seems like he got this slick lil hustle goin down
and like a circle is round we wind up back at me see
i was just tryin to order a fish filet with no tartar

when i started getting impatient
cuz you know how shot go at micky dees
"when you getting off?"
"girl how much your earrings cost?"
"i heard she's fuckin the boss!"
and I should been more patient
but i had to catch a bus
and maybe i need to get in touch
with my more sensitive side
but then i thought
fuck this shit
walked outside and split

BOBBY MILLER

My Life as I Remember It

At two years old I whistled at the mail man
and set a pattern for years to come.

At four I danced in the sunshine of our front yard
an interpretive dance to the Gods.
The neighbors swore I was retarded.

At six I told my classmates that
I was from another galaxy light years away,
Mrs. Jackson our first grade teacher
thought it necessary to alert my parents.

By ten Mr. Grady the art teacher was alarmed
by the colors I chose to paint with: red, black and purple.

In junior high I was considered weird and neat
at the same time because I dressed funny
and my parents had tattoos and Harleys.

My ninth grade report card was all D's and F's
except for art and music class.
All written reports from the faculty stated
"Talks too much. .and daydreams. ."
Some things never change.

I watched the Beatles arrive in America
and decided I wanted to go to England.
I saw hair grow over ears and down collars
and onto shoulders and backs all over the country.
I walked with the first protest march in Washington
and every other for ten years
and we still have crooks running the country.

I sat in streets, cafes, corner bars and coffee houses
and listened to the beat of a new generation being born.
I went through puberty with Janis and Jimi and took LSD
when it wasn't cut with speed or poison.
I smoked pot in fifth grade and laughed all day
at a fat substitute named Mrs. Potty
I dated black boys at fifteen in an all white Klan neighborhood.
I hitch hiked to New York from Baltimore
with three queens in hot pants, clogs, and long bleached shags
at sixteen and blew truckers all up and down the turnpike.
I've been addicted to MDA, tequilla, LSD, speed, dope,
coke, pot, qualudes, mescaline, nicotine, sex
and the mysteries of the night, all my life until I hit twenty-eight,
since then it's only night life and sex.

I've walked barefoot on twenty-four hundred degree hot coals
and not been burnt.
Greta Garbo grabbed me from behind in traffic
and saved my life.

I've had green hair, blue hair, black hair, red hair,
no hair, long hair and all before 1973.
I'm happy to still have hair.
I've walked Sunset Blvd., Polk St., Forty-second,
Hollywood and Vine, Christopher, Fire Island, Provincetown,
Key West, Bombay, Miami Beach, London, Paris, Rome, Milan,
Montreal,
and every gay ghetto listed in the book,
and I'm still looking for the perfect lover.

I've lived as a woman for a solid year and had tits. Thank you.
I've dated black men, white men, brown men, red men.
yellow men, and several delicious women
I've been engaged, married, in love, divorced
seperated and broken hearted.
I've had syphilis, gonorrhea, crabs, scabies,
hemorrhoids, hepatitis, appendicitis, dermatitus,
and the flu at least fifty times,
and I feel better now at forty-six than I did at twenty-five.

I've spent the last eleven years meditating.,
concentrating, contemplating, applicating, educating,
investigating, and instigating a higher ideal.
I've been a born again christian, a crystal holding
new age visualizationist, a Bhuddist, a Hindu,
a Christian Scientist, a universalist, a bullshit artist,
a seeker of truth, a charlatan, a holy roller,
a shamanistic dancer, a guru, a disciple, and an enigma to my friends.

I'm a triple Gemini natural blonde who loves God
and takes time out to smell the roses.
I've been around the block at least ten times,
and I'm ready to go again until these feet
won't carry me anymore.
I have always believed in the power of love
and that the groove lies somewhere
between the heart and the genitals.
I have never been deliberately cruel
and I've never hit anyone with my fist.
I hope I never have to.

I've been a whore, a saint, a sinner, a healer a heathen,
an actor, a poet, a drag queen, a straight man,
a teenage zombie, a punk rocker, a greaser, a clone,
a faggot, a street walker, a sky writer, a vegetarian,
a teacher, a student, a wanderer, a caretaker,
a wild thing, a father, a son, a yogi, and a fierce hairdresser.

I've been lost, found, confused, absolved, punished,
and rewarded.

I've stared death in the face and wondered
why not me, yet?

I've talked and listened and heard and seen
and been shown the way.

I've played follow the leader, pin the tail on the donkey,
five card stud, and Russian roulette
with a silver handled 38.
I've lost eight thousand in cash gambling
and won five hundred on a bet in less that a minute.

I've seen the eye of God,
and been touched by her hand.
I've seen miracles happen
and been disappointed dozens of times.

I've been almost everywhere, met almost everyone,
seen almost everything, done almost all of it,
and I'm still waiting to be discovered.
The night has a thousand eyes
and I'm a gypsy dancer
who's still hungry for more.

VYTAUTAS PLIURA

In the Hands of the Enemy

Their skin was ivory
The jungle was emerald
They kept me in a bamboo cage
I was given, quite mysteriously, a
     mahogany chair to sit in
A strange privilege

Because I was known to be gay
     they let me grow orchids in my cell
Orchids don't lust after much light
I also fed the monkeys and the peacocks
And was let out to make rice paper at the
     blind woman's hut

Often

When a South Vietnamese prisoner was to
    be executed

That prisoner could request to humiliate a
prisoner from the USA by making him give the condemned person
oral sex

Mark and Willard both had jet black hair
and did not impress the Montagnards

One mountain man traveled 250 kilometers to cut off some of
my blond ringlets to weave into dolls for his children

I, blue-eyed Central Illinois farm boy, a little speck
of purple-mountain-majesty among the hobbled rubber trees
and the elflike golden shimmering teak trees
Was led into a clearing
The prisoner to be shot was tied to a post, often I could
hear the women washing their clothes in the Red River singing
lullabies
    Hands tied behind my back
    I was lowered to my knees

One boy shot his semen down my throat as he lurched
                                with bullets

Loins quivering
It took him ten minutes to die
It took them that long
to free his fingers
from my hair

JEFFREY MCDANIEL

Lineage

When I was little, I thought the word *loin*
and the word *lion* were the same thing.

I thought *celibate* was a kind of fish.

My parents wanted me to be well-rounded
so they threw dinner plates at each other
until I curled up into a little ball.

I've had the wind knocked out of me
but never the hurricane.

I've seen two hundred and sixty-three rats
in the past year, but never more than one at a time.
It could be the same rat, with a very high profile.

I know what it's like to wear my liver on my sleeve.

I go into department stores, looking suspicious,
approach the security guard and say
what, what, I didn't take anything.
Go ahead. Frisk me, big boy!

I go to the funerals of absolute strangers
and tell the grieving family: *the soul of the deceased*
is trapped inside my rib cage
and trying to reach you.

Once I thought I found love, but then I realized
I was just out of cigarettes.

Some people are boring because their parents
had boring sex the night they were conceived.

In the year thirteen hundred and thirteen,
a little boy died, who had the exact same scars as me.

Logic in the House of Sawed-off Telescopes

I want to sniff the glue that holds families together.
I was a good boy once.
I listened with three ears.
When I didn't get what I wanted, I never cried.
I banged my head over and over on the kitchen floor.
I sat on a man's lap.
I took his words that tasted like candy.
I want to break something now.
I am the purple lips of a child throwing snowballs at a taxi.
There is an alligator in my closet.
If you make me mad, it will eat you.
I was a good boy once.
I had the most stars in the classroom.
My cheeks overflowed with rubies.
I want to break something now.
My bedroom is so dark I feel like an astronaut.
I wish someone would come in and kiss me.
I was a good boy once.
The sweet smelling woman used to say that she loved me.
The man with the lap used to read me stories,
swing me in his arms like a chandelier.
I want to break something now.
My heart beat like the meanest kid on the school bus.
My brain tightened like a fist.
I was a good boy once.
I didn't steal that kid's homework.
I left a clump of spirit in its place.
I want to break something now.
I can multiply big numbers faster than you can.
I can beat men who smoke cigars at chess.
I was a good boy once.
I brushed my teeth and looked in the mirror.
My mouth was a spectacular wound.
Now it only feels good when it bleeds.

Siamese Opposites

I was feeling lonely.
Phones were ringing in my fingers.
I held a light bulb to my sternum in the dark
My birthday came and went

SLAMMERS

each night without saying hello.
I sat for hours with a telescope
gazing into the stove.
Hermits looked up to me.
They piled their beards outside my window.
I was a nation of peasants.
I signed all my checks *Nation of Islam*.
I changed my name to Rated X.
My hands were siamese opposites.
I ate my eggs with a glue stick and scissors.
I pierced my spleen.
I had the word *Galapagos* tattooed on my liver.
I flirted with the wives of nuclear warheads.
I nibbled on the tonsils of emperors.
I blew my nose with a napkin signed by Joan Miro.
Each time I saw God
he had pantyhose pulled over his face.
I handed out UFO's at all the bus stops.
I walked around holding a big piece of cardboard
and told everyone I was Heaven's Door.

REGIE CABICO

Check One

The government asks me to "check one" if I want money.
I just laugh in their face and say,
"How can you ask me to be one race?"

I stand proudly before you a fierce Filipino
who knows how to belt hard-gospel songs
played to African drums at a Catholic mass—
and loving the music to suffering beats,
and lashes from men's eyes on the capitol streets—

South-East D.C., with its sleepy crime,
my mother nursed patients from seven to nine,

patients gray from the railroad
riding past civil rights

I walked their tracks when I entertained
them at the chapel and made their canes pillars
of percussion to my heavy gospel—
my comedy out-loud, laughing about, our shared,
stolen experiences of the South.

Would it surprise you if I told you my blood
was delivered from North off Portuguese vessels
who gave me spiritual stones and the turn in my eyes—
my father's name when they conquered the Pacific Isles.
My hair is black and thick as "negrito," growing abundant
as "sampaguita"-flowers defying civilization
like pilipino pygmies that dance in the mountain.

I could give you an epic about my ways of life or my look
and you want me to fill it in "one square box."
From what integer or shape do you count existing identities,
grant loans for the mind, or crayola white census sheets—
There's no "one kind" to fill for anyone.

You tell me who I am, what gets the most money
and I'll sing that song like a one-man caravan.
I know arias from Naples, Tunis, and Accra—
lullabyes from welfare, food-stamps, and nature

and you want me to sing one song?
I have danced jigs with Jim Crow and shuffled my hips
to a sonic guitar of Clapton and Hendrix,
waltzed with dead lovers, skipped to bamboo sticks,
balleted kabuki and mimed cathacali
arrivedercied-a-rhumba and tapped Tin Pan Alley—
and you want me to dance the Bhagavad Gita
on a box too small for a thumbelina-thin diva?

I'll check "other," say *artist*,
that's who I am: a poet, a writer, a lover of man.

MAGGIE ESTEP

I'm an Emotional Idiot

I'm an Emotional Idiot
so get away from me.
I mean,
COME HERE.

Wait, no,
that's too close,
give me some space
it's a big country,
there's plenty of room,
don't sit so close to me.

Hey, where are you?
I haven't seen you in days.
Whadya, having an affair?
Who is she?
Come on,
aren't I enough for you?

God,
You're so cold.
I never know what you're thinking.
You're not very affectionate.

I mean,
you're clinging to me,
DON'T TOUCH ME,
what am I, your fucking cat?
Don't rub me like that.

Don't you have anything better to do
than sit there fawning over me?

Don't you have any interests?
Hobbies?
Sailing Fly fishing
Archeology?

There's an archeology expedition leaving tomorrow
why don't you go?
I'll loan you the money,
my money is your money.
my life is your life
my soul is yours
without you I'm nothing.

Move in with me
we'll get a studio apartment together, save on rent,
well, wait, I mean, a one bedroom,
so we don't get in each other's hair or anything
or, well,
maybe a two bedroom
I'll have my own bedroom,
it's nothing personal
just need to be alone sometimes,
you do understand,
don't you?

Hey, why are you acting distant?

Where you goin',
was it something I said?
What
What did I do?

I'm an emotional idiot
so get away from me
I mean,
MARRY ME.

Scab Maids on Speed

My first job was when I was about fifteen. I'd met a girl named Hope
who became my best friend. Hope and I were flunking math so we
became speed freaks. This honed our albebra skills and we quickly
became whiz kids. For about five minutes. Then, our brains started to
fry and we were just teenage speed freaks.

So we decided to seek gainful employment.

We got hired on as part time maids at the Holiday Inn while a maid strike was happening. We were scab maids on speed and we were coming to clean your room.

We were subsequently fired for pilfering a Holiday Inn guest's quaalude stash which we did only because we never thought someone would have the nerve to call the front desk and say, THE MAIDS STOLE MY LUUDES MAN. But someone did—or so we surmised—because we were fired.

I suppose maybe we were fired because we never actually CLEANED but rather just turned on the vacuum so it SOUNDED like we were cleaning as we picked the pubic hairs off the sheets and out of the tub then passed out on the bed and caught up on the sleep we'd missed from being up all night speeding.

When we got fired, we became waitresses at an International House of Pancakes.

We were much happier there.

Jenny's Shirt

Jenny had been holing up in a tiny hotel in Paris for close to three months. She had two dresses with flowers on them, a polyester ski sweater, a pair of green corduroy pants, a pink lamp she took with her everywhere, and seven silver bracelets she never removed.

She had the equivalent of fifty dollars and no ticket home to the States. She hadn't left her room in six days.

Finally, one morning, Jenny figured she'd better get out and do something. Anything.

She got dressed and walked out of the hotel. The light hurt her eyes. The streets were teeming with a madding crowd.

She walked a few blocks then came to a little stand like many others that lined the banks of the Seine. This stand was different in that the man inside it had an incredible scar slashed across his face and he sold nothing but cheaply made button-down shirts with Eiffel Towers painted all over them.
"Hello," Jenny said to the man, "how much for the shirt?"
The man just smiled at her, picked up one of the shirts and handed it to her.

"But how much?" Jenny protested.

"On the house," the man said. He kept smiling. The sun was going down and adding pinkness to the man's already pink facial scar. This reminded Jenny of her pink lamp, the one back at her hotel room, the one she had carted with her everywhere ever since Matt's grandmother gave it to her and then her and Matt broke up and Matt ended up in Hollywood and Jenny just started drifting.

Jenny hadn't even thought about loving anybody the whole time she'd been drifting. It just hadn't occurred to her. Now, because the man's scar was as pink as the lamp that Jenny loved, now, she automatically smiled back at the man with the scar.

Later, when he closed up the stand and brought Jenny with him to the tiny room where he lived, he insisted she wear the shirt he had just given her. She stripped off everything else. The green corduroys and her white panties, She stood there naked but for the shirt with Eiffel towers on it. She touched his scar and he kissed her and they both started laughing.

They shacked up like that for a whole week. Touching and laughing. The man didn't even go open his shirt stand and Jenny didn't go back to her hotel.

On the eighth morning, they both got dressed and walked out of the man's room and onto the street. They stood for several minutes looking at each other. Then they turned and walked in separate directions.

This is how Jenny got the shirt with Eiffel Towers painted on it.

TAYLOR MALI

Like Lilly Like Wilson

> I'm writing the poem that will change the world,
> and it's Lilly Wilson at my office door.
> Lilly Wilson, the recovering "like" addict,
> the worst I've ever seen.
> So "like" bad the whole eighth grade
> started calling her Like Lilly Like Wilson.

SLAMMERS

'Til I declared my classroom a Like-Free Zone
and she could not speak for days.

But when she finally did, it was to say,
Mr. Mali, this is . . . so hard.
Now I have to . . . think before I . . . say anything.

Imagine that, Lilly.
It's for your own good.
Even if you don't like . . .
it.

I'm writing the poem that will change the world,
and it's Lilly Wilson at my office door.
Lilly is writing a research paper for me about how gays
like shouldn't be allowed to adopt children.
I'm writing the poem that will change the world,
and it's Like Lilly Like Wilson at my office door.

Lilly's having trouble finding sources,
which is to say, ones that back her up:
They all argue in favor of what I thought I was against.

And it took all four years of college,
three years of graduate school,
and every incidental teaching experience I have ever had
to let out only,

Well, that's a real interesting problem, Lilly.
But what do you propose to do about it?
That's what I want to know.

And the eighth-grade mind is a beautiful thing;
Like a newborn baby's face, you can often see it
change before your very eyes.

I can't believe I'm saying this, Mr. Mali,
but I think I'd like to switch sides.

And I want to tell her to do more than just believe it,
but to enjoy it!
That changing your mind is one of the best ways
of finding out whether you still have one.
Or even that minds are like parachutes,
that it doesn't matter what you pack them with

so long as they open
at the right time.

I want to say all this but manage only,
Lilly, I am like so impressed with you.

So I finally taught someone something,
namely, how to change your mind.
And learned in the process that if I ever change the world
it's going to be one eighth grader at a time.

HANK HYENA

William, I Giggled with Your Girlfriend

'cause I was high & she was high & you were bye-bye out of town—

William, we were both lonely without you

William, I kissed your lover's lips—I curled my paws around her hips
we cuddled on your couch 'cause I'm your closest friend, William,
I wanna feel everything you feel in this world

William, I nibbled on her thin tongue next, my fingers scampered
  'round her breast

William, we were stuffing a turkey together—that's why we got excited

William, when she borrowed my herpes lotion I knew we had a
  dangerous connection

William, I dallied with your dearest 'cause I feared she was gonna sleep
  with a creep
when you were out of town & I wanted it to be somebody you can trust

William, the last bag of marijuana you sold me was crap so you owe me
  $10

William, I held her near, she chewed my ear, I removed her pink
  brassiere

William, she rested 'gainst my shivering chest, she said you two had a
  quarrel
I said "I am ex-Catholic, sex is best when it's immoral"

William, when I saw your gal-pal's underwear I had to tear them off
  'cause
you told me there's still scars on her butt
'cause a pit bull bit her when she was three years old
you can't be telling me things like that without me wanting to know first-
  hand

William, I unclothed your cutie comrade 'cause I disrobed
some of your other darlings & I delighted in it so I decided, dang—let's
  do it again

William, I did the fling-a-ding whirl with your lovable girl
cause she was complaining that she doesn't have orgasms with you
—she wanted to find out if it was your fault or something else—
she didn't have an orgasm with me either, William
I think she's a lesbian you oughta be moving on

William, I savored the flavor of your fine friend because—
I had this sweetie named Stevie seven years ago,
Stevie said you were sexy, we spat about that, then we split,
you ruptured that relationship, William, for that, you owe me one—

William, I don't know her very well, we're kinda awkward around each
  other
—this seemed like a excellent way to break the ice—

William, I throbbed hearts with your honey 'cause it was Celtic
  holiday—
I do declare that a desperate dose of pagan power
is contained & conveyed in the Druid fluid of the amatory act
& I am, William, first & foremost, I am a seeker of knowledge

TRACIE MORRIS

Project Princess

Teeny feet rock layered double socks
Popping side piping of
many colored loose lace-ups
Racing toe, keeps up with fancy free gear,
slick slide, just pressed, recently weaved hair.

Jeans oversized bely her hip, back, thighs have made guys sigh
for milleni-year.

Topped by an attractive jacket
her suit's not for flacking, flunkies, junkies or punk homies on the stroll.

Hands the mobile thrones of today's urban goddess
Clinking rings link dragon fingers no need to be modest.

One or two gap teeth coolin'
sport gold initials
Doubt you get to her name
Check from the side,
please chill.

Multidimensional shrimp earrings
frame her cinammon face

Crimson with a compliment if a
comment hits the right place

Don't step to the plate with datelines from '88
Spare your simple, fragile feelings with the same sense that you came

Color woman variation reworks the french twist
Crinkle-cut platinum frosted bangs from a spray can's mist

Never dissed, she insists: "No you can't touch this."
And, if pissed, bedecked fist stops boys who must persist.

She's the one. Give her some. Under fire. Smoking gun. Of which songs
  are sung, raps are spun, bells are rung, rocked, pistols cocked,

unwanted advances blocked, well-stacked she's jock. It's all about you
girl. You go on. Don't you dare stop.

JUSTIN CHIN

Imagining America

If the world has seen America through the movies,
I imagine how the world has seen me.

If American has seen my homeland through the movies,
I imagine how America has seen me.

The has-been actress on the telly plumps pity with a side of Christian do-
    good. Her red finger-nails rests on the knobby head of a belly-bloated
    child,
even as the promises of the spilled semen of green cards and Amex
    holidays slash its way across the Third World.
Even as the gay community clamours to join the military, a drag queen
    in Malaysia bleeds to death after a group of soldiers hack off his penis
    to teach him a lesson.
            "Take it like a man, boy."
Even as GIs and soldiers go on R&R in the sunny Third World, screwing
    their way into the psyche of a queen named exotica,
a 16-year old boy dies because of the infection caused by the sex toy
    that shatters in his rectum, shoved there by his Big Daddy who cries
    and moves on to the next one.
            "Take it like a man, boy."
Even as AIDS inches further into wounds of the Third World, the AIDS-
    infected flight attendant lives out the rest of his life in Bangkok
    screwing without a condom and living out his dream of spreading his
    love to a bevy of beautiful boys.
            "Take it like a man, boy."
Go ahead and plumb the Third World for your sense of spirituality, your
    fuck-me-all God-head fix, rest easy in your futon feeling that you're
    making an affirmative gesture.
If you can't afford the sex tour, join the Peace Corp.

SLAMMERS

Even as the Land of Opportunity devours its poor, tired, hungry masses
yearning to breathe free, we're asked to be silent, quiet, don't make
waves, don't offend, don't do nothing, buy a new pair of sneakers, sit
back and enjoy your favourite decaffinated red, white and blue cola.

I'll take it like a man.
I'll take every inch of it like the man you want me to be, like the man
I'll never be, like the man the world wants me to be, the man Asian-
America wants me to be, the man my dog wants me to be.
Take it like I got a chip on my shoulder,—hey, what's your chip?—

If America has seen me through my cuisine,
I imagine how I would taste.
On the days when I've been the hero, the monster,
the slut, the piece of shit. Some other permutation of myself.
If I have seen myself through the movies,
I imagine how I have seen myself.
I'm tired of explaining how it feels.

EVERT EDEN

Mandela

> so this is why I've been
in New York al this time
to stand at the UN
and vote for a man
Rolihlahla Nelson Mandela
his life cut by twenty-seven and a half years
yet he said, I'm not bitter?

> up here in the north
we could learn from his south
here the smaller the brain
the bigger the mouth

> you liked New York, Nelson
but I gotta warn you
we poopscoop our dogshit

and giftwrap our bullshit
we're all prisoners in a dark sitcom
some talk revolution
but the closest they get
is to call Doctor King
an Uncle Tom

      praise-sing Rolihlahla
Nelson Mandela
your mother Nosekeni
your eldest son Thembi
they too went underground
prison-bound
unable to go their funeral
where did you go?
the last walk to hell
a deep descent
but you came back
your back unbent
you knew a nation
marched from Lagos to London
Beijing to Boston
Moscow to Cuba
Makgatho, Maziwe
Zenani and Zindziwe
how proud for them yeah
that you were *their* tata

      my father was proud
when you went to jail
he, a ten-foot crackpipe
I couldn't inhale
his idea of father
came straight from hell
he touched me only
to beat the shit out of me
and when he finished
he beat the shit as well

      all those years I made up
two fathers for me
the one I could smell
whiskey-fart near
the other one gone

island-bound, gagged
Nelson, he ain't here

      I liked having one father who was missing
he made up for the one
who was too much there
but far from my fatherland
on the isle of Manhattan
where the hype high-fives
to maroela-tree size
you get to spot self-deception
it wears a funny green hat
check it out
the cold smile of fact
Nelson, I can never dig my tata
the way I love you
but marooned in my whiteness
how long? very long
in my self-imposed exile
I know one thing that's true
the father who is my father
is my father
and the father who is not
is not
is you

      amandla!-power
awethu!—is ours
the price of freedom has been paid
in blood, in pain, in tears, in rage
hey, dad, I count the scars
you wrote on me
I price the resentment
I kept forever on simmer
I total up the rage
I ate New York night for dinner
but now today
as I make my cross
with Rolihlahla I say
sweet freedom at last

I'm not bitter

SINI ANDERSON

It's a Good Day

SITTING IN AND ON FAMILIAR SURFACES
SIDEWALKS--BARS====PISSED AND PUKE STAINED
I WANT TO BE A POET WHEN I GROW UP
I WANT MY PAST TO STALK ME EVERY CONCIOUS MOMENT
I WANT TO VIEW MY LIFE ON THE BIG SCREEN THAT
    SOMETIMES
DEVOURS MY EYES
I WANT TO REMEMBER THE SHIT OF MY EARLY YEARS IN
    SUCH
VIVID DETAIL THAT IT ALMOST STOPS MY BREATHING
I WHAT TO WALK STREETS WITH SILVER SPOONS THE SIZE
    OF
REFRIGERATORS HANGING OVER MY HEAD
SHOOT FLAMES OUT OF MY BRAIN--------AND SMILE AS IT
    COOKS
MY SELF MEDICATED FUTURE
I WANT TO PRESS PIPES THE SIZE OF MY GRANDDADDY'S
    DICK UP
TO MY LIPS AND SUCK--BITCH SWALLOW----SOMETHING
THAT TASTES LIKE BURNT METAL, OLD GUYS CUM
I WANT TO BE A POET
SO I CAN WALK STREETS AND THINK THAT I CANT TALK TO
ANYONE
MY BEST FRIEND==OVER PRICED WHITE PAPER BOUND BY
    HARD
BLACK COVERS
YEA-------THAT SOUNDS GOOD FUCKER!!!!!!!!!!!!!!
CHARMED LIFE----ASSHOLE!
I STAND AT THE BAR---SHOES WAY TOO TIGHT!!
AND I SAY TO HER WITH A ROOTED TOOTH SMILE
YOU WANT TO BE A POET???
WITH THOSE PRETTY TEETH!
SHE SEZ=====YOU HAVIN A BAD DAY?
OH----NO--NO NO--------------REALLY, IM HAVIN A GOOD DAY
IM NOT KIDDING--------------IM HAPPY . . . .

SARA HOLBROOK

Chicks Up Front

Before and After,
we stand separate,
stuck to the same beer-soaked floor,
fragranced, facing the same restroom mirror.
Adjusting loose hairs—
mine brown, hers purple.
Fumbling for lipsticks—
mine pink, hers black—
a color I couldn't wear anyway
since that convention of lines
gathered around my mouth last year and won't leave.
We avoid eye contact,
both of us are afraid of being carded.

Mature, I suppose, I should speak,
but what can I say to the kind of hostility
that turns hair purple and lips black?
Excuse me, I know I never pierced my nose,
but hey, I was revolting once too?
Back. Before I joined the PTA,
when wonder bras meant, "where'd I put that."
I rebelled against the government system,
the male-female system,
the corporate system, you name it.
I marched, I chanted, I demonstrated.
And when shit got passed around,
I was there, sweetheart, and I inhaled.
Does she know that tear gas
makes your nose run worse than your eyes?
Would she believe that I was a volunteer
when they called "chicks up front,"
because no matter
what kind of hand-to-hand combat
the helmeted authoritarians may have been
engaged in at home,
they were still hesitant to hit girls
with batons in the streets.

SLAMMERS

"CHICKS UP FRONT!" and we marched and
we marched and we marched right back home.

Where we bore the children we were not going to bring into this mad
    world, and we
brought them home to the houses we were never going to wallpaper
in those Laura Ashley prints
and we took jobs with the corporate mongers
we were not going to let supervise our lives,
where we skyrocketed to
middle-management positions
accepting less money
than we were never going to take anyway
and spending it on the Barbie Dolls
we were not going to buy for our daughters.

And after each party
for our comings and goings
we whisked the leftovers into dust pans,
debriefing and talking each other down
from the drugs and the men
as if they were different,
resuscitating one another as women do,
mouth to mouth.

That some of those we put up front
really did get beaten down
and others now bathe themselves daily
in Prozac to maintain former freshness.
Should I explain what tedious work it is
putting role models together,
and how strategic pieces
sometimes get sucked up by this vacuum.
And while we intended to take
one giant leap for womankind,
I wound up taking one small step, alone.

What can I say at that moment
when our eyes meet in the mirror,
which they will.
What can I say to purple hair, black lips
and a nose ring?
What can I say?

Take care.

DANIEL FERRI

The Scalping

Lets get this straight from the start
I'm not whining
I'm just telling you
I have sat with a polite smile
While being flogged for every crime from neolithic patriarcal warrior
society domination To leaving   the toilet seat up
And many crimes in between
Because if I didn't do it, I might have done it, or looked like someone
who mighta'
          thoughta doin' it.
How insensitive of you
You know not who you pillory
For I am part of a vast legion
Who you, and the Sun, and the rain, and every cruel child and cold
    wind
have
          conspired to humiliate.
I am a bald guy.
Your smirk stands as proof of the insensitive piece of filth that you
are.

There is no sunburn like that on the top of my head
There is no polite way to wear my hat in the house when some
conservation crazed member of the
          hair dominant culture callously cranks the thermostat so damn
              low,
          or turns the fan blasting like the propeller of a Florida swamp
              boat
aimed directly at my
          bare and shivering skull.
You cannot know the pain that a bald guy feels
When he bumps his head.
And you cannot resist smirking at the band aid.

There is a conspiracy against us—yes there is
Billions of dollars are spent each year
To degrade me
Millions of hours are spent listening

Wide eyed
Open mouthed
Blank faced
To the follicle fascists
Accepting   —   Embracing
Television's version of what bald guys are.
Hey, T.V.'s got to tell you quickly who the fool is
Who doesn't know what to buy,
What to wear
How to dress,
What to hear
Where to go,
How to get there
Or in what
They've got 30 seconds to tell their little story
And your attention span is less than three

So quick
One second to show who the fool is
And 29 for the happy haired slim lovely lady to set his ass straight and
sell you the product
One second to show who the fool is
So make 'em bald,   —no one can miss that

One-last-thing
I must warn you about the jokes
Ya, you know who you are
And so do I
So you just watch your hairy ass

No more Mr. Nice Guy
No more shame faced shuffle
No more tight lipped smile
No more Uncle Fester
I mean it
One more snicker outa you and I'll be up your ass with your own medicine
like a Rogaine enema
The gloves will be off

Nothing will be off limits
No saggy tit is sacred
No big butt, no thunder thigh
No nose, no birthmark will escape my remark

Oh yeah,
Well what's the difference?
People been figuring it's their business to mock my appearance,
About my hair's diss . . . . . . apearance since I was 19 years old.

And don't tell me you were, "Just kidding."
Don't you even dare
I'll grab you by your forty five dollar haircut and lift you up untill
your eyes pop out
I might just take your scalp
And wear it on my belt . . .
As a warning.

EILEEN MYLES

Eileen Myles' poetry emphasizes performance as an ethic and an esthetic. It isn't improvisational: living isn't improvisation, as what "comes up" isn't all out of oneself and one's artistic medium. But the proof of a life is what's done based on what happens, encounters with circumstances, other people. A poem is more controllable, but if it arises organically from living—Eileen goes out the door with her notebook, because she feels she's "on," possibly because she's upset or in a transitional life phase—a poem can become the same kind of performance that living is. Where will she go? What will she see and hear? What will happen? What will she write? This is all electric air. But in order to perform right, on the spot, you have to be a virtuoso. Eileen's poetry is very deft, and in a manner specific to her speaking voice—that specificity that's so essential to poetry and so hard to describe. It's a specificity of spirit, history, temperament, which is conducive to specific choices of sounds, stresses, intonations. There's no separating a poet's body from a poem. There's no separation between Eileen's life and poetry. That was our ethic in New York: when the two are separate, poetry tends to lie or narrow tonally and in regard to subject. Eileen's poetry is full of subject because a voice which can sing so well can handle it. The Subject and Lyricism are not fashionable right now, but Eileen is nonetheless, and in a way, fashionable. She has been faithful to her process and her sense of her deepest self for a long time, and everyone can see that, that pure fidelity. But it takes so long, and you still don't get paid much. We've always been hoping to get paid for our job, will this ever happen? We don't think so, doing it anyway. Eileen's poetry is partly about poverty: no money, small apartment, a spare set of choices, only one self or soul to be, one neighborhood, one city. How can such a one spare thing be made rich? Virtuosity, fidelity, nuance, the senses etc. . . .

ALICE NOTLEY

An American Poem

I was born in Boston in
1949. I never wanted
this fact to be known, in
fact I've spent the better
half of my adult life
trying to sweep my early
years under the carpet
and have a life that
was clearly just mine
and independent of
the historic fate of
my family. Can you
imagine what it was
like to be one of them,
to be built like them,
to talk like them
to have the benefits
of being born into such
a wealthy and powerful
American family. I went
to the best schools,
had all kinds of tutors
and trainers, travelled
widely, met the famous,
the controversial, and
the not-so-admirable
and I knew from
a very early age that
if there were ever any
possibility of escaping
the collective fate of this famous
Boston family I would
take that route and
I have. I hopped
on an Amtrak to New
York in the early
'70s and I guess
you could say
my hidden years
began. I thought
Well I'll be a poet.
What could be more
foolish and obscure.

AMERICAN RENEGADES

I became a lesbian.
Every woman in my
family looks like
a dyke but it's really
stepping off the flag
when you become one.
While holding this ignominious
pose I have seen and
I have learned and
I am beginning to think
there is no escaping
history. A woman I
am currently having
an affair with said
you know you look
like a Kennedy. I felt
the blood rising in my
cheeks. People have
always laughed at
my Boston accent
confusing "large" for
"lodge," "party"
for "potty." But
when this unsuspecting
woman invoked for
the first time my
family name
I knew the jig
was up. Yes, I am,
I am a Kennedy.
My attempts to remain
obscure have not served
me well. Starting as
a humble poet I
quickly climbed to the
top of my profession
assuming a position of
leadership and honor.
It is right that a
woman should call
me out now. Yes,
I am a Kennedy.
And I await
your orders.
You are the New Americans.

The homeless are wandering
the streets of our nation's
greatest city. Homeless
men with AIDS are among
them. Is that right?
That there are no homes
for the homeless, that
there is no free medical
help for these men. And *women*.
That they get the message
—as they are dying—
that this is not their home?
And how are your
teeth today? Can
you afford to fix them?
How high is your rent?
If art is the highest
and most honest form
of communication of
our times and the young
artist is no longer able
to move here and speak
to her time . . . Yes, I could,
but that was 15 years ago
and remember—as I must
I am a Kennedy.
Shouldn't we all be Kennedys?
This nation's greatest city
is home of the business-
man and home of the
rich artist. People with
beautiful teeth who are not
on the streets. What shall
we do about this dilemma?
Listen, I have been educated.
I have learned about Western
Civilization. Do you know
what the message of Western
Civilization is? I am alone.
Am I alone tonight?
I don't think so. Am I
the only one with bleeding gums
tonight. Am I the only
homosexual in this room
tonight. Am I the only

homosexual in this room
tonight. Am I the only
one whose friends have
died, are dying now.
And my art can't
be supported until it is
gigantic, bigger than
everyone else's, confirming
the audience's feeling that they are
alone. That they alone
are good, deserved
to buy the tickets
to see this Art.
Are working,
are healthy, should
survive, and are
normal. Are you
normal tonight? Everyone
here, are we all normal.
It is not normal for
me to be a Kennedy.
But I am no longer
ashamed, no longer
alone. I am not
alone tonight because
we are all Kennedys.
And I am your President.

Holes

Once when I passed East Fourth Street off First Avenue,
I think it was in early fall, and I had a small hole
in the shoulder of my white shirt, and another on
the back—I looked just beautiful. There was a
whole moment in the 70s when it was beautiful
to have holes in your shirts and sweaters.
By now it was 1981, but I carried that 70s style
around like a torch. There was a whole way of
feeling about yourself that was more European
than American, unless it was American around
1910 when it was beautiful to be a strong
starving immigrant who believed so much
in herself and she was part of a movement

as big as history and it explained the
hole in her shirt. It's the beginning
of summer tonight and every season has
cracks through which winter
or fall might leak out. The most perfect
flavor of it, oddly in June. Oh remember
when I was an immigrant. I took a black
beauty and got up from the pile of poems
around my knees and just had too much
energy for thought and walked over to
your house where there was continuous
beer. Finally we were just drinking
Rheingold, a hell of a beer. At the
door I mentioned I had a crush on both
of you, what you say to a couple. By
now the kids were in bed. I can't
even say clearly now that I wanted
the woman, though it seemed to be
the driving principle then, wanting
one of everything. I was part of
a generation of people who went to
the bars on 7th street and drank the
cheap whiskey and the ale on tap and dreamed
about when I would get you alone. Those
big breasts. I carried slim notebooks which only
permitted two or three-word lines. I need you.
"Nearing the Horse." There was blood in all my
titles, and milk. I had two bright blue pills
in my pocket. I loved you so much. It was
the last young thing I ever did, the end of
my renaissance, an immigration into my
dream world which even my grandparents
had not dared to live, being prisoners
of schizophrenia and alcohol, though
I was lovers with the two. The beauty
of the story is that it happened.
It was the last thing that happened
in New York. Everything else happened
while I was stopping it from happening.
Everything else had a life of
its own. I don't think I owe
them an apology, though at least
one of their kids hates my guts.
She can eat my guts for all
I care. I had a small hole in

the front of my black sleeveless
sweater. It was just something
that happened. It got larger
and larger. I liked to put
my finger in it. In the month
of December I couldn't get
out of bed. I kept waking
up at 6PM and it was Christmas
or New Year's and I had
started drinking & eating. I remember
you handing me the most beautiful
red plate of pasta. It was like your cunt
on a plate. I met people in your house
even found people to go out and fuck,
regrettably, not knowing about
the forbidden fruit. I forget
what the only sin is. Somebody
told me recently. I have so
many holes in my memory. Between
me and the things I'm separated
from. I pick up a book and
another book and memory
and separation seem to
be all anyone writes
about. Or all they
seem to let me read.
But I remember those
beautiful holes on
my back like a
beautiful cloak
of feeling.

I Always Put My Pussy . . .

I always put my pussy
in the middle of trees
like a waterfall
like a doorway to God
like a flock of birds
I always put my lover's cunt
on the crest
of a wave
like a flag

that I can
pledge my
allegiance
to. This is my
country. Here,
when we're alone
in public.
My lover's pussy
is a badge
is a night stick
is a helmet
is a deer's face
is a handful
of flowers
is a waterfall
is a river
of blood
is a bible
is a hurricane
is a soothsayer.
My lover's pussy
is a battle cry
is a prayer
is lunch
is wealthy
is happy
is on teevee
has a sense of humor
has a career
has a cup of coffee
goes to work
meditates
is always alone
knows my face
knows my tongue
knows my hands
is an alarmist
has lousy manners
knows her mind

I always put
my pussy in the middle
of trees
like a waterfall
a piece of jewelry

AMERICAN RENEGADES

that I wear
on my chest
like a badge
in America
so my lover & I
can be safe.

UMAR BIN HASSAN

Malcolm

Midwestern images threatening the horizon.
Hold back the pain. Hold back the rejection.
I can . . . No you can't! I can! No you can't!
You're not supposed to. I will!

Going against the grain. Against all reason. Becoming an outlaw
very very young. Enjoying the status. The strength is the family.
My mother's tears become my beginning and my father's end.
Brothers and sisters become the inspiration for the poem
              by any means necessary!
We will survive! I will keep the name high. They will respect my
mother. They will remember my father. I have the flag! I have the
flag! It did not touch the ground.

Learning the game. Loving the game. Obsessed by the game. And
then Harlem.
              Harlem, the only game.
Neon lights reflecting the beauty of deep dark chocolate faces. Pretty
redbone legs and tight behinds. Very African and intimate suggestive
glances and invitations. Sumptuous lips full . . . of the reality for
every man's dream. Too much sensitivity for one highly sensitive man
to bare.
Loving the game.
Learning the game.
Obsessed by the game.
And then Harlem. Harlem, the only game.

Trying to be taught what you already know. Where you niggers been?
Y'all want game? Come to Red . . . and let's play! Play . . . Lady Day!
Play these streets like I was born in the middle of them.
Play Miles!
Play these women so hard so cold only to lose myself.
Play Bird!
Play with death like waking up so easy the next morning.
Game over.
Who won?
Ooooh, what is this?
cocaine.
White girls.
Cocaine.
Whitegirls.
cocaine.
There I go . . .
There I go . . .
There I go . . .

Harlem! I love it so much I hate it. It scares me. It fascinates me. It
enslaves us! In jail. Always in jail. Letters to my insanity. Memoirs so
intelligent, so brilliant, so deranged.
I think I'm sick.
I think I should get well. I think
I should
change.
So hard to stop the game. Revelations in the darkness of the pit.
Who are you? Who are you? The little lamb knows. My savior. He
tried. He believed. He was only human.
I love you Elijah Muhammad.

I forgive the envy. I forgive the jealousy. I forgive myself for believing
in someone other than just Allah. They took my vision. But I still
have my soul.
I've always had Betty. Transcending what it means to be man and
woman. My joy was her smile. Her smile was my strength. In the
worst of times she was that small little opening to the way out. She
was that push forward to truth. She knows. She always knew. One
pride and joy after the other.

Yes! He was my man. Yes . . . I loved him! These are the answers to
all of the questions of what he meant to me. Amilah. Illyasah.
Qubilah and Attilah my partner in crime.
Smile like your daddy girl! Think like your daddy girl! Be strong like
your daddy girl!

AMERICAN RENEGADES

Death is coming. It will come in Harlem. Where else? They want to
humiliate me. To turn me into a joke. In front of my family. In front
of my friends. In front of my true love. My one and only true love.
My people. Forgive me Betty. Please forgive me. Dying in the sad
memory of brothers eye to eye. Nose to nose. I respect you. You
respect me. Let's go hunting brothers. Let's go hunting.
WARRIOR . . .
          who remembers that word, I do. I saw it smile at me in
the face of death. Bullets . . . Bullets . . . Becoming part of me. Where
is the pain? I love you brother. Self-hatred wrapped up in a twisted,
demented but well-controlled smile. Where is the pain?
I love you brother.

All I have ever been was for all of you. Where is the pain?
I love you brother.
I have always loved you. I know that tune. I grew up with that tune.
I love my people. I love my people. If they could just learn how to
love themselves. They will respect my mother. They will remember
my father.
I have the flag!
I have the flag!
          It did not touch the ground.

GERRY GOMEZ PEARLBERG

Marianne Faithfull's Cigarette
For L.

It was on the floor, being X-ed out by her long
black heel, infinite and doomed. I had to have it.

Her lips had been around it. Lipstick left on it.
I had to have it. I asked you to get it.

She was raking her fingers through her thin blonde hair.
Glancing up at the ceiling, chain-smoking.

The academics around her were talking, talking, talking.
She gazed up at the ceiling—bored, exhaling.

She rolled her eyes, then looked at us and smirked, you said.
I missed that, pondering the acropolis of fallen cigarettes
    at her feet.

How they looked like smoldering ruins—toppled, scattered.
Broken haloes of a calcified Atlantis.

Pondering chain-smoking. What a beautiful word.
I missed the look she gave us, bemused and bored.

I was thinking about the ring of lipstick on the filter.
I was thinking about the brand, and where she might've
    bought it.

Watching her light up was like seeing the Messiah.
Or Buddha's burning moment under leaves of cool desire.

First Date with the D.J.

We were in Brooklyn.
Her hand was on my thigh
when we pulled up to the stop sign.
The boys on the corner shouted
"Bulldykes!" and in a flash
she pulled a gun
from her glove compartment
and waved it like a hand-puppet
till they were history.
"They need to know we're armed and dangerous," she said.

We pulled up to my house.
There was a ruby slipper between my thighs,
a poppy field in the back of my brain
though Kansas might as well have been a globe away.
By the time she pulled my sweater off
under the street lamp
and kissed me in that glow,
I could barely remember
the name those kids had called us,
what a gun was, or how to speak

the language we'd been speaking
all our lives.

For Brandon Teena

Were you buried in your favorite slacks,
black cowboy shirt, and cowboy hat?
That's what the papers said (at first).
Or were you laid to rest in a women's
flowered print, a "ladies' " blouse,
as your relatives insisted that
the *Lincoln Journal* print
in their "correction" of the "facts"
of how you dressed—alive *and* dead?

Are any of us what our families pretend?
Our sex lives and the nature of our deaths
reclaimed, revisited, unread—
unspeakable what we do in bed
and whom we love and how we dress,
encountering eternity in our favorite slacks,
cowboy shirts and vests and hats.
Confronting eternity undisguised.
Dressed to kill. To die for. *Unrevised.*

Sailor

The girls go by in their sailor suits
They catch my eye in their sailor suits
Big or slight they all grin like brutes
In steam-ironed pants and buffed jet boots
They saunter right up my alley.

I study their easy, confident strides
Crew cuts and white hats capping decadent eyes
They shiver the pearl on nights oystery prize
They shiver me timbers, unbuckle me thighs
This alley was made for seething.

From the sweat of a street lamp or lap of the sea
A smooth sailor girl comes swimming to me

Says she wants it right now and she wants it for free
Clamps her palms to my shoulders, locks her knees
    to my knees
This alley was made for cruising.

Her face is dark coffee, her head has no hair
Her cap shines like neon in the bristling night air
She pins her brass metals to my black brassiere
Tucks her teeth like bright trophies behind my left ear
This alley is very rewarding.

She tosses her jacket and rolls up her sleeve
On her arm's a tattoo of an anchor at sea
She points to the anchor and whispers, "That's me."
And the wetter I get the more clearly I see
This alley was made for submersion.

Her fingers unbutton my 501's
This girl's fishing for trouble and for troubling fun
She slides off her gold rings and they glint like the sun
Then she smirks, rubs her knuckles, and spits out her gum
This alley was made for swooning.

Now she's pushing her prow on my ocean's sponge wall
Uncorking my barnacle, breaking my fall
And there's pink champagne fizzling down my decks
    and my hall
As she wrecks her great ship on my bright port-of-call
This alley was made for drowning.

GIL SCOTT-HERON

Evolution

In 1600 i was a darkie; Til 1865 a slave.
In 1900 i was a nigger; (at least that was my
   name.)
In 1960 i was a knee-grow; Malcolm came along.

AMERICAN RENEGADES

Then some nigger shot Malcolm down,
    but the bitter truth lived on.
Now I am a Black man; (still go 2nd class.)
But once I wanted the white man's love
    and now he can kiss my ass.

From Tomorrow

Those half moon's silly smiles
beneath my children's eyes
would not be there
    had light ever touched
    the retina of my brain.
Had I, in 1640, burned
the ships that sailed us all
to this special branch of hell,
    now would be no time to cry.
Had I, in 1840, followed Nat Turner
and field niggers everywhere,
scattering like wind-blown grains of sand,
    now would be no time to cry.
Had I, in the 20th century,
followed Garvey or Malcolm,
    King or Karenga,
    now would be no time to cry . . .
        while white men walk on stars.

LENNY BRUCE

What Is a Jew?
(from Christians & Jews)

What is a Jew?
A Jew is one who is descended from the ancient tribes of Judea.
That's what it says in the dictionary.
But you and I know what a Jew is . . .

The one who killed OUR LORD.
You didn't know?
We did that about two thousand years ago.
There should be a statute of limitations with that crime.
But the Goyim are going to make us pay dues for another deuce.
And they say, hosanna, why do we make them pay the dues,
granted that Christ was the person you say he was?
All right, I'll admit it. I know why the Jews pay the dues.
Because we copped out; we skirted the issue; we blamed it on
Roman soldiers. Yes! I will clear the air. We did it!
And not only did we kill Christ,
We're going to kill him when he comes BACK!

How to Score

I figured out a sure way to score every time.
You meet a chick and tell her:
"Look, I'd like very much to take you out, but I've got a bit of a
    problem."
"Oh? Like what?"
"I don't want to burden you with my problems. I'm happy if you'll let
    me take you out, I don't
make it with anybody. I'm celibate."
"May I ask why?"
"Well, I don't think so, once or twice I've met girls who've said 'You
    shouldn't have told me that . . .
you've ruined my night!'"
"You haven't made it with anybody?
"I don't want to talk about it."
"You can tell me, I understand people's problems."
"It's the way I'm built."
"What do you mean?"
"I'm abnormally large."
"You're that big?"
"Yeah."
"You've never had an affair with a woman?"
"13 years ago."
"What happened?"
"She's been in the hospital ever since."
"Are you really that big . . . didn't you go visit her?"
"Are you kidding, she'd have me killed . . . her brother's still looking for
    me . . . I can't wear
walking shorts."

"How big is it?"
"I can't talk about it. It's terrible if you have something like that."
"Could I see it?"
"Not a chance, it's all locked up anyway. I don't even have a key. My
    father has the key."

To Come

A scat-like poem accompanied
by drums and cymbals

"Toooooo" . . . is a preposition
"Commmme" . . . is a verb
"Too" is a preposition
"Come" is a verb
"Tooo Comme"
The infinitive form
of the verb intransitive
"To Come"
I've heard these two adult words my whole life,
even as a kid sleeping on the mohair couch . . .
"Tooooo Commme" . . .
"Tooooo Commme" . . .
It's been like a big drum solo
Didyoucome, didyoucome, didyoucome,
Didyoucomegood? Didyoucomegood? DidyoucomeGOOD!
After bein married fer 22 years, ah sure do love you.
Ah come better fer you, darlin, than with anyone
in the whole damn world. If ah come too quick,
that's because ah love you so damn much.

Everyone else in the world it's okay. But with mah own wife,
ah spend my whole life apologizin'.
Ah just can't wait for you. Ah tried
Even gettin' killed on the freeway, eaten' garbage
But . . . Don't come in me
Don'tcomeinme . . .
Don'tcomeinme mimme mimme
Don'tcomeinme mimme mimme
Don'tcomeinme mimme mimme
(cymbals) I can't come!
(cymbals) I can't come!
Cause you don't love me

That's why you can't come
That's my hang up, I can't come when I'm loaded!
Now if anyone in this room or in the world
Finds those two words
. . . decadent
. . . obscene
. . . immoral
. . . amoral
. . . asexual
If those words "to come" really make you
feel uncomfortable . . .
If it's really a hang-up for you to hear it . . .
If you think I'm the rankest for saying it to you . . .
You probably . . .
can't come

RICHARD PRYOR

Richard and I went to Kenya on Easter, 1979. We were sitting in the lobby of the Hilton in Nairobi one afternoon when Richard looked around and said, "there's no niggers here, Jen." When we came home, Richard began woodshedding at the Comedy Store for his upcoming tour. He worked on this piece, this epiphany (which became a routine he would use in his concert film, *Live On Sunset*). It was a difficult time for him: a lot of Black people said that Richard was abandoning his roots. This hurt him deeply. People were threatened by his change, by his growth.

JENNIFER LEE

Africa

Its nice to have pride about your shit. I went home to the Mother Land. Everybody should go home to Africa. Everybody. There is so much to see there in the eye and in the heart.

. . . the one thing I got out of it was magic, it was like, I was leaving and I was sitting in a hotel and a voice said to me, "Look around what do you see?

"I see all colors of people doing everything," I said.

"Do you see any niggas?" the voice said. I said, "No . . . and you know why? Cause there aren't any:

It hit me like a shot man. I started cryin' and shit. I was sitting there sayin'

I've been here three weeks and I haven't said it. I haven't even thought it. It made me say, "oh my God, I've been wrong. I've been wrong." I got to regroup my shit. I ain't gonne nevah call another black man nigga 'cause we nevah was no niggas.

SIMON J. ORTIZ

I Told You I Like Indians

You meet Indians everywhere.

Once, I walked into this place-
Flagler Beach, Florida,
you'd never expect it-
a bar; some old people ran it.

The usual question, of course,
"You're an Indian, aren't you?"
"Yes, ma'am." I'm Indian alright.
Wild, ignorant, savage!
And she wants me to dance.
Well, okay, been drinking beer
all the way from Hollywood.
We dance something.

You're Indian, aren't you?
Yeah, jesus christ, almighty,
I'm one of them.

I like Indians!

"There's an Indian around here."
What? And in walks a big Sioux.
Crissake man, how's relocation, brother?
He shakes my hand. Glad to see you.
I thought I was somewhere else.
We play the pingpong machine, drink beer,

once in a while dance with the old lady
who likes Indians.

I like Indians!

I *told* you
You meet Indians everywhere.

HETTIE JONES

Subway Poem

Yo, Spring!

We need weather baby,
    We need tulips, lilacs,
    dandelions in the grass
    and your sweet ass

In the Eye of the Beholder

Tonight she brings
            eaters!

        little black boys with purple tongues
        in the City College mulberry trees

        in Times Square a Muslim woman
        munching a Mars bar under her veil

These are Kellie's pictures you see

            she sees
            through

            her shining
        black   eyes

Words

        are keys
or stanchions
        or stones

I give you my word
You pocket it
and keep the change

Here is a word on
the tip of my tongue: love

I hold it close
though it dreams of leaving

JOY HARJO

Two Horses

            I thought the sun breaking through Sangre de Cristo
Mountains was enough, and that
                        wild musky scents on my body after
        long nights of dreaming could
                    unfold me to myself.
        I thought my dance alone through worlds of
odd and eccentric planets that no one else knew
        would sustain me. I mean
                        I did learn to move
                                    after all
and how to recognize voices other than the most familiar.
        But you must have grown out of
                        a thousand years dreaming
            just like I could never imagine you.
                You must have
                        broke open from another sky

to here, because
                    now I see you as a part of the millions of
        other universes that I thought could never occur
            in this breathing.
                            And I know you as myself, traveling.
        In your eyes alone are many colonies of stars
                                    and other circling planet motion.
                    And then your fingers, the sweet smell
                    of hair, and
                                    your soft, tight belly.
        My heart is taken by you
                    and these mornings since I am a horse running towards
        a cracked sky where there are countless dawns
                            breaking simultaneously.
        There are two moons on the horizon
        and for you
                    I have broken loose.

THOMAS McGRATH

The Crippled Artist

1.
Harsh, even to the callous ear,
He scuffs along the street in his coarse boots.
The dreaming citizens, hustling, do not hear—
Or so he thinks. And thinks them blind as bats
Were once thought blind. Propelled into the day
By racking rents, childwife and holy car
That steers them constant toward a falling star—
Mechanized Christs up on the sacred ways—
And old coots, down cats, whores and tearaways—they ramble all
    around.

2.
All around him. he thinks he must be glass,
Cloudy, perhaps; smudged, smoky—a bit crazed
Somewhere at center. And so he comes to pass—
Being occulted—where the rise is prized
By middleclass flowerfallahs gilding the gilded stalk
Of the golden lily in fence protected yards.
Above him fly the bright incontinent birds-
Milwaukee Avenue: his daily walk,
Where now the lengthening autumnal sun gives back the lacquered
                    oak leaves' luster.

3.
He'd like to take them home: the flowers, the light-
But all light falters in the narrow room
He paints in—which he wants to call his home.
Half-bat-blind, what does he want? He wants insight
or outsight: his room blazes like a noon sun-ranch.
When people lose the vision, they think lost.
He does. His paint-hand, like a willow branch,
Twitches, storm-tossed. First things become last.
Still he persists, prizing the fallen light, expendable, now dying
                    in the street

4.
And still he struggles: to take them back alive-
Flowers, birds, street, people the light that lies
Still in some alleys. It is a kind of love,
Perhaps, that sends him into those dark ways
To search the wreckage for some living thing:
To celebrate! Breath held, he lifts his arm . . .
Strength flows to hand . . . it flies . . . as if a wing!
And light illuminates all that he loves to praise!
The centuries fall asleep: the adamantine walls soften-scary-

Working, he thinks:
The lyf so short, the craft so long to lere . . .
Despair so easy. Hope to hard to bear.

JAYNE CORTEZ

Global Inequalities

Chairperson of the board
is not digging for roots
in the shadows
There's no dying-of-hunger stare
in eyes of
Chief executive officer of petroleum
Somebody else is sinking into
spring freeze of the soil
Somebody else is evaporating
in dry wind of the famine
there's no severe drought
in mouth of
Senior vice president of funding services
No military contractor is sitting
in heat of a disappearing lake
No river is drying up
in kidneys of
a minister of defense
Under-secretary of interior
is not writing distress signals
on shithouse walls
Do you see refugee camp cooped up
in head of
Vice president of municipal bonds
There's no food shortage
in belly of
a minister of agriculture
Chief economic advisors are
addicted to diet pills
Banking committee members are
suffering from obesity
Somebody else is sucking on dehydrated nipples
Somebody else is filling up on fly specks
The Bishops are not
forcing themselves to eat bark
The security exchange commission members
are sick from
too many chocolate chip cookies

The treasury secretary
                is not going around in circles
                        looking for grain
There's no desert growing in nose of
                        Supreme commander of justice
It's somebody else without weight
without blood without land
without a cloud cover of water on the face
It's somebody else
Always somebody else

The Heavy Headed Dance
For Mel & Ted

I am dancing &
on my head
is the spotted skunk
whose scent did not protect it
from Mr. & Mrs. Archibald of Texas

On my head
is the stuffed bobcat
whose facial expression was set
by the taxidermy department

On my head
is a bull caught
in the act of masturbation
& on top of that
rides the moose
stunned-gunned while wading in a lake
& on top of that
are the monkeys
entrapped while urinating
& on top of that
lay the hyena
jackal & vulture
shot while eating from zebra carcasses
& on top of that
sits the ram with
largest horn on record
donated by Henry Beck
& with all the stuffed animals piled on my head

I am dancing past
lyricist with the baboon heart

I am dancing like a dog
in front of financial consultant
implanted with pig genes

I am dancing & fluttering like a butterfly
across from novelist posing
in a beaver skin coat

I am dancing near the astronomer
who circles the floor with her
uplifted face frozen like a tiger

I am dancing against window
of artificial coyotes
& howling with contemporary African band
in the grizzly bear room

I am dancing my pangolin hairdo dance
past the river of ants in panties
of gyrating vocal groups

I am dancing so many different dances
with so many bloated animals
dead on my head
that my head is
a dancing museum of unnatural history
& I am dancing where I cannot see
myself dancing to know
why I am dancing
but I am dancing
I am dancing

MIKE TOPP

Barney Rosset and The Evergreen Review

In the early morning hours of July 26, 1968, a group of anti-Castro Cubans launched a fragmentation grenade through the windows of Grove Press shortly after a portrait of Che Guevara appeared on the cover of *Evergreen Review*. "The Canadian consulate and Japanese Air Lines were also bombed," recalls Barney Rosset, "So we were in a rather select group."

Evergreen Review was founded in 1957 by Rosset, Grove's editor and publisher. Its focus, through its various incarnations, has been a broad one, covering everything from avant-garde literature to a history of spanking to lascivious comic strips like Phoebe Zeitgeist and Barbarella. A sampling of works published in its pages includes Allen Ginsberg's *Howl*, selections from William S. Burroughs' *Naked Lunch*, and Ho Chi Minh's *Prison Poems*. Grove's "little magazine" lasted until 1973, evolving from a trade paperback-sized quarterly into a monthly in magazine format. At its peak *Evergreen Review* claimed more than 100,000 readers.

The son of a Chicago banker, Rosset turned his unwavering commitment to freedom of speech into an extraordinary career built on publishing both old and new "great outlaw masterpieces." Indeed, as S. E. Gontarski notes, "The man who began a legal crusade for the right to read was himself something of an intellectual outsider." As an eighth grader at the progressive Francis W. Parker School in Chicago, Rosset declared Benito Mussolini to be the living person he most admired. That same year, he began his publishing career with a newsletter called *Anti-Everything*. In the 1940s, after unsatisfactory stints at Swarthmore and the University of Chicago, Rosset enlisted in the Army. He managed to get himself transferred to the 164th Signal Photo Company in China, where he photographed captured equipment and the training of new soldiers for Chiang Kai-shek. In 1946 he returned to the University of Chicago. Moving to New York in 1947, he began work on *Strange Victory*, a feature film about race relations in postwar America. The film was a critical success and a financial failure; Rosset spent $250,000 of the family fortune, and lost his entire investment. In 1949 he married Joan Mitchell, an old Parker School classmate who was well on her way to becoming an internationally famous painter. The couple lived in France for a bit and then returned to New York.

In 1951 the twenty-nine-year-old Rosset paid $3,000 for a failed publishing venture called Grove Press. He ran his newfound company with a mixture of instinct and recklessness. This approach had its advantages as well as its drawbacks. During the next few years Rosset went on to publish Beckett, Genet, and Ionesco, yet turned down Lawrence Durrell's *The Alexandria Quartet* simply because he didn't like it. (A more costly decision was to later reject J. R. R.

Tolkien's *Lord of the Rings* for the same reason.) By the mid 1950s Rosset decided to publish D. H. Lawrence's long-banned *Lady Chatterley's Lover*. Although not a financial success, the book raised Grove's profile considerably. While other publishers challenged the status quo, none were able to work on such an impressive scale as Grove. The success of such books as Henry Miller's *Tropic of Cancer* (in its first year as a Grove edition it sold 1 million copies in paperback and 100,000 copies in hardcover) led Rosset down new roads.

.*Evergreen Review* burst onto the scene in the late 1950s like a bomb. It was Evergreen Review, then in its second issue, that brought to national prominence the San Francisco scene, complete with Ginsberg's *Howl* and photos of assorted hipsters posing with maximum beat intensity. After publishing such writers as Sartre, Neruda, and Kerouac, the magazine took a turn in the 1960s, when ads for Male Jeans vied for attention with soft-core pornography, cartoons, and still more works by Beckett. *Evergreen Review* stopped publishing in 1973, basically for financial reasons. Phoenix-like, it rose from the ashes last year and can now be found on-line at evergreenreview.com. Here once again Victorian erotica tangoes with cutting-edge literature. Rosset once wrote that the two things which most interested him in life were justice and pleasure. *Evergreen Review*'s antacid continues to help counteract society's bile.

BARNEY ROSSET

Ernest Hemingway

The Champs Elysees is a wide street. When it rains the wooden bricks are slippery. Today it was raining and Malin drove slowly. He liked to drive fast. Today he drove slowly because he had to enter the Ambassador Restaurant on his feet. Not in the front seat of the Citroen. Not today. Yesterday yes, after four or five Cognacs. Today he had to have propriety. One Cognac before the meeting, no more.

There was width for eight cars abreast. Nothing to it. He depressed the accelerator. He depressed it slowly. He did not want his wife to notice. She did not. The bartender at the Ambassador knew he preferred Courvoisier. He saw the bottle. The Arc de Triomphe was a big bottle of Courvoisier. The Eiffel Tower was a bigger bottle of Courvoisier.

"Malin, keep to the right."

"I am." He cursed her. To himself he cursed her. She told him that every day. Every day he kept to the right. With or without Cognac he kept to the right. Usually with Cognac. Only decent drink the Frogs had. He swerved to the right to miss a big bottle of Courvoiser at the head of the Champs Elysees.

The Little Sons of Fidel*
Dedicated to the 65,000 Miskitian Indians, enduring in Honduras, and the Cuban doctors who have gone to their aid.

In Pranza, Honduras
17 days without food
Not even sugar water
For the kids.
All 400 of them.

A top U.S. Military Official said
"The Honduran Government
Has no plans
For the Miskitia Indians region."

"It took two weeks to get here"
Said a United Nations Volunteer
"The Honduran Air Force planes
Were grounded for maintenance."

"This is the edge of the world"
Said Colonel Chuck Jacoby
Commander U.S. Task Force
In Honduras,

"We kind of diverted
For a little while
Out of Miskitia."

In Bruslaguna
A village of 3200 people
"One aid shipment came"
Said Arnold Mangara, a resident
"One hundred pounds of rice
It was about enough
For one day
Even the little sons
of Fidel
Don't come.
They've gone

To another village.
To every small town
In the area
Except here."

*Thanks to
Geoffrey Mohan,
Latin American Correspondent,
and Newsday, Dec. 14, 1998.*

ISHMAEL REED

If My Enemy Is a Clown, a Natural Born Clown

i tore down my thoughts
roped in my nightmares
remembered a thousand curses
made blasphemous vows to demons
choked on the blood of hosts
    ate my hat
threw fits in the street
got up bitchy each day
told off the mailman
lost many friends
left parties in a huff
dry fucked a dozen juke boxes
made anarchist speeches in brad
the falcon's 55 (but was never
thrown out)
drank 10 martinis a minute
until 1 day the book was finished

my unspeakable terror between the
covers, on you i said to the
enemies of the souls

well lorca, pushkin i tried
but in this place they assassinate
you with pussy or pats on

AMERICAN RENEGADES

the back, lemon chiffon between
the cheeks or 2 weeks on a mile
long beach.

i have been the only negro
on the plane 10 times this year
and its only the 2nd month

i am removing my blindfold and
leaving the dock. the judge
giggles constantly and the prosecutor
invited me to dinner

no forwarding address please

i called it pin the tail on the devil
they called it avant garde
they just can't be serious
these big turkeys

LUIS J. RODRIGUEZ

To the police officer who refused to sit in the same room as my son because he's a "gang banger":

How dare you!
How dare you pull this mantle from your sloven
sleeve and think it worthy enough to cover my boy.
How dare you judge when you also wallow in this mud.
Society has turned over its power to you,
relinquishing its rule, turned it over
to the man in the mask, whose face never changes,
always distorts, who does not live where I live,
but commands the corners, who does not have to await
the nightmares, the street chants, the bullets,
the early-morning calls, but looks over at us
and demeans, calls us animals, not worthy
of his presence, and I have to say: How dare you!
My son deserves to live as all young people.

AMERICAN RENEGADES

He deserves a future and a job. He deserves
contemplation. I can't turn away as you.
Yet you govern us? Hear my son's talk.
Hear his plea within his pronouncement,
his cry between the breach of his hard words.
My son speaks in two voices, one of a boy,
the other of a man. One is breaking through,
the other just hangs. Listen, you who can turn away,
who can make such a choice; you who have sons
of your own, but do not hear them!
My son has a face too dark, features too foreign,
a tongue too tangled, yet he reveals, he truths,
he sings your demented rage, but he sings.
You have nothing to rage because it is outside of you.
He is inside of me. His horror is mine. I see what
he sees. And if my son dreams, if he plays, if he smirks
in the mist of moon-glow, there I will be, smiling
through the blackened, cluttered and snarling pathway
toward your wilted heart.

Rosalie Has Candles

Rosalie has candles in a circle around her bed.
One night as I lay on a couch
in a tequila stupor,
she takes off my shoes and trousers,
pulls a cover over me and snips
two inches of hair from my head.
She places the hair in a glass
near the candles. I don't know why.
I don't know why she searches for me.
I don't know how she finds me in the bars.
I don't know why she ridicules the women I like
and uses me to meet men.
Rosalie usually finds solace in a glass
of whiskey. In my face she finds the same thing.
I don't know why. We argue too much.
We feign caring and then hurt each other
with indifference. With others we are tough
and mean. But in the quiet of darkness
we hold each other and caress like kittens.
She says she can only make love to someone
when she is drunk. She says she loves men

but has lesbian friends.
She loves being looked at. I want to hide.
She hates struggle. That's all I do.
She has Gods to pray to. I just curse.
I don't know what she sees in my face,
or hands for that matter. I only know
she needs me like whiskey.

Somebody Was Breaking Windows

Somebody was breaking the windows
out of a 1970s Ford.
Somebody's anger, for who knows what,
shattered the fragile mirror of sleep,
the morning silence
and chatter of birds.
A sledge hammer in both hands then crashed
onto the side of the car,
down on the hood,
through the front grill and headlights.
This Humboldt Park street screamed
in the rage of a single young man.
Nobody got out of their homes.
Nobody did anything.
The dude kept yelling
and tearing into the car.
Nobody claimed it.
I looked out of the window as he swung again.
Next to me was my woman.
We had just awakened after a night of lovemaking.
Her six-year-old daughter was asleep
on a rug in the living room.
My woman placed her arms around me
and we both watched through the louvre blinds.
Pieces of the car tumbled
onto steamed asphalt.
Man hands to create it.
Man hands to destroy it.
Something about being so mad
and taking it out on your car.
Anybody's car.
I mean, cars get killed everyday.
I understood this pain.

And every time he swung down on the metal,
I felt the blue heat swim up his veins.
I sensed the seething eye staring from his chest,
the gleam of sweat on his neck,
the anger of a thousand sneers—
the storm of bright lights
into the abyss of an eyeball.
Lonely? Out of work? Out of time?
I knew this pain. I wanted to be there—
to yell out with him,
to squeeze out the violence
that gnawed at his throat.
I wanted to be the sledge hammer,
to be the crush of steel on glass,
to be this angry young man,
a woman at my side.

Chota

Here I lie, embraced by the miasmic draft
of side-street America
as a voice cuts into the still air.
A police officer stands above me
and the gum stains on Seventh Street.

Chota.

Soon I sit battered, humiliated,
in the dankness of a jail cell;
officers wallow around
contemplating my "suicide."

But this time
they will have to kill me.
Each time a fist smashes
across my belly, pummels my face,
I reach out
to the cries of the curb,
the ballads out of broken brick,
and the smoky outline of a woman's face
burned onto a cell wall.

They will have to kill me!

AMERICAN RENEGADES

Believe Me When I Say . . .

water is the skin of the earth
trains are arteries with corpuscles of people
a sigh is an ancestor praying
a woman's body is suspended over the land
tears come from clouds in your head
writing a poem is like fathering a river
waiting is the art of desire
something about a city makes you want to kill
fetuses scribble on the walls of wombs

Meeting the Animal in Washington Square Park

The acrobats were out in Washington Square Park,
flaying arms and colors: the jokers and break
dancers, the singers and mimes. I pulled out
of a reading at New York City College
and watched a crowd gather around a young man
jumping over 10 garbage cans from a skateboard.
Then out of the side of my eye I saw someone
who didn't seem to belong here, like I didn't
belong. He was a big man, six feet and more,
with tattoos on his arms, back, stomach and neck.
On his abdomen were the words in huge old English
lettering: Hazard. I knew this guy, I knew that place.
I looked closer. It had to be him. It was—Animal!
From East L.A. World heavyweight contender,
the only Chicano from L.A. ever ranked
in the top ten of the division. The one who
went toe-to-toe with Leon Spinks and even
made Muhammad Ali look the other way.
Animal! I yelled. "Who the fuck are you?" he asked,
a quart of beer in his grasp, eyes squinting.
My name's Louie—from East L.A. He brightened. "East L.A.!
Here in Washington Square Park? Man, we everywhere!"
The proverbial "what part of East L.A.?" came next.
But I gave him a shock. From La Gerahty, I said.
That's the mortal enemy of the Big Hazard
gang of the Ramona Gardens Housing Projects.
"I should kill you," Animal replied. If we were in

L.A., I suppose you would—but we in New York City, man.
"I should kill you anyway."
Instead he thrust out his hand with the beer and offered
me a drink. We talked—about what happened since he stopped
boxing. About the time I saw him at the Cleland House
arena looking over some up-and-coming fighters.
How he had been to prison, and later ended up homeless
in New York City, with a couple of kids somewhere.
And there he was, with a mortal enemy from East L.A.,
talking away. I told him how I was now a poet,
doing a reading at City College, and he didn't wince
or looked surprised. Seemed natural. Sure. A poet
from East L.A. That's the way it should be. Poet
and boxer. Drinking beer. Among the homeless,
the tourists and acrobats. Mortal enemies.
When I told him I had to leave, he said "go then,"
but soon shook my hand, East L.A. style, and walked off.
"Maybe, someday, you'll do a poem about me, eh?"
Sure, Animal, that sounds great.
Someday, I'll do a poem about you.

Don't read that poem!
For Patricia Smith

She rises from a chair
and slides toward the stage
with satin feet over a worn-wood floor.
She bears down on the microphone
like a blues singer about to reveal
some secrets.
A fever of poems in her hand.
She seizes the mike
and begins her seduction.

I'm in the back of the bar,
my head down.
The things she does to me
with words.
I want to leave. I want her
never to begin.
She starts with a poem
about Daddy-love, and I feel

like getting up right there
and yelling: Don't read that poem!
That one that causes little bursts
of screams inside my head,
that makes tears come to my eyes,
that I refuse to let fall.

Don't read that poem!
the one about a daughter raped and killed
in the shadow of a second's dark fury.
I want to hide in the neon glare above me;
to swim away in the glass of beer
I hold close to me.
She does another poem
about her many mouths
and I want to howl:
Don't read that poem!
that one that entices me
to crawl under her skin,
to be her heartbeat.

Oh, how she plunks the right notes,
rendering me as clay in bruised hands.
No, don't do the one about
what it is to be
a nine-year-old black girl,
the truth of it trembling at my feet.
Somebody should make her stop!

I should be home, watching TV,
blank-eyed behind stale headlines,
cold popcorn on the couch,
a dusty turntable
going round and round and round.
I should be fixing a car.
Or shooting eight-ball.
But I can't leave.
I need to taste the salt of her soliloquy,
to be drunk with the sobriety
of her verse
quaking beneath my eyelids.

ALICE NOTLEY

It's Dumb to be a Member of a Dominant Species

snow falling outside the window of Procope
on windowbox paperwhite narcissus—
it stops. What language were they speaking
at the next table? I don't know

Diderot, Robespierre, and Nazis have eaten here
Silver lines impinge on the scene
invisible connections to the past and the future
the room on the second floor is rooted

in the first floor, the wine cellar, tribal dreams
such as the union of egg and sperm, the existence
of a monster like a man or a woman
the necessity of killing and of its regulation
the dream—the tribal dream—is of food and sex
after having destroyed the enemy.

————————————

World passing by in tableaux
forming from and dissolving back to
waves or clouds . . .

The pouches under Mitch-ham's eyes are so large
I'm tempted to poke them with a hatpin
and see what comes out. Liquid crystal he says or ichor,
not pus or tears—

a weak shower of spermlike snow
falls on our flames . . .

REJOICE IN THE INIQUITIES OF THE LORD

BUDDHA PRACTICES AUTOFELLATIO

MOHAMMED IS A MUGGER

such are the messages
left on the walls
just visible through fire

WE LIVE IN MYTHOLOGY BUT MYTHS ARE STUPID

THE HEART SINKS LIKE A STONE MYTH

THE SCIENTIFIC METHOD IS ONLY
THE MYTH OF THE SCIENTIFIC METHOD,
WHICH WILL EVAPORATE WITH THIS CIVILIZATION

MITCH-HAM IS A MYTH
ANY PEOPLE'S WAYS ARE TOTALLY
OFF THE WALL, THIS WALL.

———————————————

I'd like to find the humility room,
I say, though humility's a myth—

It's simply, again, says Mitch,
the room where other people starve, not a myth.

———————————————

Went to a restaurant once more. Ate a duck. Guilt.

———————————————

I dream I pull down from the sky
yards and yards of
a mesh-like silver-grey
narrow band of a fabric,
with a purse attached.
And a newspaper.
In a young tribal society
this might become the story
of how we got our ways,
receiving from heaven
our wealth and
the first great length of our
headband and belt material;
we could organize a festival
where it fell from
the sky every year
as in the beginning

and we danced, holding
the ribbon high over our heads.

I'm eating her food.

I can have any books I want from this box . . .

One's about foretelling the future from clouds,
a practice apparently found in many cultures:
Australian Aboriginal, Amer-Indian, African, etc.
Clouds are observed and painted with
unadulterated pigments in broad brushstrokes

e.g. several crimson swaths against a grey-blue mass
which subtly changes across its grainy swelling;
color renders volume and depth and the stratification
of the clouds—maybe the future's told from those qualities.
The future being ominous . . . that's the drift of this book.

A conversation. "I'm waiting for . . ."
a myth of rescuing the future

We sanction no war whatsoever
just or unjust.
As a matter of fact we do nothing
we use no more fuel, drive no more cars
because we have tied our hands
with the silver-grey fabric.
It's hard to eat, hard to write. Our enemies
can kill us if they want.
I think they're us anyway
and we were already doing that, killing us
if we wanted

KATHE IZZO

For Seattle Boy Sacred Mantle

Sometimes I remember it as if
my body was naked and so was God's.

There are hundreds of designated reincarnations
of spiritual deities around the world.

For Seattle boy, sacred mantle,
the next great teacher of Tibetan Buddhists in exile,
born, by luck or by grace, two blocks from a Pizza Hut,
for the rest of us, the holy and insecure, the need
for an extreme and coded love that will speak to us—

These moments are rarely blissful, more often like a train wreck.

Freedom was outside the window
the day I heard the angels come.
It was the end of the world,
and God had risen to the top of the telephone pole.
He held some papers above his head, everyone was breathless
and he said, "Where is my littlest apostle?"

My eyes burned as I rose to meet him, hovering first
at his feet and then by his side. I looked
into his eyes and then I looked out at everyone
that thought they knew me.

The body knows the precise spot
on the beach 100 miles away
where someone it loves is waving.
It can feel the hollow shadow
beneath their eye. It knows the clouded leaf
behind the curve of the belly,
the forgotten trees. It knows something
the size and weight of a small lemon, but smooth,
nutlike, close to the spine—

I am dreaming of a liquid world,
where the guiltless roam translucent,

like say we were in love and I was killed in your arms and then reborn
and many years later we found each other and the alien lover,
born within, would already know your body but I would not on first
    meeting—

I have a black eye and a white tattoo,
I know you will remember this,
thumbs pressed up inside
the braille of my skull,
a rose tattoo, like the inside of my eye,
a purple fragrant tattoo,
like the fugitive imprint of your hand,

the goodness of that quivering, bruised host—

From *I am in Danger Nowhere in This World*

IV
As in all relationships, a cross fertilization is implied.

In the analytic container such profound cross-fertilization occurs through
    the
transference-countertransference inevitable when the work proceeds into
    -the
magical and archaic levels of the psyche.

Typically both parties are touched.

She remembered he had taught her the method of separating words into
    syllables.

The word Daddy always stuck in her throat.

Her skin was so soft, although she would never admit to her desire to be
    touched,
above and beyond the fucking she saw as so necessary.

Her skin was so soft, you could hardly see it sometimes.

I hungered for her, although I knew the only possibility for union was
    within her body.

V

More often than not she had to check if someone were following her.

Ultimately the concept of home was passé; the pornographic images in her mind more real and posessing; her life lived most safely inside her car.

That night she loved like she had never loved before. I felt a carnival inside her pulse as she wrapped her arms around my neck. In her throat an acrobat dangled, in her wrists horses galloped on tightropes, and as her legs intertwined with mine, I felt the electrical empathy of the freak show.

The car was on the road just barely.

She had begun to get into the habit of driving without her glasses, until the night the police stopped her and without question assumed she was trying to either provoke or elude them.

They dropped to their knees and drew their revolvers without a whisper.

Within her inner chaos, a cavernous light exploded, creating an equal and opposite reaction to the crust of humiliation that had formed on her vital organs.

As she accepted them within her, graciously and without complaint, from somewhere inside came the memory of a tiny breath once taken in which the fragile cilia of her nose felt the force of life for the very first time.

JOE BRAINARD

Joe Brainard (1942–1994) was born in Salem, Arkansas, and grew up in Tulsa, Oklahoma, where he met poets Ted Berrigan, Ron Padgett, and Dick Gallup. In 1961, after a few months of study at the Dayton Art Institute, he moved to New York City. His first solo exhibition was at the Alan Gallery there in 1965. Later he had many shows and took part in a great many group shows around the country. His theater work includes set designs for LeRoi Jones' *The Toilet* and Frank O'Hara's *The General Returns from One Place to Another*, as well as sets and costumes for the Louis Falco Dance Troupe and Joffrey Ballet Co. He also designed the covers of a great number of poetry books and magazines. Brainard edited and drew *C Comics* and *C Comics 2*, collaborations with contemporary poets such as Frank O'Hara, Kenneth Koch, and James Schuyler. His work is in the collections of the Metropolitan Museum, the Museum of Modern Art, the Whitney Museum, and the Brainard Archive at the University of California, San Diego, among others. Currently his Estate is represented by the Tibor de Nagy Gallery.

Brainard was also a gifted writer and authored many books and collaborative books including *I Remember* (Penguin) and *Bean Spasms* (Kulchur, 1967) with Ted Berrigan and Ron Padgett.

RON PADGETT

JOE BRAINARD

Van Gogh

Who is Van Gogh?

Van Gogh is a famous painter whose paintings are full of inner turmoil and bright colors.

Perhaps Van Gogh's most famous painting is "Starry Night": a landscape painting full of inner turmoil and bright colors.

There are many different sides to Van Gogh, the man.

When Van Gogh fell in love with a girl who didn't return his love he cut off his ear and gave it to her as a present. It isn't hard to imagine her reaction.

Van Gogh's portrait of a mailman with a red beard is probably one of the most sensitive paintings of a mailman ever painted.

It is interesting to note that Van Gogh himself had a red beard.

When Van Gogh was alive nobody liked his paintings except his brother Theo. *Today* people flock to see his exhibitions.

Van Gogh once said of himself: "There is something inside of me—what is it?"

Sick Art

Mona Lisa's smile often causes observers to overlook the fact that she has no eyebrows.

One skin specialist offered the suggestion that Leonardo da Vinci's model was suffering from a skin disease called alopicia. Alopicia is a skin disease in which one has no eyebrows.

On the other hand, many women in those days shaved their eyebrows and Leonardo da Vinci's model may have just been following the fad.

There is no doubt, however, that Rodin's "The Thinker" has bunions on both feet.

Today, with modern art, it is not to easy to spot diseases and physical disorders.

Many doctors, however, have noticed a strong relationship between various skin diseases and the paintings of Jackson Pollock.

Fungus infections are very common in the art of the Middle Ages and the Renaissance.

Art

Looking through a book of drawings by Holbein I realize several moments of truth. A nose (a line) so nose-like. So line-like. And then I think to myself "so what?" It's not going to solve any of my problems. And then I realize that at the very moment of appreciation I had no problems. Then I decide that this is a pretty profound thought. And that I ought to write it down. This is what I have just done. But it doesn't sound so profound anymore. That's art for you.

Death

Death is a funny thing. Most People are afraid of it, and yet they don't even know what it is.

Perhaps we can clear this up.

What is death?

Death is it. That's it. Finished. "Finito." Over and out. No more.

Death is many different things to many different people. I think it is safe to say, however, that most people don't like it.

Why?

Because they are afraid of it.

Why are they afraid of it?

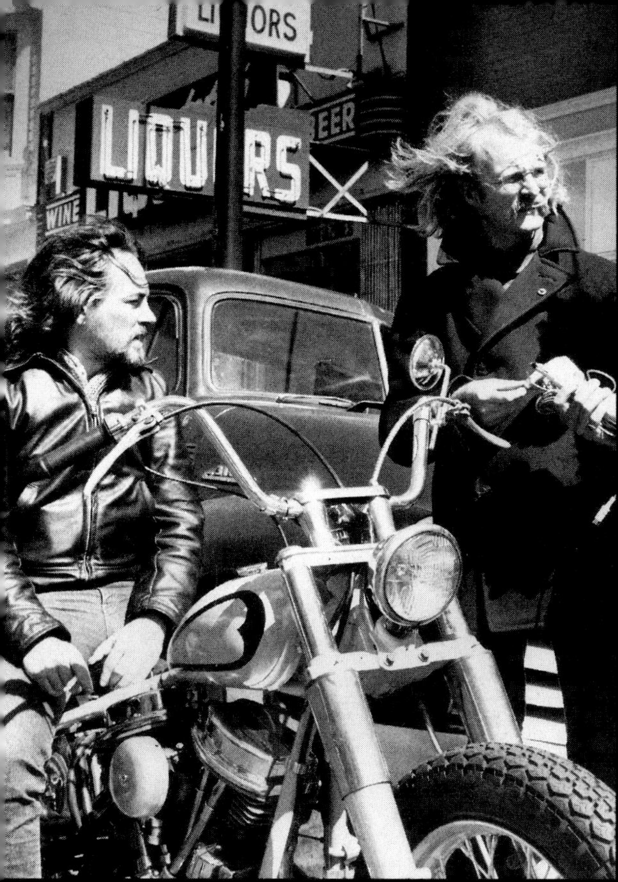

courtesy Rhyder McClure

Michael McClure and Richard Brautigan on Haight St., 1968

Ray Bremser

effrey Weinberg 1998

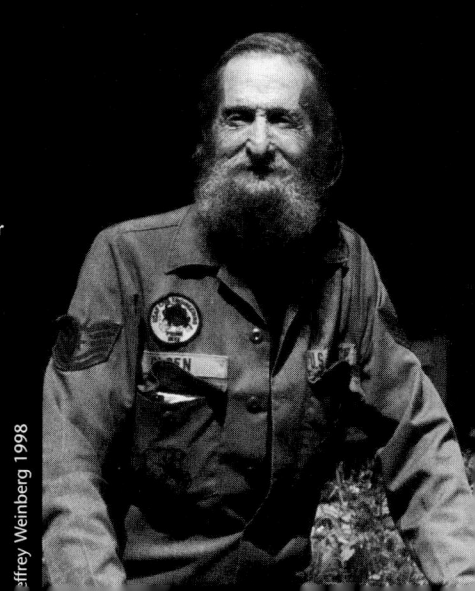

Heather Harris 1990

Wanda Coleman and Lydia Lunch

Harold Norse

Ralph Ackerman

Janine Pomy Vega

Lisa Martinovic´

Daniel Higgs' back

Pedro Pietri

Greetings from New York City, where "ya gotta have a gimmick"

Jack Micheline with Bob Kaufman,
San Francisco, 1974

Bruce Polonsky

Lawrence Ferlinghetti

Jack Micheline performing
with Charles Mingus

Babarians at Café Babar

François Janicot

Richard Gibson

singlehandedly
conventions of

s have passed
uce died. and
bably floating
ethereal plain.
th Swift. Pope
ry once in a
oarous laughter
shift in our
ing us to take a
k about who he
, Bruce left us
with much of
his brilliant
material. which
is as fresh and
inventive today
as it was during
his life

Lenny Bruce

Poet's Strike, San Francisco
City Hall, 1993. Left to right:
Neeli Cherkovski, Alan Kaufman
(holding sign), John Ross
(reading), Merle Tofer

POETRY IS FREE!

Luis J. Rodriguez and son

Julian Beck

Gerard Malanga

Ralph Ackerman

Alan Kaufman

Sapphire

Ana Barrado 1994

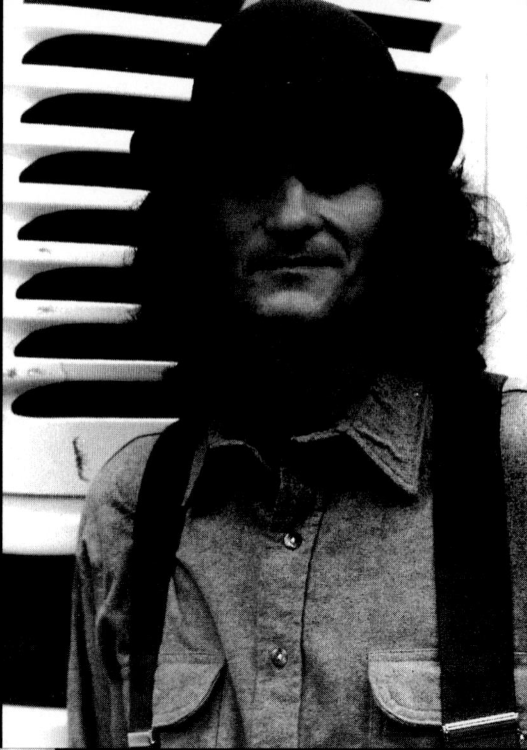

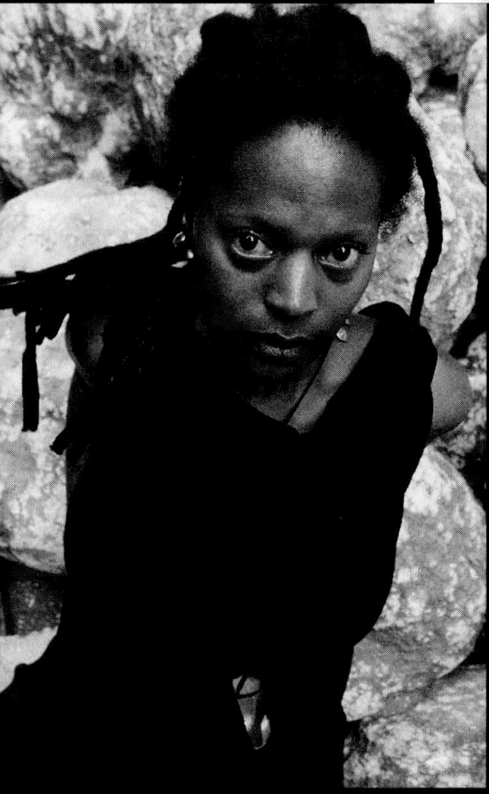

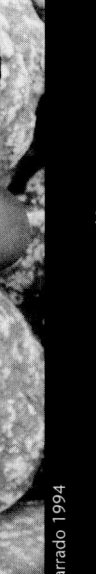

Ralph Ackerman

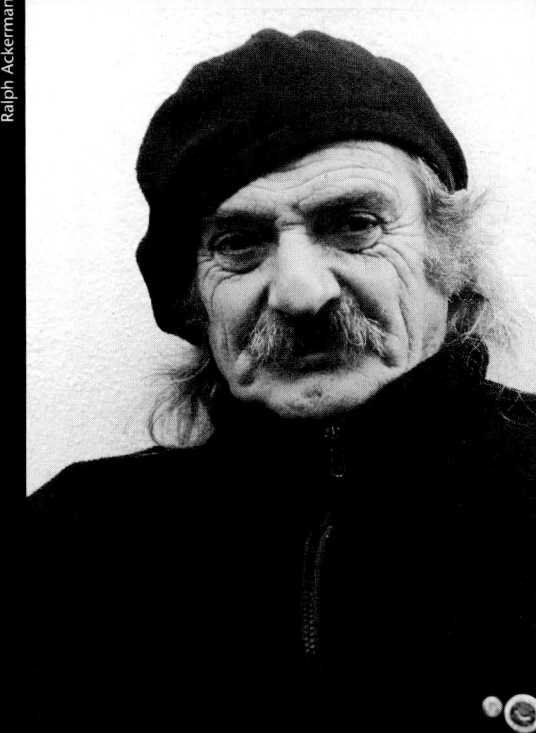

Jack Hirschman

Allen Ginsberg's poetry farm, Cherry Valley, New York, 1970. Sitting, front row, left to right: Gordon Ball, Allen Ginsberg, M De Loach, Mary Beach, Bonny Bremser. Sitting, back row, left to right: Gregory Corso, Ann B., Ed the hermit, Unidentified, Unidentified, Alan De Loach (with goatee and glasses), Miles, Liz and Pam Plymell, Claude Pekieu, Charles Plymell, Ray Bremser. Standing: Peter's girl and Peter Orlovsky

courtesy Charles Plymell

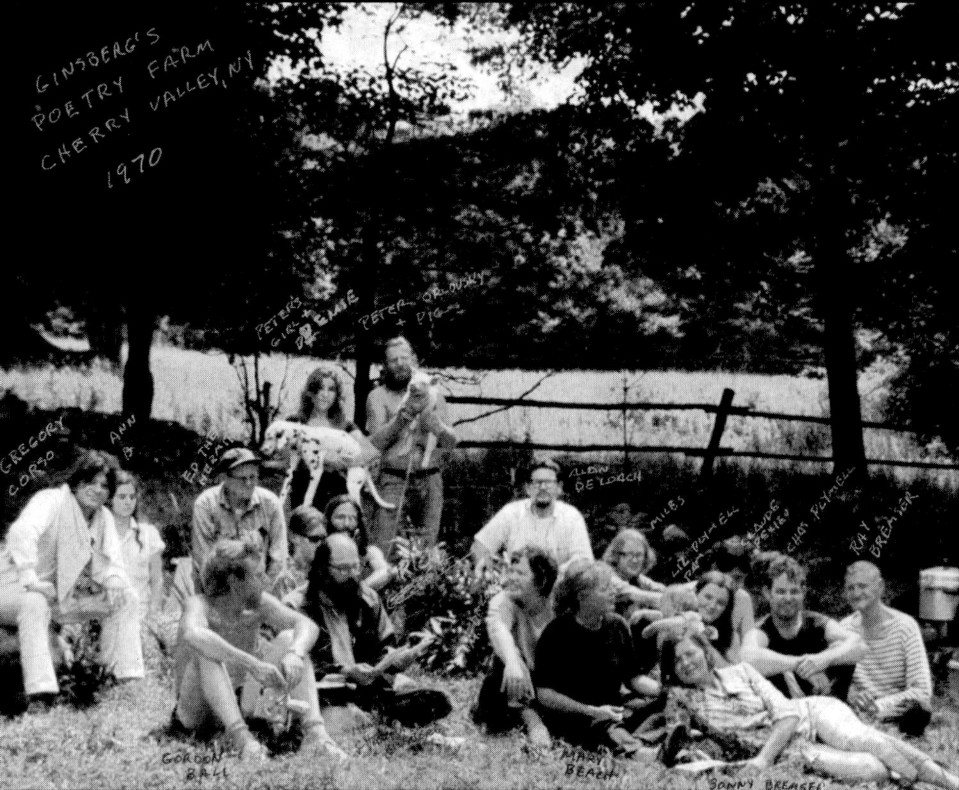

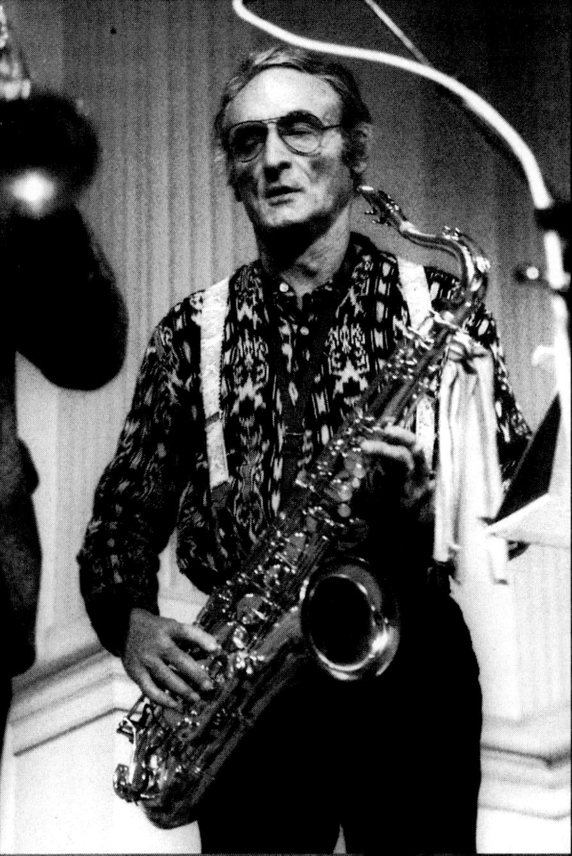

Vivian Selbo 1988

Larry Rivers

Herbert Hunke

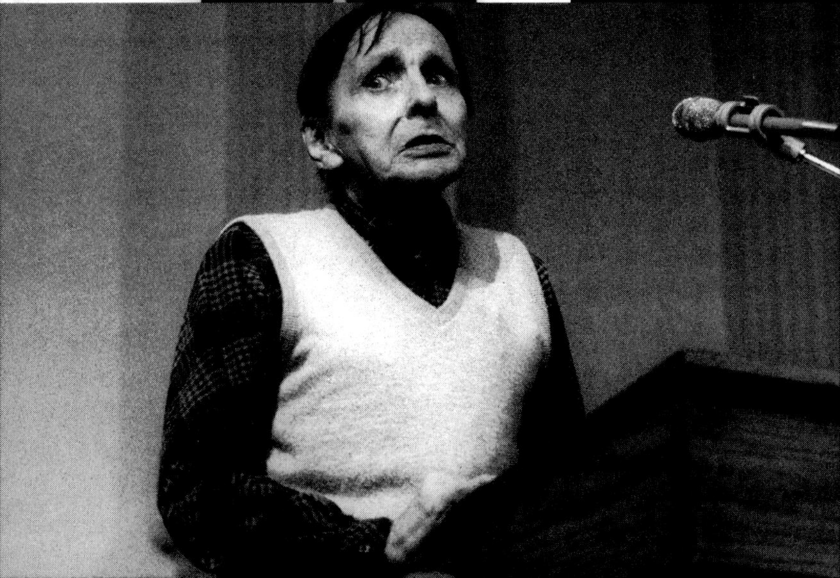

Bob Kaufman

Tracie Morris

Charles Plymell, 1954

Bucky Sinister

Join the
Undergrou

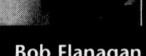

Bob Flanagan

Because they don't understand it.

I think that the best way to try to understand death is to think about it a lot. Try to come to terms with it. Try to *really* understand it. Give it a chance!

Sometimes it helps if we try to visualize things.

Try to visualize, for example, someone sneaking up behind your back and hitting you over the head with a giant hammer.

Some people prefer to think of death as a more spiritual thing. Where the soul somehow separates itself from the mess and goes on living forever somewhere else. Heaven and hell being the most traditional choices.

Death has a very black reputation but, actually, to die is a perfectly *normal* thing to do.

And it's so wholesome: being a very important part of nature's big picture. Trees die don't they? And flowers?

I think it's always nice to know that you are not alone. Even in death.

Let's think about ants for a minute. Millions of ants die every day, and do we care? No. And I'm sure that ants feel the same way about us.

But suppose—just suppose—that we didn't have to die. That wouldn't be so great either. If a 90 year old man can hardly stand up, can you imagine what it would be like to be 500 years old?

Another comforting thought about death is that 80 years or so after you die nobody who knew you will still be alive to miss you.

And after you're dead, you won't even know it.

RON PADGETT

The Fortune Cookie Man

Working for ten years now at the fortune cookie factory and I'm still not allowed to write any of the fortunes. I couldn't do any worse than they do, what with their You Will Find Success in the Entertainment Field mentality. I would like to tell someone that they will find a gorilla in their closet, brooding darkly over the shoes. And that that gorilla will roll his glassy, animal eyes as if to cry out to the heavens that are burning in bright orange and red and through which violent clouds are rolling, and open his beast's mouth and issue a whimper that will fall on the shoes like a buffing rag hot with friction. But they say no. So if you don't find success in the entertainment field, don't blame me. I just work here.

To Woody Woodpecker

I love you, Woody,
when you peck
on the head
of a bad person
and laugh and fly
away real fast,
speed lines
in the air
and clouds of invisible
dust dissipating,
I love the way
you last only seven minutes.
The heart has seven minutes
with Woody Woodpecker,
seven minutes of pure bliss.

MIKE TOPP

My usual writing method is this: after a day at the office, I come home, eat, and take a nap. I then get a vigorous rubdown from my boy Hajii. At midnight I go out on the town for a couple hours. When I come home, I like to drink Pernod and smoke opium, stroke my pet gazelle, and pound out some poems.

. . . I don't really like the Western idea of creativity, with its emphasis on originality and the insistence that everyone must be so interested in what the writer is thinking. I like the poetic diaries of the Japanese, with their free sense of border crossings between poetry and prose, and their mix of the original and received. My favorite book is Kenko's *Essays in Idleness*.

My biggest influences are Erik Satie, William Wegman, and Joe Brainard—none of them writers in the usual sense.

Mike Topp attended the University of Copenhagen and New York University. He interned at archive/performance space Franklin Furnace in New York City in the early 1980s, working with Martha Wilson, one of the original "Guerrilla Girls." During that time, he published mostly in Between C&D and Public Illumination Magazine. He met Miguel Pinero in 1984 who offered writerly advice at store/performance space Neither/Nor on Avenue D. He also met former Grove Press head Barney Rosset in 1988 and edited several anthologies. In the late 1980s and 1990s, Topp published primarily in *Exquisite Corpse* (editor Andrei Codrescu), *The Quarterly* (editor Gordon Lish), and on-line magazine *RealPoetik* (editor Sal Salasin). He was managing editor of *Artforum* in 1997–1998. His books include *Local Boy Makes Good* (Appearances, 1994), *Six Short Stories & Seven Short Poems* (Low-Tech Press, 1997) and, with Sparrow, a flip book: *Wild Wives/High Priest of California* (Beet, 1997).

Mike Topp is an aristocratic rebel whose high-spirited life has captured the imagination of Europe. He attended Harrow and Cambridge, where he was a good student and a great athlete. A deformed foot has only increased his determination to excel.

Mike Topp, born Berdichev, Ukraine, December 3/6, 1857. Joined French marine service 1874. After harrowing trip up the Congo, left the sea for good and in London 1894 turned to writing. Surmounting agonizing difficulties of composition in English, produced *Bilax, God of Gum Arabic* 1895 and *Milgrig and the Tree Wilfs* 1896. Married Jessica George 1896. Children: two sons. Wrote *Lord Jim* 1900. Began *Heart of Darkness* in 1902, finished by Joseph Conrad. Died 1924. Buried in Grant's Tomb.

The "mad poet," Mike Topp, is neither mad nor a poet. He is a self-schooled Siberian peasant who affects religiosity and dabbles in faith healing. He has a talent of sorts for hypnosis. He has an eye for human frailty. And, decisively, he has a gift for sex, or more precisely for seduction, since the act itself for Topp is an affair of moments. He has bent (literally) to his will scores of women on whom he has fixed his stare. His vigor is seemingly undiminished by a prodigious consumption of alcohol in all-night drinking bouts enlivened by gypsy choirs.

A precise description of Topp's male attributes is unnecessary here, but there is a hint in one of Michael Musto's anecdotes that these may be more than just the subject of conjecture. Having smashed up a smart New York nightclub, Topp was challenged to prove that he was who he said he was. In response, Musto notes, "Topp unbuttoned his trousers and waved his penis at the waiters and onlookers."

This piece of self-advertisement aside, one of Topp's saving graces is that he also knows when to favor discretion. He has not had a sexual relationship with Maggie Estep, for all the gossip to the contrary. Nor has he had a sexual relationship with Elizabeth Wurtzel. His ascendancy over the downtown poetry scene derives from his supposed powers as a healer. He is credited with halting three potentially embarrassing episodes of laryngitis in the poet laureate, Robert Haas, and with saving Allen Ginsberg's life after a train crash.

But healing and fornicating are merely Topp's calling cards. What makes him a power in New York is the fact that the literary agent Andrew Wylie listens to him and usually trusts his judgment. Wylie thinks Topp is a good judge of other people. He has come to rely on tips from the wild-eyed sage when making and unmaking writers. This is no small franchise. In a single year under Topp's influence, the Lower East Side has had two presidential candidates, three movies, one Broadway play, and a special on Howard Stern. Topp can fix television, too: a word from him is enough to have a troublesome author dispatched to host a fund-raiser on PBS, or a tractable one featured on MTV.

Topp's constituents, once in the media, are obliged to help him in the lesser favors in which he traffics wholesale: grants, contracts, readings, agents, merchandising and the like. In January 1998, 300 to 400 people were calling on him daily in his modest apartment on the Lower East Side. The columnists call him an almost supernatural fiend, but he is in reality one of New York City's great literary fixers.

My favorite mythological figure is Baubo, the Greek goddess of laughter, who saw through her nipples and laughed through her vulva.

Rejected Mafia Nicknames

Vanilla
Kitty
Jughead
Señor Wences
Marcel Duchamp
Archilochus
Tony the Logical Positivist

X-15
Gideon
Achilles Fang

Disappointment

6'5"
4"

What Kind of Cars They Drove

Albert Einstein	1955 Buick Century
Delmore Schwartz	1958 Mercury Montclair Phaeton
Norman Mailer	1960 Plymouth Fury
Ian Fleming	1956 Ford Fairlane Victoria
Cardinal Richelieu	1960 Cadillac Fleetwood
Sitting Bull	1956 De Soto Firedome Convertible
Jackie Robinson	1962 Chevrolet Impala
Gertrude Stein	1962 Chevrolet Impala
Ramses II	1957 Cadillac Eldorado Brougham
Ludwig Wittgenstein	1960 Chevrolet Impala
Santa Claus	1960 Ford Falcon
Richard Wagner	1960 Ford Thunderbird
Mr. Ed	1960 Dodge Dart Station Wagon
Flipper	1964 Cadillac Coupe de Ville (with water)

Just Go Fuck Yourself

Gasan was sitting at the bedside of Tekisui three days before his teacher's passing. Tekisui had already chosen Gasan as his successor.

A temple had recently burned down and Gasan was rebuilding it. Tekisui asked him: "What are you going to do when the temple is rebuilt?"

"When you're better we want you to speak there," said Gasan.

"Suppose I die before then?"

"Then we'll find somebody else," replied Gasan.

"Suppose you can't get anybody?" said Tekisui.

Gasan answered loudly: "Don't ask such stupid questions. Just go fuck yourself."

AMERICAN RENEGADES

This Mind is Buddha

Two monks were arguing about whether their train was moving. One
said:
"Our train is moving."
The other said: "The train on the tracks next to us is moving."
The sixth patriarch happened to be walking down the aisle. He
asked them: "Would I look good in short shorts?"

Tozan's Pretzels

A monk asked Tozan when he was eating some pretzels: "What is
Buddha?"
Tozan said: "These pretzels are making me thirsty."

We Have Chocolate Pudding

When Banzan was walking through the Union Square greenmarket he
overheard a conversation between a vendor and his customer.
"Do you have chocolate mousse?" asked the customer.
"We have chocolate pudding," replied the vendor.
At these words Banzan became enlightened.

KENNETH PATCHEN

What Is the Beautiful?

The narrowing line.
Walking on the burning ground.
The ledges of stone.
Owlfish wading near the horizon.
Unrest in the outer districts.

Pause.

And begin again.
Needles through the eye.
Bodies cracked open like nuts.
Must have a place.
Dog has a place.

Pause.

And begin again.
Tents in the sultry weather.
Rifles hate holds.
Who is right?
Was Christ?
Is it wrong to love all men?

Pause.

And begin again.
Contagion of murder.
But the small whip hits back.
This is my life, Caesar.
I think it is good to live.

Pause.

And begin again.
Perhaps the shapes will open.
Will flying fly?
Will singing have a song?
Will the shapes of evil fall?
Will the lives of men grow clean?
Will the power be for good?
Will the power of man find its sun?
Will the power of man flame as a sun?
Will the power of man turn against death?
Who is right?
Is war?

Pause.

And begin again.
A narrow line.
Walking on the beautiful ground.
A ledge of fire.
It would take little to be free.

AMERICAN RENEGADES

NOW IS THEN'S ONLY TOMORROW

As ever the trust of little birds
That the sky will be
Smart enough to appreciate
Their invention
Of flying

Kenneth Patchen

Ah, Yes! we'll please as we do

That no man hate another man,
Because he is black;
Because he is yellow;
Because he is white;
Or because he is English;
Or German;
Or rich;
Or poor;
Because we are everyman.

Pause.

And begin again.
It would take little to be free.
That no man live at the expense of another.
Because no man can own what belongs to all.
Because no man can kill what all must use.
Because no man can lie when all are betrayed.
Because no man can hate when all are hated.

And begin again.
I know that the shapes will open.
Flying will fly, and singing will sing.
Because the only power of man is in good.
And all evil shall fail.
Because evil does not work,
Because the white man and the black man,
The Englishman and the German,
Are not real things.
They are only pictures of things.
Their shapes, like the shapes of the tree
And the flower, have no lives in names or signs;
They are their lives, and the real is in them.
And what is real shall have life always.

Pause.

I believe in the truth.
I believe that every good thought I have,
All men shall have.
I believe that what is best in me,
Shall be found in every man.
I believe that only the beautiful
Shall survive on the earth.
I believe that the perfect shape of everything

AMERICAN RENEGADES

Has been prepared;
And, that we do not fit our own
Is of little consequence.
Man beckons to man on this terrible road.
I believe that we are going into the darkness now;
Hundreds of years will pass before the light
Shines over the world of all men . . .
And I am blinded by its splendor.

Pause.

And begin again

MIGUEL ALGARÍN

The Scattering of the Ashes: The Burial of a Poet

Many years ago, two poets made a promise to each other, and the promise was deceptively simple. One poet promised the other that by the next evening he would come back with a poem that would lay out in detail what was to be done upon his death.

> Just once before I die
> I want to climb up on a
> tenement sky
> to dream my lungs out till
> I cry
> then scatter my ashes thru
> the Lower East Side.

So it came to pass that Miguel Piñero would die, on June 17, 1988. We had been scheduled to do a reading tour of the Southwest, preparations had been made, all our Chicano friends were prepared to feed us menudo for the cruda and taquitos to go along with the tequila.

But that night, Miky did not come home. Miky belonged to the streets, on the concrete and the asphalt of New York, and his disappearances were not rare. It was his operational mode. The streets were where he felt best. It was in the early morning that a phone call came through: Miky had not been reveling and indulging in his excesses but had fallen ill and been admitted to St. Vincent's. My move toward the hospital was automatic, frenetic, and impulsive. I had to look out for my main mellow man, who was both my shadow and my angel.

There's always an eerie silence around the beds of people in intensive care. The only sounds are the electronic machinery insisting on their digital count-downs, insisting with their automatic accuracy how much or how little life is left. Miky's eyes were closed, he seemed deeply asleep, and as I approached him I remember saying to my sister that maybe we ought to wait outside, wait till he wakes, and then we can speak, and then we can visit, and then we can show him our love. But Miky, with that third eye always open to the universe, had in a flash felt my sister's and my presence, and although he could not immediately open his eyes, his fingers moved and his arms twitched, and I knew to enter, that he was conscious and I could speak and be heard, though responses were not to be easily had. I said, "Miky, my love, rest."

I moved toward the bed and put my hand in his, though it was difficult getting to his fingers through the tangle of intravenous lines. He surprised me with the strength of his grasp, and I said, "Tomorrow, we'll leave tomorrow, and if we can't leave tomorrow, we'll reschedule and leave when all is well again." His fingernails had grown long, and his grasp grew tighter and his nails dug into my palm. He wanted to say something, so I tried again: "I'm going to call Jimmy in Albuquerque and tell him that we'll come out next month." He pulled me toward the bed, I saw his eyes slowly open, and his lips barely moved as I bent down and put my ear up to his lips, and he kissed my ear, his hand grasped harder, and he said, "This is our last tour, we must keep all our dates, I will be here when you come back, and anyway, you know what you need to do if I die." I knew exactly what I had to do, and yet I couldn't imagine I would actually have to do it. He seemed impatient with me for staying as long as I did, and he gave me a glance that said everything it had to about my lingering: "Don't you have to catch a plane, Miguel? Why aren't you on your way?" I was shaken, and I knew that I didn't want to leave him. Yet his instructions were very clear.

That afternoon I left for Albuquerque to meet Jimmy Santiago Baca, to enter the holy land of the Chicanos' semiarid, drier-than-dry air and the spiritual world of Quetzalcoatl. The readings went as scheduled. Everywhere I read, everyone was moved and saddened by Miky's absence. His death was announced at 2:30 A.M., June 17, by his brother in a long-distance call from New York. My impulse was to climb on a plane to New York immediately. Miky had, however, instructed me to finish the tour, so I left Albuquerque for Taos. A poet's dying will is something that must be enacted and not foiled. So I performed in Taos, got off the stage and into a car, and on my way back to Albuquerque I thought, "I better study my instructions before I arrive in New York." The muscular, now familiar refrain of the poem kept coming at me; it both refreshed and frightened me. Miky's living will now resided in his verbs:

> So let me sing my song tonight
> let me feel out of sight

AMERICAN RENEGADES

and let all eyes be dry
when they scatter my ashes thru
the Lower East Side.

That was my task.

When I arrived in New York, I went immediately to the Wollensky Funeral Parlor, where a great poet lay in state. I knew I was to conduct the ceremonies attendant upon a Nuyorican* poet, which meant that there would be a call let out: "I want musicians, I want drummers, and may all the poets come prepared to read, to testify in heightened language to a life lived as a lifelong sonnet." I knew I had to put the poem into action, and I knew that the whole of the community would have to help me lift the poem off the page.

That night Amiri Baraka, Pedro Pietri, Jose-Angel Figueroa, Nancy Mercado, Eddie Figueroa, Julio Dalmau, Amina Baraka, Louis Reyes Rivera, Luis Guzman, and many, many other writers, musicians, and friends showed to celebrate the passing of a man who had left a legacy of poetry and theater behind.

When a poet dies, a whole community is affected, and the Lower East Side was abuzz with despair, sadness, and the keen awareness of the solitude that was coming. We all knew we would no longer see Miky on the streets of the Lower East Side, giving and taking at will whatever and whenever he wanted.

The preparations for the ceremony of the scattering of the ashes forged an unbreakable bond between the artists and the working people of the Lower East Side. Miky had asked that his ashes be scattered

From Houston to 14th Street
from Second Avenue to the mighty D

He wanted his ashes scattered where

the hustlers & suckers meet
the faggots & freaks will all get
high
on the ashes that have been scattered
thru the Lower East Side.

Miky wanted singing. He didn't want tears. As we prepared the empty lot next to the Cafe, people came from everywhere to join our procession. A wonderful installation had been created in that garbage-strewn lot by Arturo Lindsay.

*Nuyorican (nü yòr 'ē kn) (New York + Puerto Rican) 1. Originally Puerto Rican epithet for those of Puerto Rican heritage born in New York: their Spanish was different (Spanglish), their way of dress and look were different. They were a stateless people (like most U.S. poets) until the Cafe became their homeland. 2. After Algarín and Piñero, a proud poet speaking New York Puerto Rican. 3. A denizen of the Nuyorican Poets Cafe. 4. New York's riches.

He had prepared an effigy to be burnt at the site. Drummers surrounded the installation, poets were ready to offer spontaneous testimonials at the installation, and our teacher Jorge Brandon spoke the first words. Brandon, the great master of the oral tradition at the ripe young age of 85, spoke with accuracy and pitch that belied his age and appearance. It was high oratory at its finest. The effigy was lit, and as it burned, a poet stepped up, read a poem, then dropped it into the fire; as that poem burned, another poet would step forward, recite, then drop a poem into the flames. It was clear that Miky's instructions had been letter-perfect. There was simply no other place to start the procession of the scattering of the ashes than the Nuyorican Poets Cafe, which he had founded with me. The lot was perfect—not manicured, but littered and disheveled and unpretentiously alive. We had cleared only a small circle for the installation, leaving the rest in its natural state: broken glass, strewn brick, unearthed boilers, and local garbage. The poem continued:

> There's no other place for me to be
> there's no other place that I can see
> there's no other town around that
> brings you up or keeps you down
> no food little heat sweeps by
> fancy cars & pimps' bars & juke saloons
> & greasy spoons make my spirits fly
> with my ashes scattered thru the
> Lower East Side . . .

The poem began to leap off the page and become the thing itself—words were becoming action.

I was handed the quart-sized can that contained Miky's ashes. My hands trembled as Joey Castro took the can from me. I asked him to please open it. He pulled out his pocketknife and began to pry the lid gently respectfully, and yet fearfully. I'll never forget the look on his face when the lid popped lightly and we saw the ashes for the very first time. How very odd—the frame of a man weighs less than two and a half pounds of dust. And what did I have in the quart can? I had the ashes of a man who proclaimed himself to be

> A thief, a junkie I've been
> committed every known sin
> Jews and Gentiles . . . Bums and Men
> of style . . . run away child
> police shooting wild . . .
> mother's futile wails . . . pushers
> making sales . . . dope wheelers
> & cocaine dealers . . . smoking pot
> streets are hot & feed off those who bleed to death . . .

AMERICAN RENEGADES

all that's true
all that's true
all that is true
but this ain't no lie
when I ask that my ashes be scattered thru
the Lower East Side.

So the procession left the yard on the west side of the Cafe and began its voyage through the Lower East Side in concurrence with the configuration that the poem had laid out: *From Houston to 14th Street / from Second Avenue to the mighty D.* As we walked, I would scatter the ashes and people would say, "Who's that, who goes there?" The answer would initially come from me, "It's Miky Piñero." The response would be astounding, "It's Miky Piñero!" One person would cry out, and then another, "It's Miky Piñero,' and then another, "It's Miky Piñero." It was a litany, the repetition of the rosary. People passed the word out in waves of sorrow, communicating to each other that the dispersal had begun, that Miky's ashes were being spread. Piñero was having the burial of his dreams, his poem breathing moving and bonding people. By the time we reached Avenue D the procession was huge. People walking their dogs, going into stores, and standing at the bus stops would forget the object of their mission and join us. It was as if they were impelled by a force bigger than themselves. If they were on the way to work, they didn't go. If they were on their way to the store, they wouldn't go. If they were going to the park, they didn't go. If they were walking their dog, they joined us. The murmuring grew into an audible incantation: "It's Miky Piñero, it's the poet, it's the guy who wrote *Short Eyes*, it's the guy on TV, on 'Miami Vice,' it's the guy that gave me twenty dollars when I needed it." It was the man that we all knew by many names and in many places.

Great ceremonies are followed by cataclysmic changes. After the procession ended, a great food-and-drink reception had been planned at Roland Legiardi-Laura's loft. The planning for the reception had been spontaneous and exciting. Roland had permitted the use of his place for the send-off of a great poet, and I had found what I was searching for: a big, well-lit space where we could all come to make an offering after the scattering of the ashes. The wake would be accompanied by great food, drink, and recitals. In the midst of this rejoicing, Bob Holman approached me and said, "Miguel, it's time to reopen the Cafe. This is the moment, you know, and Miky is insisting on it, and we are ready. Let's move on it, let's open the Nuyorican Poets Cafe again."

Bob Holman's words later began to unravel a need that had been lying dormant in me ever since I had closed the doors of the Cafe for what had become a prolonged period. Yes, Miky's death was to be a new beginning. From the ashes, life. From the whispered promise made by one poet to another, the oral tradition was to find a permanent home at the Nuyorican Poets Cafe.

MIGUEL PIÑERO

Seekin' the Cause

he was Dead
he never Lived
died
died
he died seekin' a Cause
seekin' the Cause
because
he said
he never saw the Cause
but
he heard the Cause
heard the cryin' of hungry ghetto children
heard the warnin' from Malcolm
heard tractors pave new routes to new prisons
died seekin' the Cause
seekin' a Cause
he was dead on arrival
he never really Lived
uptown . . . downtown . . . midtown . . . crosstown
body was found all over town
seekin' the Cause
thinkin' the Cause was 75 dollars & gator shoes
thinkin' the cause was sellin' the white lady to black
children
thinkin' the cause is to be found in gypsy rose or j.b.
or dealin' wacky weed
and singin' du-wops in the park after some chi-chiba
he died seekin' the Cause
died seekin' a Cause

and the Cause was dyin' seekin' him
and the Cause was dyin' seekin' him
and the Cause was dyin' seekin' him
he wanted a color t.v.
wanted a silk on silk suit
he wanted the Cause to come up like the mets & take the
world series
he wanted . . . he wanted . . . he wanted . . . he wanted to want more

wants but
he never gave
he never gave
he never gave his love to children
he never gave his heart to old people
&
never did he ever give his soul to his people
he never gave his soul to his people
because he was busy seekin' a Cause
busy
busy perfectin' his voice to harmonize the national anthem
with spiro t agnew
busy perfectin' his jive talk so that his flunkiness
doesn't show
busy perfectin' his viva-la-policía speech
downtown . . . uptown . . . midtown . . . crosstown
his body was found all over town
seekin' a Cause
seekin' the Cause
found
in the potter fields of an o.d.
found
in the bowery with the dt's

his legs were left in viet-nam
his arms were found in sing-sing
his scalp was on nixon's belt
his blood painted the streets of the ghetto
his eyes were still lookin' for jesus to come down on
some cloud & make everythin' all right
when jesus died in attica
his brains plastered all around the frames of the pentagon
his voice still yellin' stars & stripes 4 ever
riddled with the police bullets his taxes bought
he died seekin' a Cause
seekin' the Cause
while the Cause was dyin' seekin' him
he died yesterday
he's dyin' today
he's dead tomorrow
died seekin' a Cause
died seekin' the Cause
& the Cause was in front of him
& the Cause was in his skin
& the Cause was in his speech

& the Cause was in his blood
but
he died seekin' the Cause
he died seekin' a Cause
he died
deaf
dumb
&
blind
he died
died
  & never found his Cause
because
you see he never never
knew that he was the
Cause

Twice a Month Is Mother's Day

Waitin' for the mailman to come—early in the mornin'
'fore the junkies wake—twice a month—the 16th & the 1st—
stoop draped with people hungry eyed—&
winos dying of thirst—Mama pushed back the walls of my room
hurriedly i dress—removin' dead roaches from the coffee cup
bury 'em navy style—down the kitchen sink—
with a quick eulogy spiced with puerto rican profanity

II
Again our roommate who lives rent free & eats better than me—
has successfully 'voided the snare—& takes the prize—
Mama thinks she'll use cyanide—i don't think it makes a
difference to him or her—& don't think it works either—
If lead-paint-chippin' plaster won't kill him—i think
nothin' will—Why not consider him part of the family—
like the beautiful white people on t.v. do with their
dog & cat only difference is our pet will be a rat

III
hate coffee con powdered leche—surplus—all gone—no money too . . .

IV
Sold the cheese to don florencio el bodeguero—for two containers
of milk—today he'll sell it back . . .

AMERICAN RENEGADES

doña carmen—doña adelina—comai toñita—hurry corran he comin'
el caltero—nes builin' down—don luis hurry or the tecatos will
get your check—don luis is very old & he scared of los perdidos—
how are you ladies today—everyone says—tan ju bien—an ju—ho arl ju
don't like his smile—don't like the way he says ladies
don't like the way he says it's mother's day. . . .

V
On the first—got a paper bag did number two in it—was goin' to
drop it on his bald head—as he takes off his hat & bows to the
comadres on the stoop—after he says it's mother's day—
Mama caught me—held me—held the bag till he went away—she
     smells it—
she looks inside—she screams—out the window it went—more
     screams—
with curses too—Mama still screamin' at me—yellin' she gonna
hit me—NO she holds my arms—WHY? ¿PORQUÉ? cuz i don't like
     the
way he says it's mother's day . . .
she laughs—outside they curse—Mama starts laughin' stops laughin'
now she'll hit me—No she starts cryin'—kissin my head—
don't like seein' mama cry . . .

VI
Everyone is cryin'—they all want to change the thing with Mama
but i am the oldest i will go—protect her from . . .
like the day the big guy took Mama's purse on delancey st.
i ran behind parked cars—hidin'—he stops—i snatch it from him—
ran back—was a real hero—just like john wayne . . .

VII
Mama looks real pretty today—even doña olga looks pretty—Mama says
"have to change el checke before the collectors come around—"
doña rosa y doña maría didn't get the checke today—doña maría
she says she take the nenes to the wilfredo oficina let 'em feed 'em
everyone says sí-sí-sí-sí-sí Y que más—cuz they know she comes back
for them—Mama says she will speak for her tomorrow at the center
Mama she speaks very good english . . .

VIII
oh-oh-oh here come the tecatos—los perdidos—los motos—they will
stand there on the corner with their arms around their bellies
lookin' lookin' until . . .

AMERICAN RENEGADES

IX
AHAHAHAHaaa here comes doña rosa she is pretty—NO she is
    beauuttiiiffuullll
NO she is prettier than "pretty please with sugar on top" . . . wow
she says the investigator came around last night & almost caught
don miguel—who is the nenés tío—everyone says sí-sí-sí-sí Y que más—
didn't find don miguel—pero—he found his shoes—everyone says sí-sí-sí
Y que más she says they belong to her son rikie—he says tooooo biiiggg
everyone says sí-sí-sí-sí Y que mas—she says he now wants to sleep with
her or he'll never give back her checke & this time for good—everyone
says sí-sí-sí-sí Y que mas—she says que se va hacer
when me & Mama are leavin' i ask doña rosa why the investigator wants
to sleep with her—coño I don't even like sleepin' with my two
hermanos—everyone was feelin' good cuz they all start laughin'

X
But everyone is always happy on the 1st & on the 16th no other
days—people are always sad . . . but not today—not today—
TODAY THE WHOLE WORLD IS CHANGIN' THEIR WELFARE
    CHECK . . .

DAVID HENDERSON

Poem—Miguel Piñero
there is a procession for departed poet-playwright-santo Miguel Piñero del
lower east side

> you were a fucking movie star!—Miky
> "Short Eyes," "Fort Apache—The Bronx"
> on television—"Miami Vice"
> in one season they killed you twice
>
> they scatter your ashes
> all over the lower east side
> like you say in your poem
> and they even play a fucking videotape
> of you reading the poem
> as your ashes take to the breeze

AMERICAN RENEGADES

and then they have a party, a feast for you
miguelito *cumbia para bailar*
and at this party
I saw a Latina play an African drum
along with the *cumbia* record
playing while everyone danced
and there were others playing
and others chanting in time
when the time came
drumming   chanting   dancing
at the same time
and then at once everything in the room
became another avenue of time
Santo Latino rhythms
on the fringe of the fringe
bridges between worlds
between black and white—Miky!
cumbia para bailar

Miguel Algarín

A Mongo Affair

On the corner by the plaza
in front of
the entrance to Gonzalez-Padín
in old San Juan
a black Puerto Rican talks
about "the race"
he talks of Boricuas
who are in New York on welfare
and on lines waiting for food stamps,
"yes, it's true, they've been taken out
and sent abroad and those that
went over tell me that they're
doing better over there than here
they tell me they get money
and medical aid

that their rent is paid
that their clothes get bought
that their teeth get fixed
is that true?"
on the corner by
the entrance to Gonzalez-Padín
I have to admit that he has been
lied to, misled,
that I know that all the goodies
he named humiliate the receiver,
that a man is demoralized
when his woman and children
beg for weekly checks
that even the fucking a man does
on a government bought mattress
draws the blood from his cock
cockless, sin espina dorsal,
mongo—that's it!
a welfare fuck is a mongo affair!
mongo means flojo
mongo means bloodless
mongo means soft
mongo can not penetrate
mongo can only tease
but it can't tickle
the juice of the earth-vagina
mongo es el bicho Taino
porque murió
mongo es el borinqueño
who's been moved
to the inner-city jungles
of north american cities
mongo is the rican who survives
in the tar jungle of Chicago
who cleans, weeps, crawls,
gets ripped off,
sucks the eighty dollars a week
from the syphilitic
down deep frustrated
northern man—
viejo negro africano,
Africa Puerto Rico
sitting on department store entrances
don't believe the deadly game
of Northern cities paved with gold and plenty

AMERICAN RENEGADES

don't believe the fetching dream
of life improvement in New York
the only thing you'll find in Boston
is a soft leather shoe up your ass,
viejo, anciano africano, Washington
will send you in your old age
to clean the battlefields
in Korea and Vietnam
you'll be carrying a sack
and into that canvas
you'll pitch las uñas
los intestinos
las piernas
los bichos mongos
of Puerto Rican soldiers
put at the front to face
sí!
to face the bullets, bombs, missiles,
sí! the artillery
sí!
to face the violent hatred of Nazi Germany
to confront the hungry anger of the world
viejo negro
viejo puertorriqueno
the north offers us pain
and everlasting humiliation
IT DOES NOT COUGH UP
THE EASY LIFE: THAT IS A LIE
viejo que has visto la isla
perder sus hijos
are there guns to deal with
genocide, expatriation?
are there arms to hold
the exodus of borinqueños
from Borinquen?
we have been moved
we have been shipped
we have been parcel posted
first by water then by air
el correo has special prices
for the "low island element" to be
removed, then dumped
into the inner-city ghettos
Viejo, Viejo, Viejo
we are the minority

here in Borinquen
we, the Puerto Rican,
the original man of this island
is in the minority
I writhe with pain
I jump with anger
I know
I see
I am "la minoría de la isla"
viejo, viejo anciano
do you hear me?
there are no more Puerto Ricans
in Borinquen
I am the minority everywhere
I am among the few in all societies
I belong to a tribe of nomads
that roam the world without
a place to call a home,
there is no place that is ALL MINE
there is no place that I can
call mi casa,
I, yo, Miguel ¡ Me oyes viejo!
I, yo, Miguel
el hijo de Maria Socorro y Miguel
is homeless, has been homeless
will be homeless
in the to be
and the to come
Miguelito, Lucky, Bimbo
you like me have lost
your home
and to the first idealist
I meet
I'll say
don't lie to me
don't fill me full of vain
disturbing love for an island
filled with Burger Kings
for I know
there are no cuchifritos
in Borinquen
I remember last night
viejito lindo
when your eyes fired me
with trust

do you hear that?
with trust
and when you said
that you would stand by me
should any danger threaten
I halfway threw myself
into your arms to weep
mis gracias
I loved you
viejo negro
I would have slept
in your arms
I would have caressed
your curly gray hair
I wanted to touch
your wrinkled face
when your eyes fired me
with trust
viejo corazón puertorriqueño
your feelings cocinan
en mi sangre
el poder de realizarme
and when you whispered
your anger into my ears
when you spoke of
"nosotros los que estamos
preparados con las armas"
it was talk of future
happiness
my ears had not till
that moment heard such
words of promise and of guts
in all of Puerto Rico
old man with the golden chain
and the medallion with an indian
on your chest
I love you
I see in you
what has been
what is coming
and will be
and over your grave
I will write
HERE SLEEPS

A MAN
WHO SEES ALL OF
WHAT EXISTS
AND THAT WHICH WILL EXIST.

John Bennet

Ode to My Mother

Something's gone awry askew askance somewhere, this disconcerted rhythm this discordant symphony of my brain this terrible mix of lucid light and clinical disease; alzheimer's, let's call it that, this dit-dit-dat that keeps delving thru my word bank, a strange merge of August chrome and a decaying maze of neurons, the same message that came dimly for the dim from the caved-in tunnel of my mother's life, the faint (not dim) persistent tapping, the dit-dit-dat of her urgent shutdown cry, and me listening all my days, my ear to the coaldust iron earth in my Communion virgin whites, bony-kneed child who stood spread-eagle at the threshold of her trance to keep them out to keep them from going in there with their glib insufficient tools to make matters only worse.

And now she's gone, tough old Irish saint who never took her fierce eye from the lodestar of her deepest meaning. They had her down to 80 pounds with tubes and fancy gizmos, they had her translated into Latin names they could neither hex nor find a cure for, they drank her blood and ate her flesh and turned her bones to trinkets. They mauled her noble face with rouge and sold her to the highest bidder. White boys in a limo drove her off before her skin'd grown cold and black men with a back-hoe placed her in the earth in the shadow of the nation's war room before the needle of our numbness found our vein of grief.

Life, said a colonel at her grave side, holding up an eagle clutching arrows and the cross of Jesus, must go on; and he led us like an usher from my mother's grave, her coffin still suspended in the air. I turned back and told the black men—put her down. They did, and I buried my fingers in the moist soil to which she'd soon return and sent a handful raining down upon her coffin.

Now, nine months later, the time it takes a human life to form, the first cry of loss escapes me, skinny boy in soot-black virgin white, and I raise my fist from my iron loveless past and leaping high, lock my legs around the sun and fuck it blind.

A Wish Come True

Who knows what the good Lord has in store. Just about everything. Shelves stocked to the ceiling, coiled hemp on big spikes hammered into raw timber, glass jars of soft cloying candy, dark ugly-tasting liquid to drive out gout and evil thought, nail clippers and three-mast clippers with pre-billowed sails, waiting to carry your dreams away. And under the counter, between the ball bat and chess board, a mace gun filled with disappointment. It's all there waiting for you to enter the shop with your little list that mommy made, that teachers tagged things onto, the list inspired by example, the list that once everything has been crossed out will make your wish come true.

Some angel with acne puts it all in paper bags and two more help you to your car. You slam the trunk shut, start the engine and look both ways. Still blocks from home, you're stricken blind or your heart explodes. Worse yet, nothing happens, but when you try to put the key into the front-door lock, your hand is shaking and spotted brown.

Inside, you slump down on the couch, the bags on the floor beside you. Everything is in order, has been for years. The clock is lopping off the heads of seconds on its tiny chopping block, and the cat is sunning on the window sill. You doze. Every now and then you surface, try to remember what comes next. Someone will find you there, long after your message machine hits overload and your dial tone fades. There are procedures for cleaning up a mess like this. They're followed, and life goes on.

Much Ado About Nothing

Sometimes I feel like a motherless child. The obsession with uniqueness is the one relentless constant in human evolution. We set ourselves apart and then corrode with loneliness. We invent a machine to spank our champion chess player and then fret ourselves into a frenzy. What does it mean to be human, we cry out, and being human, we're left without an answer.

Pure laughter is the highest form of intelligence. A computer will never laugh. Program one to do it and see how it makes you feel when the thing starts making its noise. Technology is how we mock ourselves.

Wanting to know yourself is the worst form of schizophrenia. You can't know what you are. You can only be what you are. Wishing to be God, we become nothing. It is, after all, as plain as the nose on your face.

Top of the morning and a tip of the hat to you, fine sir. Excuse me while I shuffle off to Buffalo in my baggy trousers. Down along the railroad tracks rusted with progress. Smelling roses and weeds with reckless indifference. Cloaked in secrets never meant to be accessed. Whistling, by God, like a bird on a wire packed tight and humming with a fast current of useless information supposed to pry my imagination. Face turned to the sun where everything is straightforward and warm.

There is no such thing as artificial insemination. A stallion mounting a mare in the greenness of a high mountain valley spawns ponies that cannot be cloned.

Reasons to Drink

Living on the edge is a way of life for the alkie, his dubious refuge, the place normies stay away from. And if they show up, they're only slumming—one taste of rusty pain and they disappear like smoke. Normies confuse pain with nobility. Pain is when nobility has been battered into garbage. Garbage in the hot August sun. Try waking up at high noon behind one of those big blue Dempsey Dumpsters with the smell of garbage the first thing that assaults your senses. Then you smell shit and piss and then you feel it and then you look down and you see the wide stain on your trousers.

This club is full of treachery and danger. Potential saints. You've got to knock Paul off his horse with lightning to get the makings of a saint. You've got to rob Augustine of his carnal ways. St. Augustine giving head to a vestal virgin on a bearskin rug in front of a flagstone hearth, when out of nowhere the Holy Ghost enters him from behind. Normies don't have the right stuff for sainthood. It takes Judas to whisper the cold facts in Christ's ear. Normies show up at the funeral after the carnage has been hosed away, after the mortician's iceman cosmetology. They circle kitsch with halos and fall down on their knees.

Molecular Conspiracy

Molecular structure. Of things, of thought. The molecules of dream. Of illusion. Fulgent fulgurations on the face of time, routing logic's drum and bugle corps. The tabernacle empty.

Wild tulips, cunt-petal pink and yellow as a cat's eye, crayon marks of Zen-snap affirmation. I have this in my day, and a coffee house buzzing like a hive, bodies arcing, hummingbird eyes darting, mouths clashing head-on. Matadors of diversion, poised to plunge the sword and win the roaring approbation, rose petals and a señorita's smile.

Each day I rise up from the world of dream into illusion, cast my bones across the nothingness that incubates both time and space and ask myself: What next? A precarious beginning for a day.

Receiving no answer, I set about the all-important task of recreating myself. Still naked, I open the front door and let the dog go bounding thru the grass. Then I pull the blinds and let the light in. Next I run hot water in a tub and brush my teeth. I walk steaming in a blue bathrobe about the house, toasting bread, brewing coffee, slicing grapefruit. I eat these things and cap them with a self-rolled cigarette.

Playing the Game

Nine-eleven-96—hike the ball to the split-end the tight-end to the end of the known world fling the fucker between your legs and prepare to meet your maker as an army of 300-pounders beefed up on steroids and quarter-pounders comes rolling over you but what the fuck what the hell let the thunder die in your ears as they go on their merry way in hot pursuit and then pick yourself up and limp over to the sidelines where the coach will slap you on the ass and the waterboy will slap you on the ass and all the guys on the bench jump up and slap you on the ass you did your job you set the ball in motion and even tho you're no 6-digit superstar you're essential to the game and people speak of you fondly if they speak of you at all which they really don't that much and ten years down the line maybe less probably more like five when you're drunk on a stool in the last of the skidrow bars even the bartender won't know your name and he's been a sports fan since before he could walk which you can barely manage yourself drunk all the time on cheap wine and one day you can't even go in there you're on a park bench in a big overcoat with no pants underneath no pants and a ridiculous pajama top and no you're no pervert this is just what it's come down to and here comes that cop on a horse again twirling his billy move on move on the words echoing in your confusion you look around but there's no place left to go and then you look up and there is this world of winter branches latticed against a blue sky. Something lifts something lifts bigtime go there you think go there and you do.

JOHN FARRIS

Some Profession

Fortunately for you the blood was clean
as you took his ear into your mouth, siphoning his sweat
as you bit down on cartilage with those iron teeth of yours, and having
gotten what you wanted, contemptously spat it to the canvas.
You might have swallowed it as did your progenitors once when they

were kings, testicles and all when they ate a man, taking in his whole
measure at a gulp, becoming what they ate thereby.

It could not have been a picnic to have become your own worst enemy,
but the way he was hitting on you, the way he danced you around,
he could have tried to take your shorts off, the robe off, cross-
dressed you right and left, belt long gone already, spanked you
as if you were a brand new baby taking his first breath, violated you.

Iron Mike—the New Kid on the Block, getting his natural ass kicked
in front of all those people—millions of them, for all
those millions of millions: what were you expected to do—be
the Marquis of Queensbury? You had to come up with something.

Brother

If you came to town right now, you would be a ghost: where
the cop stood waving away the curious was the last place
I saw you; you weren't even dead then, just hurt
that they picked you up like a stray

cat, promising to cut you down like a dog if you
moved. You said it was like having your own individual
gas chamber when they slapped you as hard as they did
into the patrol car, slapping you again when you

shouted to the black one that, Hey—your rights
were being violated, & his skin should have entitled
you to better treatment, that the battering & all the name-
calling were unnecessary. I heard him when he told you

that his skin wasn't in it, that it was your own
that was suspect, your own that you had to watch
out for, slapping you again for emphasis
as they drove off with you. I heard you cursing.

I heard that when they took off the handcuffs
& told you to strip, you struggled against
them, & they had to tie you down, they had to sap
all the struggle from you. I never heard from you after that.

AMERICAN RENEGADES

Imago

This is what I get: two minutes with you in an elevator. Going
    up was never
so fast—so dizzying—nor going down. Imagine if we had gotten
stuck together
between the twenty third & twenty fourth floors

just once, & we'd
have had to share our lunches while the maintenance men
were called
to unstick us, & after hours, our
emergences from our metal chrysalis like twins—it would have been
difficult to separate, so I would have hoped to join
    you
for another bite of something. This time
I would have your ear. You'd

have needed a hand
getting out
of the elevator. I'd have gladly
given you mine, except the

ride could not have gone more smoothly, gliding without so much
    as
a whisper, down to the lobby,
where you disgorged yourself, indicating nothing—not
a scent, not a smile; nothing.

Note to Lorca

Tourist—
        if you
had looked
into my eyes
on your great visit the caged
animal that staring back as it did
would have surprised you
would have been me, surprised
by what I could only have described
as a patronizing attitude, probably
a politician, I would have said to myself. (If
I had had

a bicycle, I would have ridden
it over your foot: if
as a consequence you would have
had to stay home
from the war, you would
probably be

alive now, most
likely, quite popular.)

SONIA SANCHEZ

A Poem for Jesse

your face like
summer lightning
gets caught in my voice
and i draw you up from
deep rivers
taste your face of a
thousand names
see you smile
a new season
hear your voice
a wild sea pausing in the wind.

On Passing thru Morgantown, Pa.

i saw you
vincent van
gogh perched
on those pennsylvania
cornfields communing
amid secret black
bird societies. yes.
i'm sure that was

you exploding your
fantastic delirium
while in the
distance
red indian
hills beckoned.

Father Daniel Berrigan

Poet, priest and social activist, Daniel Berrigan was born May 9, 1921, in Two Harbors, Minnesota, to a devout German Catholic family. His father, a railroad engineer, expected "nothing less than perfection" from Daniel and his five brothers. Daniel entered the Society of Jesus (Jesuits) in 1939 and was ordained a Catholic priest in 1952. Berrigan once wrote that he became a Jesuit because "they had a revolutionary history."

Remaining true to that history, Berrigan quickly became an "unsettler," leaving his mark on Church and country in his fight against violence and for peace. "Peace is something that has to be done," Berrigan once remarked, "with your heart and your hands like love." Berrigan was a leader of the religious opposition to the war in Vietnam. In 1968, Daniel, his brother Philip and seven others were arrested in Cantonsville, Maryland for burning draft files with homemade napalm in opposition to the war. "The Cantonville Nine" received international attention for their protest, inspiring Berrigan to write what became a successful play about the trial. In 1980, Berrigan and others (including Philip) entered the G.E. nuclear weapons manufacturing plant and hammered on an unarmed nuclear nosecone, symbolically "beating swords into ploughshares." Berrigan has been arrested hundreds of times for his acts of civil disobedience against preparations for war.

Berrigan is a prolific writer—publishing fifty books to date which include prose, poetry, and drama. He is perhaps best known for his poetry. His first volume of poetry, *Time Without Numbers*, published at the suggestion of poet Marianne Moore and later nominated for the National Book Award, was awarded the prestigious Lamont Prize for Poetry from the American Academy of Arts and Letters. Many of his poems have been composed from jail cells, safe houses and locations around the world. His work and life have inspired thousands around the world, including Thomas Merton, Dorothy Day, Rabbi Abraham Heschel and Buddhist leader Thich Nhat Hahn. Actor Martin Sheen wrote, "Mother Teresa drove me back to Catholicism, but Daniel Berrigan keeps me there." Yet, Berrigan has as many critics as he has supporters. Although he is hailed by many as a pacifist and a prophet, he has been labeled a "fanatic," a "terrorist" and a "misguided anarchist."

ALAN KAUFMAN

Prophecy

The way I see the world is strictly illegal
to wit, through my eyes

is illegal, yes;
to wit, I live
like a pickpocket, like the sun
like the hand that writes this, by my wits

This is not permitted
that I look on the world
and worse, insist that I see

what I see
—a conundrum, a fury, a burning bush

and with five fingers, where my eyes fail
trace—
with a blackened brush
on butcher sheets, black on white
(black for blood, white for death
where the light fails)

—that face which is not my own
(and my own)
that death which is not my own
(and my own)

This is strictly illegal
and will land me in trouble

as somewhere now, in a precinct
in a dock, the statutes
thrash in fury, hear them
hear ye!
the majestic jaws

of crocodiles in black shrouds
the laws
forbidding me
the world, the truth
under blood oath

forbidding, row upon row
of razors, of statutes
of molars, of grinders—

those bloodshot eyes
legal, sleepless, maneating

—not letting me
not
let blood

Children in the Shelter

Imagine; three of them.

As though survival
were a rat's word,
and a rat's death
waited there at the end

and I must have
in the century's boneyard
heft of flesh and bone in my arms

I picked up the littlest
a boy, his face
breaded with rice (his sister calmly feeding him
as we climbed down)

In my arms fathered
in a moment's grace, the messiah
of all my tears. I bore, reborn

a Hiroshima child from hell.

Rehabilitative Report: We Can Still Laugh

In prison you put on your clothes
and take them off again.
You jam your food down
and shit it out again
You round the compound right
to left and right again.
The year grows irretrievably old
so does your hair burn white.
The mood; one volt above
one volt below survival,
roughly per specimen, space
sufficient for decent burial.

Georgetown Poems (7)
The Trouble With Our State

The trouble with our state
was not civil disobedience
which in any case was hesitant and rare

Civil disobedience was rare as kidney stone
No, rarer; it was disappearing like immigrants' disease

You've heard of a war on cancer?
There is no war like the plague of media
There is no war like routine
There is no war like 3 square meals
There is no war like a prevailing wind

It blows softly; whispers
don't rock the boat!
the sails obey, the ship of state rolls on.

The trouble with our state
—we learned it only afterward
when the dead resembled the living who resembled the dead
and civil virtue shone like paint on tin
and tin citizens and tin soldiers marched to the common whip

—our trouble
the trouble with our state

with our state of soul
our state of seige—
was
Civil
obedience

ASSATA SHAKUR

Assata Shakur has been living in Cuba since 1986, after escaping from prison where she was serving a life sentence imposed in a highly disputed trial. Assata was a Black Panther, then a Black Liberation Army (BLA) leader in the early '70s, so she was a target of the FBI's COINTELPRO operation. Assata was captured in an infamous police action in 1973 on the New Jersey State Turnpike, in which a State Trooper was killed. One of Assata's traveling companions was also killed.

Assata refers to herself as a "20th century escaped slave." However the New Jersey State government has made it clear that they plan on getting her back. The State Police have stated "we would do everything we could to get her off the island of Cuba, and if that includes kidnapping, we would do it." New Jersey Governor Christine Todd Whitman has indicated that she will "not rest" until Assata Shakur is back in custody in New Jersey. Whitman has petitioned Congress, the Pope, and the President of the United States to pressure Cuba to extradite Assata. Most recently she appealed to mercenaries and soldiers of fortune. She has announced and continues to publicize a $100,000 bounty for Assata's return.

JERI SMITH

Culture

i must confess that waltzes
do not move me.
i have no sympathy
for symphonies.

i guess i hummed the Blues
too early,
and spent too many midnights
out wailing to the rain.

Story

You died.
I cried.
And kept on getting up.
A little slower.
And a lot more deadly.

HUBERT SELBY, JR.

Psalm XVI

PRELUDE
GOD SPEAKS
Whoever seeks me finds me,
Whoever finds me knows me,
Whoever knows me loves me,
Whoever loves me I love,
Whomever I love, I kill.

Sidna Ali the Moslem (9TH CENTURY)

Song of Forgiveness
Why do You hate us with an everlasting scorn?

We cry out to You so pained
There are those of us who do not survive!
Yet You remain mute.
We believe in You
Yet You turn the other cheek to our suffering.
How can You carrot so much in front of our hearts
As they wither and fall,
Desiccated into the gutter,
Defiled by Your silence,
Writhing with unsung songs?

Our blood flows,
Sparks leap from synapse to synapse,
But only to torture us,

Agonize us,
With blood cursed by our minds,
Knees not only bent
But raw and chewed with grit and vinegar, and
We too become mute
But not with indifference
But the pain of abandonment.
Endlessly we fight our demons
As they flay us
Mock us, and
Jeer
As they tear the eyes from our heads,
Powder our bones with jagged teeth, and
Spit us out in hopeful
Terrorized bits
That struggle to crawl together—
In Your name—
IN YOUR FUCKING MYRIAD OF NAMES
Trying to find that ineffable self
In, or
Beyond
The bloody and bloodied scraps,
Only to face Your Impenetrable silence, and
The drooling, relentless demons who,
Time after time tear and shred us,
Their breath befouled by our putrefying flesh.

Ive looked in Your direction
(and what direction can I look that is not Yours?)
And have been soothed with beauty,
The heaviness of my heart lifted
When I hear Your song as a stranger asks:
Can I help you?
But always . . . ALWAYS
The song turns to screeching derision
As the laughing child
And smiling rose
Twist into demons claws and
I can not run,
My legs unable to bear the weight
Of my hollow and tortured body
Because my knees are ripped
And splintered from supplication
And you strengthen me
Just enough to once again face the demons and

Smell my decayed flesh and
Dreams on their breath. . . .
O yes, You strengthen me,
But only so I can once more provide an
Object to be tortured, and
Yes, You lead me, but only to the playground
Of my tormentors, and
From time to time
I am nailed to the cross to watch
As friends are led by Your promises
Into the arena and
I see and
Hear
Their torment,
All of my being rent from their cries
As their flesh is slowly peeled, and
Hear the screams of each tear as it rolls slowly
Down their bloodied bodies
Crying, weeping
Because their God of Love,
The Source of Infinite Comfort,
Has once again abandoned them, and
Mis-lead them
Yet again, and
In my hopelessness
Vow to never again trust You,
Yet even as I do, knowing that You
Have ordained I will seek You
Until I find You and am
Filled with Love and Strength, and
Reach out and hold Your Hand
To be lead back to that arena.

The cross Dissolves
My friends agony rips my ears and heart,
Though their tortured parts and bits are
Mute and I make a vow
From the depths of my heart,
A declaration from the place
Within me that goes beyond this body,
Beyond my soul,
Beyond my understanding,
To never treat my friends the way
You do. . . .
A vow to never turn my back on them

AMERICAN RENEGADES

As you do,
No matter what the appearance.
You may
For Ever
Abuse Your children, but
I refuse to pass the abuse on.
In, and from, the depths of my tortured mind
And body
I will accept the responsibility of the decision
to respect life
ALL LIFE
And to treat Life with Love and Kindness.

No God,
NO!!!!
There is no forgiveness for You!!!!
But I will forgive the demons,
Those helpless tools of
Your assemblage, and
Love my friends,
Comfort them,
Help them find all their separated, tortured selves,
Bathe their wounded knees and
Help them stand with dignity,
Help them stand on legs with
Unbent knees, and
Together look the demons in their eyes and
Love them as
Their claws maul our flesh,
Their teeth splinter our bones
For the last time!!!!
We are Your victims
No more and
In our innocence shall
Love ourselves and
Each other to
Freedom.

POSTLUDE

I said to the almond tree: "Speak to me of God."
And the almond tree blossomed.

BILL SHIELDS

a chipped black hole

her smile
was the grave

& her eyes
the elevator to Hell

I put out my hand

she knew what I was

MICHAEL GIZZI

In the Vicinity of a Grocer

Nothing doing but squirrels
Watching crime novels
Minutes before it wasn't vintage
But the curious way wind holes in the maple
Makes me wonder Professor Moriarty wasn't
Drinking last night with the North Wind

Elsewhere a bastion of ensuing edges
Makes pledges of willpower
Over to Powerless Landing
At least we're not trepanned in Caledonia

I don't dig the kitchen table dead
And I'll pass on the brouhaha
You made a printout of, your family
Now in limbo of first apartment cutlery
But that was January which needs no secretaries

We'd like to change but continue
According to formula and heat, our greeter
Seems to be growing an ermine badger
In addition to 78 epaulets when
If anything it's an activity chimp
He's carried 30 years psi

Wonderful to discuss western potluck
On the delegate's couch, on specific nights
Wipe out people and bus the hatchet
But what about the other two arms
And legs expanding without church approval?
Hell, that's just a chair we discontinued in the
Sad defunct what else to do spread yourself green
Anybody wants to see someone
Better raise a hand, we're not
Going to heaven in a group
And more than likely your attackee
Will go to court growing pains

You can return to the coalmine now Apollo
The vanishing point is erased and my
Solitude knows yours, gave me
Quite a thrashing the other night
I'll have to mend my speech
It's getting dark around the rope
And older trances no less toxic
Like love is embarrassing

MIKE GOLDEN

Lungs of Glass

I used to live there myself
so I feel sorry for them
as their addiction cries out,
Pull, suck, bring the clouds into my throat!

Soon snipers, bounty hunters
will be on the prowl
hovering from rooftops
as the poor bastards crouch in doorways
for that forbidden fix

On the next wheeze the time will be over—
Pop goes the will! That quick
marks the time, comes the passing
of more than few good habits
lost in the nostalgia
of early morning phlegm.

Belmondo in *Breathless*
lying face down, the butt burning by his side
was an image like cool hanging out
of the lips—*Don't fuck with me, man!*
Don't fuck with me!

Can you see the vulnerability
through the lens: Life is
like this mirror
we look through
the other side of our desire
and hang out
wanting ourselves, our
coolest possible selves
to spit in the face of the void
like it means nothing,
nada, bitch,
not a thing.

WALLACE BERMAN

Untitled

Art is Love is God

AMERICAN RENEGADES

Opos

Sliding on hip knees thru cyrptic
Rose-lit circles poet Johnson
Wieners Grand Duchess of the five
Dollar matchbox   yr face reflecting
Thousands of terrestrial years now
Confined continuing in secret
Experiments no longer performed
Openly transpose & fool around
          Hippomancy, the Celtic
Trick with white horses. Out

Boxed City

My beautiful wife
Rearranges deaf photographs   talks
Rococo & dances off four walls
Son Tosh pencils the faithful
Image & ingnores the subtle rama

Stoned in black corduroy I continue
To separate seeds
          From the bulk.

First & Last Fearpoem

If only we can split
Before the Curtain drops.

The Man swings close   bust eyes
Ace with dozen heads racked
His funk his down home fink
Im clean my   buzz has its base
From the juice of the Czechoslovakian
          Nectar: Tequila.

Demonstrator and Cop

Wallace Berman 1976

Untitled
For John Birch & Karl Marx

If someone will explain Chinese perspective to me—I will elaborate on
the Choctaw & Cherokee blood in Jack Dempsey.

MAURA O'CONNOR

Gravity

Today I am fragile
pale
twitching
insane and full of purpose.

I'm thinking of my lover:
my soft hips pressing his coarse belly,
my tongue on a salmon nipple,
his hand buried in my thick orange hair
the telephone ringing.

I'm thinking we tend our illnesses
as if they are our children:
fevered
screaming
demanding attention and twenty dollar bills,
hours we could have spent
making love with the television on.

Faith is a series of calculations
made by an idiot savant.
I'm in love.
I'm alone
in this city of painted boxes
stacked like alphabet blocks
spelling nothing.

There are things I know:
trees don't sing
birds don't sprout leaves
the sky never turns to wine
roses bloom because that's what roses do,
whether we write poems for them
or not.

I concentrate on small things:
ivy threaded through chain link,
giveaway kittens huddled in a soggy cardboard box,
a fat man blowing harmonica
through a beard of rusty wires
brown birds chattering furiously on power lines.

I try not to think about
lung cancer, AIDS,
the chemicals in the rain;
things I can't imagine any more than
a color I've never seen

My heart is graffiti on the side of a subway train,
a shadow on the wall made by a child.
Nothing has been fair since my first skinned knee
I believe death
must be.

I cling to love as if it were an answer.
I go on buying eggs and bread,
boots and corsets,
knowing I'll burn out before the sun.

I'm thinking of
the days I tried to stay awake
while the billboards and T.V. ads
for condoms, microwave brownies, and dietetic jello
lulled me to sleep.

A brown-eyed girl once told me a secret
that should have blown this city
into a mass of unconnected atoms
Our sewage is piped to the sea.
Beggars in the street
are hated for having the nerve
to die in public.

AMERICAN RENEGADES

Charity requires paperwork,
Relief requires medication

as if we were the afterthoughts of institutions
greater than our rage.

Gravity chains us to the asphalt with such grace
we think it is kind.

We all go on buying lottery tickets
Diet Coke and toothpaste
as if the sky over our heads
were the roof of a gilded cage.

We provide evidence that we were here:
initials cut into cracked vinyl bus seats,
into trees growing from squares
in concrete,
a name left on a stone, an office building,
a flower, a disease, a museum
a child.

Tonight the stars glitter like rhinestones
on a black suede glove.

In the coffin my room has become,
I talk to God
about the infrequency of rain
about people who can't see the current of gentleness
running under the pale crust of my skin.

I tell him under
the jackhammer crack, the diesel truck rumble,
even the clicking sound traffic lights make
switching from yellow to red,
there is a silence
swallowing
every song,
conversation,
every whisper made beside graves
or in the twisted white sheets of love.

I tell him I can't fill it
with dark wine, blue pills,
a pink candle lit at the altar

the lover
touching my hair.

God doesn't answer.
God doesn't know our names.

He's only the architect
designing the places we occupy
like high rise offices or ant hills

I know this
the way I know
sunrise and sunset
are caused by the endless turning
of the Earth.

Testimony

These days
I cover my face with bottled skin
and scented creams
stain my lips the color of rose juice
wear black
my eyes deepen

The man who once called me
that girl in the white shirt
is my lover

He carried me home in a magician's casket
cut me in two
I came out whole

I'm a kindness to climb into
a Dresden doll found in the basement
of a burnt house

These days
I buy the book with the ugliest cover
comb the thick orange hair
of the innocent child
I never was

While my heroes are knocked down
like pinatas
while we wear surgical gloves
to the laying on of hands

I've folded suicide in four
laid it on a bare white shelf
someday it may gather dust
I might toss it away like an old dishrag
I'm young
green as bread mold

I'm seeking witness

I want the testimony of
Hitler
Stalin
the shadows on the bricks
of Nagasaki

These days
the newspapers serve a menu of clay pigeons
bring your own bullets

I want to ban the colors of the television
the perfect thighs
and plastic wishes
I want to put my next breath
in my lover's mouth
I want to burn Jesus leaflets
and wear his sandals

I'm taking it all off
in the bars of my ribcage

While the politicians find work
for each idle child
while two terminal patients
place bets on the existence of God

These days
I show the years when I didn't want to live
in the gray spokes of my iris
I'm coming apart like a ten-cent toy

I carry my head under my arm
like a rag doll

I want to sleep in the ruin
of last night's makeup
I want ancient recipes over instant rice

I want to find the hummingbird graveyard
I want to fill my mouth with black beetles
and walk the edge of Eden

I need a new commandment

I will collect single bars of old songs
I will weep a page of black ink
I will be an unprotected witness

My country serves three-day notice
to the starving
my country's hands are tattooed
on the belly of a battered child
my country sleeps in the snow of the television
after its anthem is played

Let's burn the country
and keep the flag

This night is falling in pieces
this moon is cream on a raisin sky

I will evolve thick skin and filter
I will plan my next breath

I will watch the four riders
foam their horses into glue

It isn't over yet

At the End

You sold your computer without backing up the hard disk,
    losing a novel in progress

AMERICAN RENEGADES

You set fire to the wall in your room by nodding out
        with a candle lit

Those last days you tried to convince me you had it under
        control, were only shooting a little bit, and
        the next hospital trip you'd clean up for good

I found your wasted naked body in a filthy room after
        you didn't come to the phone for three days
The coroner asked if you had cancer. I said, "No, he just
        stopped eating."

You spent your life chasing a moment without pain—
With: steaks and Ben & Jerry's
        12 step meetings and bottles of Snapple
        with Vicodan and Jack water back
        with dreams as big as Africa
As you lay alone in your room, 300 pounds of insolent child
With: three herniated disks
        hemorrhoids that bled so much you actually needed
                a transfusion
        peripheral neuropathy, sciatica,
        pounding headaches no pill could cure
        a painfully twisted wrist broken in a manic blackout

and days where you were working for God and he wanted
        you to take a fifty-dollar cab ride to some burnt-out
        East Oakland neighborhood where the pharmacy was
        crooked

and days where getting out of bed was like taking the last
        four steps to the guillotine

and a scar where a pharmacist shot you
        a scar where a crack pipe burned you
        a scar buried so deep it was a secret even to yourself

Yet somehow you believed in a sip from the Holy Grail,
        a best-selling novel that would buy you a house full of
        Himalayan cats with a yard dotted with flowers or
        one of your poems sparking a revolution of beautiful
        misfits in black or
        the kind of fame where you read your work in electrified
        stadiums with a famous rock band as the opening act

And that hopeless hope made you
    beautiful as Aphrodite in a giant seashell
    loveable as a basket of kittens
      intense as a jeweller inspecting a diamond that's
        going to make him rich

In the end it wasn't the wine that went to your head

DAVID MELTZER

When I was 11 years old I started writing poetry & was turned around by the music of Bebop & the hipster culture of Birdland & The Royal Roost; but was too young to participate in anything other than listening to the music at the clubs. When I migrated to Hollywood w/ my father I'd been writing poetry for 5 years & still thought I'd invented it. In LA I fell into the postwar artist scene, primarily under the mentorship of Wallace Berman & Bob Alexander (also known as Baza), & felt comfortable in the hipster urban marginal counterculture which had some of its roots in the earlier left Popular Front arts movements of the late 30s & war years. Read Ferlinghetti & Ginsberg & Corso at the open-air newsstand I used to work at for an old Jewish lady on Western & Hollywood Boulevard. But always felt Allen & Kerouac were "middle-aged" guys, elders, not my peers. When I got to San Francisco I'd already written too much work & my education continued at informal poetry workshops at Joe Dunn's flat mentored by Robert Duncan & Jack Spicer & in the company of contemporaries like John Wieners, Joanne Kyger, Richard Brautigan. I also started doing poetry & jazz at The Jazz Cellar during that brief Beat moment &, again, felt my elders like Rexorth & Ferlinghetti were miles away from the improvisational demands of jazz, even though I appreciated their work & especially delighted in Rexroth's range & blustery spirit. Friendships with McClure, Lew Welch, Phil Whalen, Bob Kaufman, Diane DiPrima, amplified my ongoing but unaffiliated development as a poet. By the time the mid 60s unfolded I was in my early 30s (therefore untrustworthy), even though I was involved w/ rock & roll as a performer & bandleader (a couple of albums for Vanguard & one for Capitol), I was more deeply embedded in jazz & experiment. To top it off, I became drawn to Kabbalah through the agency of Robert Duncan & Gershom Scholem & began publishing *Tree*, a bi-annual journal of classical kabbalistic translations & modernist poetry around kabbalah generated themes (e.g., Yetzirah, Shekinah, Messiah, Ra'a). Poets like Jerome Rothenerg & Jack Hirschman were supportive of this venture, but I alienated other poets. Let's just say that as an alter kaker (& still on the planet) I've been tagged by the Beat team, the SF Renaissance brokers, as well as the Psychedelic 60s mythographers. The only cadre that haven't roped me onto their ferriswheel are the Language poets, even though I'm particularly fond of Lyn Hejinian, Michael Palmer, Ron Silliman, & Clark Coolidge is a very old friend, in fact he was the drummer for our rockband, Serpent Power in the late 60s & in Mix in the mid 90s. Go figure. I'm somewhere, but also nowhere. During 1968–69 I wrote 10 agit-smut novels—4 were reissued a couple of years ago (*The Agency Trilogy* & *Orf*). For many readers, those works were hard to compute w/ the ecstatic poetry of domestic life & kabbalah. But I was always clear that the mystery is ordinary & that the ordinary is the mystery.

Who knows? Why does one have to belong anywhere in order to belong?

DAVID MELTZER

From *Beat Thing*

ka-chung

Beat ephemera fills up shoeboxes mice nest in

Beat lounge acts at Ramada Inn bars near airports

Beat cruise mingle w/ Beat survivors sit at Captain's table w/ poete du
jour & dance to elderly bebop band at night win costume-contest feed
    sharks
masterpieces harpoon beached wails have a bunch of books signed by
    blind
bard riffing disenchanties adored singing up from the waxed floor his
    high
led to

Beat correspondence school ads on TV John Saxon reads off the course
offerings

Beat fairs rent space w/ tables of books, berets, records, leotards,
videocassettes, CDs, posters, 8 × 10 glossies, period antiquities in
bakelite, chrome, tigerskin pincushion vinyl, pushbutton cherry gizmos,
classic Tupperware in stacks (it's really the looks not the books)

Beat things shrink inside outsize sweaters wedge into room corners away
from lone candle jammed in wax caked wine bottle; Beat gamins & Jack
    Spratt
artistes shade-goggled eyes above black turtleneck rims

Beat wax museums in Fisherman's Wharf downtown Lowell McDougal
     Street &
Beat Thing Hall of Fame wing of Planet Hollywood on Sunset Boulevard

Beat leftovers second-stringers impersonators at Beat fests & contests for
the best Kerouac & Burroughs while in another hotel Elvises spangle
     glitter
lip curl compete for credibility

Beat kareoke franchises

Beat Generation (the musical) touring show at burb malls & civic
     centers;
Beat 900 numbers for phone bop prosody or Mamie Van Doren clone
     phone sex
bongo

Beat flesh pixeled jigsaw bricolage CD Roms; Beat DNA flash-frozen
     sperm &
eggs at Better Baby Boutiques new stock added weekly as oldtimers give
     it
up before drying up

Beat bulk lurch to lunch through plateglass posh chez cafe doors pour
     blood
over crisp white linen tablecloths fans magic act away for wall hangings

Beat thing headbutts into corporate conference room where suits hold
     out
pens for him to marathon grab as he signs contract after contract stacks
     up
a big deal

the agent Charlie McCarthy's a propped up Beat body against press
conference wall

Beat superstar on MTV fastcut scratch 50's newsreel footage intercut w/
sitcom knows best voices over Kurt Loder asks Burroughs about killing
     his
wife

Beat CEO of media congealment spars w/ Bill Gates in razor-sharp
     khakis &
Italian soft leather loafers for global ownership of poetry on Charlie Rose

Beat creature from black lagoon dips spoon into tub of Ben & Jerry
   Kerouac
Carmel Walnut Chunk Satori

Beat nix sticks pen into toxic state of inc (orporation) to finish epic PR
for Disney Beatsville urban mall themepark

Beat infomercial Anne Waldman hosting looks cool in new do & black
   silk
sheath & stockings insouciant red beret w/ Beat bodyguards Ginsberg
Burroughs on each side of the overlit divan
Beat website with pot leaf wreathed logo of Ginsberg Kerouac Burroughs
mother son holyghost

Beat tour jackets T-shirts numbered prints of Beat photos by Redl Stoll
McDarrah framed offered round the clock on Beat shopping channel

Beat Gap line of chinos lumberjack flannel shirts Dr. Dean beat shades
   Joe
Camel unfiltered beat smokes Armani blue black basement zoots to suit
   up in
& walk down to theme bar restaurant Coolsville chain owned by three
publishers owned by a transglobal media conglomerate owned by a
   network of
oil companies owned by a consortium of arms dealers owned by a clot of
   drug
producers owned by a massive webwork of Swiss bankers & German
   brokers in
silent partnership with Japanese alchemists in collusion with Chinese
gerontologists as proxies for Reverend Moon

Beat mercenary high steppers bottom feeders set up emporia marts in
   college
towns & fast food dance halls troughs underwrit by Dr. Pepper's new
   beat
cola & MacDonald's beat meat subs espresso shakes Bongo Burgers Cool
   Slaw

Beat cross country tours in refurbished Chevys & fintailed Caddies
   driven
by fast-talking clean-cut Neal-like tour guides who park at neo-beat
   motels
stapled along 66 w/ bar jukeboxes stocked w/ hop rhythm 'n' blues &
   haiku
cocktail napkins

Beat Blockbuster shelves filled w/ old & new A & B Hollywood beat
  flicks
plus full stock of alternative beat video readings performances of survivor
beats sub-beats micro-beats in Xerox wrapper hand-lettered plastic cases
along w/ second & third generation beat-identified groups performers &
momentarily cool souls

Beat motif lap dancers beret-ribbed rubbers XXX loops gay road buddies
  XXX
dildoes rebel leather flight jackets slave jeans w/ snap open back flap for
bongo beat fisting

Beat outfits w/ gold leaf Burroughs signature on barrel, HH
  monogrammed
smack baggies, Gallo special edition Thunderbird label reproduces page
  from
On The Road scroll comes in cases of 24 poorboy screwtop bottles only
  &
isn't sold downtown, Cassady nickel & dime bags w/ mini silkscreen
  photo of
Neil in white T-shirt & deluxe kilo limited silkscreened last photo of
  Neil
on tightrope walking railroad tracks somewhere in Mexico numbered &
  signed
by Kesey, bonus presentation set of gold bullets in brass plaque plush
lined case w/ certificate of authenticity numbered & signed by William
  Lee

From **The Eyes, The Blood**

My father was a clown
my mother a harpist.
We do not forget
how close to death love leads us.

I can not forget my father
crying in the uncomfortable chair
in a Long Island Railroad car.
His first and only son unable to turn
or run from a father's public grief.

My mother crying on the kitchen floor
a carving knife she couldn't use

against her flesh. Black metal
cast away. Broken
I do not forget

from these parts a music was once made.
She at the piano, he at the cello.
Late afternoon rehearsal. Slow
remove of light from the livingroom.

Discomfort between father and son
as in each other was the other
neither could forget.

The smells of her body in nylons
undergarments, buckles. The scar
across her belly. Dark fold of Death
the Angel's touch.

I do not forget
it starts in the blood and ends in the eyes.
A Bible impossible to read.
The rabbi I turned away from.
Kittens murdered in the garage
hurled against the walls.
Sensual hips of my sisters.

He died in Hollywood. Nobody there
to say Kaddish.
His common-law wife
a Christian Scientist
insisted no music be played.

My children will never know my father.
My mother will not see nor bless my family.
I do not forget
that from these parts
a music was once made.
I heard it as a child.

who's the jew where is he she it that looms up in your face
unavoidable hiding behind the scenery manipulating agitating
convulsively difficult and wordy

who's the jew on the tree bleached into Aryan calendar art

who's the jew in tubs of intestines and folds of eroticism
overhwleming orifices with Wilhold sperm
percolating metastasizing permutations of monstrosity

who's the jew in blood of shrugs and connivance
pulling back the silken shroud
sequentially breaking wings without regard
for sound or pain

who's the jew on the freeway wheeling dealing and snxious to please to
acquire taboo eliminate all competition

who's the jew inventing America

who's the jew with perfect anonymous plastic generic mask
nose thinned lips blue contacts

who's the jew taking inventory of Taiwanese schlock

who's the jew on the tube with his dick in his mouth on overdrive
plugging product

who's the jew who knew the waiter at the place
everyone pretends not to be jews
pretending not to be

who's the jew crossing a line of pubic hairs
in mountainrange formation
elephantine tongue
roots and scaveneges for more

who's the jew on stage in putty nose
kvetching about who's the jew

who's the jew in church behind a pew
smelling of putrid knees

who's the kew kids throw ka ka swatsikas at
tearing the awning of a gauze temple

sho's the kew he she it of corpses and grossness
mulching gardens
molting meanings
constantly overturned

who's the jew wormed inside brains expanding to devour words
holding the world together in a perfect circle

who's the jew shrewd ferret weasel alien darkness
fouling paper with copyright and power

who's the jew who knew you once when there were no jews

who's the jew you told secrets to

who's the jew we feed to history

who's the jew night gives ink to

who's the jew in chalk-white pies skidding into laughing death

who's the jew who can't say no but won't say yes

who's the jew talking to

who's the jew's friend

who's the jew to you

who are you
are you the jew

JOEL LEWIS

Compensation Portrait

The factories have
burned down. The people
function in isolate
huts. The mayor
has gone home. The college
is issuing traffic tickets.
The water is wounded.

The Great Falls seek another
path. Chump change hits
the pavement & no
one picks it up.
Mormons are
selling the Pearl
of Great Price. Pay phone
ringing in a parking lot.
Your friends have fled
Paterson. No squirrels. Someone
begins an essay on concrete.
Did you get the money we sent?
Empty apartments. A jalopy
that needs a radiator hose.
The old circus hotel burns
down. No money for gas, the cars
run on static. The clock sounds
fade. Ghostly tongues of water
through the evening.

A car drops into a pothole. Dirty
statues. **Did you get the money
we sent?** T For dinner:
soda crackers, birch beer.
The book inside you
sleeps. Moody
telepathy. Streets
the color of cheap beer. The school
is burning down. **Did you get
the money we sent?** A nameless
uncarved block stands in
for your future. Paterson
is a relay of false
and true alarms. The moon
is not a thin silent key.

A chili dog squirts out of its buns
and lands on the curb
of Ellison Street.
This is **not**
an experiment
in the American
idiom. What
did one do
in Paterson,

AMERICAN RENEGADES

1956? **Get
the MONEY!**
A library
is burning
down. Your friends
have moved away
from you. Black out
& "friends"-turned-thieves
have redecorated
your loft through
attrition. **DID YOU GET
THE MONEY WE
SENT YOU?** Look up,
are those tangrams
of tint moonlight
or just street lamp
glare? Drunk wandering
through a midnight
housing project. It has
gone beyond
peculiar personal
habits.

Just enough
for a chili dog, maybe
a birch beer. On the shirtside
of this street, nothing
looks like homes. Snatch
of Jethro Tull snaps me back
to an easier way
of telling this. New rain
kool whips the street's
ripe debris. What is a mojo? Can
you pick up the house? The mailbox
is on fire. No one believes you
any more. A pizza shop radio blares
uninteresting "oldies", Streets
obliterated by black gum spots.
A hot dog cart explodes. **Did you get
the money we
sent?** Coffee
is not drunk
by mendicants.
What does
one do

in Paterson
circa 1998—
DUCK!
The children's toys
are burning. Empty bus
deadheads to
the Market Street garage.
You've become
the man
your father was. **Did you get
the money we sent?**
Your life—the open window.

STEVE DALACHINSKY

Incomplete Directions
For Bernhard Streit

to write eternity
on a piece of paper
is so easy
then everything else follows:

walls
shadows
dreams
death
life
gurus
signs that say keep off the grass
signs that say don't feed the birds
signs that say not too fast
signs that say not so slow
this new generation of ours
already grown old
this new year
nothing

when i asked the man for directions
on how to get to eternity
he said just keep walking
& then you'll come to the end of the street
& when you get to the end of the street
just keep walking & you'll come to the end of the street
& when you get to the end of the street
just keep walking & you'll get to the end of the street
& when you get to the end of the street just keep walking
you get the idea

to write eternity on a piece of paper
is so easy
then everything else follows:
poets
drunkards
lovers
flowers
paranoids
ceilings
bombs
toilets
answers
fingers pointing
picking noses

to find eternity is very hard
to be eternity is very hard
signs that say
stop you are now approaching eternity
signs that say eternity is just around the corner
signs that say school crossing
signs that say at the end of this street eternity
  slow down no alcoholic beverages no unnecessary noise
    don't feed the pigeons don't squeeze the squirrels
        at the end of this street eternity
      then just keep on walking until you get to the end of this
      street & when you get to the end of this street just keep on
      walking
                circles
                doormats
                windows
                mirrors you spoke to yourself in your mirror
                        you decided to change by changing the
                        course of the street

that's o.k.
the course we've walked
is dead
but we keep walking
the new course will be similar
to the old
in just one way
when we get to the end of the street
we will just keep walking

but maybe we'll stop
stop searching
stop walking
sit down & rest
& kiss & talk & hug & fight & love & die
& never mention eternity
when we get to the end of the street
we'll stop
maybe even turn around if it's not too late
that's nice

it's nice to look for something that's hard to find
but such bullshit to write it down
nothing pretty or romantic about this poem
nothing at all to read
these signs that say more signs
danger
slippery
falling rock zone
deer crossing
sharp turn
heaven
hell

so easy to write heaven on a piece of stone . . . .
coda:
the old tall thin grey man
in the old tall thin grey suit
came toward me arms out beckoning
holding in his left hand
a small grey card
& saying in a thin sharp grey voice
i don't wanna die yet
i don't wanna die yet
i don't die yet

AMERICAN RENEGADES

i turned & ran in panic to the white living room
slammed his fingers in the door
slammed the covers over my head

easy to write death
& then eternity follows
as easy to run away
or walk to the end of the street
& just keep walking

maybe if we reach the river
we can take the stone
& drop it in.

The Saxophone Factory
For Ben Webster

she works in a saxophone factory
she's young & pretty
all day long she sits in front of
a hole punch
punching holes in ivory
she gets the blues
tho she's never played
them
she's young
her blues are still on the
bright side

anything can be too late if it's not on time
seeing one fall
over & over again
why did god make me this way
how to explain this
how much this figures in . . . .

where have the leaves gone . . .
i'll tell you
look in your pockets

her baby was born in the factory
all hollowed out
like a reed

what's to show for it?
she's young

the man squats
facing a wall
he fingers the air
punching out a bluesy tune

miracle is the extension of wish

she's young &
pretty
her life still measured
in holes.

rewrite & combining of 2 poems "saxophone factory"
from 12/13/85
& "all hollowed out" from 10/31/96

The Bones #2

you played with my bones
now my bones lie soft and frustrated
on your platter
picked of warmth
and stunned by complete repulsion

now the sanity of my situation
screams like headaches
thru the yellowing
of what once looked like a torso
and the skull
so hard to penetrate
is the only door
between plucking and righteousness.

you shocked my system
with more volts than my system could take
and as you helped me crawl from the slab
to the car
i thought only of the soft side of life
and as you sat me in my neutral state
in the chair in front of the house

i felt only life's exodus,
watching bodies pass
on a warm fall day.

the bones
the bones
connecting what was once
a sometimes pleasant place to be

the soft and broken bones

you stuffed me in the back seat
and answered my right to birth
with medicines
and the lack of medicines
you told me not to pick my nose
not to masturbate
but to remove my bones to some healthy place
failing to tell me that the sun
only shined
when you let it shine
and that alone in a room
with my bones and
theirs
       sanity could only be found
  under the pillow   or in the shower.
with a grinning breath
you occupied my bones
yet never managed to inhabit them

you rocked my bones
the bones
the bones
so shocked and softened
by neurotic industrial wastes

the novel bones
the sonnet bones
the philosophical bones of dogs

with the structure further dissected
the frame became more insulated
insulted by its foundation,
angered by the careless reconstruction,
frightened by the entrance into its own sweet core.

the frame became unstable and rebellious
and the bones lay cramped and stunned
howling in revulsion
at their place in the world
and the bones
digested what was left of themselves
and rejected everything else
experimenting with poisons
while feeling the causes of their stricken state

now the bones yearn to break thru the flesh
and snap into place
on the hard cold air

now the bones feel nothing
but their own uncomfortable shifting about
in the tomb which you have built for them

and the bones know nothing
of the freedom you later sanctioned
for the bones
the bones
have neither the chance to speak
the strength to moan
nor the desire to run

the bones don't cry   they're too grown up
the bones won't dance   they're too shy
the bones don't want to move   they're too weak
the bones won't even love   they're too stubborn

the bones can't shoot jagged thru the tips
of my toes
they're too angry
yet always swollen with tears
the bones cannot refuse a song
they are too humble

i alter these bones
and willing or not
these bones do change
but the hard bone of skull remains
and these sounds that rip my ears
these sights that burn my eyes
carve like fine ivory

AMERICAN RENEGADES

dead light
upon a pattern of memories
that connects
faces with feelings
and the faces turn to bone
and the bone turns to pale translucent ash
yet never disappears

you gave me my bones
then you took them away.

James Dean

They talk about work
the men who have jobs
they discuss some aspect of work
some gossip
some inside joke
some technical tour de force.

James Dean
in a gallery window
we talk about sleep.

meat poets

D.R. WAGNER

The Mimeo Revolution

1965. There were no web pages. There was no Internet. There were no personal computers. There were no copy shops. There was hardly any photocopying outside of large business organizations. There were typewriters, even electric ones, but these were expensive. There were print shops but typesetting and printing were also expensive. Offset printing from relatively inexpensive metal masters was available, but too complex for use in the home. Printing presses were mostly quite large. Inexpensive means of reproducing print were few. The hectograph which used alcohol as a medium to transfer ink was ephemeral and of very poor quality. It was usually used in schools for reproducing student tests and class handouts. The only other process was mimeograph. The machines were compact, usually temperamental, printed a dark black and used typewriter cut stencils that could, with patience, be corrected. These stencils were capable of making five hundred copies without failing, and it was possible to get many more copies with extra care. They were available and were used occasionally. The stencils and ink were cheap. The paper used in the machines was thick and chunky and inexpensive for the time. It could last for some time and could be printed, collated, folded and bound easily.

It was the mimeograph (mimeo) machine that formed the backbone of a significant literary movement that began in the 1960's and lasted until the middle of the 1970's. This ten-year period saw an incredible explosion of small press publishing. It came to be called the "Mimeograph Revolution." The machines allowed an entire generation of poets and writers to communicate with one another and to an interested audience in a quick, efficient manner. Chapbooks of five hundred copies, magazines, manifestos, quick communications were all produced in significant amounts. Presses sprang up all over the country.

In Cleveland, d. a.levy, who had already painstakingly produced small letter-press pamphlets and chapbooks acquired a mimeo and began an incredible publishing venture with his 7 Flowers Press. Edward Sanders, in New York, published his literary journal, *Fuck You; A Magazine of the Arts*, featuring many local writers. Douglas Blazek's magazine OLE was produced in Bensenville, IL and began a showcase for direct, imperative poetic forms using street language and often startling imagery. Blazek called the activity "meat poetry" and while not a movement per se, included poets using many experimental forms. Ben Hiatt, in the Grande Ronde Valley of Oregon featured strong regional voices. In Niagara Falls, NY, and later in Sacramento, CA, press: today: niagara (later Runcible Spoon) published a variety of magazines and chapbooks. There were many, many other magazines and presses. Len Fulton's *Directory of Small Presses and Magazines* from the period, should be consulted for more information. An immediate form of communication was finally possible with this technology. Work written yesterday could be printed and distributed very quickly prompting intense conversation involving poetry and poetics to develop quickly. It became a network of exchanged publications and a forum where young poets could develop their voices and be joined by more established voices in an informal format.

Until the advent of the underground newspapers of the 1970's, the medium was a lifeline for poetic activity, linking small centers with larger ones and providing up-to-the-minute poetry everywhere.

As offset printing became less expensive and printing technology advanced the mimeograph machine fell into disuse and has virtually disappeared altogether. It was, for a brief period, the voice of the avant-garde in America and the world. It helped establish greater interest in poetry and provided an easily accessible medium to set publishing free from university publications and their definitions of what poetry was supposed to be. The poetry establishment was shaken to the roots by these upstarts flying into the face of literary convention. They had the presses and a forum to present their ideas quickly and emphatically. They were the "mimeograph revolution."

STEVE RICHMOND

A Bukowski Writing Lesson

It's about this time he pulls out my first book of poetry, the copy I
mailed him three months earlier. He starts reading the very first poem:

i tore my nails into
my stomach ripping a hole
big enough to put my hand
into me with blind fingers
feeling between intestines
and liver for the flower of
me, until i found it pulling
it out, holding it in my bloody
right hand until my left hand
got hold of my soul, and i
took the two and smashed them
together until they became a
solid piece of total beauty
for me to throw with all
my strength into the
stars

I'm watching close as he reads it through. He seems not
to be hurting at all so I feel it's all working nicely and then he
gets to the last word and he suddenly goes, "OOOOOOHHHH
SHIT. IT WAS GOING FINE RIGHT UP TO THAT LAST
WORD-STARS-OHH IT'S TOO DAMN BAD-WHAT
A SHAME."

I was asking myself, "What? What th'hell does he
mean? Stars? What's wrong with 'stars'? Nobody's ever said
anything bad about 'stars' to me in my life—hmmmmm."

Bukowski spoke on, "STARS is so goddamn ultra
poetic. You can't use STARS. STARS STARS STARS FUCK
TH' GODDAMN STARS! What a shame, kid. You had it strong
right up to the last word, then gone, ruined, all th'damn dead
false sewing circle poets are forever writing STARS STARS

STARS!! they can't write a line without STARS in it some-
where. I'm sorry kid."

What he was telling me made instant sense but I tried to
hedge in my mind because the 1,000 copies were already printed
and half the run was already distributed and there wasn't any
chance I could recall every copy and have Tasmania Press
change the last word of the first poem to some word, any word
other than STARS.

Now it's July 11, 1994 and it's been 29 years since
Hank tore his Lion's Claws into my use of STARS and I've
never used the word STARS or stars or stARS ever since
. . . . since ten minutes after I met Charles Bukowski, face to face.

A.D. WINANS

I've never worn the label of poet well. It's not a word I'm comfortable with. I
sometimes feel I'm possessed by demons whose voices confront me whenever I
sit down to write. The finished poem often bears little resemblance to whatever
I initially had in mind. The demon voices simply invade my thought process and
take over. I share Jack Spicer's philosophy that verse does not originate from
within the poet's expressive will as a spontaneous gesture unmediated by formal
constraints, but is "a foreign agent, a parasite that invades the poet's language
and expresses what it wants to say."

I made North Beach my home away from home from 1958 through much of
the eighties, but never considered myself a Beat poet or writer. If one must use
labels, I would prefer the label of bohemian. T. S. Eliot and William Carlos
Williams were two of the earliest poets to influence me. However, it was jazz
and jazz musicians like Thelonius Monk, John Coltrane, Leadbelly, and Miles
Davis that excited me early on. I'm not a guru. I don't go to the mountains
looking for the Dalai Lama. I create largely in isolation. I don't long for academic
recognition, but neither do I see the academic world as my enemy, as Charles
Bukowski did. I simply write from the heart.

I've published 22 books of poetry and have been published in over 500 literary
periodicals and anthologies, but that isn't what is important. What you do with
it is a different matter. I hope I have earned more good karma than bad karma
points. I hope in the end I can look death in face and say that I've played the
game honestly and that I never sold my integrity. In the end integrity is all a
poet has. Sell your integrity and you've sold your soul to the devil.

A. D. WINANS

Thinking About Then and Now

when I worked in Modesto
back in 1964
I'd drive to Stockton
and sit in the park
drinking with the winos
in Salinas it was field workers
in Crow's Landing it was with
unemployed Mexicans
at Latin water-holes
in North Beach and the Mission
I hung out with deadbeats
and losers
street people fighting cirrhosis
of the liver
junkie tremors and now AIDS
in the Fillmore
I cut my teeth on jazz
let Billie Holiday patch up
my bleeding heart
in the Portrero
I saw the last of the
factory workers growing thinner
like their paychecks
fearing for their jobs
in the Tenderloin
I drank with whores
and prostitutes
who opened their pocketbooks
as freely as their legs
on Market street
I witnessed panhandlers crouched
like common criminals
in open doorways
a short distance from
the jesus freaks
with billboards on their backs
pointing the way to heaven
at the old Southern Pacific
railway yard
I saw the last of the
brake men smoking a cigarette
eyes vacant as an empty satchel
while on the other side of town

high on Nob Hill
society ladies sat
in chauffeured limousines
white poodle dogs nestled
between their piano legs
unaware of the dredges of humanity
walking third and howard street
drinking cheap port
from brown paper bags
starving cold disheveled
as the homeless are today
waiting for god or pneumonia
to walk them to the graveyard

The System

There are old men and women
Who have worked all their lives
Who have put in three four decades
For the right to a pension
There are old people who have worked
Twenty years or more
Only to be laid off and given
Two weeks severance pay
There are old people who have
Worked their entire lives
Only to see the company go belly-up
And find there is no pension fund left
You can find them on park benches
Or wandering sterile supermarkets
Or sitting at neighborhood bars
Nursing their drinks
Like a blood transfusion
They come in assorted flavors
Like Life Savers
Some thin and balding
Some fat and sweating
Some complaining bitterly
Some too proud
To let the pain show
So proud they eat dog food
And find dessert in back alley
Garbage cans

Trapped by a belief in a system
That has abandoned them
For the most part they suffer
In silence
Duly unnoticed
To be carted off in meat wagons
Waiting to be cut open by coroners
Who see them as morning cereal
Who go about their business
Like a butcher
Thinking of dinner
Thinking of how it used to be
How it might have been
How it should have been
How it could have been
It's the way of life
It's the way of politicians
It's the way of rats and mice
It's the system where
Just trying to stay alive
Becomes a small victory

Poem for the Working Man and the Upper Mobile Yuppie

Some people guard their lives
Like a eunuch guards
The Harem door
Like a stock broker with
A hot tip
Like a banker who knows
That today's dollar will only
Be worth one-fourth what
It is today
In less time than it takes
To die
Better to linger over
A cup of coffee
Like a skilled lover with
No need for bragging rights
Remember that every newsman
On every street corner in America
That every meat packer and fisherman
Knows more about life than

Your average poet
The blind man rattling
An empty tin cup
Makes more noise than
A yuppie gunning
His BMW
On his way
to the graveyard

William Wantling

Poetry

I've got to be honest. I can
make good word music and rhyme

at the right times and fit words
together to give people pleasure

and even sometimes take their
breath away—but it always

somehow turns out kind of phoney.
Consonance and assonance and inner

rhyme won't make up for the fact
that I can't figure out how to get

down on paper the real or the true
which we call Life. Like the other

day. The other day I was walking
on the lower exercise yard here

at San Quentin and this cat called
Turk came up to a friend of mine

and said Ernie, I hear you're
shooting on my kid. And Ernie

told him So what, punk? And Turk
pulled out his stuff and shanked

Ernie in the gut only Ernie had a
metal tray in his shirt. Turk's

shank bounced right off him and
Ernie pulled his stuff out and of

course Turk didn't have a tray and
caught it dead in the chest, a bad

one, and the blood that came to his
lips was a bright pink, lung blood,

and he just laid down in the grass
and said Shit. Fuck it. Sheeit.

Fuck it. And he laughed a soft long
laugh, 5 minutes, then died. Now

what could consonance or assonance or
even rhyme do with something like that?

DAVID ROSKOS

Certain Prostitute
For John Wieners

she washed three valiums
down with a shot,
felt the need
to swallow my seed
& then to break
my heart.

MEAT POETS

I lie in bed
on the seventh day,
sink a soft needle
into the upturned
belly of my forearm,
taste sea salt
on my tongue.

I am in love with
a certain prostitute
who melts my love in a spoon,
who leaves me empty
& as sparse
as the light
of a sliver moon.

a single mattress
on a paint-splattered floor,
cigarette butts
& the bitten off corners
of condom packages.

I followed a constellation
up the crack of her ass.

Poem for Paulie

the snow is so peaceful
when its falling,
covers up the garbage.
I looked out the window
of the church after the
meeting last night
& thought of Paul B.,
"Baretta."
He's dead due to a shot
he took in his arm
on a rooftop in New York.
He said he knew the needle
was infected, realized it
a second before he sunk it,
just had a gut-feeling,
paused

& said FUCK IT.
He died in the VA Hospital
in full-blown dementia,
lesions on his skin,
pockmarked face—
snow settles on his grave.

FRITZ HAMILTON

Frozen Alley

Holy
Jesus never in
my 7 yrs just
passin' through this
fuckin' Bowery have

I
seen nothin' like
fat Fleishman sittin'
naked on this garbage can all

smilin' through his
big rubber head in
this alley with

zero degrees pumpin'
60 through
the garbage/ fat

Fleishman havin'
taken off all his clothes just
ridin' this garbage can/ his
ass sure frozen to the top

holdin'
his pint of Wild Irish peach freezin'

to death and
not carin' and

just last wk little ol'
Nick found passed
out sleepin' back here stiff like
a frozen fish/ so

I say/ near
frozen to death myself
        "Fleishman
        follow my ass on
        to the mission . . ."

but
then I seen it/ Fleishman
holdin' this bloody shattered
bottle and

blood frozen all
over his legs and
groin. . . .

Shit!
Fleishman done cut
off his own

balls
!

JIM CHANDLER

Jailhouse Dreams #1

Many years ago when I was a headstrong boy full
of piss and vinegar my misdeeds wound me up
on a southern road gang.

Every morning after a breakfast of fatback with
the hair still on it and a tin platter of gravy
we were loaded aboard an old schoolbus.

One deputy drove the bus and another sat on the
front seat with a Winchester pump shotgun
in the event any of us decided to get rowdy.

We were taken out to one country road right-of-way
or another where we were then given tools from
the big box on the back of the bus.

Not a big selection: axes, "lively lads," and
the type of scythe called a "briar blade" in the
south.

We were not forced to kill ourselves with this labor
and indeed the one-eyed old man who guarded us was
a kindly soul at heart.

He owned a little country store and on cold mornings
he would direct the driver by the store
where he would get a jar of instant coffee.
Once out on the site we'd build a campfire of sorts
and hang a big cast iron kettle full of water
over it.

We'd cut some right-of-way and then have a coffee break,
the steam rising from our cups blending with
the vapor of our breaths in the crisp
morning air.

"I'd never kill a man for running," the old man said
to us one morning. "It ain't worth it."

But he knew that we weren't a violent lot
just a pack of back check artists, petty con men,
smokehouse burglars, gasoline thieves, public drunks.

One morning this guy named Jerry told me
"I'm going today" and he did, about 30 minutes after
we unloaded by a railroad track.

Old Jerry headed for the tracks and began to beat feet
toward the west, running low because he didn't know

MEAT POETS

if the old man would shoot him or not.
The old deputy half-heartedly cried for him to stop
but he didn't and that was that.

Jerry went to his sister's in Detroit unless he
lied to me and I don't think he did.
He knew I didn't give a damn, I wouldn't tell.

His main vice in life was hanging worthless paper anyway.

At noon we stopped for lunch and it was always the same:
a thick bologna sandich and a peanut butter and jelly sandwich.
There was also the eternal Moon Pie, symbolic of
the land I loved and hated with all my heart.

The food was wolfed down, the cigarettes were smoked and
the bullshit was bantered back and forth.

And then it was an afternoon of the same
usually a bland space of time with nothing to make
it memorable unless something out of the ordinary happened.

Once, driven mad by a sapling that refused to yield to
the bite of my blade, I went totally berserk.
I struck the sapling as hard as I could and yet it
just quivered in the muddy ground.

It mocked me with its resilience, that scrubby little
piece of flora.

Finally in a fit of madness I threw myself onto the small
tree, screaming and flailing and fighting as though it
were a threat to my existence.

Somehow, I twisted it apart with my bare hands.
The other men were freaked out by this display of insanity
and no one made the mistake of joking about it.

They probably knew I would kill them with the briar blade
even the old deputy, I was that far over the edge.

Cold, muddy, exhausted with effort, but the victor
nonetheless.

Back at the jail late in the afternoon we were given
a pat-down search, the barest of frisks.

This was in a kinder, gentler age, before you were asked
to bend and spread and a hand went up your ass in search
of drugs, weapons or Hogan's goat.

I once slipped a hacksaw blade in hidden inside my sock
and that night we began to work on a section of
bars inside the cage.

The cage was erected in one of two adjacent concrete rooms
and were were locked in it only at night.

We made progress over a period of evenings, putting
shoe polish in the saw marks when we stopped until
finally one night we sawed through two bars.

There was nowhere to go outside the cage save the
two concrete rooms but it became a matter of pride—
we had to prove we couldn't be contained.

On the night we freed the bars the skinnier two of us
try to squeeze our way through them.

I was one of the thinner and a guy from Arizona was the other.
He'd been arrested for breaking into washers at a
laundromat while hitchhiking through the area, he
and his friend both.

He was supposed to be standing watch while his buddy
popped the coin boxes but the sound got to him.
"I heard them fuckin' quarters rattlin' and I had
to get in on it" he explained.

The sheriff drove up while they were sacking up the
loot and that's the name of that tune.

We stripped off naked and greased ourselves up with Crisco
but it didn't work, the hole was too small.

I got jammed with my head and one arm through and
for a while it looked as if I'd still be there come
feeding time in the morning.

MEAT POETS

With a lot of painful tugging they finally pulled me free.

We doped up the cuts in the metal and got a few hours sleep
but we had a surprise when we came in from the road
the next day.

There was a big log chain strung through the hole and padlocked
several times.

The grand jury had toured the jail that day and someone
spotted a dab of grease on the back side of a bar where
we'd failed to clean it off.

The great escape to nowhere was revealed.

The sheriff was a little pissed but not unreasonably so.

It just became more difficult to get the trustee
to bring you a half-pint of whiskey for a
few days even if you had the $2.50.

Dead Kid

struggling our way
along the trestle
clinging to the side
of a train to get
to where the body lies
crumpled in high weeds
'he went back to get
the minnow bucket'
his dad weeps
'he didn't make it
why didn't he jump
in the creek'
standing on the siding
in the moonlight
waiting for the highrail
truck i breath live air
while down the grade
the kid lies twisted
his forehead open
his mouth gaping bloody

like a shot rabbit
his eyes flat and blank
goddamn i'm glad to
be alive and running
my race in front of my
train although it's
getting closer all
the time

No Rain Sunday Morning

There is no rain this Sunday morning,
but like Carver I would live my life
over again and make the same unforgivable mistakes,
given even less than half a chance.

I feel somewhat lost this morning, as thought my
destiny may have been missed in some sleepy church house
my mind would never think of entering,
and my soul would never dream need of.

The only song in my heart is the low moaning wail of discontent,
that ragged little interior jingle that sings of desolation
and a place passed by that I failed to discover,
missed whizzing past in my rearview mirror.

No campfires of hope burning on the closed range of this heart,
only an ocean of sawgrass blowing in a wind whose direction
I can't plot across landscape I can't define in a world
too mad for my solitary eyes to record.

I have no vision this Sunday in rainless America,
only the dull ache of things done too soon,
a song near coda before the last true note flies
from the bell of a horn of less than plenty,

the dark hole of forever rising like sudden fearsome anger.

ANN MENEBROKER

Round Up

the old lady came along
like a goat herder
yelling and pushing her mad dogs
upon those of us who were behind.
she walked through the dust
after us with excessive voice,
herding us into our own slight deaths
(with no margin of escape.)
she threw a thick rope
around my neck, tightened it
and pulled until my legs dragged
behind her. I yelled
   whore! lousy bitch!
but she didn't seem concerned.
I tried making human sounds
to convince her
I was no damn goat
but the rest of the herd
was just as eager, and we drowned
each other out, a huge
sad bleating
that would have brought heaven
to our rescue, had there been one.
there might have been a better way
(noble, they say)
to die than this, trapped
with hundreds of whining commuters
who sobbed once too often
into the face of darkness.
I tried hard to remember
exactly what it was that drove me
over, but it was too late.

TODD MOORE

If the poetry of Ezra Pound had achieved the aim of his critical theories, he'd have poured out more images with a marksmanship equal to Todd Moore. Moore's images are concrete both literally and figuratively: they are the all-consuming street scenes that grumble resonant with rhythms of the digestive fluids in this country's underbelly. But forget that shit; Moore would want you to anyway—even if you were reading this in some ivory tower john.

Moore's father was a railroad man and a fireman . . . a bagman, a numbers runner, an acquaintance of Capone, and an aspiring novelist. Moore had more than just a taste of the life, growing up in a joint which serviced railroad men. The Clifton Hotel was predominantly inhabited by pussy peddlers, railbirds, inside men and every variety of NG (no good) that could ever cross a person's path. Moore himself got pretty crossed-up, becoming a street thief, then later in life a librarian and a high school teacher (for thirty years), who made sense of it through poetry. Moore illuminates the placental world that is as dark as a plum in a cold universe, because his technical virtuosity and grasp of realistic urban speech affords him the reach to open that envelope white door that few have the stomach for, be it a lack of hunger or a lack of courage.

Being that it is best to write from the gut, Moore's strength as a poet and a human being has been his ability to feed on this badly bruised heart of forbidden fruit and let the blood drip from the corners of his mouth onto the page in stripes that deserve at least fifty stars and an acknowledgment of an inner-city blues as real as shot up varicose veins. His best lines are molten steel that he lays in the grooves of the reader's gray matter, and as eyes meet image and tongue rolls off words, there is the click-clack of recognition, and the spark of inspiration that was initiated in Moore becomes a conflagration in the mind of any American who does not whimper: *I have a delicate stomach: it sours easily.*

A poet takes aim at one of three areas: the head, the heart or the crotch. Occasionally, all three can be scoped in one piece if you have an eye for poetic detail or if the poet's imagination has an affinity for the uzi. Once in awhile, a poet comes along who can take aim and ignite every atom in one's being. The removal of vowels in his verbs creates a sense of immobilization as if in a freeze frame in a place colder than Hollywood, as if the atom bomb that was made in his resident New Mexico has eaten through all we do—even write, even speak. *Dillinger* (40,000 lines, 34 volumes) and the soon to be released *Dunede* are American monoliths. Todd Moore once told me he was Dillinger. So what? I know.

NELSON GARY

From *Machine Gun*

the trick was

to wait til everyone
else was coming out
of the movies before
sneaking in the ush
ers never gave a
shit they were too
busy playing grabass
w/the popcorn &
candy girls to see
anything else &
by that time i was
already past movie
stills of roy rogers
& gene autry aiming
their good guy guns
at my skinny des
perado ass & some
how that felt good
but what felt better
was watching a movie
i never paid for
i'll always remember
what julene the
waitress in red's
diner told me she
sd honey most out
laws steal money
& i haven't got a
thing against that
but yr different
because you steal
dreams

dillinger dropped

the thompson into
a pillow & ran
his hand down
the length of
billie's skin til
he got to

her crotch
johnnie
she sd turning
to him
what
while we do it
lets pretend
we're in
the movies
hell he
sd crawling
between her legs
we are
the movies

Dillinger thinking abt

what it must feel like
to be killed by a machine
gun first pieces of clothing
fly off in all directions
like a cluster of frightened
sparrows then 45's shave
patches of flesh & bone as
tho this is the ultimate
strip show no sally rand
fans to hide this stuff the
victim remaining briefly
alive to watch the sur
prised blood spanked into
fine drops a red sneeze
the shaking body makes
those places hit by slugs
danced to a dull numbing
cold & the hands won't come
up & the heart's reduced
to a few walloped pigeon
flops inside the ribs then
language turns to maggots
in the skull

fuck poetry

ringo sd slapping a clip
into the 45 auto the

targets were whiskey
bottles we'd set out on
fence posts fuck all those
pretty little rhymes
they made us read in high
school ringo yelled
hitting jim beam the
glass exploding into
the weeds he passed the
45 across a porno mag
opened on a woman who
was holding her tits out
like a pair of six
shooters do you know
of a poem as packed as
that i fired at jack
daniels & missed & ringo
grabbed the automatic
& took jack out & fuck
metaphors & fuck similes
shit like that & fuck
kerouac & fuck bukowski
suddenly ringo pressed
the 45 barrel against
my forehead & while it
was drilling into my
skin he whispered
& amigo fuck you

spider wilson died

in front of johnny
the greek's shoe
shine stand
where father was
telling a guy
never to draw to
an inside straight
when he saw spider
fall he got down
on all fours to
feel for a pulse
in spider's neck
is he dead the
greek asked yeah

father sd when the
greek cocked his
foot back like he
was going to kick
spider in the head
father sd it ain't
fair to pick on
a dead man then he
came over grabbed
me by the shirt &
shoved me close
to spider's eyes
sd you wanna be
a writer you
can't look away

FRED VOSS

A Threat

My fellow workers and I
operate machines that cut steel blocks.

As the machines cut the steel,
my fellow workers like to stare and laugh at each other.
They are ready to piss on each other's graves.

They fear me.
They call me crazy.
They don't like the poetry I read.
They don't like the paintings I have hung
on the board behind my machine.
They look at me
like they want to cut my balls off.

Tomorrow I think I will start bringing roses to work.
Each day I will stand a rose in a jar of water
on the workbench behind my machine.
I want to really terrify my fellow workers
this time.

Termination

Feeling the vibrations coming out of the machines
with his palm flat against them,
and leaning his good ear
close to the green sides of the machines,
listening for the gears and shafts
turning in the guts of the machines,
listening for things only he
knew to listen for,
the foreman's whole body was aware
as the machines poured their decades of secrets
into his hand and ear
and he knew,
he knew what would happen to each of them,
whether there would be an accident
or whether it was all right.
His hands and jaw trembled slightly
from the 25 years
of the roars and shudders and chatterings
of steel mill drip hammers and presses and grinding wheels,
but he was still strong.

But the new hotshot manager and the machine operator
who wanted to be foreman
were into speed,
and the foreman took too long with his hand and ear
trying to keep machine cutters from blowing up in operator's faces,
so they rode him
until
each morning when he came to work and put his hard hat on
there seemed to be a heavier weight on his head,
pushing him into the concrete floor
of the steel mill,
driving his neck and his head
down into his shoulders
as if he were a shaft being driven down through concrete
by a jackhammer,
the trembling growing in his fingers
and jaws
until he had a stroke
that stopped the trembling and him
for good.

That manager and machine operator
really knew how to get the job done.

JOAN JOBE SMITH

Aboard The Bounty

Onto the bar I walked, my first day on the job,
a go-go girl in the raw, onto the bar from the
dressing room where I'd shakily painted my face
with pink and gloss, combed my hair high and
brown, straightened my black stockings smooth,
onto the bar from the dressing room from my
apartment where I'd kissed my kids goodbye,
showed the nanny how to warm the baby's formula,
onto the bar from the dressing room from my
apartment the week after my husband left me,
the rent two weeks past due and I looked around
the bar at all the men drinking beer and laughing
and smoking cigars and cigarettes and watching
Robin whose name I didn't know yet dance some
dance I didn't know how to dance yet to the
Rolling Stones singing a song about a stupid girl
on the jukebox playing as loud as it would go
and a man waved to me to come here, he wanted
some beer, so I went to him and he pointed up
at Robin, Robin whom I yet did not know, did not
know her stepfather'd raped her, one of her kids'd
been born brain damaged and the drunken man
pointed up at Robin's crotch and asked me, the
first thing a drunken man in a beerbar ever asked me
my first day on the job, a go-go girl in the raw:
Is that chick up there on the rag or is she really
a fag with her balls tied up in a jock?

Land of a Thousand Dances

When I was a little girl and watched
my mother starch and iron her short
red polka-dot skirt and white low-cut
peasant blouse she wore on her waitress

job at the Pow Wow Café or watched her
polish her white tasseled boots for her
job as a car-hop, I'd tell her how pretty
she looked and how I wanted to be a

waitress too when I grew up and she'd say
oh, no, you don't want to be a waitress,
it's an awful job. But she never told me
what I should be, solve for me the mysteries

of adulthood, so I imagined I'd be a princess
or a ballerina or an Eleanor Roosevelt. I
never dreamed, even if I'd been a Jules
Verne, that someday I'd go to a land of a

thousand dances and on my days off, I'd wash
my bikini and fringe and sequins; and the few
weeks I danced topless, I hoped my mother
wouldn't notice that I washed only the

bottoms. How I worried all those weeks
that she'd find out that I did something
more awful than being the waitress she
never wanted me to be. Why she never

noticed, I'll never know, for it's your
mother's duty, her umbilical urgency to
know when you're sick or tired or derelict.
It's a crime I'm glad she let me get away with:

a security guard with an unloaded gun looking
the other way as I loaded my sacks with strange
stuff and ran down the mountain, across the
desert, and into the Sea of Absurdity.

GERALD LOCKLIN

Beyond B. F. Skinner

i'm watching a rented video of *'round midnight*
with some local writers in a midwest city
and the young french guy has just
kicked down the lock of the door
of the hotel room in which the black
parisian landlady has been keeping dexter
gordon imprisoned for his own health,
not to mention his earning power,

and someone says, "i don't understand
the point of all this,"

and i say, "the point of the film is
freedom and dignity, precisely those
conditions that b. f. skinner says
contemporary man must relinquish."
well, contemporary man has pretty fucking
well relinquished them. but this french
kid is saying that the jazz man must be
allowed his freedom and dignity, must
be allowed to be a man, even if such freedom
virtually assures his early self-destruction.
it is what existentialism was always all about.
it is what john stuart mill was about. it
is what *clockwork orange* is about. it is what
john milton and john locke and even jonathan
fucking edwards were all about. it is what
billie holiday was about and john coltrane and
the bird and bud powell—it is simply what
JAZZ has always been about. it is what
FRANCE is supposed to be about and it is
what AMERICA was once about and maybe still
is but barely hanging by its fingernails.
but it's not what the insurance companies are
about. and it's not what communism or puritanism
or fascism or just about any "-ism" except maybe
existentialism or individualism are about.

existentialism in fact didn't just say you
could be free—it said you couldn't escape
your freedom, but millions of people are
doing their damnedest to.

and a few weeks later my friend cowboy
bob is quietly replying to a drunk lady
who is demanding to know why he is always
getting into arguments and fights, what
exactly it is that he wants out of life,
what it is that he lives for, and
cowboy bob tells her,

"i only live for two things.
the first one is freedom.
so is the second."

Paul Cezanne: Self Portrait, 1875

what sort of man
abides rose wallpaper?
what sort of man
has facial skin to match?

a rose is a rose is
a conflict with itself.

how can we be so confident,
yet not entirely.

baldness is naked, and
a beard is not.

i cloak myself in my profession
which i hope will keep out winter.

i am at one with world and
yet stand out from it.

the dog is always at the door.

i keep an eye on him.

Paul Cezanne: The Large Bathers, 1906

it was a good year to look backwards.

to when the woods were a cathedral.

to when the clouds were white as
eden, and the sky angelic azure.

shame was uninvented; men and women
were not yet at war.

world and time were endless, ageless:
we *had* world and time enough.

the wisdom of water was still with us.

god was the fountainhead:
creation was perfection.

it was a good year, 1906,
not to look ahead.

ALAN KAUFMAN

On Marvin Malone and The Wormwood Review

The greatest little magazine of all time, bar none, was Marvin Malone's *Wormwood Review*. Here Bukowski made his bones. "Wormy," as it was affectionately called, regularly carried work by such underground legends as John Bennet, Harold E. Briggs, Judson Crews, Lyn Lifshin, Gerald Locklin, Al Masarik, Ann Menebroker, Steve Richmond, William Wantling, Charles Webb and Jack Micheline. William Burroughs was a contributor.

Once a year editor Malone bestowed the Wormwood Award for "the most overlooked book of worth for a calendar year." Winners included Alexander Trocchi's *The Outsiders*, Kurt Vonnegut Jr.'s *Mother Night*, Charles Bukowski's *Notes From A Dirty Old Man*, and such required reading as Ian Hamilton Finlay's *3 Blue Lemons* and Gerald Locklin's *Poop, and Other Poems* . . .

MEAT POETS

MARVIN MALONE

Ten Commandments for How to Successfully Publish a Little Magazine

1) avoid publishing oneself and personal friends, 2) avoid being a "local" magazine and strive for a national and international audience, 3) seek unknown talents rather than establishment or fashionable authors, 4) encourage originality by working with and promoting authors capable of extending the existing patterns of Amerenglish literature, 5) avoid all cults and allegiances and the you-scratch-my-back-and-I-will-scratch yours approach to publishing, 6) accept the fact that magazine content is more important than format in the long run, 7) presume a literate audience 8) restrict the number of pages to no more than 40 per issue since only the insensitive and the masochistic can handle more pages at one sitting 9) pay bills on time and don't expect special favors in honor of the muse, 10) don't become too serious and righteous. Ignoring the above ten commandments appears to lay the ground for a mag's self-destruction.

american renegades

JIM MORRISON

The American Night

> for leather accrues
> > the miracle of the streets
> The scents & smogs &
> > pollens of existence
>
> Shiny blackness
> > so totally naked she was
> > totally un-hung-up
>
> We looked around
> > lights now on
> To see our fellow travellers

LAmerica

> Androgynous, liquid, happy
> Heavy
> Facile & vapid
> Weighted w/words
> Mortgaged soul
> Wandering preachers & Delta tramps

Box-cars of heaven
New Orleans Nile Sunset

JENNIFER BLOWDRYER

From *Resume*

EXPERIENCE AS TRICK
JOB DESCRIPTION: Eating dinner for $30, while appearing fascinated
   with complex real estate maneuvers executed by dinner partners.
   Locating exit of several good restaurants. In charge of own wardrobe.

REASON FOR LEAVING: Had already had dinner with all the men at
   the Swingers club, saw no specific career motivation for following up
   any further with any of these men.

REFERENCES: Frank and John.

JOB DESCRIPTION: Active participant in world of pornography.

REASON FOR LEAVING: Refusal to have sex or "show anything" in
   front of cameras conflicted with career goals of production staff. Paid
   with immediate dismissal.

REFERENCES: Mark "10 ½" Stevens, Harold Adler, Annie Sprinkle.

JOB DESCRIPTION: Wardrobe in Pornography world. Outfitted stars
   like Sharon Mitchell in cute fifties gowns, giving them a fey
   thriftstore look. Was in complete charge of making sure lingerie
   matched, and operator of Polaroid for lingerie continuity. Also aided
   docudrama crew on Crystal Methedrine wash as much money as
   possible in an abbreviated time period.

REFERENCES: Film with no title is in metal strong box in Germany,
   with my stage name on the credits.

SHOW BUSINESS EXPERIENCE

JOB DESCRIPTION: Singer in Punk Band. Supervision of infighting in band, location of connector chords, location of nightclub where performances were scheduled. Part of job entailed being in charge of equipment relocation, and an acquired ability to take in and retain large quantities of alcohol, tobacco, and both recreational and serious drugs.

REASON FOR LEAVING: Flight from key member of band down three stories coinciding with extremist lesbian separatist views developed and maintained by other band member.

REFERENCES: Anyone in San Francisco, California, who looks like they have been around entirely too long.

JOB DESCRIPTION: Thespian and writer of underground movies. Created works with titles "We're not Carol Burnett," "Blackie-O!," and "Suicide Line." Theme of works was a warped view and twisted outlook. Unrealistically hoped that these works would phase into being perceived as a normal and manipulable commodity by persons with more money than myself or my friends.

REASON FOR LEAVING: Aging naturally didn't meet with the rigorous standards of my Producer, who watched in shock and horror as I proceeded to turn first 21, and then 22.

REFERENCES: See Above.

Iris Berry

Punk Rock Royalty

SOMEWHERE IN SACRAMENTO CALIFORNIA
AT SOME WELL KNOWN CRASH-PAD
SOMETIME IN THE MIDDLE OF THE WEEK
AND SOMETIME IN THE MIDDLE OF THE AFTERNOON
DAY AND TIME CUSTOMARILY UNKNOWN TO
RESIDENTS OF HOUSE

AMERICAN RENEGADES

THE DISHES HAVEN'T BEEN WASHED SINCE JULY
(AND IT'S SEPTEMBER)
HALF EMPTY TO GO BOXES WITH TWO WEEK OLD
PIZZA AND TACO BELL REMAINS, 99 CENT BURGERS
FROM AM/PM AND EMPTY BOTTLES OF PLAIN WRAP
LIQUOR AND BEER CANS LAY STREWN
ACROSS THE KITCHEN FLOOR
LEAVING NOT EVEN A TRAIL
IN THE LIVING ROOM
THERE'S 4 GUYS
WHO HAVEN'T SLEPT IN 3 DAYS
TRYING TO PUMP LIFE
OUT OF A KEG THAT'S BEEN FINISHED SINCE
THE WEEKEND
AND 2 PIT BULLS GNAWING ON OLD RIB BONES
THERE'S FLIES EVERYWHERE
AND IT'S HOT
THE HICKOIDS'
TALES OF TERROR
FANG
AND JOHNNY THUNDERS
IS BLARING OUT OF BEER SOAKED SPEAKERS
THAT PERIODICALLY KEEP SHORTING OUT
THE TV IS ON BUT THE SOUND IS OFF
SHOWING "BLUE VELVET" FOR THE 5TH TIME THAT
DAY (MUST BE ANOTHER "FRANK" FEST)
AND IN THE MIDDLE OF ALL THIS
YOU'RE LOCKED AWAY IN THE BATHROOM
LIKE PUNK ROCK ROYALTY SITTING ON YOUR THRONE
JACKING-OFF TO MY PICTURE IN "FLIPSIDE"
FOR THE SECOND TIME THAT DAY
THANK YOU, I FEEL HONORED

LOU REED

Video Violence

The currents rage deep inside us
This is the age of video violence
The currents rage deep down inside us
This is the age of video violence

Up in the morning, drinking his coffee
Turns on the TV to some slasher movie
Cartoon-like women, tied up and sweaty
Panting and screaming
Thank you, have a nice day

His heart is pounding he switches the channel
looking for something other than rape or murder
or beatings or torture
but except for Walt Disney
it's a twisted alliance
This age of video violence

Down at his job his boss sits there screaming
If he loses his job, life loses its meaning
His son is in high school
There's nothing he's learning
He sits by the TV
Watching Corvettes exploding

The currents rage deep inside us
This is the age of video violence
The currents rage deep inside us
This is the age of video violence
Down at a bar some woman is topless
She's acned and scarred, her hair is a mess
While he shoves $5 down her exotic panties

The video jukebox is playing Madonna
While just down the block
At some local theater
they're grabbing their crotches
at the 13th beheading

AMERICAN RENEGADES

As the dead rise to live
The live sink to die
The currents are deep and raging inside

Our good working stiff looks a whore in the eye
ties her to a bed
while he beats her back bloody
and then back at home
drinking more instant coffee
calls some red-neck evangelist
He's seen on TV and says

The currents rage, the dawn's upon us
This is the age of video violence
No age of reason is landing upon us
This is the age of video violence

The currents rage so deep within us
This is the age of video violence
The currents rage so deep down inside us
This is the age of video violence

KAREN FINLEY

Montecito

Here I am in Montecito—vacationing and it all came back to me—how some 15 years earlier I was picked up by two men delivering mattresses and how they tried to rape me—I outsmarted them—I said I can't go down on you in the front seat—your dick is so big—I could give you better head in the back—your dick is so big. Nothing makes a man feel better than to tell him his dick is big. I pretended like I liked him cause I could tell in my teenage way that no one ever liked him. They are watching me as we get out of the truck and I say let's move the mattresses next to each other on the floor then I can suck you and your friend can fuck me or I can work you both with my hands. The mattresses were heavy and it took the two of them. I pretended to help but then I ran. I ran, I ran, oh yes I ran—we were stopped in Montecito in a parking lot overlooking the ocean and there were stores above on a hill and I ran and ran til I

got to that store—got to an entrance—and here I am on vacation now, got to get to the entrance—You see I ain't got nothing—
I ain't got money, a car, a degree—I ain't got nothing but me.

They think they can have me cause they are stronger than me.

All I got is wits

All I got is wits

I look at all the wealth. The big houses that overlook water with domestics where every spill cleaned up by someone else with the only mess is from everything you've got of so much stuff—with everything priceless—no one smells bad.

I'm still running and they are getting in their truck. Maybe they'll catch me. I hate myself for being a girl. For being young. For this costume of heels and makeup, of earrings that get caught. I'm dressed for this occasion of just being female. Being caught female. If I ever have a daughter I must teach her of this moment in a woman's life of running. Runing. Running. Caught. I'm caught.

"*You should have ran faster!*" All of the penguins had to be kept inside now since people had been known to shoot and stab the penguins.

"*Why don't you fight back*" and I answer to myself the sheep have more than one stomach and if they fall in a certain way their stomachs get all tangled up, they can't get up and they can die.

"*I know you're bleeding profusely but I need to see some identification before I file a report.*" All of the animals at the childrens zoo had extensive bruising to their vulvas and anus perhaps inserted with a blunt object. I'm back here 15 years later and today I want to talk to God but the only one he sends me is Jack Kerouac and so I tell him—that On The Road stuff that almost got me killed—I don't have the privilige of going on the road as a woman, as a mother, you glorify your irresponsibility—I bet you were the worst father in the world—You were just some drunken guy to me—then God sends me William Burroughs you are no hero to me—you shot your wife—yeah a big artsy guy—You are no god to me. I felt better but then I say to God—You make life tough—you make life hard—Then I got hit by a car but I'm crying, I'm so happy cause those mattress goons aren't taking me away. For now I'm safe and if I'm lucky my face might be smashed up and then I'll really be free. I'll really be free.

MELVIN VAN PEEBLES

On 115

Born with the fastest hands Harlem had ever seen
Thought they had 'em the next NBA star
On hundred and fifteenth

Same day his daddy split his momma had this dream
The Knicks or the Nets would be their ticket
Off hundred and fifteenth

Cross Lenox he'd dribble tearing ass in between
Jitneys muggers potholes and wine bottles
Up hundred and fifteenth

His jump was an arrow, his dunk was straight and clean
Sure as a flush junkies connection on
One hundred and fifteenth

The fool went one on one with big 'h' an got creamed
Found him stiff o. d' back of the rib joint
On hundred and fifteenth

Horse will always foul you, flagrant as he wanta be
Aint no refs calling no penalties on him either
On hundred and fifteenth

Somewhere stars are shining, hope God's got a boss team
Homeboys dont like playing 'gainst no punks when
They from hundred and fifteenth

Born with the fastest hands Harlem had ever seen
Thought they had'em the next NBA star
On hundred and fifteenth

RAY BREMSER

From *Poems of Madness*
City Madness

I used to sit often composing the manuscript
never denouncing and therefore not to be written
without preparation for trial.

I'd sit contemplating unobvious thoughts without poetry,
being the poet of adequate life
on broken brick steps full of contractions
of piles and pimply sores from the stone
and syphlis-eyed hypochondria sleep-thinking germs
bringing flu
and I caught my first cold fifteen histories ago
in the maggoty festering garbage-can alley
back of my mother's rear room.

I used to sit dreaming the dreams of accomplishment
marching in questionable cadences down to the foot
of the Harborside Terminal
into the emptying carrying cars of Spry and Colgate
Mullers outgoing spaghetti and infinite
meatballs!

counting the black-balled parolees and broken-backed
spics, Italian laborers, Polacks and sweaty
old terminal boss,
whose unknotted tie and left-wide agape collar
was motive enough to imagine the noose.

When I was ten I discovered the poet and quick
circulated great novels of spy and adventure
and killer police, whose murderous face
I didn't at first grasp
until I discovered a cop humping some young
indiscernable girl in the park.

She addressed him with delicate fits from her lips
which turned ghostly and blue and the dress tore away
and he popped with a joy every cop in New Jersey recalls.

AMERICAN RENEGADES

Since then I have hated what passes as law
and the ten-year-old grew but the poet did not
and the novels fell off into idiot poems
and madness and sight of my city,
the city of squares and the city of Pharisees
all mobbed into a mass of the lewdest advertisement,
tight denim levis—buck shoes for the silent
and cardigan jitterbug jackets with saddle stitched pockets
of rubber . . .
I've never been ready for trial.
But Carole Fugate has!
Sweet youngest ever martyr
City killer high accomplishment—
in her peaceful, pensive, elemental face
the Virgin Mary ended indecision
and elected to abide
in every sinew's whore-mastered inch
of Charlie's sweet
and favored yards of flesh.

How did he do it to you? Whispering 'mother'?
or 'little sister'? What of your idiot's eyes?
Now it is more than Charlie's sweet—
now it is every lecherous penis
legality has—every sensuous
prick of old righteousness! Lord, how they're prodding,
those moot prosecutors!

In love with your lips and in love with your belly's
white warmth, O human—O animal—heavenly
screwed little girl—in love with your crying's pure
succulent salt of the heart—hot heart of the murderess—
heart of the victim, whispering 'love' and whispering
        'please'—
and the minor-thief's heart in my own hunting skin
corresponds to your sexual lips of immaculate
white-
        I would run my cool tongue
in your mouth, eat your tears, taste your difficult
washmachine beauty!

My city envisions your breast beneath which
is the heart that addresses itself,
and the answers?
definite

crazy—
and love!

No; it wasn't odd
that night
when I went
alone—
into the streets
and out of my home,
so long out of sorts—
was I out of my mind, too,
with the dread melancholy
struck edgewise into my brain
and into my guts,
only man-guts, not pig-iron
but twisted and flanged
and eroded with rust?

So I had to walk
and I walked, way outward
onto the familiar street
where people are not always people—

And I took in my hand
in my coat and conjoined
a pistol, in case—
to decide things
                best
for myself!

But the dreary, unfluctuables pinioned me
stiff-columned into my shoes. The trigger-taut
sinewous spindle stood me up clotheslessly still
to suffer the bearable whipping of fingers
over the mutable flesh—
                the motherless
sonofabitching flac—
the criminal shots, were
pinned, like medals of thievery,
onto my breast;
                and my waxworkwings
found Icarus's pool;
and I'm here now,
                changelessly dressed!

AMERICAN RENEGADES

It is sometimes the way our necessity balks
at a curve, to be tried.
To be taken in dubious custody, chained
to a chair in the precinct called 1st
and allowed the due processes up to the neck
of the fist and the shattering bludgeoning hard-
rubber hose of an arm's length.

question and answer and hate
for the acne-nervousness paused on the face
and the please-leave-me-alone in the watery eyes
that were blue turning black from the law's
dark inscrutable glare—
whose brute badges of courage and bravery stare,
because Hart Crane might have had one of the heads
that was cracked by the graces
of nightstick and sailor Bayonne!

Now their foolish pomposity walks in the streets!
At the Hoboken wharves and the West New York Hills,
over Palisade plumage of rock and the Fort Lee
nest of the eagle—Washington Bridge Riviera—
doubtful escape on the harlotted Hudson Expressways!

One thing I found in the handcuffs was this:
Great fear of the law!
                          and a dread
of my own Jersey Cityite's farce
gone beyond the impossible truss
of a sentence too large
to impress *any* boy with its complex
of God!

I will sign the confession of monsterous crime—
I will sign
I will sign
I will sign

I WILL SIGN!

JIMMY SANTIAGO BACA

From *Martin XIV*

El Pablo was a bad dude.
Presidente of the River Rats.
(700 strong), from '67 to '73.
Hands so fast
he could catch two flies buzzing
in air, and still light his cigarette.
From a flat foot standing position
he jumped to kick the top of a door jamb
twice with each foot.
Pants and shirt creased and cuffed,
sharp pointy shoes polished to black glass,
El Pachucon was cool to the bone, brutha.
His initials were etched
on Junior High School desks,
Castañeda's Meat Market walls,
downtown railway bridge,
on the red bricks at the Civic Auditorium,
Uptown and Downtown,
El Pachucón left his mark.
Back to the wall, legs crossed, hands pocketed,
combing his greased-back ducktail
when a jaine walked by. Cool to the huesos.
Now he's a janitor at Pajarito
Elementary School—
         still hangs out
         by the cafeteria, cool to the bone,
         el vato,
         still wears his sunglasses,
         still proud,
he leads a new gang of neighborhood parents
to the Los Padilla Community Center,
to fight against polluted ground water,
against Developers who want to urbanize
his rural running grounds.
Standing in the back of the crowd
last Friday, I saw Pablo stand up
and yell at the Civic Leaders from City Hall,

"Listen cuates, you pick your weapons.
We'll fight you on any ground you pick."

CAL (WITH DANNY LYON)
Member of Chicago Outlaws and former Hell's Angel

Chopped Scooter

Everything was black lacquer, you hip to it? And then it had pearlescent under-neath that. And the tank went into metal flake on the corners of the tank. Then it was black lacquer on top of that, and the tank was flamed out from there. Then my fender, man it came up and had a weird scoop, and in the middle, that little diamond scene. It looked just like a little flower, like fingers of a flower. Sat right on my fender, man. You know, on the end, and it was so beautiful. It was like you could see the light come in this way and it seemed to flow out. You hip to that? On the tank it looked like wings of a bird. You hip to it? With little silver feathers right at the elbow. It looked like an eagle chargin' cause it had little red type seams. Then from there I had a sissy bar going up. It curved up on the top, and in the middle of it, man, I had this sword that went jagged. Straight sword that had two mother-of-pearl handles and the grip was gold. And the sword was gold, gold, fourteen-carat plate gold, you hip to it?

I dig them beautiful customized jobs. You know why? 'Cause I look at a scooter, man, that's completely chopped, man, and every part on it he either made himself or bought special for it. Now you look at that dude, man, and that dude's an outlaw. Whenever he rides, man, part of that scooter is him.

You see that old ancient piece of shit I came on tonight? Try it sometimes, its an experience, I'll tell you. Everything's a fuckin' death trap on that cock-sucker. No shit. Go down thirty-five miles an hour and you're going into a speed wobble. The fuckin' handlebars are cocked this fuckin' way. I think the fuckin' wheel's bent in the back. You can't get neutral in the motherfucker. It's a mind-blower just to ride it. Go down on the thing and you got your fishtails right up here by your ear, you know, so you can listen to the tone. Man, you just go through the fuckin' gears, you're on your own fuckin' scooter. You built this motherfucker.

Ai

The Kid

My sister rubs the doll's face in mud,
then climbs through the truck window.
She ignores me as I walk around it,
hitting the flat tires with an iron rod.
The old man yells for me to help hitch the team,
but I keep walking around the truck, hitting harder,
until my mother calls.
I pick up a rock and throw it at the kitchen window,
but it falls short.
The old man's voice bounces off the air like a ball
I can't lift my leg over.

I stand beside him, waiting, but he doesn't look up
and I squeeze the rod, raise it, his skull splits open.
Mother runs toward us. I stand still,
get her across the spine as she bends over him.
I drop the rod and take the rifle from the house.
Roses are red, violets are blue,
one bullet for the black horse, two for the brown.
They're down quick. I spit, my tongue's bloody;
I've bitten it. I laugh, remember the one out back.
I catch her climbing from the truck, shoot.
The doll lands on the ground with her.
I pick it up, rock it in my arms.
Yeah. I'm Jack, Hogarth's son.
I'm nimble, I'm quick.
In the house, I put on the old man's best suit
and his patent leather shoes.
I pack my mother's satin nightgown
and my sister's doll in the suitcase.
Then I go outside and cross the fields to the highway.
I'm fourteen. I'm a wind from nowhere.
I can break your heart.

KEN KESEY

Geometry

If you draw a line
Precisely safe and parallel to mine,
We can sail together
Clear on past the stars
And never meet.
And since the holes between
These points of distant heat
Are deep and blind,
Sight a course for collision
And hang on tight!
. . . the precision of our loving
Is the lethal kind.

CHE GUEVARA

Song to Fidel
(Translated by Ed Dorn and Gordon Brotherston)

You said the sun would rise.
Let's go
along those unmapped paths
to free the green alligator you love.

And let's go obliterating
insults with our
brows swept with dark insurgent stars.
We shall have victory or shoot past death.

At the first shot the whole jungle
will awake with fresh amazement and

there and then serene company
we'll be at your side.

When your voice quarters the four winds
reforma agraria, justice, bread, freedom,
we'll be there with identical accents
at your side.

And when the clean operation against the tyrant
ends at the end of the day
there and then set for the final battle
we'll be at your side.

And when the wild beast licks his wounded side
where the dart of Cuba hits him
we'll be at your side
with proud hearts.

Don't ever think our integrity can be sapped
by those decorated fleas hopping with gifts
we want their rifles, their bullets and a rock
nothing else.

And if iron stands in our way
we ask for a sheet of Cuban tears
to cover our guerrilla bones
on the journey to American history.
Nothing more.

LEONARD COHEN

What Is a Saint

What is a saint? A saint is someone who has achieved a remote human possibility. It is impossible to say what that possibility is. I think it has something to do with the energy of love. Contact with this energy results in the exercise of a kind of balance in the chaos of existence. A saint does not dissolve the chaos; if he did the world would have changed long ago. I do not think that a saint

Art by Hunter Thompson

dissolves the chaos even for himself, for there is something arrogant and warlike in the notion of a man setting the universe in order. It is a kind of balance that is his glory. He rides the drifts like an escaped ski. His course is a caress of the hill. His track is a drawing of the snow in a moment of its particular arrangement with wind and rock. Something in him so loves the world that he gives himself to the laws of gravity and chance. Far from flying with the angels, he traces with the fidelity of a seismograph needle the state of the solid bloody landscape. His house is dangerous and finite, but he is at home in the world. He can love the shapes of human beings, the fine and twisted shapes of the heart. It is good to have among us such men, such balancing monsters of love.

Disguises

I am sorry that the rich man must go
and his house become a hospital.
I loved his wine, his contemptuous servants,
his ten-year-old ceremonies.
I loved his car which he wore like a snail's shell
everywhere, and I loved his wife,
the hours she put into her skin,
the milk, the lust, the industries
that served her complexion.
I loved his son who looked British
but had American ambitions
and let the word aristocrat comfort him
like a reprieve while Kennedy reigned.
I loved the rich man: I hate to see
his season ticket for the Opera
fall into a pool for opera-lovers.

I am sorry that the old worker must go
who called me mister when I was twelve
and sir when I was twenty
who studied against me in obscure socialist
clubs which met in restaurants.
I loved the machine he knew like a wife's body.
I loved his wife who trained bankers
in an underground pantry
and never wasted her ambition in ceramics.
I loved his children who debate
and come first at McGill University.
Goodbye old gold-watch winner

AMERICAN RENEGADES

all your complex loyalties
must now be borne by one-faced patriots.

Goodbye dope fiends of North Eastern Lunch
circa 1948, your spoons which were not
Swedish Stainless, were the same colour
as the hoarded clasps and hooks
of discarded soiled therapeutic corsets.
I loved your puns about snow
even if they lasted the full seven-month
Montreal winter. Go write your memoirs
for the Psychedelic Review.

Goodbye sex fiends of Beaver Pond
who dreamed of being jacked-off
by electric milking machines.
You had no Canada Council.
You had to open little boys
with a pen-knife.
I loved your statement to the press:
"I didn't think he'd mind."
Goodbye articulate monsters
Abbott and Costello have met Frankenstein.

I am sorry that the conspirators must go
the ones who scared me by showing me
a list of all the members of my family.
I loved the way they reserved judgment
about Genghis Khan. They loved me because
I told them their little beards
made them dead-ringers for Lenin.
The bombs went off in Westmount
and now they are ashamed
like a successful outspoken Schopenhauerian
whose room-mate has committed suicide.
Suddenly they are all making movies.
I have no one to buy coffee for.

I embrace the changeless:
the committed men in public wards
oblivious as Hassidim
who believe that they are someone else.
Bravo! Abelard, viva! Rockefeller,
have these buns, Napoleon,
hurrah! betrayed Duchess.

Long live you chronic self-abusers!
you monotheists!
you familiars of the Absolute
sucking at circles!

You are all my comfort
as I turn to face the beehive
as I disgrace my style
as I coarsen my nature
as I invent jokes
as I pull up my garters
as I accept responsibility.

You comfort me
incorrigible betrayers of the self
as I salute fashion
and bring my mind
    like a promiscuous air-hostess
handing out parachutes in a nose dive
bring my butchered mind
to bear upon the facts.

JANIS JOPLIN

I remember you well in the Chelsea Hotel,
you were famous, your heart was a legend.
You told me again you preferred handsome men,
but for me you would make an exception.
And clenching your fist for the ones like us
who are oppressed by the figures of beauty,
you fixed yourself, you said: "Well, never mind,
we are ugly, but we have the music."
FROM "CHELSEA HOTEL" BY LEONARD COHEN

Turtle Blues

Oh Lord, I once had a daddy
He said he'd give me everything in sight,

AMERICAN RENEGADES

So I said "Honey, I want the sunshine
I'll take the stars out of the night
Come on and give it to me, babe
Honey, I want it right now!

I ain't the kind of woman
Who'd make your life a bed of ease
No, I'm not the kind of woman
To make your life a bed of ease
But if you just want to go out drinkin', honey
Won't you invite me along, please
Oh I'd be so good to you, babe

I guess I'm just like a turtle
Hiding underneath it's horny shell
Yeah, like a turtle
Hiding underneath its horny shell
But you know I'm very well protected
i know this Goddamned life too well

People call me mean, you can call me evil
I been called much worse things around
Oh honey, don't you know here
Call me mean, call me evil
I been called much worse things
But I'm gonna take good care of Janis
No one gonna talk me down

Neil Ortenberg

An Aging Radical Muses on His Conjugal Visits

Yes, she's a beauty,
breasts you wouldn't believe,
you touch them
once a month
when she visits
from the suburbs of Virginia

without husband & child.
This is what keeps you going
you say,
the way she brazenly
puts your hand
on the forbidden whiteness of bosom
and you in your seventh decade
quiver with pornographic absorption,
forgetting momentarily
the struggle,
        the revolution,
                your life of resistance.

For you there has been
no greater joy
than
living for causes,
the fifty-six arrests,
        freedom rides,
                the march to Nagasaki.

There is a story told
how you, fresh with blood
forehead to chin,
where the thrust of jackboots
entering snarls of flesh
made you only more determined,
did not wash the blood,
instead spent the rest of the day working,
ecstatic in the grip of solidarity,
the cuts & red chisels of cheek & brow
saying to the world,
"I'm an underdog,
        I am best so."
Now you are waiting
for what you call your "conjugal visit,"
there is talk of war in El Salvador,
murder in Atlanta,
but you think now only
of her erect nipples,
the bristled threads of hair
lining her thighs,
the way she makes you feel
the struggle isn't in vain.

HUNTER S. THOMPSON

In 1965 Hunter S. Thompson wrote numerous poems while covering the Hell's Angels motorcycle gang for The Nation. Thompson usually wrote these poems on a whim, a creative way to kill time at his Haight Ashbury apartment or a local Bay Area tavern. The revolutionary surrealism of 1960's San Francisco provided perfect fodder for penning outlaw poems about Ken Kesey's Merry Pranksters and LSD, the Jefferson Airplane and Berkeley's Free Speech Movement. Three of Thompson's poems were published—one in *The Nation* and the others in *Spider*, the journal for the Berkeley Free Speech Movement. "Collect Telegram from A Mad Dog" appeared in the October 13, 1965 edition of *Spider*, and Thompson would later include it in *The Great Shark Hunt*, a 1978 anthology of his best gonzo journalism. The poem was written in a Point Richmond diner after a night of heavy drinking. "It's a true story," Thompson notes. "I was sitting at the counter with a waitress having some coffee when suddenly a stranger came out of the bathroom with shaving cream on his face ranting like a madman." Bored, Thompson struck up a conversation with the strung-out delinquent and eventually brought him to Sunday brunch at the home of Richmond mayor, David Pierce where they gorged on blintzes with raspberries and Napa Valley champagne. They spent the remainder of that Sunday together at the Mariner's Tavern.

DOUGLAS BRINKLEY

Collect Telegram from a Mad Dog

October 13, 1965

Not being a poet, and drunk as well,
leaning into the diner and dawn
and hearing a juke box mockery of some better
human sound
I wanted rhetoric
but could only howl the rotten truth
Norman Luboff
should have his nuts ripped off with a plastic fork.
Then howled around like a man with the
final angst,
not knowing what I wanted there
Probably the waitress, bend her double
like a safety pin,
Deposit the mad seed before they
tie off my tubes

or run me down with Dingo dogs
for not voting
at all.

Suddenly a man with wild eyes rushed
out from the wooden toilet

Specifically Luboff and the big mongers,
the slumfeeders, the perverts
and the pious.

The legal man agreed
We had a case and indeed a duty to
Right these Wrongs, as it were
The Price would be four thousand in front and
ten for the nut.
I wrote him a check on the Sawtooth
National Bank,
but he hooted at it
While rubbing a special oil on
his palms
To keep the chancres from itching
beyond endurance
On this Sabbath.
McConn broke his face with a running
Cambodian chop, then we
drank his gin, ate his blintzes
But failed to find anyone
to rape
and went back to the Mariners' Tavern
to drink in the sun.
Later, from jail
I sent a brace of telegrams
to the right people,
explaining my position.

DAVID WOJNAROWICZ

Hobo on Flatcar
Eastbound for St. Paul
Minneapolis

I came east from Spokane Washington last night . . . been riding all night headin
to St. Paul to a mission so I can get a meal and some sleep . . . ya gotta watch
these overpasses at night . . . *It's dangerous* . . . them kids who live up around
here'll attack ya or stone ya to death . . . there's no lights in these cars and these
kids think there's nothin funnier than to jump some guy and beat him up or
hit him in the head with rocks . . . hey ya see that guy come outta that tunnel?
ya know where he just came from? Well a lot of them homosexuals come down
to this area to have what they call fun . . . those kids never mess with the ho-
mosexuals cause a lot of them are rough . . . yeah they're demonstratin in the
streets for their rights to marry one another . . . a woman marryin a woman, a
guy marryin a guy . . . hell! I don't know why they wanna do that . . . I wouldn't
get married . . . too many bills too many problems . . . now I don't mean that I
don't wanna be around a buddy . . . I just mean I don't want no wife . . . ya know
some of them women homosexuals are just as strong as men . . . one time I was
in this bar and one of them women was sittin next to me she says: Hey buy me
a drink . . . so I bought her one and then she tells me to buy her another one
. . . I said Hell no. No woman's gonna take advantage of me . . . then the bar-
tender leaned over and said: You better watch it she's a dyke and the woman
said: Yeah I'm a dyke. So I bought her a drink . . . ya gotta watch it cause some
of them are really rough . . .

The switchmen don't give ya any trouble . . . they only give the winos trouble.
The winos and tramps who are hungry give ya the most trouble. Ya got all kinds
of heads ridin these days . . . ya got pillheads, hopheads, jesus . . . they try to
catch you asleep or drunk . . . then they hit ya over the head . . . that's when ya
have trouble. I can't stand them winos. I know I look like a wino when I need
a shave but I ain't one. Who needs to get wrapped up in wine all the money it
takes to keep on gettin it. No not me . . . I just move around stop here or there
at a mission to eat and clean up. The mission over in St. Paul is real nice . . .
you fellas oughta come out with me . . . you'll get yourselves a good meal and a
night's sleep. Well here's where I get off. Listen when I jump can ya throw my
pack down right after me? it'll save me walkin all the way back to pick it up . . .
and make sure ya jump before ya get to the switchyards . . . they got guys watchin
from the towers . . .

Young Boy in
Bus Station Coffee Shop
Denver

Yeah . . . I almost got killed when I was going cross country . . . but I guess every-
body comes close to death at least once if they make that kind of distance. I
was in Las Vegas . . . man Las Vegas was beautiful . . . well I was hanging out at
this apartment with two roommates. We were all working at different hours.
One of the roommates owned a motorcycle and one day when he was at work
my other roommate turned to me and said: Hey let's take a ride on the motor-
cycle. He didn't have a license or nothing but I said: Okay and we split going
around the roads in and out of town and all of a sudden we passed this fuckin
cop car. We kept going and this cop car circles around and starts following us.
We turned down one street and then another and the fuckin cop was still fol-
lowing us. Finally he puts on his flashing lights and gave a few blasts at his siren
so we pulled over to the side of the road down at the bottom of a hill near a
fork. The cop pulls to the side and starts getting out of the car and right across
the road is this path that cuts through a forest to another highway so my room-
mate driving the motorcycle waits till the cop is a few yards away and then guns
the fuckin bike and cuts across the road onto the path. The cop made this big
scramble to get back to his car and he goes blowing out in the dust to chase us.
We were heading through to the other highway and we made it and started
heading further away from town. The cop car was coming up behind us pretty
fast with the siren screaming he was weaving in and out of traffic and so were
we. We finally cut to the side of the road to get past all the slow cars and the
cop saw what was happening and did the same. Now we're really going fast as
hell and getting further and further away from town . . . we kept cutting down
side roads and finally we turned down this one street and it was a dead end . . .
there was nothing in front of us but the whole goddamn desert so we said: Oh
shit! and we hear the cop car racing down behind us. We had been traveling up
to eighty miles per hour with this cop behind us. So my friend guns the motor
again and we cut out into the desert. We were going about twenty-five miles
per hour brrooommmm up and down these slopes and dunes and hills with this
fucking cop still behind us and we got pretty far out but then we went up the
side of this slope and it turned out to be a small cliff on the other side and the
bike dropped off and we went through the air and slammed into the sand at the
bottom. I had the wind knocked out of me and I could hear the cop coming so
I stood up and turned around with my hands in the air waiting for him to come
over the rise and get me. I figured there was nowhere else we could go because
the bike was smashed up from the fall and this cop comes running over the
slope towards me and he drops to his knees in a crouching position and aims
his gun and shouts: Halt you sonuvabitch! Halt! and I turn around and there's
my roommate running commando style across the fuckin desert dodging back
and forth. I couldn't fuckin believe it. So the cop handcuffs me and I'm lying

AMERICAN RENEGADES

there on my side in the sand and he radios for reinforcements. About twenty minutes later two squad cars show up and these big beefy bastards pull out a bunch of dogs. They were out there about two hours sniffing around but they never got the guy. I don't know how the hell he got away. So they took me back to town and threw me in jail. I was in there for three days under the charge of grand larceny resisting arrest and some other shit . . . but let me tell you it was alright in that jail . . . I just slept and ate . . . I mean I would rather have not been there but the guys in the cell block were right guys. We would write these notes on small pieces of paper and shove them through the slots in the doors and wiggle them around to try and get the guard's attention in the early morning when they walked through the cell block. You know, notes like: HEY I'M IN-NOCENT or PLEASE CALL THIS NUMBER FOR ME. After the day they finally let me make a phone call they took me into this empty room with bars over everything and they got this fuckin ugly cop leaning back in a chair against the wall smoking a pipe and a radio was playing. I called my other roommate and he came down to convince them that the bike was his and that I didn't steal it. The cops tried to get me to say who it was who was driving the bike but I kept telling them that I didn't know, that I knew he knew my roommate but that I had never seen him before in my life. Two days later I was taken to court and they let me off . . .

Man in Harbor Coffee Shop
San Francisco

When I was in prison there were these two brothers, Hugh and Roy D'Autremont, who I became good friends with. I don't know if you ever heard of them but they were in prison for life for blowing up an entire train to get the mail-car money. So every day I'd walk with Hugh in the yard . . . he was like this great mystical teacher but without getting into the mysticism, just a beautiful fella. So we'd walk along and stop every now and then because he had something to say to me like: Earl, do you see that guard tower? and I'd say, Yeah, and he'd say: Well take your fingers and measure how big it is from here, and I'd take my thumb and forefinger and place them about an inch apart so that the guard tower fit neatly between the two, and Hugh would say: Got it? and I'd say, Yeah, and he'd say without taking his eyes off the guard tower: That's how high it really is. Then we'd talk awhile more while I pondered this and realized he was talking about perspective . . . and every so often we'd pass his brother Roy and Hugh would say: My pawn to your bishop, like they were playing mental chess, didn't even have a chessboard, they knew each position of the pieces in their heads which means Hugh was teaching me things and talking about various subjects and all the while he'd be pondering the moves of the chess game in his head . . .

I had a lot of great sex in prison . . . there was always some guy at my elbow trying to persuade me to drop whatever daddy I had and go with him . . . there was one time that I had two guys at once. One was a real handsome guy but he had had a prefrontal lobotomy. Whenever we would get into conversations about the past he could only remember up to a certain point, then he'd explain his loss of memory with: That's when they cut off my horns. So I was making it with him and at the same time I was making it with this other fella who was in for murder. One day I was sewing in my cell when this queen rushed up and said: Earl, Earl, Joe and Butch are out there killing each other. They found out you've been making it with both of them! So I quick rushed into the yard and there they were punching it out and I ran up and got in between them and said: Now boys you stop fighting this instant . . . you both should know better . . . why there's surely enough of me to go around. Well after that they both thought about it and I was dropped . . . neither of them would see me anymore . . .

JIM CARROLL

8 Fragments for Kurt Cobain

1
Genius is not a generous thing
In return it charges more interest than any amount
of royalties can cover
And it resents fame
With bitter vengeance

Pills and powders only placate it awhile
Then it puts you in a place where the planet's
poles reverse.
Where the currents of electricity shift

Your Body becomes a magnet and pulls to it despair
and rotten teeth,
Cheez Whiz and guns

Whose triggers are shaped tenderly into a false
lust
In timeless illusion

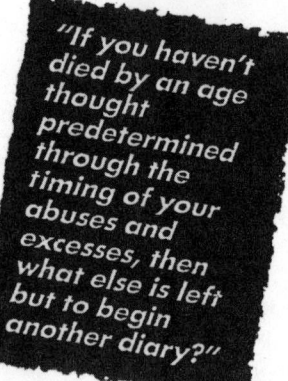
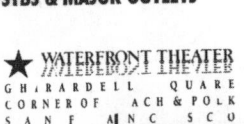

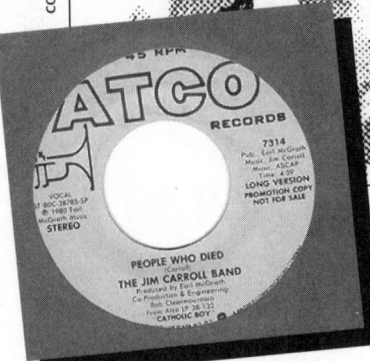

2
The guitar claws kept tightening, I guess, on your
heart stem.
The loops of feedback and distortion, threaded
right thru
Lucifer's wisdom teeth, and never stopped their
reverberating
In your mind
And from the stage
All the faces out front seemed so hungry
With an unbearably wholesome misunderstanding

From where they sat, you seemed so far up there
High and live and diving

And instead you were swamp crawling
Down, deeper
Until you tasted the Earth's own blood
And chatted with the buzzing-eyed insects that
heroin breeds

3
You should have talked more with the monkey
He's always willing to negotiate
I'm still paying him off . . .
The greater the money and fame
The slower the pendulum of fortune swings

Your will could have sped it up . . .
But you left that on an airplane
Because it wouldn't pass customs and immigration

4
Here's synchronicity for you:

Your music's tape was inside my Walkman
When my best friend from summer camp
Called with the news about you
I listened then . . .
It was all there!
Your music kept cutting deeper and deeper valleys
of sound
Less and less light
Until you hit solid rock

AMERICAN RENEGADES

The drill bit broke
and the valley became
A thin crevice, impassable in time,
As time itself stopped.

And the walls became vises of brilliant notes
Pressing in . . .
Pressure
That's how diamonds are made
And that's where it sometimes all collapses
Down in on you

5
Then I translated your muttered lyrics
And the phrases were curious:
Like "incognito libido"
And "Chalk Skin Bending"

The words kept getting smaller and smaller
Until
Separated from their music
Each letter spilled out into a cartridge
Which fit only in the barrel of a gun

6
And you shoved the barrel in as far as possible
Because that's where the pain came from
That's where the demons were digging

The world outside was blank
Its every cause was just a continuation
Of another unsolved effect

7
But Kurt . . .
Didn't the thought that you would never write
another song
Another feverish line or riff
Make you think twice?
That's what I don't understand
Because it's kept me alive, above any wounds

8
If only you hadn't swallowed yourself into a coma
in Rome . . .

You could have gone to Florence
And looked into the eyes of Bellini or Rafael's
Portraits

Perhaps inside them
You could have found a threshold back to beauty's arms
Where it all began

No matter that you felt betrayed by her
That is always the cost
As Frank said,
Of a young artist's remorseless passion

Which starts out as a kiss
And follows like a curse

Facts

Its own wisdom has
Left Holland in ruins.

If you repeat the words
                    "Medulla Oblongata"
Long enough over and over you will
Collapse to the ground and hear the sound
Of the first drum developed by homo erectus man.

When Oscar Wilde lay on his death bed,
Penniless and disgraced,
In a cheap boarding room in France,
He stared dimly to the window and muttered:
"Those curtain are absolutely horrendous;
One of us has simply *got to go*."

He then sank into the pillow, shut his eyes and died.

If Angela Lansbury sneezed
While swimming underwater
It would take exactly one second
For the sound to travel one mile
And be heard by, say, a sea otter or pilot whale

AMERICAN RENEGADES

Though they have tried to squash the facts
There is enduring evidence
That when Wallace Stevens died
An unspecified number of blackbirds
Flew through the windows
Of the mortuary where he lay
Removed his eyeballs with their beaks

And flew away, carrying both eyes
To the Florida Keys, depositing them
Softly into the green waters above the coral reef.

Jukebox
For Jim Gustafson

Now I've come to realize
That I am a jukebox

A very old jukebox
A classic you might call me

I spent my early years in the elegant saloons
Of downtown Detroit
I still recall

The cool brush of pearls
Against my glass
As women leaned over me
To read what I had to give, to discover
What I had within me, it changed
From week to week

During Prohibition I was trucked off
To a garage in the middle of a desolate winter

And for years I stood disconnected
In pools of oil and antifreeze
Beside a refrigerator
Without a door, a steering wheel
Leaning against my back

I should make this clear:
I play only 45s

Aching spirals of black vinyl
I do not play compact discs

I do not show videos

They are digital technologies

I am an analogue thing
I participate in your consciousness
As you participate in mine

When they discovered me last year
They tried to insert
A laser inside me
But I rejected it like a transplanted heart

Look at my lines
I have a right to be proud
On each side I have wide tubes
Filled with amber and green liquid
Where large bubbles form and flow
Constantly, bottom to top

It's true
My needle has turned slightly dull

And my tone arm
Skips
Across the music
Creating lovely variations and distortion
Each time they drop
Onto the turntable and play

Songs that bring memories
Painful as dry ice

Now I have been hauled to the cemetery
And placed on brittle grass

Over your grave
Instead of a headstone

My guts filled with all your favorite tunes

AMERICAN RENEGADES

Just as you wrote it out

And instead of flowers or stones
Friends bring rolls of quarters

Today a tall woman
Thin with long straight hair
Inserted ten dollars in even change
On the same song: F-6

And danced away
To my speakers blasting

"Brown-Eyed Girl"

Over and over
The morning through
In the grass grinding above you.

The Ocean Below

She was a diagnosed schizophrenic. When he walked into her apt., in fact, he noticed a document on the wall from the Social Security Dept. of the State of New York certifying her as a schizophrenic, and thus eligible for financial benefits, medical treatment, and food stamps. She had it hanging under glass in a walnut frame, as if it were a diploma or a law degree.

When she was lucid, she would speak of her ailment as if it were a blessing bestowed on her by God, or a capability that she had worked strenuously, over many years, to master. She made it sound as if she could dunk a basketball or perform jaw-dropping feats of magic. "Yes," she would speak loudly, "I am a diagnosed, fully certified schizophrenic, and I am getting progressively worse. It is a disease, you know. It has to do with the chemicals in my brain being out of balance. It's quite complicated. I have a very, very complicated disease." She said this with such pride.

As she continued to talk, however, she would slip away from the articulate, and refer to the, "Panthers that inhabit my lungs, whose paws sometimes scratch while they tell me secrets even Jesus does not know . . . there's no way you're getting me near those railroad tracks."

She would lapse from clarity into such phrases without warning, in the space of a single sentence, as if one were leisurely walking along a country road and suddenly plunged off the edge of a cliff, plummeting straight into the ocean below.

With van Gogh

I am sitting on a park bench in the neighborhood where I was raised as a boy. Van Gogh approaches me in the dark, a wide blue gash laid down his luminous cheeks. There are some thin papers folded beneath his arms, secured by a ribbon. He is wearing a cheap iridescent suit, beneath it a yellow polo shirt with the image of two small green alligators copulating sewn on above the pocket. Over his spiked red hair is a felt hat, its wide brim covered with twelve thick candles. They are burning rapidly in the wind and give off the scent of a cathedral. There is no reason I should know who he is, but I do. He tells me he is going down beyond the running track to paint the Harlem River. I ask him to sit awhile and talk with me, and in a crippled fashion he lowers himself beside me on the bench. I notice the famous missing ear and he sees this and anticipates a question—"It was an experience, right?"—and he laughs. We are both laughing. We cannot stop laughing . . . we are bent over with our fist pounding our guts and howling into the wind as it grows. Just then a woman in a dark dress approaches us in tears. Van Gogh looks up to her, as if to ask, "Why are you doing this?" The woman explains that she has come tonight to realize so many contradictions in her life, that her entire life seems a contradiction and that she is unable to bear such a notion and so has been weeping all through the evening and, now, into the night. Van Gogh and I look to each other and slowly build into even greater fits of laughter. He is pointing up at the woman and clutching my knee and his shoulders are bouncing up and down in hysterics. The woman cries harder, as if for her tears to outdo our laughter. Seeing this, van Gogh rises. Standing before her, he mutters slowly the phrase, "My many contradictions . . . my many contradictions . . ."over and over; then he closes his fist and smashes the woman across the face with incredible force. As the woman, who I see now is quite beautiful, goes down to the pavement, van Gogh falls back beside me on the bench and looks at me, laughing. Then he looks down at the woman and speaks, "There, now you really have something to cry about!" He looks back over to me, after a moment of silence, and we begin laughing again. I throw my arms around him and lay my head to his shoulders, continuing to laugh until my tears begin to fall down the lapel of his suit, which is glowing from the fluorescent light in the lamppost above us.

Rimbaud Sees the Dentist

As he had promised, the old man knocked at Arthur's door early that morning. Rimbaud was ready, and together they passed down into the fresh blocks of sunlight on the sidewalks. Rimbaud was neatly dressed, though his frail black tie, which was more like the lace of a boot, could not conceal the lines of dirt along his collar.

"You should hold no fear of the pain one often takes for granted on the way to the dentist," the old man explained, "for this particular one has lately been experimenting with a strange new form of gas, called nitrous oxide, which is, to all reports, quite successful in eliminating such discomfort."

Rimbaud nodded to that, though, as things were, he was rather looking forward to an experience which involved the purging of one form of pain by means of another, even greater, pain. By the time they had reached the office, however, the old man had made payment and Arthur had been seated in a chair not unlike that of a barber, he had grown curious about this new gas, and asked the dentist if he might inhale some as part of his treatment. The dentist, who was fat, with a stale yellow beard, was delighted this young man knew of his innovation, and he began to attach, somewhat clumsily, a black mask shaped like a cup over the poet's mouth and nose. A long rubber tube ran from the mask to a cylinder placed behind the chair. He turned a knob on the mouth of the cylinder, readjusted the mask, patted the young man's shoulder and told him to relax, that he would return in a short time. "There is no time to speak of that is short," Arthur was mumbling. "And there is a tiny German whose clothing is in flames running in circles along the back of my jaw." The dentist chortled and walked through the door to his outer office; he knew the drug was already at work. The old man had told him his young patient made claims to writing poems, and now he would allow some time to pass before he began extracting teeth, and he would let the poet dream.

So Rimbaud dreamt the nitrous dreams. Of women with black skin whose lips were like drums. Of rodents sealed in kegs of blue water. Of lightning shaped like freight trains passing vertically through the branches of a tree. Whose leaves were knives falling to the earth and standing upright. There was a speed in these visions, each dissolved to the next with thin wheels in flame dropping from the sky. And there were words painted in many colors across the foreheads of women whose arms linked like a chain. The smell of burning rubber clung with thorny fingers to the ceiling of his skull.

ABBIE HOFFMAN

School Prayer for the 80's

Lord we know you're not a Commie
    We're sure you're not a kike
We know *you're* one of us Lord
    cause they say that you're all white

We know you're not a homo
    even though you got no wife
We know you're not a woman Lord
    only man could have created life

We're not mad about disasters Lord
    cancer's just a minor fluke
And we know you'll guard our future
    thank God, you're, *not* anti-nuke

So deliver us from evil
    punish us for all our sin
But when they draw the lottery
    just remember Lord it's me that's supposed to win

TULI KUPFERBERG

"Don't ever leave home without your glue stick," Tuli Kupferberg once warned me as we walked the streets of Soho pasting up flyers on buildings and telephone poles. Although Tuli was dubbed "the Noel Coward of Bohemia" by his friend and co-founding Fug Ed Sanders, I've always thought of the multidextrous humanist-humorist as "the Tom Paine of Standup Protest Performance Art." But whatever handle you try to hang on him, it's safe to say that without ever hogging the spotlight his work deserves, this poet-playwright-editor-publisher-pamphleteer-cartoonist-mime-singer-songwriter-cable-TV-host-political-&-social-archivist-historian and father of two sons (Joseph and Noah) and a daughter (Samara), has probably subliminally influenced more underground writer-poet-artist-publishers in more different areas than any other Boho to come down the page this century. A true multi-medium Godfather of subversive-humor (to groups like the *Unbearables*), Tuli is one maestro equally as pleased hitting the brilliant highs as the groan producing lows as long as he gets his point across.

Born to Lemuel and Jennie Weledniger Kupferberg in New York City's Lower East Side, September 28, 1923, Tuli grew up in the cosmopolitan environment of Manhattan's Yorkville, and liked to say, "My father is a tailor; he puts pockets on people's clothes so other people can put money in them." At 13 he had joined the National Student Union at Townsend Harry High School, beginning a lifelong love affair with his major political influences, Karl Marx and Peter Kropotkin. Somewhere between critiquing Karl and embracing Groucho, he graduated cum laude from Brooklyn College (1944), then did graduate work at the New School for Social Research.

Though it's impossible to compile Tuli's entire bibliography in the space provided here, an abbreviated version pinpoints his publishing career, beginning in 1958, editing and publishing *Birth*, a magazine that ran three issues, and featured writing by, among others, Allen Ginsberg, Diane DiPrima and LeRoy Jones. In 1959, his *Beating: Selected Fruits & Nuts, From One Crazy Month In Spring Not So Long Ago*; and *Snow Job: Poems 1946–1959* were published. Then he and his longtime lover and collaborator Sylvia Topp put together a reference work entitled *Children As Authors: A Big Bibliography*. In the winter of 1960 and fall of 1961 they put out four issues of *Swing*, a magazine devoted to the writings and drawings of children. In 1960, he also published *Young Men Shall See Visions, A Drama in 11 Scenes*. From 1961 to 1964, he edited and published ten issues of *Yeah*, a magazine that described itself as "a sarcastic epitome," "a sardonic review," and "a satiric excursion." The magazine had an issue that authentically reproduced the racist American National Party's entire *Kill* magazine. In 1961, he published several works including his *The Grace & Beauty of the Human Form, 1001 Ways to Live Without Working* (republished by Grove Press in 1967), and *Beatnicks; or, The War Against The Beats*, a pamphlet that explained why the Post WW II square world simultaneously hated and envied the Beats for succeeding in dropping out of society—an act that illuminated the possibility of liberation at the same time it criticized mainstream American life, and concluded with the message, "Listen square . . . you may kill the Beatnik but you will not kill the Beatnik in yourself."

In 1962, he published *The Rub-ya-out of Omore Diem, The Mississippi (A Study of the White Race) Freely Adapted from The Congo (A Study of the Negro Race) by Vachel Lindsay*, and *Sex & War*, which insisted that the U.S. and the U.S.S.R. desired war because of their mutual sense of sexual mystery and frustration. In 1963 he published his satirical book *The Christine Keeler Colouring Book & Cautionary Tale*. The year 1964 saw *The Fugs*—the musical equivalent of R. Crumb's *Zap* comics, they were the one true rock band to come out of the movement, a group whose satirical-political-cultural-musical influence still hasn't been given its proper measure outside of unofficial counterculture history. Formed with lead singer-songwriter-front po' Ed Sanders and drummer Ken Weaver, Tuli's contributions were writing half the songs, playing erectorine and performing a different skit (some of exceptional complexity) to accompany each number. After a two-year mid-60's stint at The Players Theatre on MacDougal Street, *the Fugs* made over a dozen albums for a number of different record companies—including *The Real Woodstock Festival* in 1994.

Tuli put out his own double album, *Tuli & Friends* in 1989 and is still singing & performing with *The Fugs* as we approach the millennium. Among the songs he wrote, were such classic *Fugs'* standards as the melodic *Morning, Morning; CIA Man; Nothing; Slum Landlord of the Lower East Side; Supergirl; Kill for Peace; Children of the Dream; Painted Red (and Black); The New America and The Universal Housewife*. In 1965 he published the last and best issue of *Yeah* titled *Kill For Peace*, and in 1966 came the bestselling *1001 Ways To Beat The Draft*, written with Robert Ashlow, as well as his play *Caught In The Act: A Legal Vaudeville*.

He followed up in 1967 with *1001 ways to Make Love*. Then in 1971 he published his *Newspoems*, a collection of poems based on news items with many photos, cartoons, poems, ads & juxtaposed together on such subjects as the Mai Lai massacre, the trial of the Chicago Seven, civil rights, police brutality and censorship. In 1973 he published *Listen To the Mockingbird: Satiric Songs To Tunes You Know*. And that same year he and Sylvia collaborated on *As They Were Too*, another book of childhood photographs of well known people.

In 1981 he published the first of his many books of cartoons, *Questionable Cartoons*. Then Tuli followed that in 1983 with *Was It Good For You Too?* And *In Media's Feces* in 1986. And in 1987, a collection called *Kill For Peace Again*. Then in 1991 he came out with *Don't Make Trouble*. A book of his collected cartoons, *Teach Yourself Fucking* is forthcoming before the Millenium from Autonomedia, and he is presently working (with yrs truly) on his autobiography and yours (a workbook), called *Fucked Lincoln's Doctor's Cat*.

MIKE GOLDEN

The New America
Music: "America."

My country is it of thee?
Land bereft of Liberty,
Is it of thee I sing?
Land where the Indians died,
Land of the Slave-Holders' pride,
From ev'ry mountain's strip-mined side
Let Pollution spring.

My Know-Nothing country, thee
Land of Great College Fees,
Thy hair's been dyed.
We hear thy rocks and rolls
Jingled by them greedy souls
And all thru Land they stole,
Thy TV is refried.

Thy gunshots shoot the breeze,
Gooks hang from world-wide trees,
You own the Bomb.
Lied to in all our schools,
Beaten with their Golden Rules,
Treated like a bunch of fools,
Our time will come.

Their Propertied God, to thee,
Architect of Tyranny,
To thee we won't cower.
Soon may our Land be bright,
With Rebellion's Holy Light,
In daring love is our might,
Common People to Power!

Great Moments in the History of Capitalism
This song is dedicated to the Passers of the Welfare Reform Bill
Uranus (tune: "Aquarius")

When the Stools are in the Gingrich House
And Senators align with Mars
Then Greed will guide our country
Pure Ego steer our Pol-Stars.

AMERICAN RENEGADES

This is the dawning of the Age of Uranus
The Age of Uranus
Uranus, Uranus

Simony, misunderstanding
Cruelty, sad lusts abounding
Lots more lying and derision
Golden parachutes their vision
Mystic racist fulmination
Nation-soul in constipation.

Uranus, Uranus

When the Pricks are in the Clintrich House
And Congressmen are paged with bribes
Then Idiots will damn our destiny
And Shits will ruin our lives.

This is the dawning of the Age of Uranus
The Age of Uranus
Uranus, Uranus

Conspiracy and underhandling
Media control astounding
Circuses with bread omission
Downsize lives without contrition.

Uranus, Uranus

Now the Ghouls are in the Masters House
And Murderers kill us en masse
Now the Rich they Rule the Planet
And wipeout the Underclass.

This is the Sundown of the Age of Uranus
The Age of Uranus
Uranus, Uranus

Let the Moonshine
Let the Moonshine
Let the Moonshine
Let the Moonshine in!

Where is my Wandering Jew
A Song

Where is my wandering Jew tonight?
Or on the left, or in the right
Does ecstasy come in the fall of the night?
O where is my wandering Jew tonight?
  Where is my wandering Jew

Did Hitler survive in the heart of the beast?
Is happiness there where we seek it least?
Does the Baal Shem dance at the President's feast?
O where is my wandering Jew?

Is loneliness cast at the center of life?
Is peace our reward at the end of this strife?
Is our time's music the Gun and the Fife?
O where is my wandering Jew tonight?
  Where is my wandering Jew

And O where is my wandering God tonight?
Where are my children, where is my wife?
Where is the song I once called my life . . .
O where is my wandering Jew, tonight
  Where is our wandering life, tonight?
  O where is our wondering life tonight . . .
  Where is our wonderful life?

Paint It Red (and Black)
Tune: "Paint It Black" (Rolling Stones) with spoken extensions.
NOTE: Red & Black are the Anarchist colors.

I see the White House & I
        want to paint it Red
Rabbi Jesus whispers to me:
        "Besser Red zan Dead."
I see the Kremlin & I'm
        gonna paint it Black
Clinton's toasting Yeltsin:
        "Zdrovye Bourgeois Hack!"

I spoke to Tolstoy: "Emma
        Goldman's coming back!"

AMERICAN RENEGADES

He sat there writing on a
        shard of red & black
Black & Red. Coming back!
Red & Black. They're comin'
        back!

The Homeless Alien morphs to
        Newt's Sonovabitch
The Species [SOCIAL] Being's
        served up: dessert for the
        rich
The Lions of Reason strobe
        the deep grave of yr dream
The Lamb of Love hides in the
        Caves of Academe.

I hear the students as they
        wonder what comes next
They're forced to take the test
        but do not have the text

They wander thru the World
        Wild Internet
They still believe they'll find
        the Finland station yet! [In
        St. Petersburg where
        Lenin entered Russia in
        1917]

I heard Mohr [Marx] & The
        General [Engels] laughing
        in their Hell
They said Bakunyin had a fun-
        ny tale to tell:
"Anarcho-Pacifist Bolshevism never
        had its chance!"
Perhaps we cd invite St. Fran-
        cis to the dance? And hey
        St. Paul & Jacob Frank!
        [18cent PolJewCath pan-
        sexualist Messiah]
        YOWZAH!

        I see the White House & I
        want to paint it Red

Willy Reich is shouting at me:
"Better Red than Dead!"
Now Bill's roastin Yeltsin:
"So long Bourgeous Flack!"
I spy the Kremlimne Hey we're
gonna take it back!

RED & BLACK
GET IT BACK
RED & BLACK
WE'RE COMIN' BACK
RED & BLACK
RED & BLACK
RED & BLACK
RED & BLACK

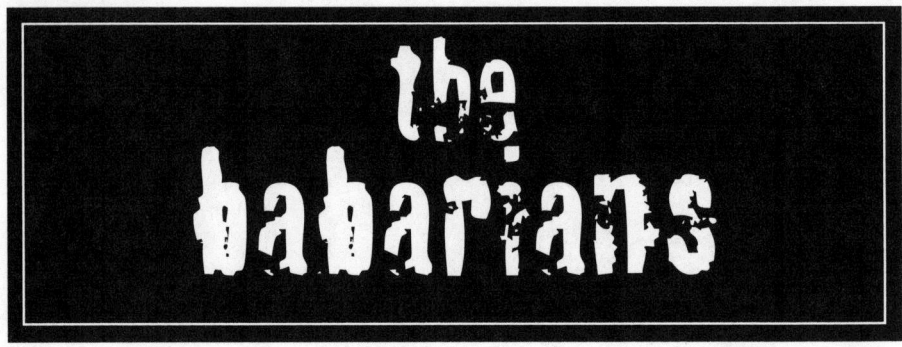

DAVID LERNER

This Is the Babarians

Some of you may know that Cafe Babar is a small club in the Mission district of San Francisco where poetry is committed every Thursday night. About three years ago, not having taken poetry seriously for years (I'd been writing magazine articles for a living), I stumbled into this joint and the sizzle in the air smelled like steak. There were kids with mohawks and elderly gentlemen alcoholic poets in twenty-year-old suits. There were strippers from various joints around town like the Mitchell Brothers, some of the most talented people in the room and now among my closest friends. There were street people and college professors, visiting rock stars and frightened debutantes. About one-third were poets, about two-thirds came to listen.

In the US poetry exists outside market forces; what results is the agony and the ecstacy, the best and the worst. Some of the poetry was amateurish beyond belief. Some was just dull. Some of it smoked. And some of it was almost too good for words, so good it almost pissed me off. A roomful of ferociously individual voices, the best of whom nevertheless seemed to be swimming in the same direction, if along different routes. It was a poetry of confrontation, subtle and otherwise, sexual, political and moral, a poetry of personal risk, of exposure verging on the indecent. It got me hot.

I realized that here, in 1987, was an almost completely non-careerist environment for the development of creative talent. There were few dreaming seriously of fame and fortune or even a living. You pretty much just had people who had somehow gotten turned on to poetry—many of those under 30 primarily through the rock lyrics of those same songwriters who'd digested the basic poetic influences of the age—and who wanted to blow.

The Babar also takes from rock a high expectation of, if not performance exactly, *presence*. Show business values are operative. Command of the stage is very important, in this tiny, noisy joint with its preturnaturally sensitive audience. If you can take the stage and hold it at Babar, you can probably do it anywhere. You have to be able to walk what you talk. It's like boot camp, only you don't have to get up so early. Our stuff has been called "performance poetry;" it's a clumsy but sometimes useful label.

The format, as with most weekly readings these days, is open/feature—anywhere from ten to infinity open slots, and a feature or two as well. The open readings function as a farm team to some extent, out of which people capable of doing features rise. Open readings, it's said in some quarters, have gained a certain respectability, acceptance, that was not quite theirs before the *Examiner* etc. started turning up and writing articles about the Babar a couple of years ago.

The open reading portion is a jam session: people get up and try out their chops. The thing about the Babar, in contrast to most other series, is that if your work is weak, you're going to find out. You won't necessarily be heckled— the room isn't really cruel—but there will be an exodus to the bar. There will be yawning and whispering and the cracking of peanut shells. Few will worry if you're an important editor or potential patron or someone on a grants committee who happens to write horribly. All that matters is the work. This crowd takes poetry as seriously as rednecks take football.

In its two years of existence Zeitgeist Press—of which I'm co-founder and an editor with—has published over twenty books (mostly through the energy of my partner, publisher and co-everything-else, Bruce Isaacson), most of them perfect bound. The press came into existence primarily as a vehicle for the Babar poets, as well as others who show up at Babar but whose orbit is far wider, Jack Micheline, for instance. And though we still have no real national distribution to speak of, our books sell well within our limited channels. And we've been successful in the most important sense; with authors primarily but not entirely drawn from the Babar pool, we've been publishing not a school but a sensibility. And myself and Bruce Isaacson, Bana Witt, Julia Vinograd, David West, David Gollub, Laura Conway, Vampyre Mike Kassel, Eli Coppola, Tommy Swerdlow, Kathleen Wood, and others not on our list, such as Joie Cook, Danielle Willis, Sparrow, Whitman McGowan, Jon Longhi, and Bucky Sinister have been putting out, as our ad copy boasts, "Poetry you can actually read."

Poetry is the rock of tomorrow, now that pop music is in spiritual receivership. And Babarian poetry—the sensibility, not the players—is the future of poetry. What the Babar does is take the fierce rebellion and impossibly lucent imagery of Ginsberg's early work, mixes it up with Bukowski's plain-spoken doom-struck melodies, cooks it all up in Bob Kaufman's spoon, throws in the Sex Pistols, a few magazine articles and something a stand-up comic said last week, and blares out a poetry that—at its best—could be spoken at midnight on a street corner and draw a crowd.

Only a sensibility distilled from mass culture can have a chance of reaching it. Only a sensibility capable of turning that poison into something magic has a chance of surviving its acceptance.

Of course, at this point that crowd—outside of a few bookstores in SF, Berkeley, NY and LA—would have very few places to buy the book.

Several years ago, when I was still doing magazine features regularly, I pitched *Mother Jones* for a piece on my friend Julia Vinograd, who's based in Berkeley. She's been writing for twenty years, does two books a year herself, 2000 per run, and sells them all. The feminists like her, she writes political poems once in a while. A solid *Mother Jones* story.

My editor even knew who she was. But then he asked the key question; "Does she have national distribution?" Ah, well, ah . . . "Then it's not a national story." He was right, of course. Catch-666: it's as hard to get national coverage with national distribution as it is to get national distribution without national coverage. . . .

But I probably learned more about writing poetry as a journalist than I ever did in a poetry workshop. I took a couple of writing workshops a long time ago, but people are just too goddamned sensitive. Writing features thousands of words long on a deadline, and then raking them over the coals with a hard-nosed line editor on even tighter deadlines, you learn about having a beginning, middle and end, about having a strong lead, about being ruthless with your work; learn how to step back from it and, with a killer's eye, cut out the fat so the gold can gleam. Most writing is cutting. The enemy of feeling is sentiment. Barbarian poetry is about feeling.

I want to read my stuff in auditoriums to thousands of people, because I know I can make them hurt, scream with laughter, and get very, very quiet. This scene, movement, family we call Barbarians, is so far off the map that until quite recently nobody in the American lit crit crapshoot has taken us very seriously. But we don't seem to be going anywhere, though the Babar these days is staying open month to month, the lease having expired. Well, fuck it, poetry's month to month too, who'd give it a lease, you got a bunch of teenager vampires and junkie moving men and music business burnouts and apostate MBAs and, yeah, the Richard Wilburs, all hunkered, whether we like it or not, under the same crappy tent that leaks from the centerpole, and it's raining gasoline, and somebody's about to light a match. Imagine the blaze it'll make. . . .

BRUCE ISAACSON

Lost My Job & Wrote This Poem

No longer will I swallow hard boiled
instructions. No longer smile at
people I'd like to bite.
Today I am free.
Today I am Mick Jagger's lips.
Today I am Kerouac's touchdown in Lowell '39.
Today I'm Jack Kennedy—*ich bin ein unemployed!*

There will be time later for assassins.
Today I am Lenin arriving at Finland Station
Napoleon back from Egypt.
Today I am Neville Chamberlain's peace
Timothy Leary's PhD
Joplin's vocal chords
I am used up—but *new*
and yesterday was my last day of work.

Now come the women who say no.
Now come New York Amsterdam Leningrad Rangoon.
Now come books I'm too undisciplined to write
poems written on white bread and toilet paper.
Now comes literature rubbing at my leg like a dog.
Now comes Christmas with its childish lies.
And I will believe all of them.
I'll make up new ones.

I'll buy Jesus a pink shirt & leather chaps
and wear them to parties of the damned.
I'm the vagrant with a purpose
the comrade in a Mercedes.
The King is dead. Long live dead capitalism!
Long live the bridge loan made of Rolaids.
Long live Hemingway's shotgun,
Milken's salary.
Long live the hand of God as it
fingers its way to your rectum
pushing you to do what you must.
You must tell the boss to treat you with respect.

THE BABARIANS

You must stand up for free speech.
You must stand up in a crowd
of an overpriced New York restaurant
and shout—*O Waste Nuclear Waste!*

Tell the emperor when the people have no clothes.
Homeless & health farms, convenience stores & medicare,
tummy tucks for pets, advertising titty hope hologram.
I am the blister on the burn
I am the golden boy turning bronze.
I am Kerouac's belly,
Howard Hughes' germs,
I am Van Gogh's knife
looking back at you in the mirror.

I wrote poems for a nation of tv stars.
I became the floating eyeball
that looks over your shoulder as if
peering off the edge of the earth.
I have strip mined love for poetry.
I cracked bones like Jesus cracked bread.
That's how poems visit me.
Like the ghost of a lover done wrong.
Like a party for a world done wrong.
Imagine Abe Lincoln and Karl Marx
in the party masks of Nixon & Stalin.
The Popes collect gold, now the Russians prefer Pepsi.
I would rather take dictation from the planets.
From the strangest bottomfish scrubbing the sea.
From the worst delusion
            of the best psychotic
                    waving poetry like a flag
                            in a wind that burns as it blows.

Poetry in Orange County

When we got to the college we were fucked.
There was no poetry-hungry throng
no collection of trendy art-punks
and no $300 check either.
There was an empty auditorium
and a professor
with a perfect Southern California body

and a firm grip
as if he was either going to
impress someone or intimidate someone.

He decided I was someone.
So when the conversation turned to
careers for poets
it seemed like time to leave.
We ended up at a bar
only this being Los Angeles
the bar was in a shopping center.
It was filled with
loud ex-football player dudes
in surfer shirts
who had all grown the exact same mustache.
As if Jung's collective unconcious
had appeared in a furry spot on the lip.
Someone explained it as the Orange County version
of rednecks.

And when a few of them heard we were poets
they taunted us to go through with the reading.
So we found a space at the corner of the shopping center.
It was a twenty foot concrete slab
only a sidewalk apart from the Pacific Coast Highway
beneath an inexplicable fifteen foot pole sign
that said "Lingerie."

We stood out there
four poets and four hecklers
reading poetry at the cars speeding past
feeling both fabulous and stupid.
When a streetperson about my age walks past
wearing an old suit like pajamas
homeless and drunk, like he was
transporter-beamed out of the Bowery
to the landscaped parking lots
of Orange County.

And as the poet was shouting at the traffic
the bum began shouting at the poet
then the audience began shouting at the bum
and then shriek skid crash
4 poets 4 rednecks & a streetcrazy
gaping at the car metal's crunch.

THE BABARIANS

JULIA VINOGRAD

In the Bookstore

I went down to the bookstore this evening
and found myself in the poetry section.
But for every thin book of poems
there was a thick biography of the poet
and an even thicker book
by someone who's supposed to know
explaining what the poet
is supposed to've said and why he didn't.
So you don't have to waste your time
on the best the writer could do,
the words he fought the darkness and himself for,
the unequal battle with beauty.
Instead you can read comfortably
about the worst the writer could do:
the mess he made of his life,
how he fought with his family,
cheated on his lovers, didn't pay his debts
and not only drank too much
but all the stupid things
he ever said to the bartender
just before getting 86'd will be printed for you
and they're just as stupid
as the things everyone says just before getting 86'd.
The books explaining the poet
are themselves inexplicable.
The students who *have* to read them
cheat.
I left the poetry section
thinking about burning the bookstore down.
Some of a poet's work comes from his life, ok.
But most of a poet's work comes
in spite of his life, in spite of everything,
even in spite of bookstores.
So I went to the next section
and bought a murder mystery but I haven't read it yet.
I find I don't want to know who done it
and why;
      I want to do it myself.

THE BABARIANS

KATHLEEN WOOD

Gregory

Gregory stumbled into the saloon.
He ordered a screwdriver.
I ordered a Beck's.
We introduced ourselves.
He said he liked my hair.
He wanted to buy me dinner
At Baby Joe's on Broadway.
We left the bar.
As we walked, he told me
All about his experiences
Fucking boys with Allen in Tangiers.
In the restaurant, we drank beer
And he told me he was
an ex-junkie and
An alcoholic and proud!
So very proud of it all.
He said everyone here gave him
a bad rap, but
Everyone loved him
In New York and
He would take me with him and
We'd stay at the Chelsea
Where Edie and Sid and Nancy stayed
and he would introduce me
To the most wonderful people.
After we finished our pasta,
He asked me if we could go
To my place.
I said okay, but I lived
In a residential hotel and
He had to leave by ten p.m.
We took a bus to Fourth and Mission
And traipsed through the ritzy lobby
Past the disapproving glare
Of the desk clerk.
Halfway up the stairs
Gregory decided we needed
Vodka. We turned around

And went next door to Merrill's
Where we purchased a pint
Of vodka and a quart
Of orange juice.
As we paraded through the lobby
Gregory was swigging
From the vodka bottle.
Upstairs, we drank screwdrivers
From the complimentary plastic cups.
He said he wanted to fuck me
I said he had to use a rubber.
I handed him a package.
He said the grillwork
of my pseudo-Victorian bed
Would be perfect for bondage.
I gave him a few of my scarves.
I removed his shirt
I asked him why there were scars
All over his arms and chest.
He told me he's been attacked
By an ocelot.
I stripped and he tied
My arms and legs
To the bedposts. Then
He fucked me.
We went and got more vodka
When we returned, he asked me
If I'd ever read his poetry.
I said no, but I would
Read it later. He said
I really should because
It was very good.
I told him I wrote poetry too.
I showed him my book
Of poems about punk rockers,
Junkies and coke fiends.
He told me it was good.
Then he said that he
Was a better poet than I was
Because he was a traditionalist.
I said I'd be sure
to read his books.
At five of ten I told him
That he would have to go.
He said he was broke

And demanded ten dollars
For cab fare.
All I had was a twenty.
He told me he would take that.
His voice was getting
Louder by the second, so
I gave it to him.
He left. I was afraid he'd call me.
He never did. A week later,
A friend of mine told me
That Gregory was in New York
At the Chelsea where Edie lived.
I discovered he'd left
His watch in my room.
I took the watch to a pawnbroker,
But the guy told me
he could only give me
A couple of bucks for it.

The Wino, The Junkie, and The Lord

I was on a bench at 18th and Val
Talking to a wino who said he believed in the Lord.
He said he needed money for dinner at McDonald's.
He said he wasn't asking for much.
I gave him a dollar.
He said he'd protect me whenever I was in the
neighborhood.
Because he always looked out
For the people who helped him.
He said he had good reasons
    for being an alcoholic.
I told him I used to have good reasons for being an addict.
He asked me where I was going.
I said to an NA meeting on Eureka Street.
He said his daughters lived on Eureka Street.
And he hoped they turned out okay.
He wanted to know which drug I was addicted to.
I said several.
He said he wanted to know where the meeting was
Because the streets were dangerous at night.
He asked God to protect me
From the crazies in the dark.

THE BABARIANS

He turned to a yuppie who stood nearby.
"I've got good reasons to be an alcoholic!"
The yuppie smiles at me and shook his head.
The bum asked the Lord to keep us all.
Then he stumbled off down Valencia.
The yuppie muttered something about crazies.
Our bus arrived.

VAMPYRE MIKE KASSEL

I'm Not *Mad*

Am I mad at you?
Of course I'm not mad, what ever gave you that idea?
Just because I'm sitting here pushing pins
into a little wax doll
with a lock of your hair in it?
Just because I burned the panties you left here
and buried the ashes
at the crossroads at midnight?
Just because I sent the nude pictures we took of you
to *Cattle Breeders Digest?*
Just because I welded the doors of your car shut?
I'm not mad, whatever gave you that idea?
Just because I wrote your name and address
on the men's room wall
of every biker's bar from here to Bakersfield?
Just because I made three hundred copies
of your apartment key
and handed them out
to every junkie and wino in the Tenderloin?
Just because I switched your birth-control pills for Ex-Lax,
spiked your shampoo with Nair,
and hid an electric cattle prod inside your favorite dildo?
Just because I pitchforked your mother,
got your kid sister turning ten-dollar tricks,
and strung out your cat on speed?
No, I'm not mad.
And, by the way,
have you got a dollar?

THE BABARIANS

KATHI GEORGES

The Real Me

The only time I want your tongue
in my mouth
is about an hour after I've eaten.
Yeah, right when the bacteria
starts to form
and take their real
gut-killing position.

The only time I want your tongue
in my cunt
is when it's bloody.
Yeah, so you can really
taste what's
inside a girl.

You see, baby, I want you to
taste the real me.

I want you to see that
I'm full of bacteria
that can eat you alive.

I want you to see that
I'm full of blood that
drips drips drips
four days a month.

I want to give you
my life.

What do you want to give me?

BUCKY SINISTER

I Was With Her Long Enough To Change Brands of Cigarettes

We had split a bottle of wine and a pint of rum
before we went into the fair.
It started with a kiss on the ferris wheel.
I didn't know that actually happened until then.
One of my favorite days of all time . . .

Six months later
I gave her money that she referred to as "fetus money."
We were long over as a romantic couple.
That day she listed why she hated me.

I had told her that I was sorry and I said so again
but those words can't take away a clumsy fuck.

The way she talked to me
it sounded like her mistakes
never hurt anyone but herself.
My mistakes have bad aim
and always seem to hit those near me.

She looked so young
I felt so old
I had driven another away
or she'd changed
or vice versa
whatever it was
it was done
and I was tired of looking.

DANNY SHOT

The Living Legend

put his dick
on the table
in the bar
on Avenue B.

I was shocked,
until I saw
what an unobtrusive
penis he owned.

Then I wanted
to put my dick
on the table,
to show him
how a true poet
was hung.

But my wife
wouldn't let me.

I drank another
beer, fighting
the urge to
plunk down
my shlong on
the wooden table.

I can see it,
everyone silent,
all eyes upon me,
the only sound
in the universe
my drunken pecker,
sloshing around in
a puddle of beer
on the table
in the bar
on Avenue B.

THE BABARIANS

Thrown out on
my soon to be
immortal ass
into the wet
darkness
of
a
drunken
night.

On Long Shot

"Long Shot: A big bet on the future." So said Allen Ginsberg in 1982. Since that time, Long Shot has been a consistent force in the countercultural movement. Long Shot emerged as a vehicle for independent artistic expression at a time when America was undergoing a rightwing backlash against the social and political changes that defined the '60s and '70s. Long Shot, the brainchild of New Jersey born and bred poet-activists Eliot Katz and Danny Shot, was launched with the aid of legendary beat poet Allen Ginsberg. When alternative voices and visions were being straightjacketed by the conservatism of academic and mainstream literary conformity, Long Shot helped breathe new life into a stagnant 1980s literary landscape. From its beginning, Long Shot attracted the interest of literary luminaries such as Charles Bukowski, Amiri Baraka, Adrienne Rich, Lawrence Ferlinghetti, Marianne Faithful, Jack Micheline, William Burroughs, Tom Waits, Jayne Cortez, Anne Waldman, Quincy Troupe, Piri Thomas, Gregory Corso, June Jordan, Sonia Sanchez, Alicia Ostriker, Sean Penn and Pedro Pietri (to name a few), who generously contributed work and support. Long Shot has been a catalyst that helped propel the current spoken word boom. Poets such as Paul Beatty, reg E. gaines, Tracie Morris, Edwin Torres, and Tony Medina count Long Shot among their first publishing credits. To its credit, Long Shot has, and continues to be, a showcase for prominent and emerging visual artists including Yoko Ono, Cindy Sherman, Larry Rivers, Sue Coe, Larry Clark, Leon Golub, Nancy Spero, George Segal, Arlene Gottfried, H. R. Giger, Patt Blue, Viktor Koen, Shelby Lee Adams and Eric Drooker. In this day when corporate culture dominates every aspect of our lives, Long Shot remains fiercely independent, never having to bend under the yoke of government or corporate sponsorship. It has maintained the punk rock ethos of "do it yourself!"

JACK WILER

It's About the End of the World Stupid

I always see the hills of Persia as brown and fading.
The processions winding through the streets of Moscow
The crack of gunfire in Sarajevo
The sound of Allen Ginsberg's voice
in the cobbled rooks of Prague.
I'm putting on the veil.
I'm remembering my place.
I'm thinking of jobs long neglected.
I'm watching for signs.
Fractals dancing in the hills.
Whirling
Sufis
Singing all the praises to the lord
Transfigured
melting

We've lit the last big Roman Candle
It's late on the Fourth of July
We're turning out the lights
Come inside while you still can.

KLIPSCHUTZ

america

I want all the women
all the money
and all the fun

I want every rainbow
all the marbles
and a personalized introduction to God

I want a death list
transparent skin
and a cat with no fur

I want everything
I have nothing
I will negotiate

Dear Ezra,

You died. Class dismissed. All that noise.
Well the Jews they're still with us—
one of 'em's my worst enemy:
                            me.
My plot to dictate the economy goes badly.
The elders screen my calls, ignore my counsel.
And goyim look down their button noses
at you, with your hypersonic booms and busts
        of meaning,
oy! your screwball scholarship du jour.
In their pacific eyes,
                    you may
be a bit of a Jew yourself.

Your schoolgirl crush on Mussolini—
poet's tears on seaside sand,
another day and no letter in return!
No wonder the sky ball leaks red fire
                and drowns itself in the bay . . .

DAVID GOLLUB

As for Us

As night falls like a blade we are
seated on benches again
goggling at each other;
lenses bend our eyes crutches of light.
Hair streams out of our heads like smoke
of thoughts
from brains on fire; our faces get
stretched to caricature
each in the other's mirror, finding each other
sweating
on the spot, forced to dot
dark exclamations
even before we speak. Rage stretches the
rein we keep on our voices taut
near to breaking,
as if our very words were
horses lacerated toward a stampede
into chaos, desperate to shed
their meanings, pulling the thunder of those
empty wagons
over badlands with ever more
panicked resentment.
Whose symptom is it,
that unrelenting spur? Look at this world,
people starve, and receive
from those with food in houses
and hands in pockets
warm smiles. Cruelty
not even for pleasure,
pleasure is punished.
Look at us: drunk, furious, with a strong back suddenly
broken, with a twisted leg,
with muscles rotting on green bones,
drug-sick, rule-sick, work-sick, 86'd,
homeless, hungry, horny, choked in bed
by the intolerable burden
of another body's muscular love,
choked on the dust

of the blossoming acacia,
longing for love and frightened of it,
wheezing, sad, pissed off,
broke. Delivering
ourselves the last wound
with knife, spike, prick, sharp
sorrow
just to be on the side of the
sharp sorrow that seems
always to win. Look at us,
each with the identification badge
of a conspicuous personally tailored
mortal wound
held closed by enchantment.

Q.R. HAND

(some) people have enough problems

he sits there   wringing his hands
so tightly   at times they pale
at the knuckle joints   where
fingers meet light brown hams

it says here   he beat up
on his wife and kids
before he was blind sided   by a local economic enterprise
one dark night in the streets   real bad
of the mission district

did he?

he was the kind of hard working man
who might consider it perfectly all right
to kick a little ass at home
after all they were his

didn't he feed them
provide them with a roof over their heads
color television

new car   he polished
to a metallic sheen
every saturday after noon
hadn't he for years

drunk and sober

in broken english   and
the kind of spanish
    i am told only the well educated
      speak like that in peru
he rants about the niggers and cubanos
who did it to him

left him in those streets   with epileptoid visions
seized   convulsing in san francisco   general hospital   emergency
coming in and out of pain full fogs
losing a piece of his mind   with each shudder
now   trying to hold on to his common sense
he touches the new metal plate in his head
first   with one hand   then   the other
they say he just found it last week

he used to carry his own weight
in sacks   loading and unloading trucks
with a green card in his back pocket
before the union would let him apprentice
prove he could hammer   saw   measure
to an exacting millimeter
fit perfectly angled wood against wood
with these great hands

now he forgets what he meant
in the middle of a sentence
ends muddled thought with a smile
    with a shrug   i am told he alludes
      to embarrassment in spanish
        which i don't understand

he thinks he must appear nice for us

he lists to the left
in a slow lop sided shuffle
after 2 years in a wheel chair
the muscles have atrophied   the ones that still could receive
as he tries to remember   accurate messages within
bring back to life   his shattered central nervous system

THE BABARIANS

fine physical intelligence
on a cane   the rest of his life

he had to sell the car a long time ago

this part is unclear to me
in any language
at home he thinks his wife thinks
he should jump out of the window
she gazes out of all the time
      is she dreaming of   what   he thinks
            The cholos and their street action
some times he thinks any one of them
one   or two   or more
could have been the ones
he never saw that night
who cracked his skull   opened
to fill their own pockets

he does not like how she looks at them
his papers say he curses at her
and threatens because of what he thinks
she is thinking

he says he gazes at her out of tears he is too slow to hide
he thinks at home they over load him with dilantin
he can never remember the right time and amount
and washes down with endless cans of rainier ale

he thinks his kids make fun of him
miming his own clumsy gestures   and fake tremors   all over
taunting   he thinks they feel safe
if they keep him slowly

i wonder if it is true

he says his family waits
at the front door of their flat
for the tribe of social workers
who tend to the needs of him self and family
through circulating paper
that is all ways late

they can go down 3 flights
to the mail box
faster than he   and only
bring what they want
to him

he knows they whisper to these clerks
he is drunk and paranoid and dangerous and
he should live some where else and soon
i believe it when he says
he dreams nightly   he's a little boy
in the hills of peru
climbing to get a look at lima
just the other side of a rise
he can never quite reach

BANA WITT

Mal de Tete
For Jean Michele Basquiat

He was a great artist
            but he was "mal de tete"
sick in the head
            like me and all my friends

            Everyone tried to help
                        and helped him get sicker instead

            They watched him die
                        at parties and openings
            and took his paintings to bed
                        instead of him

He dragged his fame around by the tail
            like a dead cat
and pierced his flesh to find
                        the perfect saturation of red
So he joined the crew
            baptized in postmortem press
and all his canvases became
            vertical shrouds
and behind them are ju-ju shrines
            filled with wickless candles
            that only burn
            when the rain is falling towards the sky

THE BABARIANS

american renegades

ALLEN GINSBERG

Homage to Hersch

Herschel Silverman's memoir of early days (late 1950's) introduction to the New York poetry bohemian beat Lower East Side Village Cedar Bar & 7 Arts Coffeeshop scene or community is touching—his faithfulness to an idea of art & excitement he projects on others tho he half denies it to himself. I'm glad he enjoyed the better part of both worlds, householder, candystore elder in W. C. William's Jersey province as well as active believer & observer & Poet in the now-historic yet-still-developing poetic scene in pre-millenial megalopolis America. He makes too much of me as poetry messiah or macher & I'm a little uncomfortable in that role, either he's found out my vanity or layed on me a stereotype. But his sincerity & the pleasure his life's taken in the poetry world encourages us all to realize that poetry does serve humankind well in giving pleasure & empowerment to people of sensitive spirit, domestic folk, enlightening their lives and relieving some of the suffering of earthly existence.

3/17/92

HERSCHEL SILVERMAN

From **High on the Beats**

I remember reading in New York Times Book Section a bit of literary gossip by Harvey Breit talking abt a visit by poets just in from West Coast with rucksacks full of poem/manuscripts. Romantic visions of troubador poets siezed my imagination, fantasized, conjectured, bled in heart to be on road also, to be on move, run away, to see differently, experience, write down impressions, O! Here at last were Real Poets, so unlike dead ones learned abt in school, the ones who were to be scanned and studied, to take tests on and memorize. O no, these rucksack poets were living poetry, not being university House Poets. I felt a kinship, wrote to Paterson, New Jersey address of Louis Ginsberg to get in touch with the young poets, invite them to my Bayonne candystore to drink malteds, talk poetry-talk & establish a friendship. Allen Ginsberg answered & wrote he would soon be over to Bayonne if he could find some free time before embarking for Europe & he would "get drunk on my malteds". I was thrilled & expectant and wrote many poems & waited for the visit, but Allen never came, too busy with personal life and knocking on publishers doors, "pushing" literary works, Kerouac's, I think. (It would be 25 years until Allen finally visited Bayonne candystore). Allen went to Europe in 1956. We wrote back & forth, 9 Git Le Coeur, Paris to 29th St. Bayonne. Allen's letters & poetry hypnotic working me up to write a lot of poetry influenced by him. He told me to "stop writing that Beatnik shit & write real poems of Bayonne." & I still wrote a lot of schmaltzy lines along with other things to project my soul knowing world-consciousness, become known, teach, climb out of anonymous candystore into literary pages of Poetry Chicago, Atlantic Monthly, Harper's, New York Times Book Review.

I read Rexroth's column on Beats, figured him literary father-figure of Ginsberg/Kerouac & early 1959 learned Rexroth was to read his translations of Chinese poetry accompanied by jazz bassist in Five Spot Cafe, Cooper Square, New York & I was thrilled to go see this mentor-friend of Poetry & I hurried over to N.Y. hoping to talk to Rexroth, find out abt Allen G. as no word from him in long time & anxious to hear abt him as a poet living out fantasy of American poet in Paris. Approached Rexroth at end of bar, introduced myself & asked if he had heard from Allen & Rexroth became surly, brusquely brushed me off with "I have a show to do, no time to discuss Allen!" Putting me down chastening me for some unknown unforgivable sin & I resented Rexroth, wanted to run out of Five Spot shouting wild curses at Rexroth but meekly stayed, & to be objective, i enjoyed Rexroth's "show," his reading and the stimulating black bassist plucking strings actually creating Oriental sounds/moods. Years later realized Rexroth's prediction of Allen G.'s becoming America's Popular Poet was reality and Rexroth had been in jealous mind in Five Spot.

AMERICAN RENEGADES

Allen's reputation had grown with success of Howl & Other Poems (City Lights), & had created a burgeoning audience for his work plus opened up young minds to modern poetry. He had been engaged to read his poetry along with Denise Levertov at NYU's Washington Square auditorium upon his return from Europe.

Most of the poets i had heard read original poetry were of the English-American School such as Sitwell, Auden, Spender, Robert Frost, Ted Hughes & others at the Poetry Center, 92nd St, N.Y. To me their poetry seemed contrived to fit a form. There was no soul in it. Allen's was more spontaneous, ecstatic, full of emotion/motion. It was Present, Direct.

After the reading there was a brief question/answer period & then Allen was surrounded by friends, members of the press, and curious on-lookers. He was busy exchanging greetings & introducing people to each other as is his way (he is great Literary Connector). We finally met, embraced warmly, looking into each other's eyes deeply seeking out the soul.

Hypnotized by reading Allen's Howl & Other Poems over & over and applying them as Great Poetry Truths in comparison with most other "modern" poetry taught in schools, i viewed Allen as Holy American Prophet almost 2000 years in making, seeing him as Yeats Creature slowly moving toward Jerusalem to proclaim 2nd Coming. I was sure that near end of 20th century, Allen's words would be recognized as Herald of New Man, a breakthru in civilization's march toward Enlightenment. I was seeking a guru thru poetry and now had found him.

Allen introduced me to Ray Bremser Donald Allen & Leroi Jones, people whom i had never heard of, interesting people with aura of new literary mystique. Leroi Jones gave me a copy of Yugen magazine which he had just published. It was issue #3 which sold for 50 cents, containing work by Gary Snyder, William S. Burroughs, Charles Farber, Barbara Moraff, C. Jack Stamm, Philip Whalen, Gilbert Sorrentino, Allen Ginsberg, Mason Jordan Mason, Diane diPrima, George Stade, Peter Orlovsky, Fivos Delfis Ray Bremser, Robin Blaser & Thomas Jackrell. The co-editor was Hettie Cohen. Leroi Jones held the handful of magazines importantly as if they were bibles of the New American Literature.

Lites in the NYU auditorium were being turned off, the crowd breaking up, & i contemplated going back home to Bayonne, full of romantic notions abt being a modern American poet. At the moment Allen said, "C'mon, we're going over to the Cedar," inviting everyone nearby him & looking at me, almost an Order to move on to further adventure. The chatty retinue began leaving the suddenly darkened auditorium & headed past the east end of Washington Square Park. I had no notion of where or what the Cedar was. Soon, after walking in complete trust of Allen, to University Place & W. 8th Street, we reached the Cedar Tavern, an old N.Y. bar, darkwood-panelled booths, New York scenes on walls, reasonably priced drinks, an owner-bartender named John who looked like a tough army top-sergeant, & wall-to-wall people, mostly mature men gesticulating wildly, their words smoking with energy burning, seeming to exist only for that moment, existential noise punctuating the Present with gusto. I had never witnessed a scene like this, these must be Giant Creative Spirits moved into man here, moving man to shine, come out of moon to revel, unwind mind in Cedar Tavern, life's exciting dialogue taking place.

Together with Bayonne friend, Ralph Gonzalez, a cub reporter working nites on the New York Daily News, i found a seat in a back booth, feeling "high" daydreaming, being a part of Cedar scene, revelling in noisy atmosphere, silent myself to others but shouting high epiphanies singing celebrating in mind, learning, turning over magic phrases, beginning to see road to expression paved with a shared energy turned loose in Cedar Tavern. A babbling yabbling gabby vociferous offering to the god of voice-expression.

Being in company of Allen Ginsberg and these interesting people so full of nitetime energy, sharing that energy, behaving as royalty, partying like there is to be no tomorrow this Friday nite, no Saturday, Time stopped, overwhelming, one becomes part of all.

In the booth in the Cedar, Gonzi & i talked with Ray Bremser. Ray came from Jersey City, the three of us products of Hudson County, N.J. I had grown up an orphan in Hague's Jersey City. Ray told us that Donald Allen was putting together an anthology & wanted some of Ray's writings for possible publication. Ray said he had been writing to Ginsberg from prison where he had been held for a teenage crime, & that Allen Ginsberg had been impressed with Ray's talent. Ray also had creative work accepted by Yugen magazine. I suppose most of the friends of the nite had been in touch with Allen and i understood what Allen had said in a letter to me that "all he was doing was meditating by the banks of the Seine & writing letters when he really wanted to be writing poetry."

A youngish red-haired inquisitive looking man introduced himself to Gonzi & i as Al Aronowitz, a reporter for the New York Post. Said he was writing an article on the Beats. He & Gonzi both sharing newspaper work had a brief conversation. Allen moved animatedly around the Cedar visiting with almost everyone. He came over to us and in a compassionate manner asked abt my candystore Bayonne family-life, whether my wife was simpatico to my writing poetry, he searching my face for Truth in my Soul, asking what was my specialty, and i in surreal mind, the beer, the din excitement and long long day, blurted out "Tuna fish." I should've said loving my wife, daughter & son, that's why i'm not on the road with you, why i'm chopping onions and celery and making tuna salad & working 80 hours a week selling newspapers in Bayonne. Allen read me. We bought Ray Bremser a beer. Ray said that a group of poets would be leaving the Cedar to go uptown to 9th Ave. & 42nd St. to a coffeehouse called the 7 Arts for an allnite poetry reading and that Allen would be there later. Go home now, be ready for tomorrow? Head for 7 Arts and Poetry? Surge of Confusion. Make most of moment! Tonite head for 7 Arts. Tomorrow take care of itself!

ANDY CLAUSEN

Wail Bar Night

Wail Bar
Wail down Night
wail thy spectral headlights
    bulleting the factory charred
        heavens neon till dawn beyond
            returning to the unworkable

Let's be women & men again
Let's be exuberantly resplendent
Let this formica be hewn oak
Let's heat with wood & sun & work
    & wind
Let's cakewalk yell & rave
    & scream eternal connotation
Let's till the young the old
    no longer resist
Let's get drunk on universe
    is its own miracle!
Let's all know and become
    we can change our lives!

Wail Bar
Wail down the all night night!
A Mad Locomotive screaming
    over singing tracks of satori
        old story not the same snow
    swelling and gelling
        our galctic conscience
in the cross country Rocky
    mountain glow
We are the cabin light in the lost
    wilderness
We are the living relics of past martyrdom
We are the motley beautiful
    protectors of stowaway Honor!
Our love is supreme!
Our Code is unrehearsed!
Our Mission is the Future!

this day of dogmatic selfishness
this virtue-izing of lookout
    for No. one
this scoffing of heroics
this demeaning of heroic accomplishment
this material priority—emotionless terror
these chemical masks unable to hide
    the crimes of totalitarian nationalism
        & paper religions founded on Fear
            of an outside Deity!
this paranoia, this body hatred
this genocidal pleasure
this doctrine of might
cannot endure our Wailing!

Wail Bar
Wail Down Night
    Halide gold lambent effulgent bright
        as light fly thru these abused muscles
                & joints & blood of smog indentured days
                & liver sick eves
O Night simple everyday magic Night
Hoist thy iron true hammer!
    of urgency
    of necessary justice
    of universal victory at last!
Hand liberating Hammer!
Hammer liberating Hammer!
The matriculating Scythians trample
    out the vintage!
Planeticide will be uninvented

    in the unevent
Slavery will be a dead word
Freedom shall mean taken for granted
God will have her name restored
and the Buddha will be everywhere

Let's be women and men again
Let this plastic be cedar
Let's put our window in the sun
Let's electrify our five senses
harnessing the unbusted horses
    powering the winds
Let's jump clean shouting

AMERICAN RENEGADES

unchewed courage
Roll giant superrealistic desires
  prepare to meld with unbeatable
    love movements to surrender it on
Let's dance till we're enlightened
Let's get high on our bodies
Let's talk about everything
Let's know and become
  We can change our lives!
Our Choice is our inviolate power!
Open up to love from Future Russia
Let's breathe without fighting
  for it!
Let's know and become it!
Wail Bar!
Wail Down the all night
New Jersey Wail Bar Night
Wail! Bar, Wail!

JANINE POMMY VEGA

Mad Dogs of Trieste
For Andy Clausen

We have never been in a war like this
in all the years of watching
the street at 3 a.m.,
kids lobbing cherry bombs into garbage cans
the last hookers heading toward home

It used to be, stopping in Les Halles cafes
after a night we could find the strong
men from the market
and the beautiful prostitutes
resting in each other's arms
Le Chat Qui Peche, Le Chien Qui Fume
alive with Parisian waltzes, his hands on her ass

We could pick up raw produce from discard bins
and have lentil stew for tomorrow

Things have never been like this.
Cops square off against teenagers in the village square
take the most pliant as lovers, and re-rout the rest
into chutes of incarceration
The mad dogs of Trieste
we counted on to bring down the dead
and rotting status quo, give a shove here
and there, marauder the fattened and calcified order,
have faded like stories

We used to catch them with their hat brims
keeping most of the face in shadow
and sometimes those voices
one by one
turned into waves
like cicadas in the August trees, whistling
receding, and the words crept under
the curtains of power, made little changes,
tilted precarious balance, and brought relief

Those packs don't crisscross the boulevards
now in the ancient cities, no political cabal
behind us watches the world with
eyes entirely
cognizant
the lyrical voices rainbow bodies
your friends my friends nobody left
but the mad dogs of Trieste as we
cover the streets.

Willow, NY
August '98

NEELI CHERKOVSKI

The Woman at the Palace of the Legion of Honor

She does not know that I am staring at her
      as she stands in her bright yellow dress
        looking at something by Rodin,
She does not know that I believe in the solemn
      things sculpted by Rodin,
Looking like poetry
      or the secret of clay.

If only I were brave and handsome,
      I would let her hear my mind
        as I equate her with the statue.
I don't think she has even glanced at me,
      and here I am, so close by,
      confused,
        listening to Rodin,
And listening to the woman
      who stands there,

looking like poetry
      or the secret of clay.

1965

BUDDY GIOVINAZZO

New York Guy in Berlin Night

It's late at night and the trees are shaking in the wind and the park is black as your heart and there's evil bloody murder in the air as I take the pick from my pocket and slowly poke holes in my arm to prepare for the mayhem and anarchy of despair that walks beside me in the bashful blue of Berlin with her fine liquid

WANTED

FOR WORD HUSTLING

JACK MICHELINE	FLOYD SALAS
JIMMY LYONS	NEELI CHERKOVSKI
MICHAEL WOJCZUK	ANDY CLAUSEN
PALADIN	JULIA VINOGRAD
THOMAS DAWSON	PAUL WEAR
BILL ROBINSON	MAX
GINNY STALEY	BOB ADLER
GARY BLACKMAN	RANDY FINGLAND
LINDA CLAUSEN	TOM PLANTE
MICHAEL SAUCIER	GREG SALAS

10-12 PM The ISLAND 16th & SANCHEZ S.F. WED. AUG. 18

REWARD

legs on wet black cement but not too fast as I sneak up behind her floating on my Cons with my arm raised high and the point gleaming in the light of the moon and as the church bells toll with a crack of ancient metal she turns to see the pick aimed straight at her eyes and as the church bells toll again she screams in picture perfect terror as I think to myself, it's just like home with no regrets. A New York guy in Berlin night.

PENNY ARCADE

The underground is inviolate. It is not a street, a neighborhood or a certain city. It is a metaphysical space located where bohemia intersects with the demi-monde. Not everyone from bohemia can descend into the underground just as not everyone in the demi-monde can find their way to either bohemia or the underground.

If you do not have a functioning criminal class in your art scene you have academia and while academia is a reflection of the art world it can never be the art world.

The Lower East Side of New York used to be filled with poets, writers, actors, musicians, photographers, filmmakers, junkies, whores and weirdos. Now it's filled with college students pretending to be poets, writers, musicians, actors, photographers, filmmakers, junkies, whores and weirdos, in other words the ten most popular kids from every high school in the world are now living in downtown New York. Those are the people who most of us who ran away to New York, came here to get away from! Nobody who was popular in high school can ever be hip. It's not possible. If you were popular in high school, that was your peak. Be satisfied.

PENNY ARCADE

Career Move

I NEVER TELL PEOPLE MORE THAN THREE THINGS
THREE BAD THINGS
THAT HAVE HAPPENED TO ME
CUZ I CAN'T STAND THE LOOK OF PITY IN THEIR EYES
I CAN'T STAND WATCHING THEM
DO THAT FAST ARITHMETIC IN THEIR HEADS
IT SEEMS LIKE TIME STANDS STILL
WATCHING THEM SHIFT
THEIR WEIGHT

AMERICAN RENEGADES

FROM FOOT TO FOOT
IT SEEMS
LIKE TIME STANDS STILL
WAITING FOR THAT SIGH
TO COME OUT
OF THEIR CHEERIO MOUTH
THAT LITTLE
PHEW
THAT MEANS
NOTHING LIKE THAT
COULD EVER HAPPEN
TO ME.

I SAW HIM FROM A LONG WAYS OFF
I WAS HIGH AND THE SIDEWALK LOOKED
LIKE IT HAD DIAMONDS
DIAMONDS SHINING IN IT.

WHEN I GOT CLOSE TO HIM
I COULD SEE THAT HE WAS AN OLD MAN
HIS HAIR WAS SILVER AND IT LOOKED
LIKE IT HAD DIAMONDS
DIAMONDS SHINING IN IT
HE LOOKED LIKE HE'D BEEN WAITING FOR ME
FOR A LONG TIME

HE SAID HI
REAL SOFT
LIKE HE KNEW ME

HE SAID
DO YOU WANT TO HAVE COFFEE?
AND I SAID OK
CUZ WELL WHAT ELSE WAS THERE TO DO?

WE WENT INTO AN EMPTY COFFEE SHOP
HE BOUGHT ME PIE TOO
WE DIDN'T TALK ABOUT MUCH OF ANYTHING
HE SAID I WAS NICE POLITE
NOT WILD LIKE THE OTHER GIRLS WHO RUN THE STREET

THEN WE WENT TO GEM'S SPA
HE BOUGHT CIGARETTES AND GUM
HE PAID FOR IT WITH THE BIGGEST ROLL OF MONEY I'D
    EVER SEEN

AMERICAN RENEGADES

IT WAS BIG
LIKE A BIG CHEESEBURGER
HE ASKED ME IF I WANTED ANYTHING
THERE WAS A WALL OF MAGAZINES
THERE WERE SO MANY COLORS
THEY WERE RUSHING IN MY EYES LIKE A WATERFALL
IT TOOK A LONG TIME TO PICK ONE OUT.

ON THE SIDEWALK HE TOLD ME THAT I REMINDED HIM OF
   A MOVIE
AND I GOT REALLY EXCITED
ON ACCOUNT OF HOW I ALWAYS WANTED TO BE IN A
   MOVIE
BUT NOBODY EVER SAID I REMINDED THEM OF NO MOVIE
THEN HE TOLD ME
THAT THE NAME OF THE MOVIE
WAS
CARMEN BABY
AND I GOT REALLY EXCITED
ON ACCOUNT OF HOW
MY MIDDLE NAME WAS CARMEN
AND I THOUGHT
IT WAS A GOOD OMEN
YOU KNOW
LIKE A GOOD SIGN
THAT SOMETHING GOOD WAS GONNA HAPPEN TO ME
THAT I WAS GONNA BE SOMEBODY
NOT STAY A NOBODY
ALWAYS
HE SAID
LETS GO SEE THAT MOVIE!
AND I SAID
OK
CUZ WELL
WHAT ELSE WAS THERE TO DO?

AND WE STARTED WALKING
AND I STARTED CRASHING
FROM ALL THAT SPEED I SHOT
AND I WONDERED
WHY WE DIDN'T TAKE A TAXI
WITH THE BIG ROLL OF MONEY
THEN HE SAID
LOOK
AND THERE WAS A BIG MARQUEE

AND IT SAID
CARMEN BABY
THEN HE SAID
SEE
AND THERE WAS A BIG POSTER
AND IT SAID
CARMEN BABY
AND THERE WAS A GIRL IN THE POSTER
AND SHE LOOKED
ALOT LIKE ME
EXCEPT SHE DIDN'T HAVE ON MANY CLOTHES
ACTUALLY
SHE DIDN'T HAVE ON ANY CLOTHES
AND HE SAID
LETS GO IN!
AND I SAID

NO . . I . . .
DON'T . . . I . . .
NO . . . .
I DON'T . . . . THINK . .
I . . NO . . .

AND HE SAID
I WANT TO INTRODUCE YOU TO SOMEONE
AND WE STARTED WALKING
AND I WAS CRASHING
AND I WAS PUTTING
ONE FOOT IN FRONT OF THE OTHER

AND HE SAID
IN HERE
WE WALKED INTO A BUILDING
UP SOME STAIRS
THERE WAS A HALF RIPPED OFF SIGN ON THE WALL
IT SAID
ALL TENANTS WILL PLEASE. . . .
AT THE TOP OF THE STAIRS HE PUSHED ON THE DOOR
I STEPPED INSIDE
THERE WAS
A BED
A BUREAU
A CHAIR
I SAID
NO NO NO

AMERICAN RENEGADES

HE PUT A GUN TO MY HEAD
HE SAID
IF YOU SCREAM
I'LL KILL YOU
AND I SCREAMED
AND HE HIT ME HARD IN THE HEAD
I FELL ON THE GROUND
WHEN I OPENED MY EYES
HIS FACE
WAS GOING
ROUND AND ROUND
LIKE ON A FERRIS WHEEL
HE SAID
GET UP
AND I WAS CRYING
AND
I COULDN'T SEE
THERE WAS TEARS AND SNOT
AND I SAID
PLEASE DON'T HURT ME
PLEASE
PLEASE
I WANT MY MOMMY
AND HE REACHED OUT AND GRABBED MY DRESS
AT MY THROAT
AND IT WAS
LIKE A CARTOON
HOW THAT DRESS
CAME OFF IN HIS HAND
ALL IN ONE PIECE

HE SAID
I'M GONNA MAKE THIS EASY ON YOU
AND HE TOOK OFF ALL HIS CLOTHES
HE DIDN'T HAVE ANY HAIR
ON HIS BODY
JUST ON HIS HEAD
HE LOOKED LIKE AN OLD CHILD
OR A LIFE-SIZE DOLL OF AN OLD MAN
HE LAY DOWN ON THE BED
ON HIS TUMMY
LIKE HE TRUSTED ME
HE POINTED THE GUN TO THE FOOT OF THE BED
HE SAID
NOW GET DOWN THERE AND LICK MY ASSHOLE

AMERICAN RENEGADES

AND I THOUGHT
OH MY GOD
I'M GONNA HAVE TO DIE
I'M GONNA HAVE TO DIE
AND
I COULDN'T MOVE MY FEET
AND
KEEP MY EYES
ON THE TWO LOCKS
ON THE DOOR
AND HE SAID
DO IT!
AND I WAS SCARED
OF WHAT I MIGHT SEE
AND SMELL
YOU KNOW
LIKE SHIT
BUT WHEN I GOT THERE
HE WAS COMPLETELY CLEAN
AND HE SAID
DO IT
AND
I PUT MY HAND ON HIS ASS
ON THE ROUND PART
AS FAR AWAY FROM THE ASSHOLE
AS I COULD
AND WHEN I TOUCHED HIM
HIS ASSHOLE STARTED BLINKING!
HE SAID
DO IT!
AND
I WET MY FINGER
AND I THOUGHT:
THIS IS NEVER GONNA WORK
HE'S GONNA KNOW
BUT WHEN I TOUCHED HIM
HE EXPLODED ON THE BED
I GUESS HIS FANTASY WAS SO STRONG

THEN HE GOT UP
HE WRAPPED THE SHEET AROUND HIM
HE LEFT THE ROOM
I BUTTONED MY SWEATER AROUND ME LIKE A SKIRT
I PUT ON MY COAT
I WENT OUT THE WINDOW

DOWN THE FIRE ESCAPE
I THOUGHT
HE'S GONNA CATCH ME
HE'S GONNA KILL ME
HE'S GONNA CATCH ME
HE'S GONNA KILL ME
ON THE SIDEWALK I SAW A BUS
I DIDN'T KNOW IF IT WAS GOING UPTOWN OR DOWNTOWN
I GOT ON
I THOUGHT
EVERYONE IS GONNA KNOW
BUT NOBODY EVEN NOTICED ME
DOWNTOWN
I WENT TO THAT CRASH PAD WHERE I WAS STAYING
I TOLD PEOPLE WHAT HAPPENED
UH NOT THE ASSHOLE LICKING PART
THEY WERE INTERESTED FOR A MINUTE
CUZ OF THE BLACK EYE

THE NEXT DAY
I SAW HIM
HE WAS STANDING ON THE CORNER OF ST MARK'S PLACE
HE WAS LOOKING AT ME
I THOUGHT
HE'S GONNA KILL ME RIGHT IN THE MIDDLE OF ST MARK'S
    PLACE
HE WAS CROSSING THE STREET
I COULDN'T TAKE MY EYES OFF HIS MOUTH
AND MOVE MY FEET AT THE SAME TIME
HIS MOUTH WAS SO TIGHT
I COULD SEE HIS TEETH
WITHOUT HIM OPENING HIS LIPS
WHEN HE GOT IN FRONT OF ME
HE SAID REAL SOFT
YOU KNOW
YOU LICKED MY ASSHOLE REAL GOOD
YOU KNOW
YOU COULD MAKE ALOT OF MONEY DOING THAT
YOU KNOW THE MAFIA GUYS?
NO I MEAN THE REALLY BIG MAFIA GUYS
THEY PAY ALOT OF MONEY TO GET THEIR ASSHOLES LICKED
THERE'S A BIG FUTURE FOR YOU
LICKING ASSHOLES IN THIS TOWN.

STEVEN J. BERNSTEIN

Murdered in the Middle of the Dance

I was lonely
my hands holding each other
tight. You think
it is never like that
for me,
but it is.
A scorched flower rested
on my forehead,
a bottle of pills rattled
as I walked from one end
of the dance floor
to the other.
You could tell I was sick;
no one wanted
to dance with me,
that night.
But, how long was the night?
And, every dance
went on and on,
painfully. Yes,
your happiness was like
a good whipping.
I laid down in a room
full of coats and hats
and umbrellas and took it.
Then, I tore off my head
and stuffed pills in its mouth.
I threw the head
in the waste basket
and walked down the hall
to the mens room.
Even though I didn't have a head,
I was still a man.
Maybe people screamed
and ran into each other
trying to get away from me.
I couldn't see or hear
anything. Blood ran

down my shirt.
Blood, or spit, or sweat.
The dance was meaningless. The head,
having taken its pills,
was all well. The rest
was riddled with disease,
but stumbled on, thoughtlessly.
Doubtless,
you were in someone's arms.
Maybe, you hadn't even heard
about the headless man
poking at the doors
in the hall.
He was dressed for love.
I was dressed for love.
It is the same as murder
when I have to dress for it.
My balls crushed
against the edge of a table.
A bowl of punch and ice cubes
splashed all over me.
That's all I know.
My hands touched one another, again,
as though they had never met.
In another room
they were giving me a shot
and tying me to the stretcher.
It is a waste of time
trying to save a man
without a head.
Tomorrow, that part will be found
empty in the coat room
with its flower
and its mouth full of medicine.
All the love
went with the body,
and the body is covered
with punch and blood. In fact,
they have taken the clothes
that I wore for love,
and put them in a bag. Now,
I am naked
and I don't have a head.
I am on the slab
and they are looking.

This one got murdered
in the middle of the dance.

HERBERT HUNCKE

Herbert Huncke was the first modern writer to protect neither the innocent nor the guilty with pseudonyms, but used real names, including his own, and actual events. A style so seemingly simple, natural and obvious, it became an ideal aspired to by Kerouac, who was denied its use by the legal exigencies of a prestigious commercial publisher—and the growing fame of his friends. Huncke, however, toiling in obscurity, wrote the way he did everything else—exactly as he wanted to.

The heart-breaking story "Elsie John" is quintessential Huncke. The eponymous character is an egregiously conspicuous and exotic ex-circus freak. Tall and large, well over six feet, lipsticked, long hair obviously dyed, mascared eyes, he is now reduced by the importunity of what Herbert called "an oil-burning" heroin habit to working flea markets and penny arcades—billing himself as the only "real hermaphrodite"—and selling drugs to keep going. They meet, Herbert moves in, they get to know one another and share a life together, talking all night, "coping" and hustling together. Then the bust.

It is a story without the slightest sensationalism or sentimentality about a world of cruelty and prejudice so institutionalized, unconscious, and pervasive as to seem, indeed, almost natural. Herbert, with neither agenda nor axe to grind, poignantly describes what happens without editorial comment or moral indignation. There is no railing against injustice. The police are simply behaving as police. The young punks are merely being themselves. Even Elise John accepts without protest his sad, inexorable fate. Herbert shares the story—and moves on.

ROGER RICHARDS

Elsie John
.

Sometimes I remember Chicago and my experiences while growing up and as a youth. I remember in particular the people I knew and—as frequently happens—I think, with people, I associate whole periods of time as indicative of certain changes within myself. But mostly I think about the people and I recall one person rather vividly, not only because he was out of the ordinary, but because I recognize now what a truly beautiful creature he was.

He was a giant—well over six and one half feet tall with a large eggshaped head. His eyes were enormous and a very deep sea-blue with a hidden expression of sadness as though contemplating the tragedy of his life as irrevocable. Also there were times when they appeared gay and sparkling and full of great under-standing. They were alive eyes always—and had seen much and were ever quest-ing. His hair was an exquisite shade of henna red which he wore quite long like a woman's. He gave it special care and I can see it reflecting the light from an overhead bulb which hung shadeless in the center of his room while he sat crosslegged in the center of a big brass bed fondling his three toy pekes who were his constant companions and received greatly of his love. His body was huge with long arms which ended with thin hands and long tapering fingers whose nails were sometimes silver or green or scarlet. His mouth was large and held at all times a slightly idiot smile and was always painted bright red. He shaded his eyelids green or blue and beaded the lashes with mascara until they were a good three quarters of an inch long. He exhibited himself among freaks in sideshows as the only true hermaphrodite in human life and called himself Elsie John. When I met him he was in his early thirties.

He came originally from somewhere in Germany and before coming to this country had traveled—travailed if you prefer—much of Europe and could talk for hours of strange experiences he'd had. He was a user of drugs, and although he liked cocaine best he would shoot up huge amounts of heroin, afterward sitting still like a big brooding idol.

When I first knew him he was living in a little theatrical hotel on North State Street. It was an old hotel and in all probability is no longer in existence. Ap-parently at one time it had been a sort of hangout for vaudeville actors. It was shabby and run down and the rooms were small and in need of fresh paint. He lived in one of these rooms with his three dogs and a big wardrobe trunk. One of the things I remember distinctly was his standing in front of a long thin mirror which hung on the wall opposite his bed—applying makeup—carefully working in the powder bases and various cosmetics creating the mask which he was seldom without.

When I met him he was coming out of a lesbian joint with a couple of friends and upon seeing him for the first time I was sort of struck dumb. He was so big and strange. It happened that one of the girls knew him and he invited us all up to his room to smoke pot—tea as it was called in those days. His voice was rather low and pleasant with a slight accent which gave everything he said a meaning of its own. When we were leaving he suggested I come back, and it was not much time until I became a constant visitor and something of a friend.

He liked being called Elsie and later when I introduced him it was always as Elsie.

We began using junk together and sometimes I would lie around his place for two or three days. A friend of mine called John who was later shot to death by narcotics bulls while making a junk delivery—they grabbed him as he was handing the stuff over and he broke free and ran down the hall and they shot him—joined us and we became a sort of threesome.

Elsie was working an arcade show on West Madison Street, and though junk was much cheaper then than now he wasn't really making enough to support his habit as he wanted to and decided to begin pushing. As a pusher he wasn't much of a success. Everybody soon got wise he wouldn't let you go sick and per result much more was going out than coming in. Eventually one of the cats he'd befriended got caught shooting up and when asked where he scored turned in Elsie's name. I will never forget the shock and the terror of the moment the door was thrust open and a big red-faced cop kind of shouting "Police" shoved into the room followed by two more—one who sort of gasped upon seeing Elsie and then turned to one of the others saying, "Get a load of this degenerate bastard—we sure hit the jackpot this time. This is a queer sonofabitch if I ever saw one. What the hell are these?"—as he became aware of the dogs who had gathered around Elsie and who were barking and yipping. "Goddamned lap dogs—what do they lap on you?" he said as he sort of thrust himself toward Elsie.

Elsie had drawn himself up to his full height and then suddenly began saying, "I'm a hermaphrodite and I've got papers to prove it"—and he tried to shove a couple of pamphlets which he used in his sideshow gimmick toward the cop. Meanwhile one of the others had already found our works and the stash of junk—about half an ounce—and was busy tearing Elsie's trunk apart, pulling out the drawers and dumping their contents in the center of the bed. It was when one of the cops stepped on a dog that Elsie began crying.

They took us all down to the city jail on South State Street and since Johnnie and I were minors they let us go the next morning.

The last time I saw Elsie was in the bullpen—sort of cowering in the corner surrounded by a group of young Westside hoods who had been picked up the same night we were—who were exposing themselves to him and yelling all sorts of obscenities.

Jeff Gordon

Path

> from inside this broken package
>   damaged goods
>   scarred and pained body
>   static blood
>   bone dissolved
> my heart dances when I look at you

American Renegades

my eyes
burnt orange on the edges
clouded by clouds
see you and
your acorn light bathes them
in wonder.
where the tree once stood-straight
now ash
but from that a new tree takes shape
harboring branches broken
and limbs twisted
but you are a giver
of soil and water and sun and moon.

JOHN GIORNO

Just say
NO
to Family Values

On a day when
you're walking
down the street
and you see
a hearse
with a coffin,
followed by
a flower car
and limos,
you know the day
is auspicious,
your plans are going to be
successful;
but on a day when
you see a bride and groom
and wedding party,
watch out,

be careful,
it might be a bad sign.

Just say no
to family values,
and don't quit
your day job.

Drugs
are sacred
substances,
and some drugs
are very sacred substances,
please praise them
for somewhat liberating
the mind.

Tobacco
is a sacred substance
to some,
and even though you've
stopped smoking,
show a little respect.

Alcohol
is totally great,
let us celebrate
the glorious qualities
of booze,
and I had
a good time
being with you.

Just
do it,
just don't
not do it,
just do it.

Christian
fundamentalists,
and fundamentalists
in general,
are viruses,

and they're killing us,
multiplying
and mutating,
and they're destroying us,
now, you know,
you got to give
strong medicine
to combat
a virus.

Who's buying?
good acid,
I'm flying,
slipping
and sliding,
slurping
and slamming,
I'm sinking,
dipping
and dripping,
and squirting
inside you;
never
fast forward
a come shot;
milk, milk,
lemonade,
round the corner
where the chocolate's made;
I love to see
your face
when you're suffering.

Do it
with anybody
you want,
whatever
you want,
for as long as you want,
any place,
any place,
when it's possible,
and try to be
safe;
in a situation where

you must completely
abandon yourself
beyond all concepts.

Twat throat
and cigarette dew,
that floor
would ruin
a sponge mop,
she's the queen
of great bliss;
light
in your heart,
flowing up
a crystal channel
into your eyes
and out
hooking
the world
with compassion.

Just
say
no
to family
values.

We don't have to say No
to family values,
cause we never
think about them;
just
do it,
just make
love
and compassion.

                                        1995

IRA COHEN

Electronic Multimedia Shamanism

As Angus MacLise once said, "Shamans are not like other people." In fact, Shamans are in some sense outside the law & are, by their vocation, regular travelers to unseen worlds. Among the poets there are those whose work & lives touch deeply the shamanic prerogative. I would call these intrepid voyagers Outlaws of the Spirit. They might also be numbered among the Radical abusers or Akashic messengers. So we opened the door of Electronic Multimedia Shamanism—I saw it as a diamond in the sixties . . . Lone wolves of the future impossible we dared to lean into the unknown to cast a spell over the crumbling cities. From poetry to prophesy. From Light—clairvoyance! You know who you are.

Letter to Caliban

This is my history, New York City, 1998
There are blind spots everywhere
Someone stands on a stage begging for help
What is it eating my vitals and the vitals
of my friends?
Selling death is the business of the capitalist
state No longer loves cannot rise above the subway
Looking through the bicycle wheel one remembers
a pyramid
The prophets push up the sewer covers and enter the
streets by night
We are crowded into small rooms which cannot contain
us
A young mother dreams of wrecking crews
yet the children find the sun, the leaf, the bird
Make the tongue rare to fill the space
with meaning in the text we presuppose keys,
hope to find wetness
Once people slept in gardens
Now not even photography can get you out of prison.

JULIAN BECK

From *Songs of the Revolution*

metallic blisters thats what theyve got on the mind
tanks are contagious building protective walls around everything
no more semi permeable membranes
just fortresses looking down

telling it isnt enough
walls dont hear
and only a few kids have their ears pressed agains the plates
straining to hear

wagner knew nothing but he gave a lot of people gooseflesh
painting his sunsets with soprano volcanoes
and oceanic contours
but not a word of truth about mrs goodman and her petty bourgeois
    tragedy

wagner represents every travesty
grandeur without merit
and opinions count for nothing
when youre pleading with the sky
for louisiana and all its promises

wagner is the state over and over
the state is our fathers humming
his love his order his order his natural need to sit at the head of table
and listen to wagner
while the opera house burns

paris
5 october 1982

JUDITH MALINA

Leaflet for soldiers
(Written in Italian by Judith Malina, translated by Uri Hertz)

> This poem was distributed on
> The International Antimilitarist
> March to soldiers who were prohibited
> from accepting leaflets
> but were permitted to accept and read poetry.

To Our Friends the Soldiers

In every country in the world
There are men like you,
Trained and prepared
For combat where you must kill
Other young men like yourself,

Who are called upon like you
To defend the national borders,
To protect certain political and economic systems,
To maintain civil order.

Have you ever considered
That these national borders
Are the mark of our failure
To learn how to share
The planet, its earth and resources?

Have you ever considered
That these political and economic systems
Are all failures
Of our potential to satisfy
Needs and desires, one with the other,
By practical and possible means
Through mutual aid without tyrannical structures?

Have you ever considered
That the ones who maintain civil order
Take too heavy a part in the cycle of fear?

Have you ever considered
That armed force is never the best solution
To any human problem?

Let's talk about this together.

In every country in the world
There are men like you
Who are talking about this together.

Cagliari, Sardinia
August 13, 1976

GERARD MALANGA

Poem in the Manner of Paul Blackburn

Hitching up trousers
from just having gone to the can,
leaving the door purposely ajar—
beautiful, young girl
suddenly rushes in without knocking—whataya 'spect—
        shocked
at her surprise to find me there,
excuses herself "That's all right" I say—
and suddenly leaves, a few seconds shared
in one lifetime of separate realities,
an erotic aftertaste.

      In another phantasy,
she wd've stayed,
got on her knees and sucked me off.
Her head held in my hands,
My hands running thru her hair

. . . . shows what a cup of coffee can do in the morning.

AMERICAN RENEGADES

EVE WOOD

First Lady

I've snuck into the White House.
I carry a huge vase of lilies
in front of my face
so no one will see me.

I have a friend in the secret service who owed me a favor.
He cased the place for me, made a map of the east wing
complete with pencil drawings of every object
in Hillary Clinton's bedroom—
measured each window,
her bedroom's diameter, calculated how many minutes
it would take me to get there
from the main hall entrance.

I wrote to the government demanding
they put Hillary's face on a stamp;
I said I believe she is honest.

All this unoccupied space makes me nervous,
though I keep moving from room to room
followed only by the prints of my feet
on the slate-colored carpet,
wanting to believe I can fill the space up.

My friend Lenora said Hillary held auditions
once a year for a new female lover,
and if interested, I would need to investigate.

I've taken the White House tour
eighteen times since Hillary was elected.
Every week the White House staff reorganize
the Presidential paintings—today Woodrow Wilson's face
hangs above the fireplace in the study,
while in another picture, FDR, flanked by Pekinese,
poses near an open window.
My favorite tour guide's name is Kamar,
we've become close friends, though I still haven't told him.

A jester in the queen's bed chamber,
I get down on all fours,
bury my face in the carpet,
hide behind the life-size ceramic tortoise nearest the door,
imagining Hillary barefoot, catching the scent of her here,
a mixture of perfumed talc, cat hair and iodine
for a cut on her little toe.

I smell perfume
which makes me hungry.
The lilies I carry seem to lunge
at my face with each step.

A door opens behind me,
and the room falls away
the moment she steps into it
with her helmet of hair signifying
power, or this perfection is not who I am, but how I got
here.

She knows why I am here,
says many women have been interviewed,
and if I am hired, I will work solely for her pleasure,
to make her loneliness a ghost.
I'll be paid in lobster, my favorite foreign films,
twenty-four hour limousine service
and the occasional excursion of the Presidential jet.

Telling her she is beautiful
will not win me points;
"flattery," she says, "is the surest way to get fired."
She hands me a pair of tight, leather gloves
and repeats I can touch any object in the house
as long as my hands are covered.
My mouth is dry.
We are alone for almost ten minutes before
I put on my jacket and walk
to the high, white door
at the opposite end of the room, saying,
"Last night in my dream you had a freckle
inside your right ear,
and I was the only person who could find it."

HENRY J. MORRO

Marilyn Monroe Is Dead

When Marilyn Monroe stepped on that iron grate,
her skirt billowing like a parachute,
I fell in love with her white skin and her blond hair,

and when I returned home
I broke the mariachi music on the stereo,
songs of women sleeping in buses,
buses filled with men lugging chickens and knives
through Panama and El Salvador,
migrating across the immense Mexican desert
to the fiery border.

We had come to this country for the TVs and the Cadillacs,
for the money and the skyscrapers.
When I saw Marilyn's shimmering legs,
I was ashamed of my dark skin
and ashamed of the latinas
and their sweet-fifteen debutante parties,
where girls became women,
without ever touching a man's body,
without ever touching my brown body.

And whenever my Uncle Reynaldo
showed up with his blond wife,

his brothers would flirt with her,
in their thick accents,
in their busboy English,
offering her their own crooked words,
shaped while working sixteen hours a day
in the kitchens, in the boiler rooms, in the factories,
working sixteen hours a day

to break through the language.

Marilyn Monroe is dead and I feel the dark
Indian blood that has run

silent for hundreds of years,
coming back;
I feel the language of peasants and machetes,
of machine guns and priests,
of gods and flesh,
the language that built the pyramids and temples,
cathedrals and plantations,
that sacrificed virgins,

that fought the Marines,
I feel that dark
language coming back.

Barbie

Long after the head was ripped off,
the shoes lost,
her huge, pointed tits were still hard.
I used to grip her ankles, hammer her tits
on the table like a woodpecker.

I would slide her long, skinny legs
into a wild split,
lift them straight
into the air, but her legs
wouldn't spread open.

And she wouldn't kneel.
I could get her to raise her arms
as if she was going to bow,
but she wouldn't kneel.

I stripped her, tossed her
under the bed with the hair balls.
I chucked her into the freezer naked—
she came out cold to the touch,
her skin still perfect.

I sat her on a fence rail
in her cheerleader outfit,
took out my B-B gun, cocked it.
The first shot caromed off her wrist.

The next one grazed her cheek.
The last shot rapped her in the chest
and bucked her off the post.

When I picked her up, her cheek crushed,
her blue eyes glittered in the sun.
I strode for the garage; on the workbench
was the adjustable vice.
As I cranked the steel jaws against her skull,
and reached for the hacksaw,
her mouth puckered into a kiss.

ERIC BROWN

You Fucking Cunt

They kept the relationship fresh by greeting each other with "Hello, you fucking cunt." Each morning she would tape notes to his windshield saying that he was the product of a rape and so was his mother and both her parents. He would wrap her parrot in kite string, stick it in a bowl of guacamole up to its neck and teach it to say, "Is that your nipple or a scab?" and "Your dreams are paltry bullshit."

The idea was that this hostility would eradicate the frustrations of living in this large smelly rectum that surrounds us, and that one day they could embrace, unite in serene bliss, juices and bloods relocating, salivary glands glancing, with a music box shaped like love sitting on the night table playing "Raindrops Keep Falling on My Head."

And the rain did come; it came in torrents, drenching their lawn and dripping through their leaky roof while they called each other fucking cunts.

The abuse gave them confidence and a sense that they weren't like everyone else, that they would not fit in any demographical survey, they couldn't be described in any intersection of columns.

He would send Hare Krishnas and Jehovah's Witnesses over when her favorite television program was on; she wrote his work phone number on toilet seats frequented by the S&M bondage crowd.

For twenty years they diligently thought up new ways to belittle in sickness and in health, then one day they got into a battle and knocked each other out, peacefully crumpled unconscious and bruised on the floor, dreaming of the morning when kindness would be the only thing left to give.

Billie and Satchmo or, You Fucking Cunt II

"Good morning" said the black-eyed wife to the black-eyed husband and he replied the same. "Pleasant dreams?" asked man of woman and she replied oh yes.

They agreed that the dreams could be realized, and entered into a phase of prelapsarian beatitude, kissing with morning mucky-mouth, immune to stresses implied by the job, impending war, or economic collapse.

They taught sonnets to their parrot, walked together at midnight on hills over-looking the urban turmoil, and did away with pitiless coping mechanisms.

She sang to him in the voice of Billie Holiday: "Your cock, is a non-stop, cock-a-doodle-doo;" he responded in the throat of Satchmo Armstrong: "I feel at home in your henhouse."

All was well in Denmark and they even began to consider a child. A child. The conclusive yes I said yes I will yes, the trophy of the existential insanathon, a gob of spit in the face of an unloving god.

But the world laughed at them. The world flung shit at them. And they with-stood it for a while.

But like all products guaranteed to last a lifetime, they broke.
To avoid incarceration in a rubber Motel Six, too unbrave to steal the right from the aforementioned unlover and take the brave way out, too weak to withstand the reproach for plagiarizing the Montague and Capulet kids, they reverted to their old ways—

She drove home fast from work, as did he, and as the front ends of their cars collided at the mouth of their driveway, they leaned on their horns, zipped down the power windows and screamed: "Hello, you fucking cunt!"

ED DORN

Harvesting Organs: *On the Head-Injury Death of a 24 Year Old Boy in Vermont*

Several Specialists "flew" in from Pittsburgh.
Please pardon the anthropomorphism there.
I don't mean to suggest raptors—
they're just carrion birds.

Whereupon they tore the fucker apart,
called him Skin & Bones.
They freezedried his butt,
chilled his skin. Somebody else
is wearing it now—who *is* wearing it now?
Probably some lawyer in Topeka.
Or maybe a wag in Wichita.
The fat from his posterior
now fills out an anorexic gal in Scranton.

The heart went to Houston as usual.
There is sense in this—
Houston needs all the heart it can get.
The boy's eyes went to Denver
a place as plain as the nose on your face
in dire need of vision.

And what did Pittsburgh get?
The most perishable goods, the liver
and maybe the spleen—
whichever, you can bet Pittsburgh can use it.
Look at its history, think of its past— .
it has always been a big consumer of organs.

All the other parts, right down
to the toes, all the way out to the branch banks
to someone in need of a new set of knuckles,
the boy's parts were scattered through
the vast black market of the medical abattoir,
thrifty now as the Hormel slaughterhouses
of Austin Minnesota. Yet very few, if any,
of the "recipients" would be black.

Note: the very first attempts to put
the hearts of baboons in the human breast
occurred in South Africa—the surgical anxiety
to find a primate substitute
for the scandal of the obvious.

Ah well, even as we repose here
studying the ramifications
of this cryogenic express,
they're out there, under the flashy lights,
gleaning the fallen fruit, the strange fruit—
and this time it's the bourgeoisie who are gathered.
After all, they run around the most,
they are the fittest.

ELLYN MAYBE

When I moved to Los Angeles a few years ago, the poets I met kept saying, "You've got to check out Ellyn Maybe." After about the tenth time, I began wondering "Who the fuck is Ellyn Maybe?" Eventually we were introduced at a spoken word gig outside a since-closed record store in Santa Monica. I wondered if I was the victim of some massive practical joke, because there was no way in the world that this spaced-out cross between a squealing deadhead and a giggling bag lady was the best poet the city of angels had to offer. I ran into her a couple nights later at the Hammer Museum, as we both straggled in late to a Jorie Graham reading, and my curiosity was aroused—very few poets find it necessary to attend bohemian events in coffeehouses *and* high-brow literary shindigs. Perhaps there was more to Ellyn Maybe than met the iris, perhaps my initial conclusion was rash and pig-headed—it wouldn't be the first time.

Ellyn Maybe lumbers nervously to the microphone, swinging a hand-held tape recorder, which she plops down on the stage. She talks with a mumbling lisp about what an honor it is. I expect the worst and WHAM—she busts out with images that make my brain do double takes, and on the spot, as the audience feeds her love, I'm hastily revising my notions of poetry and its possibilities. Ellyn Maybe has played me like a sucker, roping me in to thinking she's a dunce, betting my small fortune against her, then laying down the aces, one by one.

Ellyn Maybe has been called "the daughter of Allen Ginsberg" (by Peter Rabbit of the Taos Poetry Circus), and despite the fact that she's never done drugs, still lives with her mom, and is saving her virginity, the comparison works on a

number of levels. Ellyn has Ginsberg's remarkable ability to bring people to-
gether. Los Angeles' poetry scene, like the city itself, is tremendously cliquish,
and Ellyn is the point where parallel lines inevitably meet. At the same time,
she's the antithesis of the Hollywood archetype. She is the antonym of Pamela
Anderson. She has a Beat sensibility, rarely revising (something more "academic"
writers criticize her for), her poems are lengthy (some might say excessive), and
she's not afraid to wear her liberal politics on her sleeve. Until recently Ellyn
was one of LA's best-kept secrets, but the publication of *The Cowardice of Am-
nesia* has cast her into the national spotlight, and she's proven up to the task,
touring relentlessly, dazzling audiences in over 15 cities in the past six months
(both on the spoken word circuit and in more traditional venues).

Many journalists liken the contemporary spoken word/poetry slam phenom-
enon to the Beats. This comparison however is deeply flawed. The Beats were
anti-establishment, whereas the slammers, for the most part, are eager to "get
paid" and be assimilated into the corporate structure. Slammers are generally
more interested in high scores from the randomly chosen judges than speaking
the truth. Ellyn Maybe is the exception to the rule. The fact is, she may be
more gifted than Ginsberg or his hallucinating peers. Her work is filled with
outstanding insights, arresting images, and hysterical word play, all in a voice
that is entirely her own, defying the gravity of stereotypes.

JEFFREY MCDANIEL

Ball & Chain Record Store

Someone came into the ball and chain
    record store I work at
    and said no bags
    a waste of plastic.

I said yes.
You must be a granola-eating, left-wing,
    dig-gothic, post-modernist, watch a lot
    of Billy Jack movies, Arlo Guthrie type.

He said yes.
I smiled.
I dream of Tom Waits fingerpainting
    lightbulbs on my holiday wreath
    and I'm Jewish, pretty weird huh?
    I celebrate Tiny Tim's birthday
    with a parade of dancing deadheads
    some who never sleep and some
    who never go to the bathroom.

His T-shirt said have you hugged
    a rainforest today?

I said I love the planet
    but it's unrequited love.

He told me babe, you're bringing me down.
When I was born my first word was ohmmm . . .

In kindergarten I organized the pacifists
    to demand we didn't have to read
    from Dick, Jane and Spot books.
    Too generic.
I demanded we get American Indians
    to talk about what's real.
And I gave them my nap mat
    cause it's their land and
    I gave them my peanut butter
    and jelly sandwich cause
    the buffalo have been murdered
    and they need protein.

He blushed with passion and said
    tell me you.

Well, the first 15 years of my life
    I thought Barry Manilow was a sex symbol.
Needless to say I got a sort of late start
    at being at one with the cosmic heartbeat.

He gave me one of those looks
    like I better get this girl
    some Jack Kerouac books to read fast
    before she suffers the confusion
    of not knowing there's other existences
    beside the banal.

I put my hands on my hips and squealed
    I read *On The Road*
    and the letters of Allen Ginsberg to Neal Cassady
    and vice versa.

He said on Monday, Wednesday, and Saturday
    I'm a part time Marxist.

AMERICAN RENEGADES

He took out a beanie
put it on his head
and began to chant.
This definitely turned me on.
All of a sudden he began to sing
    the minimum wage workers' song
    "the walls are full of faces
    the mini-malls are full of neon
    the bitter bite the hands that feed them
    the food is a mixture of bone, blood
    and snails
    man is a cannibal."

I said wow! you are the sort of guy
    who says right on and really means it.
You probably only drink the milk
    of socially conscious cows
    who voted Crosby, Stills, Nash and Young
    for president.

He screamed, oh chick, my life changed
    in 1962 when I realized the Constitution
    was written without women, blacks,
    indians, and poor white men in mind.
That was not o.k.

I became the Jackson Pollack of feminism.
I threw paint of outrage everywhere.
I was a man who identified
    with Billie Holiday and Ernest Hemingway.
I was a traveler.

So what brings you into this
    San Fernando Valley air conditioned
    intellectually malnourished record store
    with the exactlys?
We open exactly at 10:00
Close exactly at 10:00
No matter what our karma
Damn it's so crass,
    you can't even rent *The Last Waltz* here.

He said I'm in a competitive mantra makers
    bowling league.
We have weavers, chess players,

avant-garde stamp collectors
and Hell's Angels.
Inventors all.
We bowl whenever the fuck
the spirit moves us.
With any luck we'll be playing the
New Age/lawyers/used car salesman league
again real soon.

Hippies and New Age people are like
the difference between Bob Dylan and Bob Hope.

He smiled and said do you want to bowl?
We are definitely into strikes
for the betterment of the worker.
We need someone who looks
like she could walk into the woods
and find incense without getting poison ivy.
You look like Van Morrison
when you pout your lips.
You could be a part of the father, son and
the holy ghost meshuganeh athletic league.
Besides I love you.

I started to weep.
Tears of Bas Mitzvah cake
and tears of being the last kid picked
for field hockey in gym class.
Authentic tears.
Nobody ever said all that to me before.
I guess I kind of do have Van Morrison's mouth.
Why hadn't anybody ever noticed?

I said I love you.
But every free moment I moonlight at
Hairy Krishna Organic Coiffures
and Tea Salon.
We use
no chemicals
no dyes
no sprays
no combs
no brushes
Hell, you look pretty much the same going out
as going in.

AMERICAN RENEGADES

He said what's a nice girl like you doing
      living in a Republican administration
      like this?

The manager of the record store comes over
      and says
You know the movie *Fahrenheit 451?*
Corporate has ordered us to burn it.
Get to it!
Don't give me your damn whimpering
      Joan of Arc eyes.
Lots of people would love to have your job.
I screamed pig! PIG!
You are giving barnyard animals a bad name.
Cops are Pigs!
Intolerants are Pigs!
Bigots are Pigs!
Everybody who does it and says
      they're just doing their job is a Pig!
Everybody who does it to someone else
      knows what they are.

This is my first day at the record store.
I guess if they want to have a quiet
      complacent yes sir type of employee
      they ought to ask different questions
      on the application.

Like do you conform?
Like do you care that this is stolen land?
Like do you believe in playlists?
Like do you believe in yourself?
Do you mind waking up alone
      rather than being beat up with fists?
Do you see the government is beating us up
      as bad as a knife in our elbows
      as bad as a slur in our ears
      as bad as a rape
      when we just wanted to be held

And all they ask is
      can you work part-time?
      and what days can't you work?
      and they say whom do we contact

in an emergency?
I said
    cause you need to ask that
    constitutes an emergency.

The hippie said my name is Hell's Bells
    but you can call me hope.
He said I dug you.
Now I dig your whole being.
It's strange,
No matter how many nights I wake up unhappy
    there is still a possibility of rising
    into a change so easily.
The outlaw lives in a world where
    when he sees a mirror he sees a hero.
And all heroes put their bellbottoms on
    one leg at a time.

Let's face it,
How can you trust money when
    there are politicians' faces printed on it.
Money is sexist.
The only woman on so-called American currency
    which is really Turtle Island to the Indians
    is Susan B. Anthony and they stopped making those
    real fast.

Is money worth killing for?
Is money worth killing for?

I ran through the store singing
    about William Blake's eyebrows
    and Walt Whitman's bellybutton
    saying everything is alive
    and everything is sort of adorable.
I took paperclips and gave them
    to loving vegetarian families
    who needed someone.

I took the bathroom sink and gave it a hug.
I freed all the rubberbands!
And I said to all the plastic bags
    I will never burden you
    with films weighing you down,

Perry Como cassettes,
or even a piece of Jerry Garcia's beard.
Well maybe.

But I will never staple a bag
for you brought love.

Most people tell me
it was all the pop tarts I ate.
Some people tell me
it was because I was a liar.
And I said I'm too honest
to be anybody's best friend
But at times nobody believes
this hippie ever even came by.

There are
no lingering peace signs
no incense
no tea bags
no fuck the fuckers pamphlets
Yet I still can't even believe
Abbie Hoffman is dead.
So my strengths and pains
are in my sense of wonder.
All I know is I don't believe in
wearing sandals and argyle socks together.
And when I needed it most, hope was here.
Change must not be too far behind.

FRANCEYE

Asteroid Poem #15

Today's news is that "Corpus Christi,"
a Terrence McNally play that depicts Jesus and his disciples
as gay
can't be shown in New York for fear of Christians,

who want to burn down the theater
and exterminate gays, Jews, and McNally.

Digesting this
on my way to breakfast,
I saw the billboard that says
ARMAGEDDON
July 1.
Well, shit, I said,
it's about fucking time.

ANNE WALDMAN

Pact

      alias commandantress
alas commends
 and then
    proffers
    (a smoking gun)
cigarillo, por favor?
alas, an alliance an extra
   sigh
       sucks in with her eyes
sign / pack / pact
retire? alas, never

RUTH WEISS

For Madeline Gleason

"do your poems haunt you?"
oh Maddie
is not the poem of our life
a haunt
drawing us
releasing & drawing us?
A stronger line each time
drawing us the artist
drawn & quartered
into seasons, elements . . .

CHARLES PLYMELL

Was Poe Afraid?
To commemorate reading with Huncke and Bremser at The Cross St. Bar in Baltimore

On these same brick streets of
Baltimore tonight—was Poe afraid?

Afraid of the florescent eyes of dogs,
the raven's reflection, the rats scat
through sawdust in Hollins Market,
the smell of rot and burlap thick as fur.

Afraid of roaches, disease, of poverty,
loud poverty boom-box crackle crack whip
poor ponies pulling carts full of greens
up Greene Street—overloaded with greed.

Afraid of the thick sky over foggy tavern door
On Cross Street's cloud-draped rummaged
crimson cloak, threading from the hill
down to the curling dark water bay.

Afraid of statues with iron poet capes flowing
in formal rapture and cast hollow spirit
looking down cold upon those animated
walking and talking past old doorways

Afraid of the wine, the drugs, the vault
of alcoholic shoreline's fractal ragged fault
floating in a dream grave afraid to yell
smug disciples repeating versions of hell.

The whirl of a wash, a tangled thread
sets an alarm that turns to dread
makes the vision flow instead into
creation and how such grace is fed.

Life is a poor host grabbing guests who came
swirling great pleated sheets wrapping the stars
leaving, streaming party coils to their last cars
some on twilight's slightly twisted cane.

Cool Hobohemian's 1950's Bennies from Heaven Poem

Sam Shusterman, the shoe store man, under the overpass over the manholes in old downtown updone Wichita has like a cast iron front store you'd see like on the Bowery. He sold dem used shoes to da old folk, poor folks and dos hipsters bopping down de street on Douglas Avenue, main drag, hip to de tip, a few blocks from the Great White Way Snooker Hall—long time gone. He gots da used shoe store where da Florsheims shines and da floor shines too. He gots time and da togs to climb any gamey frame. He gots da Wingtips, hightops, blues suedes too. Off-size, replete, repaired, recast, retread, rebuffed, runover, factory rejects for da dejected, rejected, the prejudged multitude, da crude, da recluse, da dolly moppers and be-boppers, and suburb sinners at the door.

He stretches da off size, puts Sholls's in da too-wides. Black and white shoes for blacks and whites too. Pointy toes too for dos wid a point of view, pegged pa-chuco trousers, silver watch-chained deja vu, oxfords for da saddle or da golf goof course, even penny loafers for a memory of swing.

High heeled boots for shit stompers and whammied out galloping sluts. Hip boots laced in place, glittering fast socks clean up da alley cooch. Plastic pumps wid taps on de heels, patent leather for da patch pond n' gators galore.

I'm going down to Sam Shusterman's store across the Santa Fe tracks and get me something to bop the night train in, rack back my sack and lay my nod in da the bog before da sod, so fonk it and honk it, and trim the slim trinket 'cause I gots my new used kickers on, shufflin' and scufflin' down the street swift as a sneaker's shoestring, long time before Doc Martin made the scene.

PAUL LANDRY

Displaced Poet

I go to the country
and while there
I can't write
about trees
or turnips.
Sunlight seems like
a steel car
falling off a hill.
Trees?
What names should
I give to these girls
in green dresses
prom queens
who will never know
I exist at the edge
of their gowns?
I go nowhere
going out of my mind.
And the city arrives.
And the city sits down
and the city wants
the country
to serve tea
and pork chops

simple as that
unconfused
green light already
shining on top
of the hill.

GEORGE TSONGAS

The States

it's an
amazing
place, where
no one enjoys

life

but they
all want
to live

forever

MIKHAIL HOROWITZ

In Memoriam: Charles Mingus

I sat be
side the man / his
ruined, round

AMERICAN RENEGADES

body / eyes of a
sultan, sandweary & all
encompass

ing / fat, black
pudgy fingers ancient
eyes

   : you know me for

sure
Charles Mingus / got
nuthin to

say got nuthin
to ask of your vastness
Your sadness

old as notes
the soul neglects / got
nuthin to

give you back
for what you blew

Got
nuthin but
the slow, sad weight
of

2
huge
hands

2 urns
to hold the ashes
of

a
man's
gesture

moving pensively
on the dense piano
like

God's
presence on the
still face of the

hushed
waters

KAYE McDONOUGH

For Frank

You took all those things,
you know you did.
You broke Alix's door and Paul's door and Roger's window.
They remember you at Abe Cohn's pawnshop:
        typewriter
        record player
        radio
        one pearl necklace
        one gold ring
Then you lied about it even after I asked you.
You drank too much, too, and you weren't honest at all.
I can't remember a single good thing we ever did.
You scared the holy hell out of Dan Cassidy that night
we went hunting for methedrine.
He ran up the street while you broke holes in the wall
and threw my pocketbook out a closed window.

I knew all about death until I met you.
All the things I'd figured out, you undid—
told me I was full of shit.
I had to think all over again and wonder why you and Rich
sat and cried over "Fern Hill" one late afternoon.

Auntie Kaye died a hard death with you, boy.
I'll bet you thought when *you* died I'd pretend as though
nothing ever happened.

All the rush of words and ways come running back
from past a midnight house or two.
I'm lost again thinking of you the way I used to do.
You could sit in the big brown chair again in Berkeley.
I could sit on your shoulders and hug your head
while we read the paper and listened to the rain.
Baby, baby, come back and jump on my typewriter
I want to see the keys fly.

1967

MARC OLMSTED

From *Bones*

One week after
Ginsberg's death
  get up with
the alarm to
 say a special
prayer exactly
at the time
he died 2:39 AM
-tradition says
he'll wake every
    7 days
(for 49 days)
at that same time
 and realize
 he's dead
instead of dream-like
    confusion-
at this moment
 he can be

       told quite
    directly how
       to liberate
    his mind into
    clear empty
space
 -burning
    candles in the
       shrine room
    reading in
    the dim
    flickering glow

 -he'll be
    fine, is fine
 all these
    prayers-
 my way of
    grieving

DAVID AMRAM

Collaborating with Kerouac

Jack and I first performed his words and my music together at varous Bring-Your-Own-Bottle Parties, held in painters' lofts throughout lower Manhattan in 1956. We immediately tuned in to each other. Accompanying him as he read (or spontaneously rapped) was as natural as when I played with Dizzy Gillespie, Charles Mingus, Sonny Rollins, Thelonious Monk, and all the great Latin American, Middle Eastern, Native American, and symphonic musicians with whom I had already performed. All of these artists like Jack and like myself had paid their dues for years and because of their great discipline and connection to the souls of others, were able to do anything with anybody and make it a memorable experience. Jack shared that same effortless intensity and purity of intent that pulled new ideas out of the air. He was both inspired and inspiring. We were like the proverbial birds of a feather who flock together.

Jack had absorbed the gorgeous reading styles of Dylan Thomas, Lord Buckley, and the lyrical genius of the music of the Catholic liturgy, traditional Jewish chants, the sanctified sounds of Gospel music, Native American singing styles, and the haunting refrains of French Canadian folk songs, lullabies, and stories. He was as musical as he was literary. Sometimes he would play the piano and I would make up scat vocals, rhyming on the spot the way rappers do today. We would often trade off four bar duets, as all musicians of the fifties did with one another. Sometimes he would play the bongos, and I would accompany him playing French horn, piano, a bagful of flutes, or whatever was available.

We became friends before *On the Road* was published and stayed friends through those early glory days and nights and the subsequent turmoil and heart-break that followed the success of his monumental book. When we gave the first-ever jazz poetry reading in New York City in the late fall of 1957 at the Brata Art Gallery, we were having as much fun as when we would spontaneously entertain ourselves and a handful of others at the Café Figaro, with my band at the Five Spot at 3 AM when most of the customers had left, on an empty bench in Washington Square Park accompanying chess players, at Lucien Carr's apart-ment in all-night jam sessions or when Jack crashed at my place on Sixth Avenue.

When we wrote the song "Pull My Daisy" and collaborated on the film of the same name with Robert Frank, Alfred Leslie, Larry Rivers, Gregory Corso, Allen Ginsberg, Delphine Seyrig and other friends, we were always treasuring the enjoyment of the moment. I accompanied Jack in the two extraordinary narrations that he improvised on the spot, in 1959.

Because all the serious artists of our era believed that the treasures of the European tradition could be enhanced with the philosophy of American Jazz, we never rehearsed anything, and it always came out right. That was because we trusted each other and were always searching, collectively and individually, to share a shining magic moment that we knew would never happen again. We also tried to infuse our formal works (Jack's novels and poems, my symphonies and chamber music, Robert Rauschenberg's paintings) with the same energy and natural feeling, draw from our own real life experiences.

Above all, Jack was a man of Spirit. He was also a great scholar of literature, music, religion, sports, painting, language, and humanity. He had as much love for the poetry of Celine, Rimbaud and Baudelaire as he had for the work of Dylan Thomas, Langston Hughes, Carson McCullers, Thomas Wolfe and Lord Buckley's spontaneous gems. He could sing the themes of Haydn and Bartok string quartets with the same accuracy and zest as when he scatted the recorded solos of Charlie Parker and Dizzy Gillespie.

In 1964, he helped me to find the texts for my cantata for chorus, solists and orchestra, "A year in our Land," which included part of "The Lonesome traveler." Jack suggested fifty books to read to find the text for this work that used Vivaldi's idea of The Four Seasons, set in America. Spring in the East, Summer in the West, Fall in the North, and Winter in the South with a prologue and epilogue set to music from the texts of the authors James Baldwin, John Dos Passos, Jack Kerouac, Thomas Wolfe, John Steinbeck, and Walt Whitman.

I was lucky enough to know Jack and spend memorable times with him. I'm still collaborating with him forty-three years later, as the millenium approaches.

My current composition, "Giants of the Night," a flute concerto, commissioned by James Galway, and Jack Kerouac. The second movement of the concerto, dedicated to Jack, includes two French Canadian folk melodies that Jack used to sing to me in late-night, early-morning adventures that we shared. I am also creating new music, some improvised on the spot, some composed for chamber ensemble to accompany unreleased archival tapes of Jack reading his own work, lovingly preserved and available over forty years later on a series of CD's produced by Jack's nephew, Jim Sampas. Every time I hear Jack's voice, I expect to see him come into the room.

As I approach my seventieth year, coinciding with the year 2,000, I feel Jack's spirit in the joyous faces of the young people I see all over the world whenever I mention his name before performing some of the works we created together. Those few of us from our generation still here all try to bear witness to his generosity of spirit, and the shared energy of all the unsung men and women who made it possible for us to somehow continue to pursue our dreams when most of the society of the 1950's rejected us. Because of this experience, a small group of us were always *in*clusive, not *ex*clusive, and always left an extra plate of whatever we had to eat, a smile and a hug, and most important, a word of support for our brother and sister artists, old and young alike.

I believe Jack would also share my hope that what we did together long ago can inspire young people today to collaborate and share their talents and blessings with each other and the world.

JAN KEROUAC

Hey, Jack!

Hey, Jack! Hey, Jack! Is that you?
This is Jan Michele, your daughter.
Remember?
This is your daughter, remember?
I believe we met twice down in the Stew Pot.
Yeah, it's me.
I'd like to talk to the cat that begat me, you dig?
I heard your voice come over the line
From out there in black telephone universe land
And I felt like the RCA Victor dog.
Yeah.

AMERICAN RENEGADES

Oh, to be a gleeful Mad Boy back to the mists of innocence
A Beat still incubating in the unsullied womb of Beathood
Where the only specters of doom were "two bald-headed cats
Who, like, could push a button and blow us all outta here, man!"
And now, those imagined antics of Khrushchev and Ike
Have long since dissolved in the serum of history.
Immortalized by Mad Magazine
Which I used to steal from the corner candy store
H bombs drawn in so many cartoons
It's become a cartoon, or at most the smallest measurement
Of nuclear firepower on earth.
No one seems to realize it, but I'll tell you a secret:
The H bomb, I think, is the success secret of Japan.
Yeah.

If one of those sweet Beatitudinous Babes of yore
Had stood up and prophesied that in three decades
An Iranian fanatic would hold the entire publishing world hostage
If he had said
That there'd be Haitian drug gangs called posses in Kansas City
Or condoms advertised on TV
Computer viruses
Hypos handed out on street corners
If he had dared to suggest
That in the late 80s
Soviets would be more peace-minded than the Americans
And that there would be a huge hole in the ozone from spray cans
They would have put him in a straitjacket
And carted him away to an asylum.
And there, in the nuthouse,
He might have written a monstrous work of fantasy science fiction
To make George Orwell's *1984* look like the *Wizard of Oz* by
    comparison.

Ah, my poor father
He was such a Big Baby Noodlebrain
Too noodlebrained to exist in this world of geometric fear
Too animal saintly-headed
Too animal saintly-hooded
He was too saintly to crawl through those concrete rat mazes of tortured
    thought.
I know.
I'm the same kind of Baby Noodlebrain.
'Cause I can feel him in my bones

I'm getting to know him.
I'm getting to know Little Boy Blue from the inside out.

Racing down, down madness-awkward
On Madison Avenue to Madhattan today
Freezing in the cruel cold, I wrap myself up like an Arab
Blue hat and scarf like veils and, while rushing,
Caught a glimpse in store windows.
I looked like a mad Tuareg or Berber tribesman of the Sahara
Hurtling at full tilt on a horse
Or maybe even a camel
Turquoise shrouds and veils flapping in the hot desert wind.
Only this was cold city wind
Here on the other side of the Atlantic
Which reminded me of the ancient, sunken home
Of continental driftwood
Continental breakfasthood.

Ah, we humans must be a pretty hardy lot
to swarm all over this poor old globe, time after time
Strong as dynasties of cockroaches
In those tenements I used to live in.
Remember, Jack?
You came to visit me in a tenement.
I bet you didn't see any cockroaches
No, you were too drunk.
Well, never mind.
Anyway, so
You say,
All your fathers wore straw hats like W. C. Fields
Well,
I wish I could say that
But, you see,
My father was the Invisible Man
But I won't hold that against you.

GERALD NICOSIA

Jack Kerouac Returns to Lowell After 25 Years

Nobody recognized him
Without a checkbook and an Oscar-winning grin
They stole his Mercedes and hid it
In some old friend's garage
Nobody expected he'd still be walking
With his eyes on the crooked tarry cracks
In the sidewalk of a run-down neighborhood
They were expecting him in a dazzle
Of blinding marquee lights
With film crews from several major networks
Vying for multiple media rights
They all claimed to represent him
Except for the ones who actually had his blood
And everyone loved him except
For a few of the women who'd slept with him
He was looking for the Moody Street Bridge to jump off of
But they'd changed the name
And put up a bland white university
To protect his old neighborhood from the ghosts
Of former beatnik agitators
Not even the chance for a dirty glass of whiskey
In Nicky's now that it had been resurrected
Into a bright French restaurant
But down in an alley off Gorham Street
He found a Vietnamese kid whose English was bad
With no money in his torn jeans
And they shared a cigarette
Remembering when America was still a foreign country
To all the bastards who now own it
And they smiled because
Even in the worst of times
Kicks still come for free.

LAUREL ANN BOGEN

The Door for Love and Death

You push the shadow against the wall.
Open the door for love and death.
What rooms are rented there?

In the Room of Exquisite Torture,
A woman watches her lover shave.

In the Room of Hopeless Romantic,
A man weeps before a portrait of Voltaire.

In the Room of Maternal Instinct,
The rose is embalmed.

In the Room of Amorous Adventure,
Both doors hide the tiger.

In the Room of My Life,
I give up one and love the other.

STUART Z. PERKOFF

stuart oft remarked that it is not only what poems the poet left, its also who he may touch in life. in the history of the craft, there are untold numbers of word-whackers u never heard of, but they, in their turn, might have touched a patchen or an olson, been an inspiration to others u may not know, to carry forth this vision. he loved the lineage of the craft, felt part of a huge army of the dedicated who came before. u cd laff & joke abt anything except there wd be no mocking of poetry. too many had died of it in pursuit of the craft. about the lady, who is in many of stuart's poems: we had talked of how man from the ooze has worshipped many gods & all of them, the gods, were not men. the lady was assigned, in many cultures, to the fecund spring & the bountiful harvest. in zeus times, the muse was a lady. & on balmy nite beaches, we wd marvel how 4 bozos really, cd have been given this gift of the poem. & stuart sd it was the lady who enlisted us, that it was a lifetime gig, & we must never betray the craft or she wd take it back, becuz it was hers. the lady was no mythic presence in the sky, (altho on one hallucigenic nite on the beach, we indeed did see her that way), no, the lady was here, walking the streets checking, always checking. the lady gave us a dignity we had never known before & sometimes, watching the hand move the pen across the page, i acknowledge stuart & the lady & am so very grateful. about the poems u will see: stuart wuz a master wordman. he cd be o so very witty funny or, hear him read something he deeply cared abt, the hair on yr head wd stand & u just might weep. stuart was a devastating reader & he always knew just when to stop. his 1st poem is as good as his last poem. his adage: "just write abt something u care abt to someone u care abt" & he did. the little times of magic in an otherwise ordinary day, he wd write abt telling how he felt & did it change his life in any way. too many poets u read or hear string together many pretty images but then u think: yeah, thats cool, but what are u saying & how do u really feel abt it. stuart had the courage to throw out a brilliant image becuz it didnt fit the poem or wuz merely gloss. even in his longer poems, there is that same economy of like: say what the hell u got to say & get off, anything else is ego (she dont like that, either). i wish i cd pass the joy of perkoff on to the very busy reader but i can only say: what the hell, take a chance take a minute, read, this is a book u know. stuart, like wally berman, the other poetmaker in our lives, died way too soon, too damn early in this cursed life. a line from stuart i will always remember: "life is a disease we are infected with at birth" & i think, yes, i am here today & i will carry on, pass it on, & in the lineage u live, u will always live.

for more stuart: his brother Gerry, has done a masterful job of collecting & editing all of stuart's known works, ramrodded the issuance of "voices of the lady: collected poems" from the national poetry foundation at the univ of maine. i know u need this book.

TONY SCIBELLA

Untitled

peace peace
we too shall
rest.

& in the air
         no breath
& in the eye
         no birds
& in the black
         no needs

then when we are nothing & one
& our flesh is eaten
by trees that thrust to the sun
& our blood is drunk
by lizards with flickering tongues
& all that we are is nothing
& all
& being born.

then over the fields of quiet wheat
the wind will caress
& there will be peace
& we too
shall rest.

The Suicide Room

I have within the head a room of death:
brown walls (the death of spring), a vague breath of
seasmell, a ring of knives of every kind
circling a centered mat.
                              The failing lives
to be accompanied by flat drums,
dovecooing horns, plucked strings.
                              The supplicant comes,
he sits upon the mat. Attendants bring
paper and pen. He wills his philosophy
to the world and binds his eyes. And blind he dies.

This is the room I go to when my mind
extends no further than its hidden doom.
I weld the music and the knives into
a power over deaths.

                              I leave the dead
within this room when I have held power
for long enough to go beyond the point
beyond which one cannot possibly go.

Love is the Silence

love is the silence out of which
woman speaks. the female
country, the grieving country.

         i stole
those images from a
wild girl's mouth. i am a
witch. i deal with
death. she sd. i
struggle against it.
the poem
is my struggle, i sd. a different
craft.

      the once i hungered
where the two crafts cross
to take within my hands
that power
& heat it
at will.

her lips moved in the dark room. blue with
kissing that cold thing. woman is
silence, she sd.
a different craft

Untitled

poets of the world, be
      careful. i can't say it
strongly
enuf. i know
i know
i tell you i know
that she stands on every street corner waiting & watching
that she looks into the dark doorways & empty windows seeking
that she tirelessly walks up & down the hard streets of the world calling

   watch out, you fools, you are blind
as well as deaf, that's one of the things she hates.
be careful, poets.

its not enuf
to put a pretty word
next to another one.
a real image or two
studding yr verse
won't save you at this reckoning.
this is the real
thing, take
cover, poets.
she is knocking on the door
are you shivering in yr shit filled shoes?
have you roses growing out of yr nostrils?
she is coming
she is coming
she is coming thru the door
she is coming up the stairs
she is coming opening the doors of the bedrooms & the eyes, looking in
she wants to hear no stories
she wants to hear no songs.
i think she's had her belly full of singing.

she is merciless.
she knows what you have done
there is no use crying abt it, making up fancy tales
you've gotten too good at that
anyway.
    she'll take it back. it's hers. she wants it back.
run poets, run.
hide poets, hide.
be careful
take cover
i warn you
i know. i tell you, this i know.
she's coming. up & down the streets, in & out of the houses, in the
    dark & the lite, seeking, looking, crying, mercilessly
    examining every soul.
i warn you
she is as relentless as you wd expect her
to be.
it's hers. you know it. when she finds you
she will take it back.

TONY SCIBELLA

Venice West

there was a north beach there was a greenwich village there was no venice called "slum by the sea" venice was a warren of extremely cheap housing & work space, perfect for poets & painters, anonymous neighbors to nod greetings to. in 1958, stuart z. perkoff opened the venice west cafe & suddenly there was a place to meet, hang, yr work, read yr poems out loud! & in pre-tourist days we mostly read to each other, but that was most important to us starting out: the acknowledgment of our peers in the summer of '59, after the publication of the holy barbarians, by lawrence lipton, hordes of backpacking beards, w/a paper copy of on the road in their pocket, showed up on the beach, & then there was venice.

i didn't mind, at first, when the beat generation began being bandied (it was kin to the lost generation which we knew), because it gave a sense of *us* to us, we were not alone in our pursuits. & yes, we were beat by 2 wars, a new cold war, the bomb. & we did plunge into verse totally, above all else, poet was a noble profession in crew cut america, where status was if yr butler fit in yr bombshelter

amazingly, 40 years later, those of us still alive, are still singing words in a flash/bang world, surviving drugs, alcohol, broken marriages, frantic affairs, meager bare-bones existence of bread sandwiches & empty hopes. none of us would change anything in our life of verse, feeling duty too strongly, knowing we must pass it on to the new blood: that it can be done: poetry & magic & they must be true until it is their time to repeat after me.

the voices presented here are the cadre of venice west. it is striking out of this incestuous community, that each voice is so individual w/not one sounding like the other. (o how inspired we were chanting w/the moon, blowing be-bop verse, riffing great guffaws of glee & joy down midnight promenades, just so damn grateful we were spun thru lot & circumstance to be in venice together.

i love these people: john thomas, the large, the smartest man i have ever known. philomene long, plucked from the convent to land at the perfect place at the perfect time. frank rios, out of the bronx in black blowing his broken word verse. jimmy morris, end stool at the bar longshoreman, mortared in korea, sent home w/a giant thirst. stuart z. perkoff. we all owe stuart. he told of the joy of verse & a calling. & he lived it everyday one foot before the other. example is golden, to see that it can be done.

in most intros, the introducer will urge you to read the poems for the betterment of yr lore & feeling. not here. this verse is the day it was written, like: here it is, kid, do what yr gonna do. these then, are "the voices heard in venice".

Untitled

i look at stuart
i say: are we a myth?
as about a mile
he sez
eternal toiler
in the fields of shit
we spread it
we kick it
we eat it
we mix in our beliefs
& spread it over our bodys
hoping the stench will keep away
any human contact
the stuff that closeness needs

i expect any bodys
that been together
for a while
fall into a semi-coma
& stay
& if nothing extraordinary happens
waking up some where
down the line
wondering what happened
to life
& the promise of love

& we were promised love
& happiness
that we were to attain
but no body explained how
i see a vast space crowded w/naked people
milling blindly crashing into each other
bouncing off crashing into
& when two fall into a pile
they are lashed together at the ankle
& thrown into hell

AMERICAN RENEGADES

i can see a day
i pray
that i may understand
how such beginnings
can make a love
to last a lifetime

PHILOMENE LONG

Memoirs of a Nun on Fire
(Beat generation poet behind convent walls)

"You are worldly, Sister Marie Philomene,"
the Mother Superior had said in the parlor
bent over me, tall, angular, aristocratic
like the silhouette of a praying mantis.
"Even your voice, its inflections. Worldly."

At that I was to kneel on the spot.
Kneel with no excuses.
Blind obedience.
Drop to the floor like a swatted fly.

Eyes lowered, lips closed.
I wiggled. My veil fluttered.
My knees bent a little, then locked.
I would not.

Back straight, head erect,
my eyes wide, cool, and I hope vacant,
I stared into her triangular face. I turned. Left
through the dim corridors of no time or season.

In my room I reached through the silence, and
as if from a great height,
watched my hands take the scissors,
begin to cut name tags off veils,
stockings, underwear. Everything.

All over the room,
threads and scraps of my name,
"Sister Marie Philomene" like tiny white clouds
far beneath my feet.

I knew I would leave that night.
Just walk out.
Five years within this cloister.
An enclosure of silence.
Latin. Eyes fixed to the floor.
Black robes, medieval gestures.
In the most secret recesses,
a thousand daily deaths.

At the end of the hall the life-size crucifix.
Christ's bruised knee,
the level of our lips.
A well-kissed knee.

Through these corridors
we glide through our own ghosts.
Muted light. Fluid movements.
Everything clean. Silent and clean.
"I have loved, O Lord, the beauty of Thy house."

But here some things feel dirty.
Like in my dreams.
In the convent I do not dream of the good sisters.
Each night it is a dark man who follows me.
He is tall, thin, and wears black. All black.
His half smile is repulsive.
He wants to kiss me. Every night in my dreams.
Sometimes he removes my veil,
runs his fingers through my hair.
Once he does kiss me.
I am frightened. I tell another sister.
She says the dark man is myself.

And then—the night I was seduced
by God disguised as a fat black fly.
As a Bride of God I was told to experience the Mystical Union
I must make my mind empty, an erased blackboard.
I contemplate the blackness of space,
the millions of light years between the stars.
I stretch my mind until it is no longer fixed anywhere.

I became the Bride of the Expansive Black.
I kiss it. Marry it. Its deep silence.
But it is difficult to contemplate the Immensity
while enduring a small but persistent itch.

Daily I work shoveling the convent's garbage into the incinerator.
The flies and yellow jackets are very friendly.
At times the golden insects cover my black serge habit
like a jeweled mantle, as the flies circle my head.
At first I do not know a fly, that one fly has crept into my ear to rest.
I suppose it has awakened, confused, and is trying to escape.
Lost deep within my ear canal, it buzzes with mounting intensity.
Its buzz is as loud and wide as the universe I am contemplating.
Finally, I know it is not God, but only a fly.
Or is it God disguised as a fly? Is it the buzz of God?

Not only is it a hot summer day, but I am having my period.
I begin to twitch and squirm on the sanitary napkin.
The fly buzzes with growing desperation.
My twitching on the pad increases.
As the fly's delirium grows, so does mine
given the heat, the perspiration,
the itchy habit, the sanitary napkin, and
the frantic buzzing of that fly. That Fly?

When it emerges into my outer ear
I open the side of my head gear and the fly flies out.
At this moment, this very moment, I have my first orgasm.
I know what it was because
I have felt the sensation begin once before
while kissing my high school sweetheart.
While I bounce on the pew, I see it at the corner of my eye
an enormous black fly.
It hangs in mid-air as if to look at me for a moment.
The most beautiful fly I've ever seen

But what did the nuns see as they sat silently behind me-
everyone motionless except one bouncing nun and
a hovering fly besides her?
I will never know. No one ever mentions it.
No one ever mentions anything personal.
And if they do, what would they say,
"Excuse me, Sister Marie Philomene,
but did I see you having an orgasm
during five o'clock meditation?"

Beat. Beaten. Beatific.
I am on my knees before the bed, the crucifix.
This particular night is exceptionally dark.
It is this night I am to understand I am a poet.
Saturday night. Time to whip ourselves again.
I wonder is Cardinal McIntyre doing this?
But I will do it right this time.
Five years within the convent and I have not yet done it right.
Each time the hand that holds the chains has exerted its own will.
I say to the night, "I will tonight. I will beat myself until I bleed."

My body, mind—one thing
I raise the chain high up. Higher.
That way it will come down with greater force-
to beat, beat. To beat, to be beaten. Higher. Faster.
Body, mind, chain—one thing. One will.
To strike repeatedly. To beat to blood.

It ends.
I run my fingers over my back.
There is blood.
For the first time—blood.

A small amount. But I did it.
"Beautiful blood," I say.
I remove my habit.
I run my fingers over the spot.
Yes. It is blood.
Beatific blood. Beatific spot.
Slowly, I turn in awe to see it.
It, indeed, is beautiful.
But it, my beatific spot . . .
is a mosquito bite!

I stand in the center of the room. Let loose a mighty laugh.
"Beatific mosquito! Beatific bite!"

I, who have been the Bride of flies,
have become the Bride of mosquitoes.
"Holy proboscis! Probe of fire!"
(Didn't Saint Rose of Lima, out among the mosquitoes
so that they might bite her, say their hum sounded to her
like a choir of angels?)

AMERICAN RENEGADES

"O Holy Night! The mosquitoes are quietly biting
Little fly. Great night."

If you would have looked into this dark corner,
you would have found Philomene naked as if by the night,
a Philomene who no longer hid her heart under crossed arms,
but who excitedly held her breasts in her hands as if
she were offering them to her beloved.

Hers was a song of ... .
No, it was deeper even:
it was a prayer, as the priest mutters
from the altar holding up the Host.
Her heart thumping in this forgotten corner as she prayed.
You would see her dare to look at her own body,
in the stark black night
Her body, golden serpentine,
glowing cheeks, glistening eyes, crimson tongue
In this night of black finger, her slick long body rising
rising in the blackness-slowly, very slowly turning,
turning in the unseeing dreadful hole of night.
The night, its burning lips, the night of kisses.
She danced. Naked burning bride of God.
In the Grand Silence, you could hear Philomene whisper,
"I am a poet."

But I will always be a nun.
Always in my dreams I am a shabby nun.
There are flies under my habit
and my robes are in bits and pieces.

I will always have an affinity for the extreme.
Even now I prefer the company of a St. Francis of Assisi
taking his clothes off in public,
or St. Simeon Stylites
who sat for years atop a high column,
or St. Joan of Arc
who heard voices and dressed in men's clothes.
Even now I prefer to live among
the poets, saints and mad ones of Venice West.
I know no other way but to strip and leap naked
into the Holy Fires.

Burn. Burn. Must burn.

NELSON GARY

Skull

Spent some time
sculpting the devil's face
with earth, wind, water, and fire.
Spent some time
within myself,
legislator of loose rules
and inventor of new forms
of instantaneous contentment.
Like an apocalyptic saint proper,
I played chess and wrote poetry
in the shadows of the mad and damned.
I carried a candle
through corridors, see-through deja vus
of a paradise botched, now forgot.
I was alive by virtue of stimuli
that forced me to expand, levitate,
then explode high in the sky
like fireworks on the fifth of July.
Beautiful children and adults
looked up and bolted down the ground
when I realized my soul
through the gates of prisons and institutions
for what I felt an eternity,
but what was only the present echoed by the past
when I realized the physics of our psyches
which causes each of us to strive for independence—and dance!
The skull and the bottle
are turned upside down.
My candle still aflame in the neck of it.

JAMES RYAN MORRIS

7th Sound for John Garfield

O how long have I lived
the image of John Garfield . . .

John Garfield with Jennifer Jones
machine guns blazing as Cubans
climbed all over the house he held up in . . .

"In 1933
Tony Fenner said to me—Gilbert Roland
predicting—
let's strike a blow for Liberty!"

Long after the theatre lights went on
I sat in my seat feeling my image of self
change, walking New York streets with his walk
which changed always after watching him,

cigarettes constantly lit, dangling from the corner
of my Garfield mouth.

And always, a fist-fight/street rumble with some-one
within a few hours after a Garfield movie . . .

John Garfield you were a strong influence upon me.

The day I heard you died while fucking
I got drunk and scored my 5th piece of ass
in my youthful hunger.

Now I am older and you are younger in yr Death
and I wonder just which one of us made out the best—

& Cuba, you'd never recognize it, John, yet I'm sure
there are many who wish your cinematic machine gun
would return . . .
                    it would be great, John, to go there,
You and I and Fidel
smoking big cigars, drinking large glasses of rum

all of us practicing our aim
on a picture of John F. Kennedy.

John Garfield: know that my generation still
                holds onto your image & that your
                cigarette smolders in my mouth

                day in / day out.

RAFAEL F.J. ALVARADO

Untitled
For my Grandfather, Maximo Maurielo Muller

This will not be the last poem I write
for my grandfather
Because my grandfather
was a great man to me
fuck what my father says
I consider the source
which has always been shaky
I drown in his memory
as I believe I should
a great man
is not measured by the size of his wallet
if this was true, my father would be a great man
I went by the Sav-On today
where my grandfather used to take me for ice
cream
when I was little
it was gone
like my grandfather
I miss him
more than I thought I could ever miss anybody
he lived in Silverlake
with my grandmother
years before the hip takeover

Now I can't seem to place the house he lived in
Teresa & I searched for it today
I want to put more feeling in this poem
what the fuck can I say
I already see the flood
of I'm sorry to hear about your
grandfather
I really don't want to hear it
I understand friendship
& love
I can't explain this
it will take a while
before I accept anything
so if you ask me how I'm doing
if I say fuck you
please understand
if you can't produce my grandfather
it's pointless
'cause nothing will make me feel better
'cause my grandfather & grandmother
gave me love
if not for them
I would be a hell of a lot meaner
now that he is gone
a part of me is dead
what part I won't know for a while
Last night I saw him for the last time
the one thing I didn't say
is how much I loved him
I regret too much to write down
I want every memory catalogued
I do not want to lose one moment
more than anything
I want him back

January 26, 1997

JOHN THOMAS

You'll Despise Me for This, But
I'm Going to Say It Anyway

I think, you know, I think my poetry could become very popular among the idle rich. It's just odd and dramatic enough, you know, just arty enough. All my little touches of the macabre, the grand mantle of Byronic gloom I can throw over everything. The little whiffs of obscenity and sin. My third-rate artificial enigmas. You know? Don't laugh. I think I could be, you know, the rich man's Charles Bukowski.

Oh, agreed, the idle rich are all assholes, but I could pretend I liked them, shamelessly pretend I thought they were interesting. I could do that, no sweat.

And they would back expensive little editions of my work. Sometimes, discreetly, they would give me money. That would be a fine thing, you know, the discreet money. I'll be able to buy Philomene a long dress and a pair of shoes. Christ, but I'd love to buy Philomene some pretty purple shoes.

That's the way it would be, you know? While I lived, the idle rich would fete me, and they would all be sorry and sentimental when I died.

First though, I'd need some pretty expensive cosmetic dental work, you know? You just can't hang out with the idle rich if you have teeth like mine. I only have thirteen or fourteen left, you know—thirteen, I think—and they're a kind of deep amber color. Too disgusting, too disturbing, for the eyes of the idle rich. I'm talking about eight or ten thousand dollars worth of dentistry here, and I'll never have that much money in my life.

It's fucking sad, you know? Because I have this recurring fantasy in which I say to Philomene, "Come on, get dressed. We're going to a party with the idle rich!" And she wails, "But what'll I wear?" And I grin, showing all my new white teeth, and I say, "Just check the closet, my love." And she runs to the closet, you know, and gives a little squeal of amazed delight. Because there in the closet hangs a lovely long white dress, all lace, and on the floor beneath it sits a pair of Italian handmade purple shoes. Then off we go, you know, to the idle-rich party. I, flashing my teeth, Philomene in her beautiful purple shoes. And at the party I'd read my flash little enigmatic poems, and it's all just crap, anyway. Why do I go on like this? My teeth will never be anything but uglier, and everyone knows you can't buy happiness, right?

But I tell you, I'd trade my soul tonight, this very minute, no hesitation, for that pair of perfect little purple shoes.

WILLIAM J. MARGOLIS

Venice

Getting to know Venice is like getting to know a woman . . .
one or two lumps of sugar in the coffee? . . .
a many-faceted wench, this town.
I begin to get a grip on my vision of her & she turns over,
presenting a round thigh of quiet rapport in the VW,
digging whatever sound, cool sound, is there . . .
and I begin to think I've begun to understand,
but in a moment the mood is gone. . . .

Venice is a woman.
Not so worldly-wise as the Village, not so sophisticatedly European.
Here there is a wildness of an anything but pacific, surging sea.
North Beach was a man, a virile thin-hipped cat, a hipster town.

Venice is a strange, mysterious woman.
Perhaps it's the nearness of the ocean—
Venice really *is* a beach. . . . that mothering tide. . . .
There are old women on the Ocean Front Walk,
sitting on the dim sunned benches, old womanish men;
but the varieties of femininity are endless . . .
the lesbians stalk, the week-end chicks slink in from Hollywood,
the hip & the beat young women who stand on their own feet
that fit no glass slipper, anywhere. . . .

I suddenly recall that I know I'm not the first
to be aware of the women of Venice . . .
Stuart Z. Perkoff's *Venice Poems* . . .
& John Thomas had that series of word sketches, too. . . .
But analogies & metaphors are finite vessels,
they can handle only so much pertinence—
overfilled they become silly.

Suffice it: Venice is a weird woman.
I dig her. She is very cool & unassuming.

FRANK T. RIOS

Invocation

My muse burns
a holy candle
to the nite
as She lies
quiet
in the other room

the space
between us
a mystery
like walking
on air

what I know
fits
in my closed hand

the rest
a vision
& my Muse
guiding me.

& Sometimes it all hangs crooked

Sometimes
the noise is
       everything
hanging crooked

not fear
      but something
empty
       like your hand out

a naked offering
       hung on someones door
like dead flowers

not pain
but getting killed on the way
       butterflies

& all those instant moments
looking away
        forgetting
turning up a dead end street
        not saying hello
coming out into the sunlight
        reaching for her
when she's not there
        everything
in the next room
        packed away
waiting to be shipped
        the noise
like everything
        getting louder
disappearing inside yesterday
        face to face
with yourself

& the nite all broken
        & alive
knowing the morning light
        will come
beginning everything.
        all over again.

Ritual

The ball
is thrown
in the world
bounces to where
no one is

in the most perfect sky
she picks me
tosses me about
explosing

I hold the ball
tight in my hand
afraid to let it go

She is
moved
by ritual
the man
is act
the ball
the child plays
against the wall
is black.

the carma bums

Carma Bums tour handbill

S.A. Griffin

S.A. GRIFFIN

The Carma Bums
(Because This Is What America's All About)

Rising from the ashes of precision drill team performance poetry ensemble The Lost Tribe (1985–1988, '92), The Carma Bums first toured the southwestern United States in 1989 from behind the wheel of their 1959 Cadillac Sedan "Farther" lifting off from the amazing BeBop Records in Reseda, California. As The Lost Tribe and The Carma Bums, we were always page poets looking to break thru the glass ceiling of academic poetry using mind, matter and muse. The Bums, the antithesis of The Tribe, often likened to a "happening" much like The Living Theatre, were/are a touring group of performing poets gambling from the inside using empathy and deliberation to walk the artistic high wire of public performance, sometimes at the risk of great danger, as in the case of Vancouver, B.C. at The Smash Gallery when, during the course of a gig, a group of young drunk leather clad punkers attempted to "take over" the show in order to drink all the free beer. The climax of the evening was a young punkess diving fang first into my chest like a zealous pit bull. That hurt. A local club owner rushed up after the show and exclaimed that it was the most honest and beautiful thing he had ever seen and began offering us drugs, money and women if we would just come to his after hours club and do it all over again.

He got it, but he didn't get it.

We are poets. We are process.

We have always argued and disagreed and this has been our agreement. This social experience-experiment was designed to prove that people that don't always get along can somehow get along thru above said devices. Much like The Grateful Dead, we weren't the best at what we did, we were the only ones. We brought with us (always) a copy of Thoreau, The Beat element of "be here now" or "the moment," the Meat element of "don't try," and the Da da rocking horse of absurdity hanging ourselves on bathroom walls like damp towels with eyes closed as we worshipped our own strange desire to be poetry where the rule was: there are no rules. We invested in the jazz where there can be no mistake: WE ARE NOT AND NEVER WERE SLAM POETS. This is another creature altogether. We relied upon rap-spontaneous verbal assault—in combination with "set" pieces written only for the page. We were words, words, words and group action without a net.

Like many a traveling poet, we played coffee houses, colleges, bars, theatres, galleries, open fields, sidewalks and bookstores; but mostly performed in the five-niner Caddy agreeing that the performance was ongoing and that everything we did when together *was* the performance. We made money, but lost thousands. We often played the house from inside-out as at The Black Bart

Playhouse in Murphys, the scene of the great "fuck" debate, where we entered from the back of the house and then took the time to greet everyone in the audience, never actually stepping in or onto the proscenium arch. Unlike actors in search of a mark, we were the mark. At The Henry Miller Library in bohemian Big Sur, we began the show on the grassy lawn in front of the library, and when everyone thought that the show was over, we descended into the beautiful giant redwood forest below, audience in tow, to vibrate with the history of pulp like characters in a lost Shakespearean play that depended upon white sunlight breaking thru the eaves of skyscraper high branches for the next line.

Enter laughing, exit singing. Eat air, breathe water . . .

Between 1989–1996, we accomplished 5 tours in the '59 Cadillac, one very expensive and unfortunate tour in a '66 GMC city bus (The Nowhere Tour of Words) covering the western U.S. and Canada, and one trailblazing tour of the Internet which began at The University of Washington at Seattle during the summer of Natural Born Killers in 1994.

Ellyn Maybe, giggling goddess of word and lone Carmababe, joined us at Albuquerque in 1989 to open our sets for the duration of our first No Seat Belts Tour of Words, and was there for us each subsequent tour until our final road tour, The 1996 Twisted Tour of Words, celebrating the publication of our book *Twisted Cadillac* on Sacred Beverage Press with an afterword by Ellyn. She was always stellar and could work the crowd for all the love they were worth. She is The Lady incarnate.

In 1997, under the direction of R. Bruce Dickson came *The Luxurious Tigers of Obnoxious Agreement: The Carma Bums Movie* with original music by actor/poet/angel Viggo Mortensen in spontaneous collaboration with X band members Exene Cervenkova and D. J. Bonebrake. Additional tunes by L.A. psychodelicloungewizards Double Naught Spy Car.

The time I have spent with The Carma Bums, the time we have spent together, has always been the highest highs and the lowest lows. We are truly, best friend bad brothers of word.

Presently, we ride the Internet on our International Superhighway Tour of Words and remain, words without end.

THE CARMA BUMS

MICHAEL BRUNER

Cartoons Are My Life

Cartoons are my life (GENERAL CARTOON SOUNDS)
Things come out of other things without explaining themselves
   to me
The farmer unzips his body and he is a duck (QUACK)
or another man (HI THERE!)
My friends tell me they are attacked on the streets
and my car slides out of control (TIRES SCREECHING, LOOK OUT!
CRASH)

There are too many things to think about
There are too many ways I dream to be

Cartoons in life we do stick to this earth
flying at a thousand thoughts are gone
in a particle wind echo (ECHO, ECHO, ECHO)
and there are those who accumulate these thoughts
in nets of schools and languages
they fly through the particle sky to the moon safely
(WHEEEEEEEEEEE)

But I like the old cartoons more than the new.
Cartoons that mean nothing compared to Minnie playing the cow
(MOO) or the ostrich with its head in the sand (SSSSSUCK) or an
ancient picture whose creator is gone, watching
laughing at the smashes and the bumps (*#@%*#)
the stars flying out of the Scuff (*%A!#$%@)
the children at my door (TRICK OR TREAT)
the truth

For cartoons are my life
Things come out of other things without explaining themselves
   to me

S.A. GRIFFIN

I Ate Fig Newtons Until I Puked

back when I was a kid
sitting in the pantry
I downed 3 or 4 pounds of the
gooey things
never ate them again
in fact
I can't stand the thought of them

did the same thing with meatloaf and pizza

when we are together
she and I
we just can't seem to get enough

I get down there
into her little cookie jar
and blow the dust off
eating her has the feel of a
good book
a classic
with the musty smell of gold leaf

I work the corners and study it well
commit the best of it to memory

then we fuck
make love
long and hard
we do the old in and out
sweat like summer in the south
then she sucks me until I am crazy
and I mount her like a dog
ignorant to anything but her box

as the cars roll by
the time ticks away
the neighbors argue
and children poke and play

THE CARMA BUMS

the grass grows a little longer
and we just can't do it enough

she wants me to cum
like a whale on a roller coaster ride
so I roll her over and give her my ticket for the big ride
and I watch

only imagining how good it is

she quakes like a volcano that has been inactive for years
she seems to have a fault line
running
thru the continent of her body
the landscape of her cities
collapse and burn
we lie in the ruins

my dick is getting raw
but her tuff little pussy is ready for more

so am I

I got over on the meatloaf
and pizza

took years

but I still cannot stomach the thought of
Fig Newtons

she tells me I am
with her
on the clock
we are caught somewhere in the
difference between us
I tell her the same

we call our obsession passion

we binge and purge
and it hurts so fucking good
that I don't think I can stand to go

thru it
again

until the next time

when I can work her with my fingers
she does her levitation thing and we are
trick together

she told me that she found my fingers on her
shoulders
soft bruises
like the dark spots on a banana

we call them love

America Poem

it was the pledge of allegiance
everyday
to the flag
it was the pledge of allegiance
it was our country 'tis of thee
New Yorkers that never saw a cow
cows that never saw a city
mothers fathers sons and daughters
the born and unborn
it was a house that was always there
like wood and brick eternity
it was gold silver oil
it was T.V. that was American
it was "made in the U.S.A."
it was small towns that was somewhere else
big cities that was everywhere else

that was somewhere

it was a wheel
it was wheels
it was the Wizard of Oz white man ethic that
snuck into grandma's womb and exploded like
Pandora's box over the
rising sun

THE CARMA BUMS

all hail the "glory that was God"

it was deliverance
lovers and lies that were promises
birds piloting over silent streams of sky
. it was dreams and dreaming
and it was flying higher than God
it was faith
pure and uncut
it was spent cartridges that hammered our dreams
fast to reality
it was Monroe Garbo Harpo Chico Groucho
Presley
Gone With The Wind
The Babe and baseball
hearts filled with hotdogs and homeruns
jazz pouring out of speakeasies like
hot pepper sauce over flat tongues
F.D.R.
J.F.K.
Gary Cooper and High Noon
Hank Williams Pete Seeger Huddie Ledbetter and
America
was an eager young debutante
in soft white and pink crinoline and taffeta dresses
and waves of waterfall tresses
in love with
storybook princes and princesses
it was
"I have been to the mountaintop"
assassinations and angry black clouds of riot
it was the coming of age of Harlow and Hitler
and the bastardization of Nietzche by
Hilter and Hollywood
blonde breasts sagging into fading hairlines
it was desperate to be un-understood leaders
who wanted to follow
it was a generation of giants and giantesses
spawned by
chrome gods and goddesses in the backfields of
glorious horse
Chevys Fords Mercurys Oldsmobiles Chryslers and Buicks
that longed to become
Cadillacs
it was men who hated men

pathetic pawns of power
begging for manhood
borne of paper
thrusting accusations of
"*communist, red faggot, nigger, wop, spic, kike, white trash, whore*"

it was a time
it is a time

it is America

it is a can opener
a microwave
a long distance telephone call
satellite Jesus crucified by capitalist commanders
hip new fads of neon nostalgia
sitcoms T.V. dinners
used used cars
fast fast cars
55 miles per hour
fast fast food
and the killing that rages unresolved in the
french fried inside and outside

the headlines the hairlines the waistlines
it is the dead inside of a quarter pounder with cheese
and the masturbated sesame seeds of love that
should have
it is valleys of vines
plains of corn and wheat and dyed red meat
cut picture perfect
estrogen-fed chickens with centerfold breasts
it is a single stalk of corn
growing out of a crack in the sidewalk
on a Hollywood streetcorner
it is forty years of fallout
and four hundred more
it is the one that got away
the soulmate perfect one
it is the perfection of imperfection
and the searching for truth
it is the heartland
it is America
it is the great love and admiration
the stifling addled ambition

The Carma Bums

it is the people and the truth
which is somewhere searching in a
rambling car that only stops for
dollar gas
hot coffee
then races off again over the stoic face of
what is
America

There Is a River

there is a cheerful ignorance
a chance meeting and
luck like gold that cannot be
mined or
stolen

a common atom

a dance

and stars that trick the
water with their
certain
magic

do not wash your wars in it
take your holy rituals to the
precious fountains built by your
agencies of fear

press your
wine from the fallout
and drink your
bitter victory

for yes

there is a river
a giving river that will
sing you safely

a river of
light

final
fast
and
free

where you can
disrobe
and leave your casual sadness
walking sideways at the
shore

meet me there
whoever you are
and we will agree to
swim it
together

DOUG KNOTT

Sunset Strip Self Improvement Affirmations

There is always the feeling of wind
even when there is no wind
the coat wants to turn up
young women in tight black clothes
project cold blond sex
slip out in gum-chewing 3's and 4's
from dark fertility-cars

They are fires waiting to jump
fire lanes, to enter the music smog
in the club owned by the famous movie actor
in front of which the famous kid movie star
died of too much good will
and cheap thrills from his good friends;

THE CARMA BUMS

on the sidewalk stood altars from his fans
like kaleidoscopic stoneware Mexican gods
with flowers in their hair

The guys take off their shirts
and show their tattoos at closing time
in front of the tattoo store
the girls look at them with
smiles like eclipsing planets
all the way down in their bellies
their faces turn up to the stars

The religious coffee house has folded, of course-
people drive more wildly on this street
holding phones to their ears in their cars,
feet jammed down tight close together
figures on big billboards peer down
like row of giants on a drawbridge
who appear intimate but are
secretly filing for divorce

And the Whisky and the Roxy clubs
feature rock bands that are named after toilets,
boomerangs, and kitchenware;
And I want a motorcycle
I have never had a motorcycle

And everybody here is a little bit behind or in front
of the cameras: in the bookstore, I stood in line
beside Donald Sutherland, one of my favorite actors
and I almost vaulted the aisle to grab his arm
and tell him how much I admired his work, particularly
in Nicholas Roeg's dark Venetian drama
But I held back my racing heart
to give him space to breathe alone
in the illusory world where he is not recognized

In the gas station I pump gas
next to the famous male model
with the blond hair-extensions and big pectorals

I knew it was him when a girl with huge sweater breasts
approached and pulled his autograph while we pumped
and I said: "It's you, right, you're that movie guy?"
and he said, "No, not him," and I said "OK,"

THE CARMA BUMS

because it was funny enough to me that he denied it,
but then he stood behind me to pay at the cashier
and I turned and said again, "C'mon, you're the guy,
aren't you?" And he said, "Yeah . . . it's me, it's me,
it's me" and we were both gratified

And the Mesopotamians behind the payment grill
also brandished their mustaches at the big-star action;
I had just seen this male model
as a life-sized comic cardboard cut-out
in the greeting card store window up the street

This is the city of movies, not *films*—
of package, persuasion and negative pickups
in the financing of all life, including executives
who seek preference in restaurant seatings
like packs of militant seals
and this is the city that serves up
its own name as part of the deal

The High Holy Hype of litmus audience test
Sunset Boulevard in the dog breath night:
the long cars line up in lacy steel brocade
outside the restaurants to be loaded
with people who generate international states of mind
and dubious cultural symbols

And it's time for the hit men, the pitch men
the agents and the one-line guys
and to roll the big cameras like dice
and no one forgets to be seen leaving a big tip
or to throw themselves with a big round of applause
and chopped liver under the wheels

Which roll down the street
walking distance from the health club
ragged with the dregs of rock and roll
The traffic lights blink and car shadows
move across me like a movie that kicks in
when I close my eyes—
its the movie where I'm always the star
waiting for the light to change
waiting for the big change
city of stars
neighborhood of strangers

THE CARMA BUMS

it will happen for me
it will happen for me
it will happen for me

Scott Wannberg

No Mercy

You got no mercy in your hair the way you
shake it in traffic and cause all those
blinded drivers to slam on their bewildered
brakes
       the way your eyes invite one to
suddenly snap in half with
the thought of it all
     oh, those horrible wondrous nasty
thoughts of it all
        no mercy on a stick
you buy it at the corner convenience
             no mercy on the tip of your tongue
as the air forces of all the belligerent nations
involved
pile into each other during rush hour
when the sky is full of ornery birds
back talking each other in
strident glee
       no mercy in the dark room
where everyone gets exposed
even the quiet ones
sitting there by themselves in
the oh just let them alone and they will let you live
corner
you know how it goes
they say your name enough times
and even you sooner or later begin to believe it is
actually your own
       no mercy in the headlines
grabbing you by the throat and the pupils

all you wanted to do was digest your goddamn meal anyway
but you had to go and open up the paper
and the TV turned itself on and spat at you
with bullshit and the pretty anchor people
were all dead inside and
all you could do was fall onto your knees right
in front of it all and
sing
  No Mercy in the blood stream
     No Mercy in the chorus line
        No Mercy in the richter scale
I just wanted to come and play in your sandbox of mercy
  I just wanted to climb into a comfortable bed alongside
your wise sacred mercy
No mercy in the playground of nameless children
we are their fathers we are their mothers we
go and rinse them out of our skin but the rinse cycle
never ends
No mercy in the toothpaste
you scrub and brush and scrub and floss but your teeth are
not elected your teeth don't get the lead part they don't
even get a walk on
     i came here years ago
for the mercy
i'm sorry, all the mercy is gone
we ran out last night
we have it on order
how long will it take for my mercy to come in
oh, well, the local distributor is out of it
they have it on back order
no mercy school just opened
the tuition nonexistent
you just stand in the middle of the door
and if someone is stupid enough to walk up to you
and ask you to let them love you
all you have to do is either kill them
with a weapon or even worse
kill them with your heart
the one with the sad resume
stuck in it
soon the underpaid legals and the
not paid at all illegals
come and sweep up the mercy
they put it in plastic bags
they seal it so none escapes

AMERICAN RENEGADES

they mark it toxic
this sad mercy
and they bury it deep
in the hallow ground
you know where the hallow ground lives
the hallow ground has clean underwear
on and can buy its way out of any trouble
i don't have any hallow ground to throw at you
when i pick it up it burns my hands

Mike Mollett

I Am the Bomb

I am the bomb.
There's nothing you can do about me.
Or the others.

It's all over with.
Not a chance even for a "fuck you."

I am the bomb.
Made to live forever. & when I
die, everything's new.

I am the bomb.

Stop me sucker. You can't.
Your heads are filled with pennys.
Your hands play with genitals.
Stop me sucker.
I am out of your hands, in the
hands of presidents & generals & technicians & preachers.

I AM THE BOMB.

Cats & refrigerators nothing.
Instantaneous fires. I command

wind like god.
My moment is millions of degrees.
Concussion cities.

The cats & refrigerators slam
Thru space with the buildings & cars.
I vaporize all those habits.

I AM THE BOMB.

I go all the way. Come. Come.
I will even find those presidents in time.
I am the bomb. The ultimate earthly lover & necrophile.
I am the bomb.
I penetrate the billions with my orgasm.

I am the bomb.
I am most wise.
I play for keeps.
I am the unimaginable.
I have not been created for nothing.

The Word

The Word throbs &
inflates behind the opening   bursting
from the mouth
shattering
into
dangerous fragments

The Word is fat and spry

The Word hooks itself to the airways
grapples into its food
the vital walls of all sides
so it cannot be expelled

Over there
at the mall   the Word is rotten.
soft & squishy
sorta fuzzy   blue-like
it reeks!

shoppers grimace & walk around it
then spend even more
money on things.

The Word has impact.

The Word is a virus
entering the arteries of great cities
where it thrives & replicates

The Word she speaks
is like what he speaks
but it's different

his Word is loud & sharp
her Word is also loud stretches like a couch
his Word grabs her hips trying to throw her
down
her Word winds around his heart like a spy
then winds around again . . .
The Word becomes President.
has 4 great years.
everybody loves the Word
even the bad guys   they
change tactics.

but in the next term
The Word is assassinated each time
& burned in public places
such as laundromats & sports stadiums.

The Word springs from the shadows of the bed &
bites my neck. OUCH!
GET AWAY FROM ME I scream
we struggle.
I beat the damned thing off
back into the shadows
from where it came
until the next
full
moment

american renegades

ALLEN COHEN

The San Francisco Oracle: A Brief History

It was the spring of 1966 and there was something new in the air. The Haight Ashbury neighborhood in San Francisco had begun to move from a bohemian enclave with low housing costs, large Victorian and Edwardian apartments and proximity to Golden Gate Park to a self-recognition that a new potential for humanity was being born there. Artists, writers and musicians shared houses, formed communes, and explored their minds and each other in states of consciousness expanded by the use of marijuana and LSD.

One night that spring I had a dream that I was flying over the earth like a satellite with a view of the whole globe but with telescopic vision that enabled me to see events happening on the planet. As I flew, I passed over different landmarks like the Great wall of China, the Eiffel Tower, and Times Square in New York. Wherever I looked people were holding and reading a newspaper with rainbows on it.

In the morning I told the dream to my partner, Laurie. She went out, crossed the Panhandle of Golden Gate Park and went to Haight Street where she told our friends about my dream. When I went to the street everyone said, "a rainbow newspaper, lets do it." Ron Thelin, owner with his brother Jay of the Psychedelic Shop, offered the startup money. Handbills were put up all over the Haight Street calling a meeting to discuss starting a newspaper.

At the meeting a factional battle began between those who wanted a traditional political newspaper reporting on police brutality and the anti-war movement, and a group of artists and poets who wanted to publish something that was unique in form and defining of a new culture with new thinking about human nature and social institutions. After a couple of months of meetings and inconclusive arguing, the political group made up largely of members of the progressive labor party and ex-newspapermen published *P. O. Frisco*. Its title was based on the name, *Psychedelphic Oracle* suggested by Bruce Conner, an already admired moviemaker and artist. *P. O. Frisco* landed on the street with a thud. There was a naked girl with a swastika armband sitting on a couch on the front page, along with an article on the concentration camps awaiting us in Arizona. The editors' T-squares were taken from them and they left town. The next two issues were edited by John Bronson and George Tsongas in a more Mc-Cluhanesque direction but the call for an aesthetic and content change persisted and Gabe Katz, a dropped out New York advertising artist, and I began steering the ship toward a new kind of newspaper.

What I envisioned in addition to rainbows was a breakout from the rigidity of column space that I felt was a reflection of industrial monotony and the programming of social conformity. I also wanted to merge art with the written word, and reserve the front and back pages and the centerfold for art. On the content side there was a great need for information and guidance useful for the LSD journey through the labyrinth of the human mind and new thinking on how to construct a more humane society outside the crumbling shell of a war torn society.

In issue #5, the Human Be-In issue we used our first color, purple, which we screened to get different shades of purple. In issue #6, the Astrology issue, Oracle artists divided the web press's ink fountains into three parts with wooden blocks and put three separated colors in it (the split fountain). Where the colors met they self mixed other colors and we produced the rainbow I had dreamed about. Then we got more sophisticated and used color separations in addition to the split fountain.

In its twelve issue life *The Oracle* published many new and well known writers, poets and thinkers including Gary Snyder, Buckminster Fuller, Allen Ginsberg, Lawrence Ferlinghetti, Michael McClure, Lenore Kandel, Bob Kaufman, Lew Welch, Phillip Whalen, Stephen Levine, and Robert Theobold, Artists who designed pages for the Oracle included Bruce Conner, Rick Griffen, Michael Bowen, Alton Kelley and Stanley Mouse.

To determine what was going to go into each issue we used a standard criterion, "Is it Oracle Material?" By which we meant that it should make our journey and our destination more beautiful, smarter and more harmonious with the human mind and soul.

The San Francisco Oracle was a neighborhood born, grass roots creation that reached out in space and time to turn humanity on to some sense of the world's wondrous unity and beauty. May it be so!

MICHAEL McCLURE

The God I Worship is a Lion

and I pray to him for

SPEED

POWER

&

COURAGE

I pray that I sing
the music of my meat
not that which I eat
but that I am made of
while I pray for the mildness of a dove
and a tapping foot in the earthly venture.
I shall become a lion—beyond censure,
In the meekness of May
I'll sing all the day
in the throne of my flesh
freed of the mesh
and the gins and the traps
that bind me!

THE SYNAPSE BINDS THE MUSIC IN
THE DULL BAR HOLDS IT OUT.
The meter is there, calm as a hair,
in the shiplash of the throat.

There shall be a new image of god!
There shall be a new image of god!
There shall be a new image of god!

The flesh is light and the heart leaps up
The spider dives into the cup
to sail his ship in the wine.

AMERICAN RENEGADES

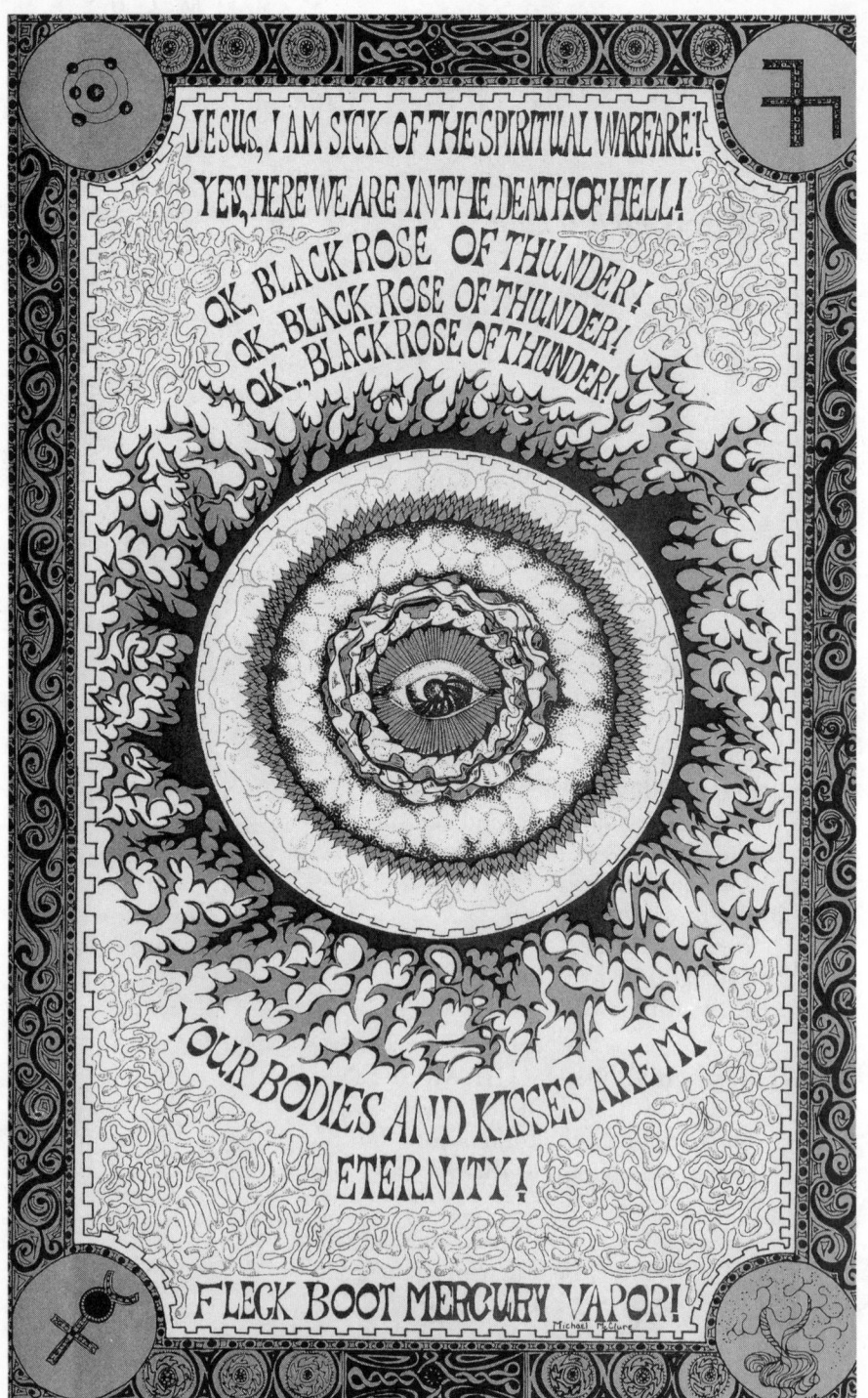

Jesus, I Am Sick of the Spiritual Warfare!

THE UNIVERSE REFLECTS A LION'S FACE TO ME
The spider tacks in the sugary sea,

Divine!

Divine!

Divine!

Divine!

Divine!

Jesus I am sick of the spiritual warfare!

Yes, here we are in the death of hell!

Ok, black rose of thunder!
Ok, black rose of thunder!
Ok, black rose of thunder!

Your bodies and kisses are my
eternity!

Fleck boot mercury Vapor!

LAWRENCE FERLINGHETTI

After the Cries of the Birds Has Stopped

Hurrying thru eternity
after the cries of the birds has stopped
I see the future of the world
in a new visionary society
now only dimly recognizable
in folk-rock ballrooms

AMERICAN RENEGADES

free-form dancers in ecstatic clothing
their hearts their gurus
every man his own myth
butterflies in amber
caught fucking life
hurrying thru eternity
to a new pastoral era
I see the shadows of that future
in that white island
which is San Francisco
floating in its foreign sea
seen high on a hill
in the Berkeley Rose Garden
looking West at sunset to the Golden Gate
adrift in its Japanese landscape
under Mt. Tamal-Fuji
with its grazing bulls
hurrying thru heaven
the city with its white buildings
"a temple to some unknown god"
(as Voznesensky said)
after the cries of the birds has stopped
I see the sea come in
over South San Francisco
and the island of the city
truly floated free at lost
never really a part of America
East East and West West
and the twain met long ago
in "the wish to pursue what lies beyond the mind"
with no Place to go but In
after Columbus recovered America
and the West Coast captured by some Spanish Catholic
cagily getting the jump by sea
coveredwagons crawling over lost plains
hung up in Oklahoma
Prairie schooners into Pullmans
while whole tribes of Indians
shake hopeless feather lances
and disappear over the horizon
to reappear centuries later
feet up and smoking wild cigars
at the corner of Hollywood and Vine
hurrying thru eternity
must we wait for the cries of the birds

AMERICAN RENEGADES

                                        to be stopped
                              before we dig in
          after centuries of running
                              up and down the Coast of West
          looking for the right place to jump off
                                             further Westward?
          the Gutenberg Galaxy casts its light no further
             the "Westward march of civilization"
                comes to a dead stop on the shores
                   Big Sur Portland & Santa Monica
                   and turns upon itself at last
                        after the cries of the birds has stopped
          must we wait for that
                                 to dig a new model
                                 of the universe
                                 with instant communication
                                 a world village
                      in which every human being is a part of us
                though we be still throw-aways
                                    in an evolutionary progression
          as Spengler reverses himself
                        Mark Twain meets Jack London
                           and turns back to Mississippi
                              shaking his head
          and the Last Frontier
                              having no place to go but In
               can't face it
                              and buries its Head
          Western civilization gone too far West
                                    might suffer a sea-change
                into Something Else Eastern
                                          and that won't do
          the Chinese are coming anyway
                                    time we prepared their tea
             Gunga Din still with us
                   Kipling nods & cries I told you so!
                      the French King hollers Merde!
                      and abandons his Vietnam bordello
          but not us
                we love them too much for that
          though the Mayflower turned around sets sail again
             back to Plymouth England (and the Piltdown let down)
             misjudging the coast & landing in Loverpool
                American poets capture Royal Albert Hall
                   The Jefferson Airplane takes off

AMERICAN RENEGADES

> > > > and circles heaven
> It all figures
> > in a new litany
> > > probably pastoral
> after the cries of the birds
> > > has stopped
> > Rose petals fall
> > > in the Berkeley Rose Garden
> where I sit trying to remember
> > > the lines about rose leaves
> > in the Four Quartets
> > > > Stella kisses her lover in the sunset
> > > > under an arbor
> > A Los Angeles actor goes Zap! Zap!
> > > at the setting sun
> It is the end
> > I drop downhill
> into the reception for Anais Nin
> > > with a paperbag full of rose leaves
> She is autographing her Book
> > I empty the bag over her head from behind
> > Her gold lacquered hair sheds the petals
> > > They tumble red & yellow on her signed book
> > Girl again she presses them between the leaves
> > > delightedly
> > > > like fallen friends
> > Her words
> > > flame in my heart
> > Virginia Woolf under water
> > > she drifts away on the book
> > a leaf herself blowing skittered
> > > > over the horizon
> The wish to pursue what lies beyond the mind
> > > lies just beyond
> > Ask a flower what it does
> > > > to move beyond the senses
> > Our cells hate metal
> > > The tide turns
> > We shoot holes in the clouds' trousers
> > > and napalm sears the hillsides
> > > skips a bridge
> > narrows to a grass hut full of charred bodies
> and is later reported looking like
> > > "The eternal flame at Kennedy's grave"
> A tree flowers red It can't run

Shall we now advance into the 21st century?
   I see the lyric future of the world
     on the beaches of Big Sur
       gurus at Jack's Flats
    nude swart maidens swimming
       in pools of sunlight
Kali dancing on the beach
   guitarists with one earring
lovely birds in long dresses and Indian headbands
          What does this have to do with Lenin?

     Plenty!
Die-hard Maoists lie down together crosswise
          and out comes a string
         of Chinese firecrackers
     and after the cries of the birds
            has stopped
    Chinese junks show up suddenly
     off the coast of Big Sur
    filled with more than Chinese philosophers
    dreaming they are butterflies
  How shall we greet them? Are we ready
          to receive them?
    Shall we put out koan steppingstones
         scrolls & bowls
   greet them with agape
   Tu Fu and bamboo flutes at midnight?
   Big Sur junk meet
     Chinese junk?
Will they ride the breakers into Bixby cove?
Will they bring their women with them?
  Will we take them on the beach?
  like Ron Boise's lovers in Kama Sutra
  face them with Zen zazen & tea
  made from the dust of wings
   of butterflies dreaming
    they're philosophers?
Or meet them with last war's tanks
  roaring out of Fort Ord
   down the highways & canyons
   shooting as they come
flame-throwers flaming jelly
     into the Chinese rushes
   under the bridge at Bixby
The U.S. owns the highway but is Big Sur

AMERICAN RENEGADES

in the USA?
San Francisco floats away
beyond the three-mile limit
of the District of Internal Revenue
No need to pay your taxes

The seas come in to cover us

Agape we are & agape we'll be

June 22, 1996

PHILIP WHALEN

characteristically
Saturday, April 22, 1967
at Kyoto

characteristically
characteristically compressed
compressed

characteristically
space bewixt and between
and so it should easily take
on a columnar shape. The
problem of composing the lines
into a pleasing pattern of
black and white also becomes
less under the circumstances
mentioned above we tend to
find a number of lesser ques-
tions of space and
layout. These
must come
later

YES.
"Come on," I said.
Try again one more time.
It was the telephone &
not the lark that whis-
pered in the bough of
that sovereign tree—
O do not go and leave
me here in the mad
green light of dawn &
the purple wings of mor-
ning flap the crystal
airs and the silkworm
scarfs all the mulberry
leaves and none is left
which can shade my
giddy head alas!

SHAPE UP!
I said to my soul,
Come. Do not write
so fucking big. try
to fit the pen and
the letter shapes together.
what's wrong with
you anyway?

I said to my Soul,
"Come. Let us flee
into the distant
rain—bow hued clouds
of infinite beauty

and delight Arise
and go while yet
the swallow slumbers
        in the aloe
            tree

much later
        19: v: 67

I have lots of answers; all the questions
                elude me

AMERICAN RENEGADES

That was Donald Duck on the phone
a minute ago—

Is this Porky Pig?
Remember:
    tomatoes   DANCING IN THE DARK
    post office   BESSA ME MUCHO
    sincerity   DINNER FOR ONE, PLEASE, JAMES

Claribel Cow?
Joris-Karl Husymans!

LENORE KANDEL

In Transit

Question: Locate the center of infinity
Answer: Anywhere
IT NEVER STOPS MOVING!

The ceaseless alchemical permutations, gold into history,
rain into strawberries, strawberries into my bloodstream,
my blood into flowering dreams

the dream into absolute perception, into coruscating visions of
THIS IS WHERE IT IS BA-BY into
infinity

It is necessary to search the spirit through the light of
one's own bioluminescence

THERE IS NO SUCH THING AS STANDING STILL

the balance is that of a gyroscope
motion existing within motion
the balance of a bird listening to its heartbeat, wings poised
against the currents of the air, eyes tracing the turning of the
earth, the planet circling the sun, the sun spinning its golden

path in the universe and the universe breeding life and death
in infinity

and the bird hangs halfway up the sky
infinite motion at rest
                    within infinite motion

        LET IT GO!

whatever you see that is beautiful
    don't hang on to it
whatever you see that is terrible
    Don't hang on to it

            LET IT GO!

the balance is that of sunlight on water, the sunlight
moving as the earth turns, the water following its gravity
path into eventual raindrops and hope to another river
the sunlight-and-water being one and together
for the duration of their parallel flow

there is no way to stop water
if you lock it up it will evaporate and reach the clouds anyhow
there is no way to stop the sun
it holds its own galactic balance and moves according to the
nebulae of outer space

            LET IT GO!
        IT NEVER STOPS MOVING

there is movement within a mountain, a rock, a thought,
a flower, a lightbulb, a cat, a star, a rice-bowl, an arrow

            LET IT GO
        IT NEVER STOPS MOVING

there is no such thing as standing still
the direction of motion is frequently a matter of choice
when you try to stop other things from moving
you give yourself an impetus toward backwards motion

            LET IT GO!

most of the time
you will be the it
being let go of

GARY SNYDER

Seed Pods

seed pods seen inside while high.
trip of fingers
the farthest limits of the thigh

waft of sticky fluid, cypress resin
from peach valley
            under walls of rock

    Ferghana horses archt
    rearing, fucking

tiny seed pods
caught and carried in the fur

  foot-pad fetlock
                slipping tongue

A pawtrack windfall
if my seed too-
float into you—

colored blood and apricot

    weaved with thread
      girls
  moons
later let it be
          come-
      stained

on their soil ledge tilth
     fucking bed

seed pod burrs, fuzz, twist-tailed
     nut-babies.
  in my fucking head.

PHILLIP LAMANTIA

Astromancy

The stars have gone crazy
and the moon is very angry
The old civilization
that rolled the dice of Hitler
is surely bumbling
into a heap of catatonic hysteria.
Another civilization
secret for six thousand years
is creeping on the crest of
future, I can almost see the
tip of its triangular star
I'm writing this from lost Atlantis
I wonder when I'll get back
to the alchemical castle
where I can rebegin in my work
left off in the Middle Ages
when the Black Beast roared down
on my weedy parchments and spilled me
into an astral waiting room
whose angels, naturally in flaming white robes
evicted me for this present irony
idleness, mancy & the Dream
instead of getting down to
the super-real work of
transmuting the Earth with love of it
by the Fire prepared from the time of Onn!
No matter, I'm recovering

from a decade of poisons
I renounce all narcotic
& pharmacopoeic disciplines
as too-heavy 9 to 5-type sorrows
Instead I see America
as one vast palinode
that reverses itself completely until
Gitchi Manito actually returns
as prophet of a new Iroquois Brotherhood—
this needs further development—
I foresee a couple
of essential changes:
a Break-Out Generation
of poet-kings setting up
The Realm Apart
of sweet natural play
and light metal work
matter lovingly heightened
by meditation, and spirit
transmuted into matter,
the whole commune conducted by
direct rapid transcription
from a no past reference
anti-rational, fantastically poetic
violently passive and
romantically unprejudiced
Each one his own poet
and poetry the central fact
food & excrement of culture
I see you smilingly tolerantly
O liberal lip (another utopian
bites the dust) but no! you just
can't see what I'm reading while
in the act of transcribing it
I know at least three other
supernatural souls who envision
much the same, under different names,
but the nomenclature's not more than
the lucid panorama I telescope
as, on this summer night's
torpor, it passes from under my eyelid and
grabs you, earth returned,
into the middle of Aquarius, one millenium forward.

TED BERK

Manifesto for Mutants

Mutants! Know now that you Exist!
They have hid you in cities
And clothed you in fools' clothes.
Know *now* that you are free!
Their graves have time payment
Opened for you for centuries.
Now you will show them
How to keep the graves
Closed forever!
They used your brains
To build burping missiles—
Now you will open your
Powerful eyes and penetrate
The Star and the Atom
And grow the new crops!
Bringers of darkness
Look to the newly awakened!
Dancers of the NOW
Look to the humming
Machine of light.

MICHAEL LALLY

My Life

I ate everything they put in front of me
read everything they put before my eyes
shook my ass, cried over movie musicals
was a sissy and a thug, a punk and an
intellectual, a cocksucker and a mother
fucker, helped create two new people,

AMERICAN RENEGADES

paid taxes, voted and served four years
and a few weeks in the United States Air
Force, was court martialed and tried
civilly, in jail and in college, kicked
out of college, boy scouts, altar boys
and one of the two gangs I belonged to,
I was suspended from grammar and high
schools, arrested at eleven the year I
had my first "real sex" with a woman
and with a boy, I waited nineteen years
to try it again with a male and was sorry
I waited so long, I waited two weeks to
try it again with a woman and was sorry
I waited so long, wrote, poetry and
fiction, political essays, leaflets and
reviews, I was a "jazz musician" and a
dope dealer, taught junior high for two
weeks, high school Upward Bound for two
years, college for four years, I got up
at 5 AM to unload trucks at Proctor and
Gamble to put myself through classes
at the University of Iowa, I washed
dishes and bussed tables, swept floors
and cleaned leaders and gutters, washed
windows and panhandled, handled a forty
foot ladder alone at thirteen, wrote
several novels not very good and none
published, published poems and stories
and articles and books of poems, was
reviewed, called "major," compared to
"The Teen Queens," mistaken for black,
for gay, for straight, for older, for
younger for bigger for better for richer
for poorer for stupider for smarter for
somebody else, fell in love with a black
woman at 18, kicked out of the family
for wanting to marry her at 20, I sucked
cock and got fucked and fucked and got
sucked, I was known for being a big
jerk off, a wise ass, for always getting
my ass kicked so bad neighborhood kids
would ask to see the marks, for running
for sheriff of Johnson County Iowa in 68
on the "Peace and Freedom" ticket and
pulling in several thousand votes, for

winning people to the cause with emotional
spontaneous speeches at rallies and on TV,
for being a regular guy, a romantic
idealist, a suicidal weatherman, a bomb
throwing anarchist, an SDS leader, a
communist, a class chauvinist, an
asexual politico, a boring socialist,
the proletarian man, a horny androgyne,
a junkie, a boozer, a loser, a nigger
lover, a black woman's white man, a
race traitor, a greaser, a fast man
with my hands, a hood, a chickenshit,
a crazy head, an unmarked thoroughbred,
a courageous human being, a Catholic,
a fallen away Catholic, An Irish American
Democrat, a working class Irish American
writer from a family of cops, a skinny
jive time street philosopher, a power
head, an underground movie star, a
quiet shy guy, a genius, an innovator,
a duplicator, a faker, a good friend,
a fickle lover, an ass lover, a muff
diver, another pretty face, a lousy
athlete, a generous cat, an ambitious
young man, a very tough paddy, a macho
hippie, a faggot gangster, a faggot,
a big crazy queen, a straight man, a
strong man, a sissy, a shithead, a
home wrecker, a reckless experimenter
with other peoples lives, a demagogue,
a fanatic, a cheap propagandizer, a
fantastic organizer, a natural born
leader, a naive upstart, an arrogant
jitterbug, a white nigger, an easy lay,
a pushover, a hard working husband,
a henpecked husband, the black sheep,
a crazy mixed up kid, a juvenile delinquent,
a misfit, a surrealist, an actualist,
an Iowa poet, a political poet, an open
field poet, a street poet, a bad poet,
a big mouth, a voice of the sixties,
a pretty poet, a gay poet, a clit kissing
tit sucking ass licking body objectifying
poet, a gigolo, a jerk, a poor boy, an
old man, an assman, unsteady, immature,

charismatic, over confident, over 30,
impetuous, a rock, a pawn, a tool, a
potato lover, a great teacher, loyal
friend, concerned citizen, a humanist,
the bosses son, Bambi's old man, Lee's
husband, Matthew's ex-lover, Terry's
partner, Slater's main man, the bishop's
favorite altar boy, the landlady's pet,
the class clown, the baby of the family,
the neighborhood stranger, the hardest
working kid, with the rosiest cheeks, who
was an instigator, a trouble maker,
too smart for my own good, too soft,
too distant, too honest, too cold, too
tactless, uncommunicative, anal retentive,
self-sufficient, shameless, unsophisticated,
too butch, too skinny, too white, too
defensive, too hungry, apologetic, in-
decisive, unpredictable, I never hit a
woman or woke up gloomy, I'm a light
sleeper, an affectionate father, a bad
drinker, a city boy, paranoid, compulsive,
and a terrific body surfer, I love the
hipness in me I thought was black back
in the 50s, the vulnerability I took for
feminine in the 70s, I hate the poor kid
act I've pulled on strangers and friends
to start them out owing me, I learned to
cook and to sew, stopped chewing gum and
biting my nails, I was a weather observer,
a map maker, a printer's devil, a
carpenter's helper, a glazier, a locksmith,
editor, publisher, promoter and critic,
I stopped dancing at 15 and started again
at 30, math was my best subject, languages
my worst, I've been knocked out several
times but only one black eye and one
fractured thumb, I've totaled several
cars but I'm an ace driver especially
in cities, I haven't had an accident since
I stopped drinking, knock on wood, I'm
extremely superstitious, don't speak too
soon, I gave up cigarettes and coffee and
using the words chick, spade and asshole,
I've read Confucius, Buddha, Lao Tzu,

The Upanishads, The Bhagavad Gita, The
Koran, The Bible, The Prophet, Thus Spake
Zarathrusta, Marx, Trotsky, Stalin, Lenin,
Mao, Che, Hesse, Proust, Firestone, Fanon,
Castenada and Davis, I read all of Joyce
and all of Dostoevsky in translation
at least two times through on night shifts
in weather towers through 1961 and 62,
I love all of William Saroyan, Van
Morrison, Jane Bowles, Samuel Beckett,
Joe Brainard, and Bertold Brecht, I'm
finally getting to know and like some
"classical music," I went to my first
ballet, opera, and concert this year and
loved all of it, took my first trip out
of the country and was glad to get back
although it was great, I love the USA and
many of the people in it, I'm afraid of
my own anger, and any kind of violence,
I've been the same weight since 1957 though
I have an enormous appetite, my hair's
turning gray, I've had it cut three times
since 1966, I spit a lot and pick my nose
too much, I could buy new shoes, eat ice
cream, chicken or chocolate pudding anytime,
I'm afraid of dogs and hate zoos, I'm
known for my second winds especially
when dancing or eating, I used to think
of myself as a dreamer, I had a vision
at 9 that I'd die between 42 and 46,
the image was me doubling over clutching
my stomach, whenever I'm embarrassed I
see that in my head, some of my nicknames
have been Faggy, Rocky, Spider, Brutus,
Paddy Cat, Newark, Irish, and The Lal,
I'm a father, son, brother, cousin,
brother-in-law, uncle, record breaker,
war child, veteran, and nut about Lauren
Bacall, James Cagney, Robert Mitchum,
Bogie and Brando, "Last Tango" and "The
Conformist" are the favorite movies of
my adult life, I've fallen in love with
eyes, asses, thighs, wrists, lips, skin,
color, hair, style, movement, bodies,
auras, potential, accents, atmospheres,

clothes, imaginations, sophistication,
histories, families, couples, friends,
rooms full of people, parks, cities,
entire states, talked to trees since
1956 and the wind since 52, between 56
and 59 I had few friends and a "bad
reputation" which made it difficult
to get dates with "nice girls," in 1960
and 61 I had more friends and several
lovers, I was at the SDS split in Chicago
in 1969 and didn't like either side's
position or tactics, I almost cried
when I heard John Coltrane had died,
and Ho Chi Minh, Babe Ruth, Jack
Kerouac, Eric Dolphy, Roberto Clemente,
Moose Conlon, Frankie Lyman, Fred
Hampton, Allende, Clifford Brown,
Richie Valens and Buddy Holly in that
plane crash, the four little girls
in that Alabama church, the students
at Orangeburg, the "weather people"
in the town house explosion which I
always figured was a set up, my uncle
Frank and my uncle John, my grandparents,
lots of people, I did cry when I thought
about the deaths of the Kent State and
Jackson State students, when I heard
Ralph Dickey had "taken his life" or
the first time I heard Jackson Browne
do his "Song for Adam" or when Marlon
Brando as Terry finds his brother Charley
(Rod Steiger) hanging dead on the fence
in "On the Waterfront" and before going
to get the murderers says something to
Eva Marie Saint like "And for god's sake
don't leave him here alone" or when he
talks to his dead wife in "Last Tango"
or finds Red Buttons and his wife
have committed suicide in "Sayonara"
I've cried a lot over movies especially
old ones on TV, I've never cried at a
play but I still haven't seen many, the
only Broadway plays I've seen were "My
Fair Lady" and "Bye Bye Birdie," I
watched my mother die, I've paid my dues,

been through the mill, come up from the
streets, done it my way, had that once
in a lifetime thing, had trouble with
my bowels ever since I can remember
then in 72 my body became more relaxed,
I've had the clap, crabs, scabies,
syphilis, venereal warts, and unidentified
infections in my cock, my ass, my throat,
all over my body, I've been terribly
sunburned and covered with scabs from
fights and accidents, I only had stitches
once at 4 when I had my appendix out,
I've been earning money since I was 10,
supporting myself since 13, others since
22, I got "unemployment" once, been
fired several times, never paid to
get laid, I lost money gambling but
quit after I had to give up my high
school ring in a poker game at the Dixie
Hotel in Greenville South Carolina in
1962 waiting for my friend Willy Dorton
to come out from the room where he was
proposing marriage to his favorite
whore who always turned him down after
they fucked and she got most of his
paycheck from him, some of my best
friends were hookers and strippers,
postal clerks and shills, supermarket
managers and factory workers, heavy
revvies and punks, actresses and junkies,
who were and are the most difficult
of friends, art dealers and artists,
musicians and hustlers, dykes and critics,
shit workers and liberals, gringos and fags,
and honkies and bastards, queer and old
and divorced and straight and Italian
and big deals and dipshits, I know at least
six people who think they turned me on
to dope for the first time in 1960 in
New York City, in 1962 in Rantoul Illinois,
in 1964 in Spokane Washington, in 1966 and
67 in Iowa City, in 1969 in Washington
DC, I once was high on opium and didn't
want to come back, I was a recreational
therapist at Overbrook Hospital in Essex

County New Jersey in 1966 where James Moody
wrote "Last Train From Overbrook" before
he was discharged, in 1960 I had a tremendous
crush on Nina Simone, I always wanted to
name a child Thelonious, I was sure
I was an orphan at 10, I wished I was
an orphan at 18, my father's alive so
I'm still not an orphan at 32, I know
a lot of orphans, I once had an
orphan for a lover, I suppose my kids
could be orphans some day, I was never
good at planning the future for more
than a couple of days, friends have
told me I always do things the hard way,
my family's response to tough times or
catastrophes was usually humor, I'm
grateful to them for giving me that,
I find cynics boring although there's
a lot to cynic in me, I find
depression dull, mine or anyone else's,
I'm no good at small talk, I feel
an undercurrent of violent tension
in most "straight" bars and on late
night city streets that intimidates
me, I find jealousy useless and
depressing, I know people who find
jealousy exciting and even rewarding,
something to live for, I'd love to
make love all the ways I haven't yet
or haven't thought of yet, with all
the people I haven't yet or haven't met
yet, although sometimes I could care
less about sex, I write everyday
and listen to music everyday and cant
imagine living without either,
libraries and hospitals intimidate me,
being around people who seem to feel
comfortable anywhere used to make me
feel insecure, I'm getting over that,
I used to feel obliged to apologize
for or defend people whose goals I
shared even though I might not like
them or their tactics, I'm getting
over that too, I've learned to love
or at least appreciate a lot of things

AMERICAN RENEGADES

I used to despise or ignore, I've had
trouble getting it up and trouble
keeping it down, I'm tired of a lot
of things but curious about more, I'm
tired of this but that's history now.

March 1974 DC

JULIA STEIN

Downtown Women

I come from downtown women,
        not uptown ladies,

I came from Bessie Abramowitz,
        the shtetl in Russia,
        not Elizabeth Cady Stanton,
        a WASP judge's daughter,
        when the matchmaker came for me
        after marrying my four older sisters,
        I said, "Not on your life,"
I came over the sea to Chicago,

I come from sewing on coats in the sweatshop,
        piecework rates at the factory,
        complained to the boss, blacklisted,
        when the uptown ladies came downtown
        with their charity baskets
        I threw their baskets at them, said,
        "Go to hell," got another shit job,
I came back under a phony name.

I come from they cut my piecework rates again,
        petitioning the boss, got ignored,
        I walked out of Shop No. 5
        of Hart, Schaffner, and Marx,
        8,000 sweated there in Chicago,

I got a band of thirteen immigrant girls
            to picket three weeks,
I came back to storm the fort.

I come from the men workers laughed at my band,
            burst through my picket line,
            they laughed and laughed for a month
            when 8,000 workers walked out,
            two months later 40,000 workers struck
            stomped out of the factories,
            we stopped the men's clothing industry,
I came back to shake Chicago,

I came from packing my suitcase,
            at the convention
            of the United Garment Workers,
            the UGW had cops on duty,
            refused to seat us immigrants,
            I led a walkout,
            began a new union,
I come from the Amalgamated Clothing Workers of America,

I don't come from the ladies tea parties,
            not from the debutante balls,
            not from the ladies of the book club,
            not the Ivy League girls' colleges
            not from the sororities,
            not from the ladies luncheons,
I don't come from sitting around.

I come from the May Day parades,
            at the head of the 1916 parade
            down Harrison St. in Chicago
            arm-in-arm with my fiancée, Sidney Hillman,
            thousands of garment workers marched behind us,
            I said "no" to the matchmaker,
            chose my own husband,
I come from raising hell.

I come from downtown women,
            not uptown ladies.

TONY MEDINA

Ten Commandments of a Street Poet

I
Let all books be remaindered for a dollar.

II
Bring out a postage stamp with Harold Bloom
and Gary Soto doing 69.

III
What's this PC shit? The whole goddamn country's
politically incorrect, anyhow! More like PCP to me.

IV
Arrest the IRS & Leave the IRA alone!

V
Fuck Proposition 187! Let's go back to 185 & 186
& get rid of these dead white corny motherfuckers
from the libraries & anthologies & panels & curriculum
of American colleges and institutions.

VI
Don't let then anthologize your soul
or tears on Saturday night re-runs
in run-down abandoned welfare hotels
on TV, clean-cut w/ new kicks & a lisp
to go with the (exhaust) pipe you suckin.

VII
Poetry shouldn't only be important because you talk
          to walls,
dust yellowed pages off beneath bedsprings, drink
          yourself blind
& silly & shove your head in ovens.

VIII
If your words can't be baked into bread,
paper knitted & sewn to make coats
or balled up into bullets & grenades,

ironed flat into switchblades to aid
the poor & working class to dis
mantle & bust some bumba clot bourgeois
ass, then it aint shit,
                     it aint shit.

IX
Treat the untouchables like they treat you,
like they got the plague: don't call 'em
don't write 'em don't read 'em don't go
out to see 'em don't touch 'em don't pray
to try to be 'em,
leave them in bookstores & TV
& magazines where they belong, collecting
dust. Seek out the humble & human
poets who believe that poetry
is public property.

X
Don't let the 20th Century end with a panel discussion.

BOB FLANAGAN

I was lucky enough to meet Bob early on in the game. Saw him do his poetry thing at the old Factory Place in downtown Los Angeles. It was a show I would never forget. Among other things, Bob was one of those performers with "it," a person with natural gift, charisma.

Born with cystic fibrosis, he struggled with the disease his entire life before finally succumbing in 1996. As a child, he had conceived of himself as a super-hero because of his ability to overcome his disease and to endure pain. In his words, he chose to "fight sickness with sickness."

Over the years, it was apparent that Bob was not only a gifted poet and performer, but a gifted human being as well. The oldest living individual with cystic fibrosis and a trailblazing performance artist with an international reputation. He also ran the Beyond Baroque poetry workshop for years impacting the lives and work of all those that he came in contact with. He only produced five books of poetry in his lifetime: *The Kid Is The Man, Fuck Journals, The Wedding of Everything, Slave Sonnets* and *Taste of Honey* with David Trinidad. He was also the subject of the RE/Search book *Bob Flannagan: Supermasochist* and the film documentary "Sick: The Life and Death of Bob Flannagan, Supermasochist."

S.A. GRIFFIN

The following are the words of Sheree Rose Levin recorded on the evening of Yom Kippur, September 29, 1998. Sheree was Bob Flanagan's life/art partner for the last fifteen years of his life.

I first met Bob at a party for poets, he opened the door and we sort of looked at each other and it was truly, love at first sight . . . the Italians have a wonderful phrase for it, lightning in my heart or something like that . . . I wanted to know who he was, I had never seen him before. I said: "Who's that guy just came in thru the door?" And the woman whose house it was (at the party), Alexandra Garrey from Beyond Baroque said, "Oh that's Bob Flanagan, he's a wonderful poet." That was the first thing she said to me about him. Then she said, "Oh, and he's been published too! He has his own book and everything!" I said, "Really?" All of a sudden, my interest got a little higher. "Oh come with me. You have to see this . . ." And she dragged me out and pulled me into this other room and pulled out this book and it was *The Kid Is The Man.* So, for me, just as a person, a fan of poetry, I thought that was like so cool, I really did. It meant that he cared enough about it, the work was thought enough about, everything was done; it was a beautiful little book, every attention to detail, it was like a perfect little Fabrege egg for the mind. I think that was something, that connection to the world that poets can give . . . the first poem I opened to was "The Nails Drove Home" and my heart started pounding like the hammer pounding the nails and I just felt a connection with Bob . . . a deep connection to him thru his words. I think that's the impact that he could have on people when you read his stuff for the first time or heard him speak or whatever your contact with Bob he made a profound impression on you. He was able to put his mundane activities in such a beautiful, perfect, structured way, which is what I think all great poets do. He was not a very prolific writer, he really worried, and babied and fidgeted with every word; sometimes even every syllable of his poems they were that important to him, they were definitely his artistic children.

Somehow he was able to turn everyday life into something that revealed the holiness of the moment of doing something while you're alive and I think a lot of people would connect with that. I was definitely his muse and as it turns out, he was definitely mine. He was very consistent in his values, he wasn't a wobbler, he knew right from wrong and he had a very strong set of values. His message was important: his simplicity, his honesty, his wildness, his sexiness, his courage . . . you name it and he was it. He was sort of like this holy person in his own very bizarre way.

SHEREE ROSE

Bukowski Poem

I started writing this poem
where Pamela and I
are sitting in a bar in Santa Monica
and she shows me some of her new poems.

I tell her they're not very good

and she starts yelling and throwing
glasses and all of a sudden I realize
it sounds a lot like
a Bukowski poem.
Shit, I say, it sounds a lot like
a Bukowski poem.
What am I doing writing like
Bukowski?

I rip it up and toss it on the floor
beside the ants and the empty bottles
and Pamela's candy wrappers.

What's wrong with *you?* she asks.

Oh, nothing, I say, it's just that
I'm starting to write like Bukowski.

Well, what's wrong with that, she says.
He's a nice guy. I talked to him on
the phone one time. I asked him if he'd
like to do a reading. He said no but
to keep buying his books.

There's nothing wrong with Bukowski,
I say. I just don't want to write
like him. I have a hard enough time
writing my own stuff, let alone
Bukowski's too. And besides, he's
doing an ok job of it on his own.

I go to the refrigerator for a beer
but there's just a lot of milk and
Pepsi-Cola. How come we don't have any
beer? I ask.

Don't be an ass, she says. You know
we never buy beer. Since when
do you want a beer? I think you're going out of your mind, she says.

You may be right, I say.

And I go into the bathroom and feel
like vomiting but can't.
I fill the tub with hot water.
CHRIST! I yell.
I don't take baths; Bukowski takes
baths; I take showers!
I shut the water off and sit down on
the crapper. I'm constipated and
I have hemorrhoids and Pamela is
pounding on the door.
Hurry-up in there, she says;
I HAVE TO TAKE A PISS!

Ok, I say, it figures—somebody has to
piss in this poem; it wouldn't be right
without pissing.

Handcuffs:

With my wrists locked in front of me, no matter what I'm
doing, it always looks like I am deep in prayer. Thank
you, God, for these beautiful black handcuffs, and the
hard-ons they inspire. Thank you for the titillating click
click click of their internal ratchet mechanism. Thank
you for the security of knowing that each and every
movement is restricted by a force much greater than mine.
And thank you for inhabiting me with a soul that not only
expects, but thrives on such handicaps, man-made and
otherwise. Although I can barely make it up the stairs
with these bad lungs you gave me, I still say thank you as
I lie here, unable to move, except for the slight
thrusting of my hips against the sheets, my penis
throbbing in spasms of unrestrained pleasure, coming, as I
quietly speak your name.

AMERICAN RENEGADES

From *Slave Sonnets*

1

I've been a shit and I hate fucking you now
because I love fucking you too much;
what good's the head of my cock inside you
when my other head, the one with the brains,
keeps thinking how fucked up everything is,
how fucked I am to be fucking you and thinking
these things which take me away from you
when all I want is to be close to you
but fuck you for letting me fuck you now
when all that connects us is this fucking cock
which is as lost inside you as I am, here,
in the dark, fucking you and thinking—fuck,
the wallpaper behind you had a name,
what was it? You called it what? Herringbone?

7

I'm an instrument. I'm a clarinet.
Maestro, I'm an oboe if you say so.
An animal if music's not enough.
Dog on command, shepherd or Chihuahua.
Eat when the dinner bells chime: Ms. Pavlov,
these experiments you've unleashed on me
hurt and strip me of everything human;
even dogs live better lives than I do.
Confession: truth is my life's a picnic.
Here I am, the ant you're about to squash.
"Ow!"—Make that "Ooo."—My lips the letter "O."
I'm a zero; nothing lower than I.
Confine me or crush me—but like magic
each reduction makes me all the more huge.

10

The name stamped onto the lock says, "Master."
But the keys are yours, Mistress. My body,
wrapped in this neat little package, is yours.
Do I dare call myself a present?
I'm the one who's on the receiving end.
You took me on, taking in my stiff prick
and swelling my head with your compliments,
your complaints, even out and out neglect.
Nothing—when it comes from you—is a gift;
wrapped in your aura of authority

even shit tastes sweet, and the void you leave
leaves me full.

It's Christmas whenever you put your foot down,
and the stars I'm seeing must be heaven.

The Wedding of Everything

Today looks much like
the rest: simple,
a handy kind of a day,
a meat and potatoes day.
The bright buildings of the past
are launched upward
into an unrumpled sky, ordinary
beyond our wildest dreams.
Personality takes off
into the blue. No mail
today: things: everything
groping towards us
like 3-D. Oranges
as orange as crayons.
A moldy piece of bread.
Junk. And the birds
will sing sing sing.
I can almost understand
a day like this.
My troubles seem so puny.
Delicious day, I will eat you up
like a mountain of white cake,
chunk by chunk.
I've got new shoe laces.
My feet slip into my shoes
over and over again.
So easy. Everything
pleasing me, sliding down
my throat (those soft
boiled eggs) the way I slide
into this day. CRACK!
That's what I mean.
CRACK! the way a baseball
smacks a bat. And THUMP,
the way it snuggles into a mitt.

A day is as a day does,
and this day, like the rest,
is leaving, and everything
grows sleepy.
The sun rises to a place
in the sky, and leaves;
and behind it leaves
a blind spot:
the purple sun, blooming,
cut down and tossed like a bouquet.
Congratulations, everything.

STEVE CANNON

This Is the Land of Missed Opportunity

This is the universe
where fortune
finds itself
in love
with misfortune.

This is the territory
of slackers,
where nothing changes
but change.

This is a place
in space
where everyone says
to the other,
"you blew it,"
and nothing,
if ever,
gets done.

REBECCA FRANSWAY

Suzanne Goes Down

My name is Suzanne.
I am learning military words.
The father of my abortion was in Special Forces.
He killed people in hot jungles.
My brain is a hot jungle.
We deal in amphetamines and weapons.
We have a machine gun in our trailer.
It leans against the same couch
with me and someone else's year-old baby.
I am drunk.
I play patty-cake with the red-haired baby
while the father of my abortion
bargains in Spanish with devils.
His wife jumps from the kitchen
and nerves about the room saying "honey"
pretending I'm a better friend to her than he.
What a son of a bitch he is.
My love is a disease.
I am learning military words.
Reconnaissance means rounding up your man
who's been captured by the cops.
Leave McDonald's wrappers by the tunnel
a mile from Folsom Prison.
Siege means you've been up five days on crank,
barricaded in your trailer. Enemies
crawl the roof and rattle the vents.
My name is Suzanne, I think.
I am a military cunt.
Look at my chest—no slacking here, sirs.
I carry my pride in a lump behind me
to be saluted while I die of drunkeness.
It's Apocalypse Now, folks.
My brain gives orders from its hot jungle.
My body is on automatic.
It marches down the lunatic lines
from trailer to liquor department at Safeway.
See the robotic arm reach out for tequila.
See the bottle drop into the handbag.

Here is my body at the A.A. meeting.
There there dear it'll be okay one day atta time
and it's NOT OKAY
My body is on automatic.
My brain gives orders from a thick hot jungle.
I am dying a military death.
I am dying with military dishonors,
in ripped underpants.
Someone is going to see my underpants.

JANINE POMMY VEGA

On Prison Poetry

Prison poetry bears a great resemblance to the spoken word we are witnessing around the country. They are both rooted in the urban neighborhood, in a political astuteness, in an awareness of the current climate of violence in America— "the voice of a crying nation" as one prisoner recently said. Both have an underlying metaphysics, a basis, you might say, in comparative religion. After twenty-three years of working and writing with prisoners in ongoing poetry workshops, and having outside writers come in and share their work, to be greeted in turn by words from the prisoners, flaming words—I can say they sound the same to me. Using the words and rhythm to drive home a message, to rock the house, to change the heart or mind of the listener, to galvanize him or her into action, that's what this poetry does. Truth celebrated so clearly and so well, so that even the enemy gets up and salutes, is poetry on the move. Where it differs from rap or hip hop is it doesn't need the m.c. to convince you. This poetry sings whether you hear it or read it on the page.

But this is not new. Jayne Cortez has been doing it, Allen Ginsberg has, Sekou Sundiata does it, so does Hettie Jones. The thing about us as a people is we've made anyone who spurns the system into an outlaw—like every kid who rebels, who has to; like anyone who sees the king is buckass naked and ugly to boot and states it plain. Our prisons, to paraphrase Dostoyevsky, expose the underpants of a nation and are not for the squeamish. How does prison poetry differ from the spoken word? Considering how we're all in opposition to the present state of things, perhaps the only difference is that one of us got caught, the other one didn't.

MUMIA ABU-JAMAL

To Those

nameless ones who came before
   and are no more,
to those who leapt
   to dark, salty depths,
to those who battled
   against all odds,
to those who would give birth
   to gods,
to those who would not yield—
To those who came before,
to those who are to come,
   I dedicate this shield.

ALEJO DAO'UD RODRIGUEZ

Sing Sing Sits Up The River

How alive,
the rhythm that waves move at,
    it's as though they're breathing,
in and out,
like seasons change, nature
    itself inhales and exhales a spirit
that air too breathes
almost human and kind,

how the wind comes to visit me,
    blowing past curls of razor wire.
Rows & rows of it—razors
wrapped around the top of electronically juiced fences

AMERICAN RENEGADES

intended to shock
until they kill.
Yet the wind still has not abandoned our visits,
       even after having been cut a million times,
       the wind bleeds, we become blood brothers

How humane & touching
That the bars feel the openness,
       the freedom outside, the space beyond
the other side of where I stand—Upstate New York.
Where underground railroads once ran & ran
cold, tired, & hungry in the night
      but can't stop
          gotta keep movin'
             gotta get to a Black freedom
and now there's prisons in these hills,
             how thoughtful.

How sparrows still remind me there's a spirit
free. And that it breathes.
Even where winters are the coldest
      & holidays are just a thing from another life.
Even in this cold that burns,
the sun still kisses my forehead
      as if I were as pure
         as a day breastfeeding in my mother's arms.

How unimaginable,
how freedom comes alive
touching the sun
between bars.

Cecil Boatswain

After All Those Years

After being punished
for ten, fifteen, twenty-five or more years,

do you think that you'll want to leave?
Can you imagine anything more terrifying
than walking through those gates
without looking back at that great square wall
that kept you in all those years?
Punishing you and comforting you!
Punishing you and comforting you!
Do you think that you will at least miss it?
That somehow, inside, you loved being here
under the tooth mother's wings?
You ain't got to worry about a damn thing!
You ain't got to worry about a damn thing!
You're Amerikka's greatest son,
the tooth mother's greatest capture.
She has taught you how to bend your knees,
stand up curve back and mop her welcoming floors,
given you paint to embellish her halls of terror—
more terrifying!
And you're been smiling all these years at her morbid green,
her institutional colors, her slavery that fits you.
So do you think after all those years of being trained
that you can just un-train yourself and leave?
That you can enjoy the wonderful colors you've only enjoyed
as a crayoning child?
After all those years behind these gray walls—
the monotony!
The Sunday pancakes, refried french toast and greasy chicken,
the Mondays you wish they had something edible,
the Tuesday Yakasorbi murder burgers,
the Wednesday killer liver,
the Thursday everything from the last four days mixed
together,
the Friday lumpy oatmeal and fluorescent Kool-Aid,
the Saturday cold cuts you go down to the mess hall just to
look at.
The cycle begins again on Sunday;
and you've gone to the mess hall for every meal,
didn't miss a single meal in all those years.
Now why do you think you can get used to real food?
Home cooking, a gourmet restaurant,
after you've only had seven minutes to eat
and an ulcer bigger than your heart.
After all those years you still think you can just leave?
Well, maybe, but remember—even though you leave the prison
the prison will never leave you.

AMERICAN RENEGADES

FRANK FISSETTE

Fugitive

Fleeing across country in a pair of beat up old wingtips stolen from a back porch that was a little too close to the prison to be worried about thieves and other men of honor.

Upstanding citizens screaming for my head. A head that's losing hair, lumpy, and empty of any concern for their health, wealth, and welfare. Another head to stuff and put over their bars and admire as they drink their whiskey and beer.

Gin martinis and smoking jackets are what I crave right now. Silk ascots embroidered with my initials—F. T. W.—in each corner, and razor blade slippers to remind me of the joy of my youth.

Icebergs are warmer than my thoughts of home. I have no home to run to anymore, but as long as I keep on running I'll always have someplace to go. Never stop. Never rest. Never give up.

Taste the difference in the air. The rain, the mud, the sweat all taste better when there's no wall around them. Walls taste like hair loaded down with so much pomade you keep slipping behind them. Further and further away from wanting to be free.

Idle hands really are the devil's workshop. They have nothing to do so they chase me. Keep coming demon boys, because today I'm a god. A Viking warrior god. Meaner than Odin and better looking than Thor.

HANNAH AQUAAH

My Room

It's small. It has one window, with a pink sheer curtain, one front door with a pink curtain. The walls are peach and full of pictures, and a big mirror faces the door. The floor is made of tiles. One bed, one sink, one toilet cover with a pink cloth cover, one chair, and one long bar for hanging clothes. Two cabinets: one for my television, the other for my provisions. The fish tank is on the television. I watch them both at once. There is a heater on one wall. A shelf on the other, over the sink, that's where I put on my cosmetics.

A plant on my window.

On my bed is a pink sheet, a pink comforter, and a pink satin bedspread.

This room is like my own house, even though it is a cell.

HERBY EHINGER

Lap 15512

Again

we walk in circles

Our eyes focused on the concrete in front of us.

Sometimes I look up to see concrete walls, barbed wires, towers. infrared cameras, and robots in uniforms, green, blue and grey.

They are shooting a movie again. Somebody is waving at the tower. He wants to be in the picture.

I keep walking in circles.

Most of the time I even run. Only 20988 laps before I will be deported. I wonder if somebody keeps count. Can't trust them, you know?

Look at this guy. He is walking in the opposite direction. Doesn't he know he is increasing his sentence.

If I had any time to spare I would tell him.
If I had any time to spare I'd look up at the sky.
If I had any time to spare I'd look at their faces and cry.

August 1996

MARK "9-BOX" BENYO

My Father

Always on the edge,
His ways, his life, his job,
My Mom and us kids.
All of us.
I seen him cry twice—
Once when he slammed my Mom's hand in the car door,
Once when his brother Terry died.
I wanted so badly to reach out but didn't know how,
Lost in the confusion of me.
Running across the cornfield in back of the house,
The rain hitting the ground
Like my tears on this paper.
Perfection was the rule of all days, every day
And I was always the imperfect one,
Trying so hard to please the man I love so much.
Failing miserably time and time again.
I couldn't even hear his beat,
Much less march to the drummer he wanted me to.
And then I'd feel the other beat,
As my sister and brothers would beg him to stop
And pull him off me.
Taking his frustration out on my imperfection,
Feeling rage I didn't understand then
And still don't now,
At the one who done it all for me:
Scouts, baseball teams, jobs—
Provider extraordinaire,
Self-made man,
Whose only failure was the imperfect son.
Home was fear and fear was home;
Left there when I was twelve—
Never returned or even looked back.
Scared for my mother, my baby sister and my brothers.
Now my whole life has been one series of prisons or another.
After the last eleven year stretch inside these walls
That are just like home,
I tried to go home again,

Though I'd heard it couldn't be done,
But only for a visit,
To pay my respects, confront my past, face my fears;
I asked myself how is it that I hold my ground
Against enraged psychopaths intent on my demise,
Steel flashing all around like moonlight off puddles of blood,
And I tremble at the thought of a ninety-five pound man
And our past.
I seen him last Easter, '94.
I asked him straight up what he wanted from me—
Anything I had to give was his to have.
My braid was sixteen inches long and I loved my hair
But he told me:
Behind every horse's tail is a horse's ass.
I cut the braid off right then and there
With a pair of scissors and handed it to him.
He hung it up on the mantle of his fireplace—
Glad it wasn't my balls,
Or was it?
He's dying now,
Cancer is eating up the one who'd put so much fear in my heart.
Regrets nibbling at my soul
For a sad shell of what was once my old man;
He can still call the shots for me.
It never changes, does it?
His upcoming death,
Like his life,
Still has me on the edge.

July 1996

ISRAEL FERNANDEZ

Trapped

An entire china set in pieces on the kitchen floor.
What is going on?

Judgmental eyes peer down upon me. The unspoken words:
What a Klutz!

Hot flashes, embarrassment, anger, confusion . . .
What is happening to me?!

A dirty suit, lost time, questions thrown at me from every direction:
"Who are you? Where do you live? Can you remember anything?"

No. Wait! Yes, it's all coming back now.
Curse the alienation, this dreaded burden upon my shoulders!

I want to be free to do the things I love; I want to be the best person
I can be, but instead I am trapped in a prison.

Envy, Pain, Isolation, Limitation, Exasperation,
Paralysis, Suffering, Yearning, Epilepsy.

the prison of limitations, of isolation, of pain, of epilepsy.

MARVIN TAYLOR

Introduction to the Unbearables

The Unbearables, a loosely organized collective of downtown writers and artists, see themselves as "poetic terrorists" who attack mass culture literary production and the commodification and commercialization of the literary scene. The weapons of their guerilla aesthetic warfare are two anthologies, scores of zines and chapbooks and a strategic campaign of readings, performances and events on everything from "self-help" to gender bending to the eroticizing of the Brooklyn Bridge. Among the Unbearables more memorable interventions are their much-touted protests of *The New Yorker* for its lame selection of poetry. Referring to *The New Yorker* as "the Empty Yawn Between Meaning," they picketed its offices demanding that the magazine publish work more relevant to everyday life in words the common person could actually understand. Perhaps one of their most interesting artifacts is The Unbearables Manual of Style. Using a copy of the Chicago Manual of Style—a text with which most of them were intimately acquainted from their work as proofreaders, data entry specialists and office temps on the margins of the marketplace—they assaulted the rigid rules of grammar and punctuation. Literally ripping the book apart, each participant took a section of the Manual and exploded the conventions (read: restrictions) it places on "style." The result is a voluptuous, sometimes Dada, sometimes post-Punk icon that subverts sanctioned language. These actions critique the constant repression of creativity mainstream society reinforces through market control. Using irony, explicit sexuality and humor, the Unbearables deconstruct the mainstays of the media-academic-literary establishment clearing the way for the larger community of writers, artists and performers to produce new works.

BONNY FINBERG

Archaeology

Young sexy women, an eternal fount of
sleek skin, alabaster and onyx,
honeyed eyes, yielding mouths.
But I prefer the avatars of elemental things.
Jill, baby faced irony and iron ass to boot.
Dangerous Diane, ineluctable eyes
that pierce the crust of bullshit.
Alice, in the wedding night blizzard of '93,
short moonfaced rascal in mink coat
and plastic rain hat, likes her vodka.
Suzie the floozy, stripper turned chef,
kept the neighborhood kids full of
jello and homemade pizza.
Linda, weighted down with cheap pearls and
expensive taste, in paint smeared jeans,
a fallen arches history of pick up porn.
I will gladly lounge with them when poachers
come to pick our bones and steal the tusks
we brandished in our cool resolve.

TSAURAH LITZSKY

Dead Louis

No more rhumba,
no bright blue robins' egg,
No abracadabra.

RON KOLM

Factory Still Life

Eduardo, my night shift partner,
Shovels another load
Into the blazing furnace.

He cups his nuts
As the flames spew out
And circle around his face.

His eyes glow
As he tells me a dirty joke
That goes on approximately forever.

SPARROW

Kurt Cobain

Kurt Cobain
Kurt Cobain
Backwards his name is
NO I BAC TRUK

Kurt Cobain
He never backed up the truck

He was young
He often sung

He was in Nirvana
They never played Havana

THE UNBEARABLES

If he had embraced
Marxist revolution,
he might still be alive today

But then he would've
had to give
all his money away

Better to be rich and dead
than poor and alive,
so said Kurt Cobain

Kurt Cobain
He should've backed up the truck

Michael Carter

God is Here

This city collects like a roach-motel
Architects and poets
(Frank and Rainer far from least)
Whose spires aspirate

unmundane desires,
make one want to shout
thru barred windows at the bare trees
'O God wherefore no pity?'
Or wrack the night with text and symbol
Conjuring arcane coniunctio, or
Search for Bohemia's chimeric image
in the sudden face of some real women:
The architecture of her lips
The rococo curling of her Ophelia's smile
The knowing innocence of her laugh
So youthful now, yet
ancient in her soul

Tarrying over the Charles
to a future nourished by futher questings

MERRY FORTUNE

Moral

Days acting like nights
come and go
like unjust profanities
casual and vain
louse ridden
like a good whore
not quite easy
not quite all there
the only one
in a half-lit room
crying for exposure
tempting you to exist

MAX BLAGG

The Bus Driver's Secret Song

O today my love I don't feel like dying
my pedal to the metal
heart pounding with health insurance
glib moments when I have the upper hand
and though they said we can go back
to our rooms
I think we will stay on this bus
as the sun pours down
on the streets of Manhattan where nobody

notices a man handstanding
his heart beating out a cleancut rhythm
his organ stiff and marvelously purple
and you on the end of it, smiling.

Patricia Freed Ackerman

Orgasm

O love give it to me unplucked
Ripe as a pear I'll show you where!
Grapes of shiny succulent skin be sucked—
Against the nature of your horizon thighs—
Such skin be rapture to endure—
Melodious whispers turned to sighs

Janice Eidus

Sound Effects

the sound waves of our orgasms could destroy
entire Japanese villages
in horror movies

and one of us could make a fortune
coming as the tornado in a remake of
the wizard of oz

JIM FEAST

Q/A

Q. Why is the goddess so sexy?
A. Tracer elements.
Q. Why is the goddess so chilling?
A. A brown-red mark on her ankle.

MIKE GOLDEN

Write a fucking poem

every fucking time
you don't know what to do.
You'll have a body of work
despite yourself.

DAVID HUBERMAN

Slave

Tell me
Who was that lady
with those spiked boots
cause I wanna get kinky
Let me
sink into the ground
that she walked on

THE UNBEARABLES

Please everybody
Turn around
Yes I even love her
with that whip
But love is like that
to a slave

C.X. Hunter

Them

I stole anything useless
made my lair in the basement
diddled the junk
on the floor in the closet
listened to show tunes
on a wooden radio
licked the dust from the windows
hid from the crow
hid from the bluebird
imagined bugs in the plumbing
dreaded the ring
of a big black telephone
feared I might be related
to a family of monsters
went without sleep for
fourteen years

JOE MAYNARD

The Professional

"That's the good thing;
about my profession,"
she said
putting her hand on my arm
while her other hand
gestured
palm up
with lipstick clad filter
sandwiched between her index
and bird finger
like a smoldering
clitoris.
"All you have to know
is how to use the phone."

SHARON MESMER

Cafe Ennui

Are we the result of some bizarre narration
of the pleasure principle?
Are we versions of desire, but not desire itself?
Do you often find yourself awash in these vague ideas?
Then nip it in a budding grove.
You should be able by now to discern the good from the stupid.
If not, what you really need is vodka. Vodka. Polish vodka,
& the 99 sacred and profane versions of "Louie, Louie."
As for me, what I don't understand I will loathe,
and what I loathe I will fuck.

JILL RAPAPORT

Panoplistic Traditions in Memphis

A perfume I tried Monday
after shoes and soap
had a great, enduring smell though
it was only imitation Oscar de La Renta.
Strange woman smiles at you on
the Lexington Avenue escalator:
"Rough day?" and you respond with a smile
like death by box cutter
how fucked up I think you are
sometimes

THADDEUS RUTKOWSKI

Yardbirds of Vermont

A woodpecker hammers its brains out
    against a weathered tree
    that looks like local cheese.
A crow robs a robin's nest
    next to a colonial inn
    and eats the stolen eggs
    in the shadow of clapboards.
A squadron of swallows
    dive-bombs for flies
    over a town pond
    surrounded by green mountains.
An English sparrow taps the ground
    with both feet
    and catches New England worms
    by sound with its beak.

A down-north heron veers off
    in the direction of Boston
    when it sees me.
A two-note songbird
    takes in the late spring air
    by answering my chilly call.

SUSAN SCUTTI

Manhattan

The first time I came up to you my
Father held my hand and
I tasted your exhausted breath,
Felt the rush of your steam against
My thighs and looking up
I saw your dark sky's squared
By buildings rising up, up
Higher than heaven could go.
I pulled my hand from my
Father's then and hearing the
Grumble of your subway voice
My fearful heart curled inside of me.
Smaller, smaller
I grew backwards: seven then six, four, three, one,
Fetal again, finally only
My soul remained,
A pale spirit adrift in your dark streets,
My heart was silent
As if I was yet to be born.
Father Manhattan:
Burst your pain inside a womb of pleasure,
I want to be your daughter.
I want to echo your siren speech.
I want to survive you when you're sold.
Father, Father
(Art in heaven)
I still haunt your skyscraped nights.
O, Manhattan: conceive me.

HAL SIROWITZ

Thursday Night in the Park

From this distance I couldn't tell
whether he was kissing her
or just taking a bite out of her pizza.

MIKE TOPP

Business District

Advice.
Lemonade.
Toy Hats.
Closed.

CLAUDE TAYLOR

Spanish Girls

Oh, she said, Spanish girls can do whatever
they want to a man. They're witches.
I said, I've seen the ones
with dark skin and blond hair
turn to smoke before you can even blink
In my heart, I wanted her to touch me then
Her large black eyes said she would
These things take their own sweet time

The wind blew the matted cardboad
Across the night and the falling rain
From down the street distant footsteps
were approaching
Above us, through a shuttered window, someone played
"Where the Rio de Rosa Flows"

DAVID L. ULIN

Mendel's Law

As I watch my
parents grow
older,
I am reminded
that there
is mental illness
on both sides
of the family,
which makes
me wonder
what the
future
holds.

ALBERT VITALE

I Want the Nobel Prize

"I am a black woman."
I've always wanted to say that.

THE UNBEARABLES

CARL WATSON

Teeth & Totemism

Then there came a time when I was seeing
Jaws in everything: in my hand,
Can-openers, pruning shears,
Doors, window jambs—everything.

The animal heads of old gods had returned
To the inanimate world & I was seeing their
Anger effectively filling all voids, all shells
The common woodsaw, even, had an eye,

But more important, it could kill.
In such a world as this, it's not unusual to measure
Dominance by number, for instance:
The number of keys slung from the belt of a sadist

For keys too have teeth & when they fit
Like a cock in a lock & turn, it can be so, shall we say, ecstatic
To know one is not imprisoned or pariah
And is welcomed home at last to many mouths

DIWAN-I HAYAN KIRMANI

Untitled
(translated by N. Pourjaundy and Peter Lamborn Wilson)

Last night glad news came to the tavern:
I heard from the messenger of the Unseen
'Why do you sit here so hopelessly sober?
Rise, take the cup from the Saki's hand and drink!
If your purse is empty
Pawn your puritan's robe to the vintner.

Why waste your strength in self-denial?
Try one hour with wine and the musician.
When the sea of forgiveness reaches full tide
It will wash away the mountain of your disobedience.
Does the bird of the heart mourn each dawn in his garden?
Does the cockerel crow from the throne of heaven?
If like Hayati you drain the grail of love
Poison will become honey in your mouth.'

Tehran 1349 S

CAROL WIERZBICKI

Red Snappers

Whatever fish were,
I did not know these
mottled red/gray
spray-painted tubes
nose-down in the bucket. My five-year-old hand
grabbed a tail; its slipperiness
anchored it.
My grandfather and his
mariner friends
let out loud guffaws
at my first encounter
with the unfairness of weight.

Poets to Come

Poets to come! orators, singers, musicians to come!
Not to-day is to justify me and answer what I am for,
But you, a new brood, native, athletic, continental, greater than
    before known,
Arouse! for you must justify me.

I myself but write one or two indicative words for the future,
I but advance a moment only to wheel and hurry back in the
    darkness.

I am a man who, sauntering along without fully stopping, turns a
    casual look upon you and then averts his face,
Leaving it to you to prove and define it,
Expecting the main things from you.

WALT WHITMAN

Naropa

Mind
is shApeLy

Art is shApeLy

— ALLEN GINSBERG

Writing & Poetics Dep

B.A. Writing & Literature

M.F.A. Writing & Poetics

STREET POETRY

Featuring:
Bob Kaufman

Jack
Micheline

A. D.
Winans

NEIGHBORHOOD ARTS THEATRE — JUNE 9th, 9 to 10:30 PM
220 BUCHANAN STREET, SAN FRANCISCO
TICKETS $3 — AVAILABLE AT 165 GROVE STREET (Upstairs Office) Phone 431-8856, THROUGH ALL ARTS OUTLETS, OR AT THE DOOR

CITY LIGHTS
REVIEW

An Annual Review of Literature & Politics
Edited by Lawrence Ferlinghetti & Nancy J. Peters

RECENT CONTRIBUTORS: Edward Abbey ✦ Noam Chomsky ✦ Andrei Codrescu
✦ Lydia Davis ✦ Robert Gluck ✦ Susan Griffin ✦ Marilyn Hacker ✦ Alberto Savinio ✦
Henri Michaux ✦ Marie Ponsot ✦ Roland Topor ✦ Todd Gitlin ✦ Edward Said ✦
Alexander Cockburn ✦ Sue Coe ✦ Abbie Hoffman ✦ Jonas Mekas ✦ Karen Finley ✦
Kathy Acker ✦ Heathcote Williams ✦ Edmund White ✦ James Purdy ✦ Diane di Prima
✦ Roy Schneider ✦ Victor Serge ✦ Leon Golub ✦ La Loca ✦ Gary Indiana ✦ Clayton
Eshleman ✦ Diane Michals ✦ Sharon Doubiago ✦ Victor Serge ✦ Cookie Mueller

Available at better bookstores &
through City Lights Mail Order:
261 Columbus Avenue, San Francisco, CA 94133

contributors

Mumia Abu-Jamal, author of "Live from Death Row," is awaiting execution on Death Row in the SCI-Greene Supermax (maximum security) prison in the State of Pennsylvania. Charged with killing a policeman, Abu-Jamal was sentenced to death in a trial that many feel was marred by irregularities. Today, the cause to free him extends worldwide, and demonstrations of protest continue from Quebec to Denmark. Nonetheless, National Public Radio chose to drop Abu-Jamal's series of commentaries under pressure from the Philadelphia Fraternal Order of Police, while efforts continue from within the penal system, as well as at the highest levels of State government, to silence this former head of the Philadelphia Association of Black Journalists.

Kathy Acker invented the post-modern novel with genius and aplomb. Her books include *Hannibal Lecter, My Father, Blood and Guts in High School, Don Quixote and Pussy, King of the Pirates*. Writers and readers around the world mourned her recent death in Mexico from cancer.

Ai is the author of five books of poetry. She was the recipient of the Lamont Poetry Award from the Academy of American Poets for *Killing Floor* (1978) and an American Book Award for *Sin* (1987). She lives in Tucson, Arizona.

Miguel Algarin is a founder of the Nuyorican Poets Cafe in New York City. A distinguished poet and critic, with nine collections to his credit, his work is included in numerous anthologies including *Love Is Hard Work, Memories De Loisaida* and *Aloud: Voices from the Nuyorican Poets Cafe*

Rafael F. J. Alvarado is co-editor of *(SIC) Vice & Verse*.

David Amram collaborated with Kerouac on the first ever jazz/poetry reading in New York City in 1957. He wrote the musical score and the title song for the groundbreaking Kerouac film *Pull My Daisy* in 1959. His symphonic works with Kerouac include excerpts from *The Lonesome Traveler* in his cantata, *A Year in Our Land—Four Seasons in America*. He has been recently commissioned by James Galway to write a flute concerto, *Giants of the Night*, dedicated to Charlie Parker, Dizzy Gillespie and Jack Kerouac.

Rudolfo Anaya is the author of *Bless Me, Ultima* and *Albuquerque*.

Sini Anderson is co-founder with Michelle Tea, of Sister Spit: "a freewheeling gaggle of loudmouthed girls, kicking for revolution and calling it like we see it." They tour the United States in a bus, inciting Spoken Word riots wherever they go.

Hannah Aquaah is serving time in a New York State penal institution and studies writing with the poet Hettie Jones.

Penny Arcade debuted at 17 as an original member of John Vaccaro's explosive Playhouse of the Ridiculous, the seminal rock and roll, glitter political theatre of the New York 60s. She was a teenage superstar for Andy Warhol's Factory featured in the Morrissey/Warhol film *Women in Revolt*. She has created solo performance work since 1982 and group performance work since 1989. Her sex and censorship show, *Bitch! Dyke! Faghag! Whore!* has toured the world twice as both an international festival and commercial hit in twenty cities around the world including two tours of Australia. She is part of the pirate radio rebellion, heard on "STEAL THIS RADIO," the Lower East Side pirate station.

Amiri Baraka (Leroi Jones) entered the Greenwich Village poetry scene through his association with Allen Ginsberg and the Beats in the 1950s. Fame came in 1964 with the New York production of his Obie-award winning play, *Dutchman*. The death of Malcolm X converted him to Black Nationalism. He has produced plays, jazz operas, nonfiction books and thirteen volumes of poetry.

Julian Beck, born in 1925 in New York City, was a multitalented genius who left his enduring mark on the culture of this century. A gifted painter, he showed in the major abstract-expressionist shows, alongside Jackson Pollack, Franz Kline and others. With his wife, the poet Judith Malina, he founded The Living Theater. Also a poet of astonishing range, as well as a committed political activist, his books include *Living in Volkswagen Buses and Other Songs of the Revolution*.

John Bennet, who has been praised by everyone from Tom Robbins to Henry Miller, was a major force in the underground of the sixties, where he became known as the "King of the Mimeo Revolution." A model of literary independence, he has authored dozens of small press classics, including *The New World Order, Tripping in America* and *The Night of the Butcher*. He is the publisher of Vagabond Books and lives in Ellensberg, Washington.

Mark "9-Box" Benyo is incarcerated in the Eastern New York State Correctional Facility in Napanoch, New York.

Ted Berk was a well-known poet in the sixties hippy movement in San Francisco.

Wallace Berman (1926–1976), was a major artist and significant influence in the Los Angeles and San Francisco countercultural ferment. Berman, noted for his distinctive collages and constructions, also edited and hand-printed *SEMINA*, a unique enterprise featuring works by Michael McClure, Allen Ginsberg, Cameron, I. E. Alexander, William Burroughs, Cocteau, Meltzer, aya tarlow, Robert Duncan, John Wieners, and his own poems under various pseudonyms.

Steven J. Bernstein was an icon of the emerging Seattle Grunge scene and an underground cohort of William Burroughs and John Bennett, before his tragic death in October 1991. Today he is considered the finest poet ever to come out of Seattle. His poems are collected in *More Noise, Please*.

Father Daniel Berrigan's books include *And the Risen Bread: Selected and New Poems, 1957–1997; Homage to Gerald Manley Hopkins; Daniel: Under the Siege of the Divine*.

Iris Berry is a founding member of The Ringling Sisters, an L.A.-based poetry and music group. She is widely anthologized, has written for several literary publications, has performed spoken word on MTV and at Lalapalooza and has appeared in several independent films. Her CD "Life on the Edge in Stilettos" is out now on New Alliance along with her book of short stories and prose, *Two Blocks East of Vine* (Incommunicado Press). She is currently working on her forthcoming book, a verbal history of the Tropicana Motel.

Umar Bin Hassan was a member of The Last Poets, a group of poets and singers who emerged out of the Black Arts Movement during the Civil Rights struggles of the sixties. Other members included Abiodun Oyewole, Jalal, Siliaman, Felipe, Gylan Kain and David Nelson.

Max Blagg is a member of the Unbearables.

Jennifer Blowdryer, taking her name from a punk band she performed with in the seventies, became well-known in the underground as a poet and a monthly columnist for *Maximum Rock 'n' Roll*. Her books include *Modern English* and *Where Is My Wife?*

Cecil Boatswain is incarcerated in the Eastern New York State Correctional Facility in Napanoch, New York.

Laurel Ann Bogen is the author of ten collections of poetry and short fiction, the most recent of which is *Fission* published by Red Dancefloor Press in 1998. She is literary curator at the Los Angeles County Museum of Art and an instructor of poetry and performance in the Writer's Program at UCLA Extension.

Joe Brainard's books include *I Remember* and *Bean Spasms*.

Richard Brautigan(1935–1984), poet and novelist, is regarded as one of the seminal voices of the 1960s. His publications include *The Galilee Hitchhiker, A Confederate General in Big Sur, All Watched Over by Machines of Loving Grace, The Pill Versus the Springhill Mine Disaster, In Watermelon Sugar, Rommel Drives on Deep into Egypt, Dreaming of Babylon: A Private Eye Novel, 1942, The Tokyo-Montana Express, The Abortion: An Historical Romance, The Hawkline Monster: A Gothic Western, Revenge of the Lawn, Loading Mercury with a Pitchfork, Willard and His Bowling Trophies: A Perverse Mystery*, and Sombrero Fallout: A Japanese Novel.

Ray Bremser, called by Bob Dylan "the true Beat Poet," has published several books of poetry including *Poems of Madness & Angel* and *The Conquerors*. The poetry he wrote during his twelve years in prison gained him such admirers as Robert Graves, Ezra Pound, and, most especially, Allen Ginsberg and the Beats. Considered one of the finest jazz poets of the post-war era, his poems appear in many anthologies that deal with the literature of jazz.

Douglas Brinkley, a historian, is editor *of The Proud Highway: Saga of a Desperate Southern Gentleman 1955–1967* (Fear and Loathing Letters/Hunter S. Thompson, Vol 1). His most recent book is the *American Heritage History of the United States*.

Jim Brodey's brilliance, displayed while studying with Frank O'Hara, brought him into contact with the poets of the "New York School" which took him under its wing. In 1966 he won the Dylan Thomas Poetry Prize. Traveling between coasts, Brodey wrote on music for *The East Village Other* and *Creem*, launched presses and magazines, taught workshops, published his own books and encouraged other poets. He was deeply influenced by jazz, particularly that of Coltrane, Coleman and Ayler, and created a formidable body of verse, some of which is collected in *Heart of the Breath* (Poems 1979–1992 edited by Clark Coolidge). His other books include *Blues of the Egyptian Kings, Piranah Yoga* and *Judyism*.

Eric Brown is a madman and angel living in Highland Park with his wife Tori. He has produced a countless number of chapbooks and has been published in as many zines and literary journals. He is one of the founders/editors of *Rats w/ Keys* which has been scurrying about in the underground scene for over 10 years.

Lenny Bruce rose to the heights of the comedy profession during the fifties and sixties, but he was much more then a comedian. He was a brilliant artist and passionate champion of personal freedoms who, through largely improvised monologues purposely peppered with "obscene" language, both challenged restrictive mores and laws and deflated the sacred cows and pompous taboos of the day. For this he underwent a brutal regimen of arrests and trials which contributed to his decline and no doubt hastened his eventual death from heroin overdose.

Michael Bruner is a co-founder of the nationally recognized performance poetry troupes The Lost Tribe and the Carma Bums. Michael went on to receive a masters degree in performance theory and a doctorate in critical rhetorical studies and now teaches courses on identity construction and performance at Babson College in Wellesley, Massachusetts. Besides dozens of performance poems, he has published articles related to social philosophy on identity ethics, collective memory and nationalism. It is all a controlled rebellion against terrorist citizens everywhere.

William S. Burroughs was the dark genius of the classic Beat group that included Allen Ginsberg, Jack Kerouac, and Gregory Corso. Among his best-known books are *Junky, Naked Lunch, The Soft Machine, The Ticket That Exploded, Nova Express, The Wild Boys, Exterminator* and *Yage Letters*, his collected correspondence with Allen Ginsberg.

Regie Cabico is the co-editor of *Poetry Nation: A North American Anthology of Fusion Poetry* (Vehicule, Montreal 1998). He is a cyberjay on Go Poetry.Com and participated in the 1993, 1994 and 1997 National Poetry Slams and took a first-place prize with the winning team, Mouth Almighty, Manhattan.

Cal, whose real name was Arthur Dion, was a member of the Chicago Outlaws motorcycle club and former member of Hell's Angels.

Steve Cannon is editor and publisher of *Tribes*, a groundbreaking New York City-based avant garde magazine that promotes multicultural modernism.

Jim Carroll, a poet, musician and diarist was born and grew up in New York City. Talented at both basketball and writing, he attended Trinity High School in Manhattan on a scholarship and was an All-City basketball star—a period in his life vividly described in his widely praised book *The Basketball Diaries*. Carroll's first collection of poetry, *Living at the Movies*, was published in 1973 when he was twenty-two. His other books include *The Book of Nods* (1986), *Forced Entries* (1987) and *Fear of Dreaming* (1993). As leader of the Jim Carroll Band, he recorded three albums for Atlantic Records: *Catholic Boy, Dry Dreams* and *I Write Your Name. Praying Mantis*, a spoken-word recording, was released by Giant Records in 1991. *A World without Gravity: The Best of the Jim Carroll Band* was released by Rhino Records in 1993.

Michael Carter is a member of the Unbearables.

Neal Cassady served as the model for Dean Moriarity, the legendary hero of Jack Kerouac's *On the Road*. Later, he drove the bus for Ken Kesey's Merry Pranksters. His rapturous, nonstop monologues and sporadic writings artistically and spiritually influenced both Kerouac and poet Allen Ginsberg. By the time of his death in Mexico in 1968, just four days short of his forty-fourth birthday, he had already entered the annals of American folklore forever.

Jim Chandler, one of the few Meat poets to successfully make the transition into the computer age, is a powerful writer whose poems often deal with his harrowing early years as a convict and social outcast. His innovative online poetry zine, "Thunder Sandwich," has been a rallying point for some of the best poets of the last two decades, including Gerald Locklin, Lyn Lifshin, Virgil Harvey and Cheryl Townsand.

Neeli Cherkovski's biography *Hank*, remains the definitive work on his friend, Charles Bukowski. The two poets shared many misadventures that were, by turn, hilarious and inspiring. He is the author of a book of critical memoirs, *Whitman's Wild Children*, a biography of Lawrence Ferlinghetti and eight books of poetry.

Justin Chin, the author of *Mongrel: Essays, Diatribes and Pranks* (St. Martin's Press) and *Bite Hard* (Manic D Press), is one of the finest writers produced by the spoken-word movement. He lives in San Francisco.

Andy Clausen is one of a group of Neo-Beat poets, including Antler and Marc Olmstead, whose works were advocated by the late Allen Ginsberg. His books include *Without Doubt* and *Fortieth Century Man: Selected Verse 1996–1966*.

Allen Cohen founded and published the *San Francisco Oracle*, considered to be the best hippie publication of the 1960s.

Ira Cohen, a photographer and poet, has exhibited in museums throughout the world.

Leonard Cohen has published nine books of poetry, two novels, and has made eleven records, including "Various Positions," "I'm Your Man" and, most recently, "The Future," during the forty years of a career that took him to the heights of the music world.

Wanda Coleman is the most electrifying stage performer ever to explode out of Los Angeles. She revived the tradition of performance poetry that had waned after L.A.'s flirtation with the Beats. Her impact on the Los Angeles poetry scene has spanned three decades, during which she has published eight books from Black Sparrow Press, including *Mad Dog Black Lady* and *Heavy Daughter Blues*. Her recent books include *Native in a Strange Land: Trials & Tremors* (1996) and new poems in *Bathwater Wine* (1998). She also appears on many CDs, including "Twin Sisters" (with Exene Cervenka), "Black Angeles" (with poet Michelle Clinton) and most recently, "Black and Blue News." From 1981 to 1992 she co-hosted "The Poetry Connexion" (Pacifica Radio), with husband Austin Straus; they currently live and work in Los Angeles.

Gregory Corso was part of the cultural revolution known as the Beat Generation. Allen Ginsberg called him "a rascal poet Villonesque and Rimbaudian." His books include *The Happy Birthday of Death, Elegiac Feelings American* and *Mindfield: New and Selected Poems*.

Jayne Cortez is the author of ten books and performer on eight recordings of poetry. Her poems have been translated into many languages and published in journals, magazines and anthologies, such as *Daughters of Africa, Women on War, Jazz & Poetry, Free Spirits, Black Scholar, Sulfur* and *Unesco Courier*. Her most recent book is *Somewhere in Advance of Nowhere* and her latest CD recording is "Taking The Blues Back Home."

Peter Coyote's memoir, *Sleeping Where I Fall*, published in April 1998, is about a fifteen-year period in his life during the sixties and seventies when he roamed in an anarchic West Coast counterculture. A well-known star of stage and screen, Coyote's credits include *Patch Adams, Execution of Justice, Bitter Moon* and *Unforgettable*.

Steve Dalachinsky's chapbooks include *One Thin Line* and *People/Places*. His work has most recently appeared in *Long Shot, Big Hammer* and N.Y. *Arts Magazine*. He has just published a book of poems entitled *The Final Night*.

Maria Damun is author of *The Dark End of the Street: Margins in American Vanguard Poetry* and a member is of the National Writers' Union.

Alejo Dao'ud Rodriguez, Cecil Boatswain, Frank Fissette, Herby Ehinger, Mark "9-Box" Benyo and Israel Fernandez are all members of Janine Pommy Vega's prison writing workshop and are serving time in various penal facilities in the State of New York.

James Dean was the brilliant star of such film classics as *Rebel without a Cause, East of Eden* and *Giant*. His death at a young age has lent to his name a tragic mystique that has endured to the present day.

Ken DiMaggio is one of the founding poets and estheticians of the contemporary resurgence of Spoken Word poetry. Allen Ginsberg first took note of him in the early eighties. Later in that decade and into the nineties, during the nascent days of New York's budding downtown scene, he earned the unqualified admiration of fellow poets at ABC No Rio and the Nuyorican Poetry Cafe. His performances of highly original poems combine punk and pop sensibility with high art. Though his stubborn integrity often deprived him of opportunities for greater prominence, undaunted, he continued throughout the last decade to churn out novels, poems, a newsletter and to perform from coast to coast. With Steve Hartman of Pinched Nerves Press he has created limited edition books that are the last word in visionary underground art.

Diane diPrima, one of the founding poets of the Beat Generation, was arrested with co-editor Leroi Jones (Amiri Baraka) for alleged obscenity charges against *The Floating Bear*, their newsletter. A longtime champion of civil liberties, as well as an active Buddhist, she is one of a group, with David Meltzer and Robert Duncan, that established the Poetics Program at New College of California. Her books include *Memoirs of a Beatnik, Pieces of a Song: Selected Poems and Revolutionary Letters*.

Edward Dorn was born in 1929 and grew up in eastern Illinois, on the banks of the river Embarrass (a tributary of the Wasbash). He never knew his father. His mother was of French ancestry, his grandfather a railroad man. He attended a one-room school, while in high school played billiards with the local undertaker for a dime a point, and after two years at the University of Illinois and two stops at Black Mountain College, traveled through the trans-mountain West following the winds of writing and employment. From 1965 to 1970 he lived in England, where he lectured at the University of Essex. He has since lived and taught in Kansas, Chicago and San Francisco; throughout the 1980s he has taught in the Creative Writing Program of the University of Colorado, Boulder, and, with his wife Jennifer Dunbar Dorn, edited the newspaper *Rolling Stock*. His major works include *The Newly Fallen, Hands Up!, Geography, Recollections of Gran Apacheria, Gunslinger, Hello La Jolla* and *Yellow Lola* (poetry), and *The Rites of Passage, Some Business Recently Transacted in The White World* and *The Shoshoneans* (prose).

Lawrence Durrell (1912–1990), the English novelist, first encountered Henry Miller's writings in an outhouse in Greece, where he found a soiled and discarded copy of *Tropic of Cancer* and began to read. He soon wrote to the American and began a literary friendship and collaboration that lasted nearly four decades. Regarded as one of the greatest British novelists of the twentieth century, he is best known for a series of novels entitled *The Alexandria Quartet*.

Bob Dylan has been called the major poet/songwriter of our time. Dylan was born in 1941 in Hibbing, Minnesota.

Evert Eden is a South African who moved to the U.S. in 1980. In 1979 his play, *A Very Butch Libido*, was banned by the white regime in South Africa. He toured as a poet with Lollapalooza in 1994, placed second in the 1996 individual Slam, and was on the winning Slam team in the 1997 International Slam. His one-person show, How to Cook a Man, debuted in Germany in 1999.

Herby Ehinger is incarcerated in the Eastern New York State Correctional Facility in Napanoch, New York.

Maggie Estep's first novel, *Diary of an Emotional Idiot*, was published in 1997. She has made two spoken word CDs and her writing has appeared in various magazines including *Spin, Harpers Bazaar*, the *Village Voice* and the *New Yorker*. Maggie's second book, *Soft Maniacs*, will be published by Simon and Schuster in September 1999, and she is currently working on her third novel, *The King of Coney Island*. She lives in New York City.

Janice Eidus is a member of the Unbearables.

John Farris, a legendary poet of New York City's Lower East Side, is the author of *It's Not About Time*.

Jim Feast is a member of the Unbearables.

Lawrence Ferlinghetti, one of the central figures of the Beat Generation and The San Francisco Renaissance is the author of dozens of books, including *Pictures of the Gone World* and *Far Rockaway of the Heart*. As publisher of City

Lights Books, his decision in 1956 to publish Allen Ginsberg's "Howl" led to the obscenity trial that brought both Ginsberg and himself great prominence as poetic radicals and defenders of artistic freedom. Still one of the most widely read poets in the world, he is the reigning Poet-Laureate of San Francisco.

Israel Fernandez is incarcerated in the Eastern New York State Correctional Facility in Napanoch, New York.

Daniel Ferri, a 6th grade teacher, participated in the National Poetry Slam tournament from 1994 to 1998, his teams taking second place twice. He developed and is Head-to-Headmaster of the Head-to-head Haiku competition form and is the 1997 Uptown Poetry Slam Champion at the Green Mill Lounge in Chicago. He is also a commentator for Public Radio. He featured in the film *Slam Nation*.

Bonnie Finberg is a member of the Unbearables.

Karen Finley rose to national prominence as one of four artists who were denied National Endowment for the Arts funding on the grounds of obscenity. Since then she has received the highest international acclaim for her performance art, while her paintings hang in museums throughout North American and Europe.

Frank Fissette is incarcerated in a penal facility in New York State.

Bob Flanagan (1952–1996) was a poet and performance artist. He was the author of five books of poetry: *The Kid is the Man, Fuck Journals, The Wedding of Everything, Slave Sonnets* and *Taste of Honey* with David Trinidad. He was the subject of the RE/Search book *Bob Flanagan: Supermasochist* and the film documentary *Sick: The Life and Death of Bob Flanagan, Supermasochist*.

Merry Fortune is a member of the Unbearables.

FrancEye used to be someone else. Who knows who she'll be later on? Right now she's happy, so let her alone. She is the author of *Snaggletooth In Ocean Park, Selected Poems 1940–1996* on Sacred Beverage Press. She has been published in many literary magazines and anthologies including *Das ist Alles, Charles Bukowski Recollected*, Pearl Editions 1995.

Rebecca Fransway who lives in Riverside, California is a frequent contributor to *Long Shot* and is cited by the magazine's editors as one of their favorite poets for all time.

Patricia Freed Ackerman is a member of the Unbearables.

Reg E. Gaines is a Grand Slam champion of the Nuyorican Poets Cafe, winner of the Bessie Award, a Grammy nominee and a two-time Tony winner for best book/lyrics for *Bring in Da Noise, Bring In Da Funk*. He latest book is *The Original Buckwheat*, a collection of poetry.

Nelson Gary (Panorama City): Halloween baby, diplomatic liaison for Voodoo Lounge and part of accounting staff in Amsterdam for The Rolling Stones, Motown computer hack, tennis professional, parade vendor, drug-rehab counselor, juvenile-delinquent guardian, Federal government employee, door-to-door perfume salesman, fashion show grunt, poet, playwright, novelist, storyteller, casino worker, and CSUN student. He is co-founder of Low Profile Press with wife Lil.

Kathi Georges owns and operates the Marilyn Monroe Theatre in San Francisco, with Peter Carlaftes, where they have been producing plays for the past seven years together. She has been widely anthologized and is the co-editor of *The Verdict Is In* (Manic d Press), an anthology dealing with the aftermath of the Los Angeles riots in April 1992.

Amy Gerstler is a writer of fiction, poetry and journalism, who lives in L.A. Her books include Crown of Weeds and Bitter Angels.

John Gilmore is the author of *Live Fast—Die Young: My Life with James Dean.*

Allen Ginsberg reclaimed for American poetry that visionary tradition which extends from the Old Testament through William Blake to Walt Whitman, in two astonishing full-length poems, "Howl" and "Kaddish," and a rich body of shorter work. Beginning with his almost single-handed launch of the Beat Generation in the 1950s, and until his death in 1997, Ginsberg was the defining poet-statesman and public oracle of post war American counterculture. A dedicated Buddhist as well, he committed himself to serving as an outspoken critic on behalf of oppressed peoples and minorities.

John Giorno, the self-proclaimed "originator of spoken word and performance poetry," has elevated poetry reading to a high art form. Since founding Giorno Poetry Systems in 1965, he has produced 40 LPs and CDs from such legendary underground figures as Laurie Anderson and William Burroughs. He is the author of "You Got to Burn to Shine" and founder of Dial-A-Poem.

Buddy Giovinazzo is a filmmaker/author from NYC. His films *No Way Home* and *Combat Shock* are disturbing portraits of society's underbelly. His books *Poetry & Purgatory* and *Life is Hot in Cracktown* are even more disturbing. He's a disturbed man, but is kind to small animals.

Michael Gizzi, author of nine books of verse, including *No Both* and *gyptian in hortulus*, edits the Profile Series for Hard Press.

Mike Golden's *Smoke Signals*, an arts zine of the 1980s, laid tracks for today's New York downtown scene. His book on Cleveland poet d.a.levy, The Buddhist Third Class Junkmail Oracle, is forthcoming from Seven Stories Press. He is a member of The Unbearables.

David Gollub is author of "As for Us" and editor of *Bullhorn*, the official poetry broadside of the Babarians.

Gerry Gomez Pearlberg is a poet and editor whose writings have been widely anthologized in such places as *Women on Women 3*, *Hers 2*, *Queer View Mirror 2*, and *Sister and Brother*. A winner of the 1993 Judith's Room Emerging Women

Poets Award, she has edited three poetry anthologies: *The Key to Everything: Classic Lesbian Love*, *The Zenith of Desire: Contemporary Lesbian Poems about Sex*, and most recently, *Queer Dog: Homoe/Pup/Poetry*.

Matt Gonzalez's FMSBW Press publishes Jack Micheline's *Sixty-Seven Poems For Downtrodden Saints*, a remarkable limited edition assemblage of the poems of Jack Micheline spanning forty years. He works as a public defender in San Francisco.

Jeff Gordon is a poet, painter and woodcut artist. He lives in downtown N.Y.C. with the abstract painter Path Song. Together they are raising four large outdoor plants: three wisteria and one jasmine.

S.A. Griffin published in many poetry zines and anthologies; he is also the author of *Heaven Is One Long Naked Dance* and *A One-Legged Man Standing Casually on Hollywood Blvd. Smoking a Cigarette*. Driver of the '59 Cadillac Sedan, the '71 Bick Riviera and the bus. Along with partner Rafael F. J. Alvarado, publishes and edits *(Sic)Vice & Verse*. Toured with poetry supergroups the Carma Bums, the Lost Tribe and White Trash Apocalypse. He is a father. He is descended from drunks, used car salesmen, bookies, card players, angels and other assorted forms of madness. He has been seven stories tall in Las Vegas. He is a crash vampire and breathes the air in Los Angeles.

Che Guevara (Ernesto Guevara) was a Latin American guerrilla leader and revolutionary theorist who became a hero to the New Left radicals of the 1960s. He was captured by the Bolivian army and shot near Vallegrande on Oct. 9, 1967.

Woody Guthrie lived the life described in his songs, from Dustbowl wanderer to labor union man and in so doing created some of the most authentic folk songs of this century. His influence resonates in the music of everyone from Bob Dylan to Bruce Springsteen.

Fritz Hamilton, a former wino heroically risen from the skid row depths, has gone on to publish dozens of books, over 1,000 poems in magazines, and a novel, *Love, Debra*. He is one of the original Meat Poets. *Love, Debra* is currently under option in Hollywood.

Q.R. Hand, born and raised in Bedford-Stuyvesant is a poet and instrumentalist with the nationally acclaimed spoken word/jazz quartet, Wordwind. Hand is an early innovator of music-backed stand-up poetry recitation. He performs on Don Paul's "Poetry for The People" and Alejandro Murgia's "Native Tongues". His poems are published in *Black Scholar*, *Appeal to Reason* and *Beatitude*.

Joy Harjo, one of the country's finest Native American voices, is an enrolled member of the Muscogee Tribe and author of several volumes of poetry, including *The Woman Who Fell from the Sky* and *She Had Some Horses*.

Helen A. Harrison is director of the Pollack-Krasner House and Study Center.

Kurt Heinz is director of the Chicago Institute of Telepoetics and creator of the website, "An Incomplete History of the Slam."

David Henderson is author of several books, including *De Mayor of Harlem* and *Excuse Me While I Kiss the Sky: The Biography of Jimi Hendrix*. He has published three volumes of poetry and writes extensively on reggae and rap.

Gil Scott-Heron, writer, poet and musician, influenced an entire generation of rap musicians through his attitude, poetry and "bluesology." Renowned in the seventies and eighties as the "Minister of Information," his latest album is "Spirits."

Victor Hernández Cruz—a frequent champion of the Taos, New Mexico, Heavyweight Poetry Bouts—infuses his poetry with the rhythms, colors and textures of Puerto Rico, his homeland, and the Lower East Side of New York City, where he grew up. Cruz says, "I write about myself as a Caribbean man, a man within a larger tapestry; and I try to see the connections between everything— between myself and history." Cruz has taught at the University of California in San Diego and is the author of "Red Beans."

Daniel Higgs, born in Baltimore in 1964 and founder of the Ignorance Research Institute has acquired an international following as a poet and also lead singer for the band Lungfish. Regarded among poets as the successor to Kenneth Patchen, he is also an extraordinary visual artist and occasionally works as a professional tattoo artist. His books include *The Doomsday Bonnet* and *From the Mouth of Union*.

Jack Hirschman's books include *A Correspondence of Americans, Black Alephs, Lyripol* and *The Bottom Line*.

Abbie Hoffman was one of the important activists of the sixties. A flamboyant showman, Hoffman galvanized the nation's rebellious hippie youth and served to mobilize the anti-Vietnam War protest movement through his own incendiary brand of street theater. He was one of the notorious "Chicago Seven" who were tried for the disturbances that broke out during the 1968 Democratic National Convention when Mayor Daly's riot police ferociously attacked the demonstrators. He was born in Worcester, Massachusetts in 1936.

Sara Holbrook is a performance poet and author of "Chicks Up Front."

Mikhail Horowitz, considered one of the premier performance poets alive today, is the author of "Big League Poets" and, most recently, "The Opus of Everything in Nothing Flat."

David Huberman is a member of the Unbearables.

Herbert Huncke was the archetype of the Beat, and may have coined the term. He is the author of *Huncke's Journal*, and *The Evening Sun Turned Crimson*.

C.X. Hunter is a member of the Unbearables.

Hank Hyena, Slam poet, journalist and theater entrepreneur, writes for *Salon*.

Bruce Isaacson is co-founder of the notorious Cafe Babar Reading Series and publisher of Zeitgeist Press. His books include *love affairs with barely any people in them* and *Mad Dog Blues*.

Kathe Izzo is the founder of the Shadow Writing Project, a traveling outreach arts program for youth-at-risk. She is a poet, filmmaker, mother, performance artist and editor of *Flicker*, a journal of teen writing. She lives in Provincetown with her three daughters.

Joan Jobe Smith, founding editor of *Pearl*, worked seven years as a go-go dancer before receiving her MFA from the University of California at Irvine. Her seventeenth collection of poetry, *The Pow Wow Cafe*, was published in 1998 by the U.K.'s The Poetry Business.

Hettie Jones is author of a celebrated memoir of the Beat scene, *How I Became Hettie Jones*. Her poetry books include *Drive, Having Been Her* and *For Four Hetties*.

Janis Joplin, born in 1943 in Port Arthur, Texas, became one of the idols of the sixties. She began her career singing in bars and coffeehouses in Texas and in 1966, following a move to San Francisco, became the lead singer for Big Brother and the Holding Company. From there, her rise to stardom was swift. She died on Oct. 4, 1970 of a heroin overdose.

Lenore Kandel, born in 1932, came on the scene of San Francisco Renaissance in 1960 and became an associate of Lew Welch and Robert Duncan. In 1965, her controversial work, *The Love Book*, a collection of "holy erotica" sent shock waves through the Bay area and was the subject of police raids, especially at The Psychadelic Shop and City Lights Bookstore. It was declared pornographic and obscene by the courts. In its defense, Kandel defined it as "her belief that sexual acts between loving persons are religious acts." Since 1970 she has been incapacitated from a motorcycle accident with her then-husband, Hells Angel William Fritsch.

Vampyre Mike Kassel, author of such diabolical works as "Graveyard Golf," "Going for the Low Blow" and "I Want to Kill Everything" has punctured the necks of screaming audiences from San Francisco to Berlin. His writings and performances combine a savage Swiftian sense of irony with high-style vaudevillian camp.

Alan Kaufman's books include *Who Are We?*, *American Cruiser*, *Before I Wake* and an anthology, *The New Generation: Fiction For Our Time From America's Writing Programs*. He is the founder and editor of the journal *Davka: Jewish Cultural Revolution* (online as TattooJew www.tattoojew.com) and the author of the forthcomign memoir, *Jew Boy*.

Bob Kaufman's books include *Solitudes Crowded with Loneliness* and *Golden Sardine*.

Jack Kerouac's *On the Road* is one of the greatest American novels of the post-war era. Although he is widely identified as a fiction writer, he was really a poet in prose. Considered the father of the Beat Generation, Kerouac cut a solitary, beautiful figure in the sterile landscape of the Eisenhower era, living the occasional hobo life of hitchhiking and hopping freights with a backpack loaded down with the manuscripts, Buddhist prayer books and canned foods. A prodigious writer, his other books include *The Dharma Bums, Desolation Angels* and *The Subterraneans*.

Jan Kerouac first met her father Jack when she was nine years old. He arrived at her mother's apartment in the East Village and immediately asked: "Where's the liquor store?" Jan took his hand and led him to the shop. He bought some Harvey's Bristol Cream sherry and drank the entire bottle that afternoon in their living room. In a mental hospital at the age of fourteen, Jan read *On the Road* for the first time. "I read it all in one night instead of ringing for another seconal," she wrote in *Baby Driver*. She also wrote, "Now that I had a picture of what he'd been doing all this time, all over the country, it made more sense that he hadn't had the time to be fatherly." She is the author of two novels, *Baby Driver* and *Trainsong*, published before her death to wide critical praise. Despite the physical hardship imposed by kidney failure in 1991, she continued to work on a third novel, *Parrot Fever*, that will be published posthumously in 1999. She died in Albuquerque, New Mexico on June 5, 1996, at the age of forty-four.

Ken Kesey, one of the Outlaw legends of the sixties psychedelic revolution, led his Merry Pranksters on a bus steered by Neal Cassady. He is the author of *One Flew Over the Cuckoo's Nest* and *Sometimes a Great Notion*.

Klipschutz, a San Francisco poet and songwriter for the Living Wrecks, is author of *Good Neighbor Policy*.

Doug Knott, a graduate of Yale and Harvard Law School and professed world traveler, discovered the excitement of the written and spoken word in underground clubs. As a long-time member of the Carma Bums/Lost Tribe, he has been at the forefront of performance poetry since 1984. As a performer and poet, he believes that poetry should entertain people as well as move them and make them think. An award-winning poetry video director, he is the author of *Small Dogs Bark Cartoons* and his work has appeared in numerous anthologies.

Ron Kolm is a member of the Unbearables.

Tuli Kupferberg of the Fugs has published several books, including *1001 Ways to Live without Working* and *Grace and Beauty of the Human Form*.

Michael Lally's landmark reading of "My Life" at CBGB in the seventies has been likened to Ginsberg's reading of "HOWL" at Gallery Six. His books include

It's Not Nostalgia, and *"Can't Be Wrong,"* which won Oakland PEN's Josephine Miles Award. Ted Berrigan has declared Michael Lally "America's most notorious sexual outlaw and poet."

Philip Lamantia is often associated with the Beat Generation and the historic reading at Gallery Six, but it is really as one of America's foremost surrealist poets that he has made his most important contribution. His books include *Bed of Sphinxes* and *Becoming Visible*.

Paul Landry, a North Beach poet, composed his poems by hand set letterpress and lived, as he died, untainted by self-compromise. His books include *Kept in the Pocket of My Poems* and *After the Island*.

Jennifer Lee is Richard Pryor's ex-wife and currently friend and manager.

David Lerner's books include *Why Rimbaud Went to Africa*, *I want a New Gun* and *Pray Like the Hunted* (all Zeitgeist Press.)

d.a. levy's selected poems and art are available in a definitive edition of his works, *Zen & Concrete*, etc., edited by Ingrid Swanberg (Ghost Pony Press).

Joel Lewis's unfolding poetic epic, "Immigrant," a work of Joycean proportions and is already the buzz among poets from New York to San Francisco. Lewis is the author of *Nervous Fabric: New and Selected Poems* (Talisman House), *House Rent Boogie* (Yellow Press) and *North Jersey Gutter Helmet* (Oasis Press). He has edited the selected poems of Walter Lowenfels, selected talks of Ted Berrigan and an anthology of New Jersey poets.

Tsaurah Litzsky is a member of the Unbearables.

Gerald Locklin took up an academic post at California State University, Long Beach, as a professor of English in 1965 and has been there since. He has published over eighty books and chapbooks including *The Toad Poems* (1970), *Poop and Other Poems* (1972), *The Criminal Mentality* (1976) and *The Firebird Poems* (1992).

Philomene Long, beat legend, was born in Greenwich Village and cut her literary teeth listening to poets verbally sear the paint off the walls of their private hells. Later, after escaping a five-year sentence in a Los Angeles convent, she migrated to Venice, California, wrote poems and was crowned "Queen of Bohemia." Author John Maynard, in his book *Venice West: The Beat Generation In Southern California* describes Philomene as dark, mercurial and very Irish. "She was a regular feature of the Ocean Front in her tennis shoes, black thrift-shop dresses, long, straight hair, alarm-clock pendent, and heavy silver cross . . . still, somehow, considering herself a nun, she joined the world . . . and still lives the old ethic and upholds the old dream of salvation through creativity and counts poverty as a sign of grace." Philomene Long is an internationally published poet and film director. Her films include *The Beats: An Existential Comedy* with Allen Ginsberg and *The California Missions* with Martin Sheen. Among her books of poetry are:

The Book of Sleep and *The Ghosts of Venice West* with John Thomas. Her most recent biographical book is "Bukowski in the Bathtub." She has just completed her autobiographical *Memoirs of a Nun on Fire*. Philomene Long lives with her husband poet John Thomas at the desperate edge of the Pacific Ocean.

Sylvere Lotringer was a longtime associate of Kathy Acker and is an editor for Autonomedia Books.

Dominique Lowell, acclaimed in the U.S. and Europe, is known to many poets of this decade as "the Janis Joplin of spoken word." Drawing on a theatrical background and her experiences in the "contemporary urban wasteland," as she puts it, she performs her works with fury and finesse, leaving audiences ecstatic and exhilarated. She is the author of two books, *Pile* and *Bitch*.

Danny Lyon is the author of *The Bikeriders*.

Norman Mailer, acknowledged to be one of the most controversial American writers of the last half century, has walked a tightrope over public opinion, often with a dagger in his teeth. From his hipster manifesto "The White Negro" to his literary sponsorship of the criminal Jack Abbot, Mailer has fascinated and outraged bourgeoise sensibilities. His books include *An American Dream, The Naked and the Dead* and *Armies of the Night*.

Judith Molina, poet, playwright and actress, co-founded (with Julian Beck) The Living Theatre, America's most influential avant-garde theatre ensemble.

Gerard Malanga was associated with Andy Warhol from 1963–70 as a collaborator and superstar. His books include *Three Diamonds* and *The Last Benedetta Poems*.

Taylor Mali is known as the villain of the poetry Slam community for three reasons: 1) he takes competition more seriously than he takes himself, 2) he likes to win a lot, and 3) he does. Featured in the film *Slam* Nation, he is a member of the Mouth Almighty Records Slam Squad. He lives in New York City with his wife, where he teaches English, history and math at the Browning School.

Marvin Malone was publisher of *The Wormwood Review*.

William J. Margolis is one of the founding editors of *Beatitude*, an upstart magazine of the San Francisco Beats. Later, he became identified with the Southern California group known as the Venice Beats.

Lisa Martinović, the notorious "Slam Queen of the Ozarks" writes poems that are, by turn, savagely honest and warmly comic. She is the self-made voice of a whole region and way of life. Her poems are collected in a volume entitled *Poemedy*.

Ellyn Maybe is the author of *The Cowardice of Amnesia* on 2.13.61 and *The Ellyn Maybe Coloring Book* (Sacred Beverage Press). She has read her work on many public radio stations and has been heard at Bumbershoot, Lollapalooza,

Taos Poetry Circus and the MTV Spoken Word Tour. She has toured with the Carma Bums and Spoken Rodeo and reads all over the place.

Joe Maynard is a member of the Unbearables.

Michael McClure, reading in 1955 at Gallery Six, joined with Allen Ginsberg, Phil Whalen, Philip Lamentia and Gary Snyder to launch the San Francisco renaissance. During the Summer of Love, he composed the original words on which Janis Joplin's song "Oh Lord, Won't You Buy Me A Mercedes Benz" was based. A prolific writer, his books include A *Fist Full, Jaguar Skies* and *Selected Poems.*

Jeffrey McDaniel lives in Los Angeles where he teaches poetry writing workshops at UCLA Extension, and as part of Poets-In-The-Classrooms sponsored by PEN West. He has read his work at the Smithsonian Institution, and on National Public Radio's Talk of the Nation. He has two volumes of poetry, *Alibi School* and *Forgiveness Parade* both on Manic D Press.

Kaye McDonough came of age as a poet in San Francisco's North Beach district, during the explosion of readings that occurred there in the late sixties and early seventies. She was regarded as the most gifted woman poet of a circle of North Beach poets that included Bob Kaufman and Jack Micheline.

Thomas McGrath was born on a North Dakota farm in 1916, served in Aleutian Islands during World War II and was a Rhodes Scholar at Oxford University before being blacklisted during the McCarthy era. His *Selected Poems* (1938-1988) received the Lenore Marshall/Nation Prize. He died in 1990.

Tony Medina is author of "Sermon" from *The Smell of a Carcass Condemned to Begging.*

David Meltzer is the author of numerous books of poetry, the most recent being *Arrows: selected poetry 1957–1992* (Black Sparrow Press). He's edited many theme-related anthologies including *The Secret Garden: The Classical Kabbalah* (Station Hill Press) and *Reading Jazz* (Mercury House). His most recent agit-smut novel is *Under* (Rhinoceros Books). He teaches in the graduate poetics program at New College of California.

Ann Menebroker is one of the few women included among the predominantly male, hard-living "Meat Poets" that included Charles Bukowski, A. D. Winans, Jim Chandler, Douglas Blazak and others. She has authored some seventeen books, including *Mailbox Boogie* and *Surviving Bukowski.*

Sarah Menefee, born in Chicago in 1946, has been writing poetry for over thirty years and has been widely published in such magazines as *American Poetry Review, Conjunctions* and *Beatitude.* As a political activist she has been deeply engaged in working for the homeless in San Francisco. She is author of *The Blood about the Heart.*

Sharon Mesmer is a member of the Unbearables.

Jack Micheline, a street poet, authored dozens of books and chapbooks including *River of Red Wine, Last House in America* and *Street of Lost Fools*. Sixty-seven *Poems for Downtrodden Saints*, his selected poems edited by Matt Gonzalez, has just been issued in a special limited edition by FMSBW, San Francisco, in conjunction with Vince Sliver and the Jack Micheline Foundation.

Bobby Miller has been called "The Lenny Bruce of Beat Poetry." A performance poet, actor and photographer, he is the author of three books, *Benestrific Blonde, Mouth of Jane* and *Rigmarole*. He can also be heard on Epic Records CD "Home Alive" with Pearl Jam, Nirvana and others. His most recent book is *A Photographic Diary of Studio 54*.

Henry Miller is the crawdaddy of American literary outlaws. His poetic novel, *Tropic of Cancer*, while banned in America, was smuggled into the States by GIs returning from the Second World War. Editor Barney Rosset of Grove Press issued the first American edition which led to a Supreme Court ruling overturning its ban and turning Miller into a cause celebre. His other books include *Black Spring, The Tropic of Capricorn, Sexus* and *The Air-Conditioned Nightmare*.

Mike M. Mollett, Carma Bum, member of the Lost Tribe, mailartist, Dadaist/fluxist, father of the L.A. Mudpeople, Los Angeles Unified elementary school teacher, professional gardener and much-published poet.

Todd Moore began writing poetry in 1970. He edited *road/house*, a poetry magazine from 1975 to 1978. From the author: "Then published chapbooks as road/house press for another ten years or so. I taught high school english for thirty years. Spent my childhood in a flophouse hotel that had a whorehouse running on the second floor and had as childhood friends, con men, burglars, gamblers, killers and assorted thieves. I practically lived on the streets for years. Broke out of the cycle of poverty by getting a bachelor's degree. Started writing poetry when I was thirty-three. Discovered that my true subject in poetry was the dark side, noir, crime, a fascination with outlaws. Have had seventyplus chapbooks published since 1970. Major work of poetry is *Dillinger*, a long poem about the Depression-era bank robber, approx. 40,000 lines in length. This poem is still unpublished."

James Ryan Morris, active on the West Coast, Venice and Seattle, arrived in Denver in the late sixties. He jump-started the moribund poetry scene, held readings anywhere three or more people gathered, opened a book store, an art gallery, published Mile High Underground, Croupier Press and eight volumes of his own work. He died much too early. His face is on the "wall of fame" along with the other pioneers of Denver. That there is vibrant poetry in Denver is his legacy.

Tracie Morris, dubbed by the press "Queen of the Nuyoricans," has toured extensively throughout the United States, Canada, Europe and Asia as a multimedia performance poet. Widely anthologized as a poet, her words appear in "*360 Degrees: a Revolution of Black Poets*", "*Aloud: Voices from the Nuyorican*

Poets Cafe," and *"Soul."* She is the author of two poetry collections, *Intermission* and *Cat-T-her-Won.*

Jim Morrison, lead singer of the Doors, was born in 1943. A gifted poet, he was one of the most creative talents produced by rock. While at UCLA, he studied poetry under Jack Hirshman and became friendly with Ray Manzarek, a fellow student who was earning his keep by singing in a jazz group on weekends. Morrison had already started writing song-poems and in 1965 they formed their group. Signed on by Jack Holzman of Elektra after he saw them at the Whiskey-A-Go-Go in L.A., their first album "The Doors" was one of the best-selling of the era. Morrison died suddenly in Paris in 1971, after years of heavy drinking and drugging. He was buried at Pere Lachaise cemetery beside Balzac and other giants of French literature. His poems are collected in several volumes, including *The Lords, Wilderness* and *The American Night.*

Henry J. Morro has published poetry in *Seneca Review, New Letters, Black Warrior Review, Pacific Review, Jacaranda Review, Bakunin, Chiron Review* and other journals. His first poetry collection, "Somoza's Teeth," was recorded on CD by New Alliance Records.

Eileen Myles has been reading and performing her work locally, nationally and internationally since 1974. Her most recent book of poems, *School of Fish* (Black Sparrow, 1997), won a Lambda Book Award. Other recent publications are *Maxfield Parrish/Early and New Poems* (1995) and *Chelsea Girls* (1994). She co-edited *The New Fuck You/Adventures in Lesbian Reading* (Semiotext(e), 1995). Eileen Myles was Artistic Director of St. Mark's Poetry Project from 1984–86. She writes about art and literature in *Art in America, the Nation, The Stranger, Out* and numerous other publications. Currently she is at work on a non-fiction novel, *Cool for You.*

Gerald Nicosia is the author of many books including *Memory Babe*, a definitive biography of Jack Kerouac. His tireless efforts to liberate Kerouac's writings for public enjoyment and scholarship, and his advocacy on behalf of Kerouac's recently deceased daughter Jan, have earned him Oakland PEN's Josephine P. Miles award.

Harold Norse has published twelve volumes of poetry, a cutup novel, *Beat Hotel,* with a preface by William Burroughs, and an autobiography, *Memoirs of a Bastard Angel,* with a preface by James Baldwin. A National Book Award nominee and recipient of an NEA grant, Norse is one of the major figures of the Beat Generation.

Alice Notley, born in Bishee, Arizona in 1945, author of more then twenty books, lived, as she describes it, "a peripathetic, rather outlawish" poets' life during the sixties and seventies, before finally settling on New York's Lower East Side. There, for the next sixteen years, she became the best-known voice of the eclectic second generation of the New York School of poetry. She lives in Paris, with her husband, the British poet Douglas Oliver, with whom she co-teaches creative writing and co-edits the international journal *Gare du Nord*. She was recently nominated for the Pulitzer Prize. Her books include *Mysteries of Small Houses* and *The Descent of Alette*.

Maura O'Connor, author of *The Hummingbird Graveyard*, is the youngest member of the notorious poetry gang known as the Babarians. She lives in San Francisco's seedy Tenderloin District, in a run-down hotel straight from the pages of Tennessee Williams.

Frank O'Hara was assistant curator at the Museum of Modern Art and one of the founders of The New York School of poetry. His books include *Meditations on an Emergency* and *Lunch Poems*.

Marc Olmsted, a Neo-Beat Buddhist poet, is the author of *Milky Desire*. Allen Ginsberg hailed him as one of the rising stars of the new generation.

Neil Ortenberg is currently publisher of the imprints Thunder's Mouth Press, Marlowe & Company, and Blue Moon Books, including The Nation Books and Adrenaline Books. He lives in New York City with his Norton Commando.

Simon J. Ortiz is widely regarded as one of the country's most important Native American poets. His books include *MoonStone* and *A Good Journey*.

Ron Padgett's books of poetry include *Balls of Fire, Bean Spasms* (with Ted Berrigan), *The Big Something*, and, most recently, *New and Selected Poems*. Padgett is also the translator of *The Complete Poems of Blaise Cendrars*.

Kenneth Patchen's poems of love and social protest, as well as his visual art, have earned him the ongoing devotion of many generations of poets, artists and social activists. In such books as *Before the Brave, Panels for the Walls of Heaven* and *The Journal of Albion Moonlight*, he restored the pure imagination, the need for justice, belief in a universal God, and the exquisite lyricism of romantic love as themes deserving of contemporary address. His books have been translated and published in France, Italy, Germany, Sweden and Holland; and several have appeared in England. He was a painter as well as a poet and before his death had created over five hundred volumes in his "Painted Book" series. A truly progressive and original voice in his time and in the present, Mr. Patchen was often vilified by the critics and the poetry establishment alike. He remains a unique and powerful voice in American verse.

Stuart Z. Perkoff was the main man in Venice. Poet/teacher, he preached the poem, the poet, the responsibility of the craft, the class of the act. He was published early on in the best of the periodicals that arose during the very fructive time of the word. He has nine volumes and broadsides of verse published. His collected works, *Visions of the Lady* has just been issued. He received a posthumus lifetime Tombstone Award for his contributions to the craft.

Pedro Pietri's books include *Puerto Rican Obituary* and *The Masses Are Asses*, a play.

Miguel Piñero was the co-founder of the Nuyorican Poets Cafe. His 1977 play, *Short Eyes*, about life in prison, is a theatrical landmark. He wrote twelve full-length plays.

Vytantas Pliura is a first generation Lithuanian who grew up on a farm in Central Illinois. He is a UCLA graduate and an elementary school teacher. He is completing his first novel, *Tenderness In Hell*.

Charles Plymell arrived as a young poet from Kansas to San Francisco in 1964. He was one of the tough, new generations who made City Lights their rendezvous point. His memoir of late-stage Beat life, *The Last of the Moccasins*, has been compared to the writings of Nelson Algren and Jack Kerouac. Of his many volumes of verse, two in particular, *Apocalypse Rose* and *Neon Poems*, have established the importance of his voice to American poetry.

Jackson Pollack was the leading painter of the Abstract-Expressionist school.

Janine Pommy Vega, one of the most gifted of the second generation Beats, has published and performed throughout North and South America and Europe. Her books include *Tracking the Serpent: Journey to Four Continents Morning Passage* and *Threading the Maze*. She is the director of Incisions/Arts, an organization of writers working with people behind bars.

N. Pourjaundy is a member of the Unbearables.

Richard Pryor is the winner of the Kennedy Center's first Mark Twain Prize for American humor. The award forever links the white Southern writer who created Nigger Jim and the black Midwestern comic who named his best album "That Nigger's Crazy." Pryor's response to the award was, "Two things people throughout history have had in common are hatred and humor. I am proud that, like Mark Twain, I have been able to use humor to lessen people's hatred."

Jill Rapaport is a member of the Unbearables.

Ishmael Reed, poet and novelist, has been nominated for the National Book Award and is a recipient of a prestigious MacArthur Foundation "genius" fellowship. His books include *The Free-Lance Pallbearers* and *Mumbo Jumbo*.

Lou Reed is rock's answer to Charles Baudelaire. Reed is a street-smart, sexually ambiguous paradimgn of cool who first studied under the poet Delmore Shwartz before teaming before up with the Andy Warhol-annointed band, Velvet Underground, in the mid-sixties. Since leaving them in 1970, he's branched out in innumerable albums cut over three decades, including "Lou Reed," "Transformer," "Sally Can't Dance" and, most recently, "Perfect Night: Live In London." His own self-regenerating one-man revolution, Reed's poems are collected in *Between Thought and Expression*.

Roger Richards, a long-time friend and confidante to Herbert Huncke and other authors of the Beat Generation, is executor to the Herbert Huncke estate.

Steve Richmond is one of a group of Southern California poets associated with the early career of Charles Bukowski. His collected poems, *Hitler Painted Roses* (1963/1994) was recently issued with a foreword by Charles Bukowski.

Frank T. Rios, a street-smart kid from The Bronx, came to Venice in the late fifties, startled everyone with his black vision of holy pain. He is a survivor who has kept at it with a dignity and wisdom that has inspired those who think it just might be done: a life of poetry. Mr. Rios has published seven books and is now working on his collected works. In 1992 he received the Joya C. Penobscot Award for excellence in verse and furtherance of his craft. He also was the recipient of the Tombstone Award for poetry in 1988.

Larry Rivers is a leading American painter.

Luis Rodriguez's widely acclaimed memoir of L.A. gang life, *Always Running*, is the focus of a current national debate over the banning from classrooms of books deemed controversial by the public schools. A Lannan Foundation Award recipient, Rodriguez has authored three poetry collections, including his most recent, *Trochemoche*. He is also founder-director of Tia Chicha Press in Chicago, publisher of cross-cultural, socially engaged poetry.

Sheree Rose was Bob Flanagan's life and art partner for the last fifteen years of his life.

David Roskos is the editor of *Big Hammer Magazine* and Iniquity Press/Vendetta Books. He lives in New Jersey with his wife and two sons.

Barney Rosset was awarded the PEN's biennial Publisher's Citation for fostering "the freedom and dignity of artists." He is currently at the helm of the new cyberspace incarnation of the *Evergreen Review* and editor for Blue Moon Books. He fought for first amendment rights with such censorship battles as *Lady Chatterly's Lover*, by D. H. Lawrence, and Henry Miller's *Tropic of Cancer*.

Thaddeus Rutkowski is a member of the Unbearables.

Sonia Sanchez was one of the boldest voices of the Black Nationalist movement of the 1960s. Co-founder of one of the first African-American studies university programs in the U.S., she has traveled extensively to read and present her poetry. Her books include *Homegirls and Handgrenades*, *Does Your House Have Lions?* and *Shake Loose My Skin*.

Jimmy Santiago Baca rose from hard beginnings as an impoverished mestizo or "detribalized Apache" to become a poet who writes with "an intense lyricism and . . . transformative vision" (Denise Levertov). He is the author of *Black Mesa Poems, Immigrants in Our Own Land and Selected Early Poems* and *Martin and Meditations on the South Valley*.

Sapphire's books include *Push* and *American Dreams*.

Tony Scibella, too poor to afford a middle name, nonetheless has maintained a commitment to verse for over forty years. In conjunction with Bowery Press he has published over thirty-five books and broadsides; under his own press, Black Ace, he has lost the exact count. He edited the first four issues of *Black Ace Book*. He has shunned the spotlight, preferring to lie in the weeds, leaping out to urge, prod, insist and threaten for respect of the craft. He has no awards, no grants, just always remembering: "If we can find him, we can kill him."

Susan Scutti is a member of the Unbearables.

Hubert Selby Jr.'s first novel, *last Exit to Brooklyn*, incited shock, admiration and controversy for its stark portrayal of people driven to extremes of violence and desperation, upon its release in 1964. The novel was the subject of an obscenity trial in England. His other novels include *The Room, The Demon, Requiem for a Dream*, and *Song of the Silent Snow*. Selby often performs in spoken word shows with Henry Rollins.

Assata Shakur lives in political exile in Cuba.

Tupac Shakur was the target of a public crusade against gangsta rap, in 1984, headed by U.S. Education Secretary William Bennet. His record-breaking albums include "Me Against The World" and "All Eyez on Me." In 1996, at the age of 25, he died from gunshot wounds suffered during a Las Vegas drive-by shooting.

Bill Shields served as a Navy Seal in the Vietnam War for three years. He lives in Pennsylvania. "I put my life in the books. Four titles available from 2.13.61 Publications—*Human Shrapnel, The Southeast Asian Book of the Dead, Lifetaker* and *Rosey the Babykiller*. Also a new one from 50 Gallons of Diesel Press, *Cordite*. Everything else is pretty meaningless."

Danny Shot is co-founder and editor of Long Shot.

Herschel Silverman, a longtime associate of Allen Ginsberg and the Beats, rose to a new prominence in the nineties in New York's downtown scene. A jazz poet of great skill, he was adopted by the younger poets as an inspiring example of the tenacity and courage needed to live an artistic life. Today, his widely published and translated poetry is read from San Francisco to Tokyo. Publisher of Bee Hive Press, he is the poet laureate of Bayonne, New Jersey.

Bucky Sinister is an underground youth cult hero and former host of the notorious Chameleon Club open reading (where medically uninsured nationally acclaimed poets from around the U.S. swan dived from a high stage into empty beer mugs). He is the author of "King of the Roadkills."

Hal Sirowitz is a member of the Unbearables.

Marc (So what?) Smith, founder of the poetry performance movement known as Slam is also affectionately called "Slampappy" by thousands of poets from New York to Chicago to Berlin. Smith, who featured in the film documentary

Slam Nation has performed at Lincoln Center for the Performing Arts, the Smithsonian Institute and the Art Institute of Chicago. His most recent book is *Crowdpleaser*, a collection of his early performance poems.

Patricia Smith has not only won an astonishing four National Poetry Slams but her razor-edged performance style and exacting verse are the very prototype of Slam poetry. It is safe to say that if Marc Smith invented the competition format, Patricia Smith created its poetic style—one that is now deployed by thousands of performance poets across America. She is the co-author with Charles Johnson of the acclaimed PBS special and companion volume *Africans in America: America's Journey Through Slavery, Close To Death* and *Life According to Motown*.

Patti Smith has become the emblematic avant-garde figure of our time, moving easily between the worlds of literature, performance art and rock. Her debut album, "Piss Factory/Hey Joe," funded by her then-partner Robert Mappelthorpe, signaled the arrival of a major talent. This was followed by the brilliantly cathartic "Horses." Her other albums include "Ain't Nuthin' But a She Thing," "Gone Again," "Peace and Noise" and the 1996 Masters, a box set of six CDs. Her most recent book is *Patti Smith Complete: Lyrics, Reflections and Notes for The Future*.

Gary Snyder grew up in northern Washington. In college, he found academic writing limiting and was drawn to writing poetry because, "there are things you cannot say except in poetry, and those are the things I need to say." Originally a member of the Beat movement, his poetry often reflects his practice of Zen Buddhism. He lives in the Yuba River watershed of the northern Sierra Nevada and teaches at the University of California, Davis. His books include *No Nature: New and Selected Poems, The Back Country* and *Turtle Island*.

Sparrow is a member of the Unbearables.

Julia Stein has published two books of poetry: *Under the Ladder to Heaven* and *Desert Soldiers*. She has widely published literary criticism about working-class and women's American literature. Her work is in *Calling Home: Working Class Women's Writings: An Anthology* (Rutgers University Press) and the two working-class studies issues of *Women's Studies Quarterly* (Feminist Press). She won a Puffin Grant for essay writing in 1997. And she fought a censorship case against Guess Inc., which she won in 1997. She has written a novel *The Magic Circle* about the 1960s, and an excerpt was published in the "Flashback" issue of the magazine *Saturday Afternoon*. She is a founder of the Los Angeles local/National Writers Union.

Claude Taylor is a member of the Unbearables.

Marvin Taylor is a member of the Unbearables. He is special collections curator for the New York University Library System.

John Thomas was born in Baltimore. During his second day in kindergarten, he was caught trying to steal a small piece of scrap lumber. It's been downhill from there. Thomas attended Loyola College in that grim and dirty city, but received no degree. After not quite three years among the Jesuits, he was expelled for "moral turpitude." As Father Drayne, the dean of men, put it "We don't tolerate monkeys like you around here." In 1959, Thomas hitchhiked from Baltimore to Venice West, where he began to publish his poetry in *Floating Bear*, the *Evergreen Review*, and other important literary magazines in the U.S. and abroad. John Thomas has just completed his autobiographical novel, *Paradise*. He has published many books, most recently *Nevertheless* (Illumaniti), *The Book of Sleep* (Momentum) written with his wife, the poet Philomene Long, with whom he lives in Venice West.

Hunter S. Thompson is a supreme prose stylist and the undisputed king of gonzo journalism. As the chronicler of an American soul ravaged by its own excesses, Thompson has been a one-man counterculture, riding with the Hell's Angels, running for sheriff, serving time in a Louisville jail or numbing his speed-typist hands while fist fighting in Greenwich Village. His books include *Fear and Loathing in Las Vegas*, *Hell's Angels: A Strange and Terrible Saga* and *Great Shark Hunt: Strange Tales from A Strange Time*.

Mike Topp, born in Washington, D.C., and a member of the New York-based Unbearables, has remained on the cutting edge of the avant-garde. Besides being widely published in prominent literary magazines, he also self-publishes books and journals that spoof the very genres they inhabit with an unfailing eye for the absurd. Most recently, he served as special editor of the *Evergreen Review Reader 1957–1966*. He lives in New York City.

David Trinidad's nine books include *Pavane* (1981), *Monday, Monday* (1985), *November* (1987), *Hand over Heart: Poems 1981–1988* (1991) and *Answer Song* (1994). A native of Los Angeles, Trinidad has lived in New York City since 1988. He currently teaches poetry at Rutgers University, where he curates the Writers at Rutgers series, and is a member of the core faculty in the MFA writing program at the New School.

George Tsongas lives in North Beach, San Francisco.

David L. Ulin is a member of the Unbearables.

The Unbearables is a movement of postmodern poets, writers and artists concentrated mainly in New York City but with members in places as far-flung as Amsterdam and San Francisco. Collectively, they appear in their own anthologies, including *Unbearables*, *Crimes against the Beats* and the forthcoming *Help Yourself!*

Melvin Van Peebles, filmmaker and author, is the director of *Sweet Sweetback's Baadasssss Song* and author of *Panther: The Pictorial History of the Black Panthers and the Story behind the Film*.

Julia Vinograd, a Berkeley street poet, has published thirty-five books of poetry and won the American Book Award of the Before Columbus Foundation. Her poetry recently earned a Pushcart Prize.

Albert Vitale is a member of the Unbearables.

Fred Voss has been a machinist for twenty years, picking up the pen and the wrench to chronicle what goes on between tin walls. His first book of poems, *Goodstone*, was published in 1991. His work has been featured prominently by the magazines *Bete Noire* in Britain and the *Wormwood Review* in the States, and he won the 1988 Wormwood Award. *Love Birds*, a collaboration with his poet wife Joan Jobe Smith, won the 1996 Chiron Prize. He lives in Long Beach, California and works in a nearby factory.

D. R. Wagner is one of the leading figures in the Concrete Poetry movement in the United States and was a close associate of d.a.levy during the sixties.

Tom Waits conjures the demi monde of a souring American Dream in a raspy, gin-soaked voice set to music. His albums include "Closing Time," "The Heart of Saturday Night," "Heart Attack and Vine" and "Black Rider," based on his darkly comic opera collaboration with director Robert Wilson and Beat writer William Burroughs. With Paul Carroll and Charles Bukowski, Waits is an important early influence on many of the spoken word poets who rose to prominence in the nineties.

Anne Waldman is founder with Allen Ginsberg of the Jack Kerouac School of Disembodied Poetics. Her books include *Baby Breakdown* and *Fast Talking Woman*.

Scott Wannberg, Carma Bum, has a master's degree in English from San Francisco State University, which affords him a fine job at Dutton's Books in Brentwood behind the counter. He has been published in numerous publications and has four books of poetry, all out of print. Scott was the eighth dwarf, and is a big fan of *Homicide: Life on the Streets*.

William Wantling, who died at the age of forty-four, went from hardened convict to underground poet to full-fledged academic versifier. A writer of brilliance, his work is undergoing a long-overdue reassessment and revival. His books include *Seven On Style* and *Alive, Alive*.

Carl Watson is a member of the Unbearables.

ruth weiss emigrated to the U.S. after her narrow escape from the Nazis in 1939, eventually settling in Chicago where she gave her first reading with jazz at the Art Circle in 1949. An outstanding performer, she has published nine books of poetry, produced six plays and appeared in dozens of anthologies and magazines. Since her appearance in Brenda Knight's groundbreaking anthology, *Women of the Beat Generation*, Weiss is riding the crest of a new wave of popularity that has already taken her on reading tours across the U.S. and Europe.

Philip Whalen is the author of *Heavy Breathing: Poems 1967–1980*. One of the founding voices of the Beat Generation, he is abbot of the Harford Street Zen Center in San Francisco.

Walt Whitman served as editor of the *Brooklyn Daily Eagle*, worked as a carpenter, and during the Civil War as a government clerk and a nurse. In 1865 he was dismissed from his post in the Indian Bureau because of the immorality of his poetry. His books include *Leaves of Grass, Specimen Days* and *Democratic Vistas*. He was born on Long Island in 1819.

Carol Wierzbicki is a member of the Unbearables.

Jack Wiler is author of "I Have No Clue."

William Carlos Williams, one of the masters of 20th century American poetry, turned his back on Ezra Pound's Europe to stake his artistic claim on native ground, in his case Paterson, New Jersey. A friend to younger writers, Williams formed a true modernist bridge to the Beats when he wrote the introduction to Allen Ginsberg's "Howl," while also championing Harold Norse and Jack Kerouac.

Peter Lamborn Wilson is a member of the Unbearables.

A. D. Winans is one of the original "Meat Poets" and publisher of Second Coming Press, which, in the sixties and seventies, issued works by Bukowski, Wantling, Micheline and others. He is the author of twenty-two books of poetry and is published in over five hundred literary periodicals and anthologies.

Bana Witt, a former sex slave and rock singer, is the author of "Mobius Stripper," "Eight for Artie" (poems for pornographer Artie Mitchell) and "Eclipse of Reason."

David Wojnarowicz, who was hailed during his brief life as a visionary genius, rose from a hard-bitten street hustler to a major visual artist and equally powerful memoirist (*Close to the Knives; Memories That Smell Like Gasoline*). Launched through his graffiti art collaborations with Keith Haring, Wojnarowicz's fight for free expression sparked high-profile face-offs with everyone from the NEA to New York's Cardinal John O'Conner. Yet, in his art, as in his writings, he was intensely tender and elegiac, a poignancy earned, in part, through battling AIDS, which killed him.

Eve Wood has published poems in the *New Republic, Poetry*, the *Antioch Review*, and *The Best American Poetry of 1997*. In 1997 she was also the recipient of a Brody Grant. Her chapbook *Paper Frankenstein* was published in 1998 by Beyond Baroque Press.

Kathleen Wood, a celebrated star of the Cafe Babar scene, is author of *The Wino, the Junkey and the Lord*.

index

copyright acknowledgments

Mumia Abu-Jamal. "To Those" from *Death Blossoms,* © 1997 Plough Publishing House.

Kathy Acker. "Devoured by Myths" an interview with Sylvére Lotringer and "I Begin to Feel" reprinted by permission of Semiotext(e).

Ai. "The Kid" from *VICE: New and Selected Poems* by Ai, © 1999 by Ai. Reprinted by permission of W.W. Norton & Company, Inc.

Miguel Algarín. "The Scattering of the Ashes" and "A Mongo Affair" reprinted by permission of the author.

Rafael F.J. Alvarado. "This Will Not be the Last Poem . . ." reprinted by permission of the author.

David Amram. "Collaborating With Kerouac" reprinted by permission of Sterling Lord Literistic, Inc. © 1998 by David Amram.

Rudolfo Anaya. "Walt Whitman Strides the Llano of New Mexico" from *The Anaya Reader.* © 1995 by Rudolfo Anaya. Published by Warner Books, New York. Originally published in Aloud, Henry Holt, 1994. Reprinted by permission of Susan Bergholz Literary Services, New York. All rights reserved.

Sini Anderson. "It's A Good Day." Reprinted by permission of the author.

Hannah Aquaah. "My Room" © 1999 Hannah Aquaah. Reprinted by permission of the author.

Penny Arcade. "Career Move." Reprinted by permission of the author.

Jimmy Santiago Baca. "Martin XIV" from *Martin and Meditations on the South Valley.* © 1987 by Jimmy Santiago Baca. Reprinted by permission of New Directions Publishing Corp.

Amiri Baraka. "A Short Speech to My Friends" from *The LeRoi Jones/Amiri Baraka Reader.* © 1964, 1991 by Amiri Baraka. Reprinted by permission of Thunder's Mouth Press.

Julian Beck. From "Songs of the Revolution" © Julian Beck. Reprinted by permission of the author.

John Bennet. "Ode to My Mother" "A Wish Come True" "Much Ado About Nothing" "Reasons to Drink" "Molecular Conspiracy" "Playing the Game" © John Bennet. Reprinted by permission of the author.

Mark Benyo. "My Father" © 1999 Mark Benyo. Reprinted by permission of the author.

Ted Berk. Manifesto For Mutants © 1991 Allen Cohen. Reprinted by permission of Allen Cohen. "Untitles" "Opos" "Boxed City" "First & Last Fear Poem" "Untitled" from Semina by Wallace Berman. Reprinted by permission of the Wallace Berman Estate.

Steven J. Bernstein. "Murdered in the Middle of the Dance" © Estate of Steven J. Bernstein. Reprinted by permission.

Father Daniel Berrigan. "Prophecy" "Children in the Shelter" "Rehabilitative Report: We Can Still Laugh" "Georgetown Poems." Reprinted by permission of the Fordham University Press.

Iris Berry. "Punk Rock Royalty" © Iris Berry. Reprinted by permission of the author.

Umar Bin Hassan. "Malcolm" © Umar Bin Hassan. Reprinted by permission of the author.

Max Blagg. "The Bus Driver's Secret Song" © Max Blagg. Reprinted by permission of the author.

Jennifer Blowdryer. "Resume" © Jennifer Blowdryer. Reprinted by permission of Zeitgeist Press.

Jackson Pollack. Handwritten statement by Jackson Pollack, undated (about 1950) © Jackson Pollack. Reprinted by permission of Jackson Pollack Catalogue Raisonne Archives, Pollack-Krasner House and Study Center, East Hampton, NY.

Richard Pryor. "Africa" © Richard Pryor. Reprinted by permission of Jennifer Lee Pryor for Richard Pryor.

Jill Rapaport. "Panoplistic Traditions in Memphis" © Jill Rapaport. Reprinted by permission of the author.

Ishmael Reed. "If My Enemy Is a Clown, a Natural Born Clown" © Ishmael Reed. Reprinted by permission of the author.

Lou Reed. "Video Violence" from *Between Thought and Expression: The Selected Lyrics of Lou Reed* © 1991, Metal Machine Music, Inc. Reprinted with permission by Hyperion.

Roger Richards. Introduction to Gregory Corso, Introduction to Herbert Huncke © Roger Richards. Reprinted by permission of the author.

Steve Richmond. "A Bukowski Writing Lesson" from *Spinning Off Bukowski* © 1996, 1999 by Steve Richmond. Reprinted by permission of the author.

Frank T. Rios. "Invocation" © Frank T. Rios. Reprinted by permission of the author. .

Larry Rivers. "How to Proceed in the Arts" © Larry Rivers/Licensed by VAGA, New York, NY. Reprinted by permission of VAGA.

Alejo Dao'ud Rodriguez. "Sing Sing Sits Up the River," previously published in *Rattle Magazine* (1998-99) © Alejo Dao'ud Rodriguez. Reprinted by permission of the author.

Luis J. Rodriguez. "To the police officer who refused to sit in the same room as my son because he's a 'gang banger' " "Rosalie Has Candles" "Somebody Was Breaking Windows" "Chota" "Believe Me When I Say . . ." "Meeting the Animal in Washington Square Park" "Don't Read That Poem!" ©1998 Louis Rodriguez. Published in *Troche Moche*, 1998 Curbstone Press. © 1991 by Louis Rodriguez. Published in *The Concrete River*, 1991 Curbstone Press. © 1989 Louis Rodriguez. Published in *Poems Across the Pavement*, 1989 Tia Chuch Press. Reprinted by permission of the author.

David Roskos. "Certain Prostitue" "Poem for Paulie" © David Roskos. Reprinted by permission of the author.

Barney Rosset. "Ernest Hemingway" "The Little Sons of Fidel" © 1999 Barney Rosset. Reprinted by permission of the author.

Thaddeus Rutkowski. "Yardbirds of Vermont" © Thaddeus Rutkowski. Reprinted by permission of the author.

Sonia Sanchez. "A Poem for Jesse" "On Passing thru Morgantown, Pa." from the book *Homegirls and Handgrenades* by Sonia Sanchez © 1984 by Sonia Sanchez. Reprinted by permission of Thunder's Mouth Press.

Sapphire. "Wild Thing" "Rabbit Man" "1989 cont./Gorilla in the Midst #6" © 1994 Sapphire. Published by High Risk Books/Serpent's Tail, London England. Reprinted by permission of the author.

Tony Scibella. "Venice West" "Untitled" © Tony Scibella. Reprinted by permission of the author.

Susan Scutti. "Manhattan" © Susan Scutti. Reprinted by permission of the author.

Hubert Selby, Jr. "Psalm XVI" © Hubert Selby, Jr. Reprinted by permission of the author.

Assata Shakur. "Culture" "Story" from *Assata: An Autobiography* ©1987 by Assata Shakur. Reprinted by permission of Lawrence Hill Books, Chicago, IL.

Tupac Shakur. "In the Event of My Demise" © Estate of Tupac Shakur. Reprinted by permission of the Estate of Tupac Shakur.

Bill Shields. "a chipped black hole" © Bill Shields. Reprinted by permission of the author.

Danny Shot. "The Living Legend" "On *Long Shot*" © Danny Shot. Reprinted by permission of the author.

Herschel Silverman. From "High on the Beats" © Herschel Silverman. Reprinted by permission of the author.

Bucky Sinister. "I Was with Her Long Enough To Change Brands of Cigarettes" from *King of the Roadkills* by Bucky Sinister. Published by Manic D Press. © 1995 by Charles Jones. Reprinted by permission of the author.

Hal Sirowitz. "Thursday Night in the Park" © Hal Sirowitz. Reprinted by permission of the author.

Joan Jobe Smith. "Aboard the Bounty" "Land of a Thousand Dances" © Joan Jobe Smith. Reprinted by permission of the author.

Marc Smith. "Lucky Strike No Strike Back" "The Stroke" © Marc Smith. Reprinted by permission of the author.